HTML PUBLISHING ON THE internet

FOR WINDOWS

Create Great-Looking Documents Online:
Home Pages, Newsletters, Catalogs, Ads & Forums

Brent Heslop & Larry Budnick

HTML Publishing on the Internet for Windows: Create Great-Looking Documents Online: Home Pages, Newsletters, Catalogs, Ads & Forums

Library of Congress Cataloging-in-Publication Data

Heslop, Brent D.

HTML Publishing on the Internet for Windows : create great-looking documents online: home pages, newsletters, catalogs, ads & forums / Brent Heslop. -- 1st ed.

p. cm.

Includes index.

ISBN 1-56604-229-1

1. Electronic publishing. 2. World Wide Web (Information retrieval system) 3. Internet (Computer network) I. Budnick, Larry. II. Title.

Z286.E43H47 1995

686.2'2544536--dc20 95-4218

CIP

Book design: Marcia Webb
Cover design and illustration: Tom Draper Design
Vice President, Ventana Press: Walter R. Bruce III
Art Director: Marcia Webb
Design staff: Dawne Sherman
Editorial Manager: Pam Richardson
Editorial staff: Angela Anderson, Jonathan Cato, Tracye Giles, Beth Snowberger
Developmental Editor: Tim C. Mattson
Project Editor: Jessica Ryan
Print Department: Dan Koeller
Product Manager: Clif McCormick
Production Manager: John Cotterman
Production staff: Patrick Berry, Cheri Collins
Index service: Richard T. Evans, Infodex
Proofreader: Valeria Nasir
Technical review: Brian Little, Imagination Workshops

First Edition 9 8 7 6 5 4 3 2 1
Printed in the United States of America

Ventana Press, Inc.
P.O. Box 2468
Chapel Hill, NC 27515
919/942-0220
FAX 919/942-1140

Trademarks

About the Authors

Brent Heslop has co-authored over 14 books on a wide range of computer topics. He is a partner in Bookware, a technical writing firm with offices on the East and West coasts. Brent is a frequent contributor to *PC Magazine* and other computer-related magazines. Currently he is co-writing *Publishing on the Internet for Mac* to be published by Ventana Communications in mid-1995. He lives in Mountain View, California, with his lovely wife Kim and their devoted dog Cassius.

Larry Budnick has had more than 15 years of computer systems experience as a systems engineer, developer and systems integrator. He holds a B.S. in Systems Engineering from Rensselaer Polytechnic Institute, and an M.S. in Computer Engineering from Boston University. He has worked on a variety of computer and communications projects ranging from ISDN telephony to wireless data to online documentation systems. He is currently involved in designing wireless data communications systems.

Acknowledgments

No one person can tackle as fast changing a topic as publishing on the Internet. Numerous people supplied us with valuable information for which we are extremely grateful. First and foremost we want to thank Elizabeth Woodman at Ventana Communications, Inc. and our agent, Matt Wagner, at Waterside Productions for having the foresight to publish this book. Two people we want to thank in particular for their research and contributions to this book are Ray Werner and David Holzgang. Ray helped draft a few of the preliminary chapters and David Holzgang helped us complete this project by writing the HTML reference. David, by the way, is the co-author of the forthcoming Macintosh edition of this book.

Essential to writing a book on publishing on the Internet is an Internet connection and a solid TCP/IP package. We are in debt to Bob Berger at InterNex and Rich White at Best Internet Communications for letting us use their services to test the examples in this book. We want to thank Bob Williams and Donna Loughlin at NetManage for keeping us up to date with Chameleon and Ann Krauss at Frontier Technologies for her help with Super TCP Pro.

Many thanks to Clif McCormick at Ventana Communications, who was instrumental in setting up the CD-ROM, and all the companies and individuals that let us include their software on the Companion CD. At SoftQuad, we want to thank Lucy Ventresca for supplying us with HoTMetaL PRO and late-breaking news, Liam Quin for his technical review and Donald Teed for answering our many questions. Thanks to John Hahn at Netscape Communications for letting us include the commercial version of Netscape Navigator. We were overjoyed that Robert Denny let us include the HTTPD Server and Chris Adie let us include the EMWAC HTTPS server and WAIS utilities. Thanks to Adam Tratt at Microsoft for letting us include Microsoft Assistant. We are grateful to Tammy Wing at Image Club Graphics, Inc. for letting us include some impressive clip art and digital photos. Ann Burgraff at CMCD helped by supplying us with some great digital photo samples. On the subject of graphics we are indebted to Bill

Dickson and Jonathan Ort at JASC for letting us include Paint Shop Pro, a powerful graphics editor. Jon was a fountain of information on working with graphics on the Internet. Thanks to Tom Boutell for letting us include his MapEdit program, which is sure to save users time creating image maps. We appreciate that David Koblas at Home Pages Inc. let us include giftool as well as create a windows front-end for his giftool program. We also appreciate Andreas Ley letting us include the giftrans program. Thanks to Chris Craig for letting us include his GoldWave sound editor. Thanks also to Rick Brown for letting us include Adobe Acrobat Reader. We also want to express our thanks to Dan Baumbach at Canyon Software for letting us use his company as an example throughout the book and letting us include Drag And File, Drag And Zip, and Drag And View.

Numerous companies gave us information and products related to Internet publishing. Thanks to Bob Hatton at Fast Electronics for letting us use Movie Line for the chapter on video editing and Ralph Bond at Intel for letting us use the Intel Smart Video Recorder Pro. There are a few people that we would like to thank at Adobe: LaVon Peck for her help with Adobe Premiere, and Patricia Payne and Sonya Schaefer for Adobe Photoshop. We also want to thank Rick Brown and Pam Deziel for help with Adobe Acrobat products. Thanks to Rolf Rudestam at the Rudestam Group for the information and preliminary version of Quarterdeck's Web Author. We want to extend our gratitude to McLean Public Relations, specifically Kimm Haas and Laurie McLean for Fractal Design Painter and trueSpace, as well as Jill Ryan for Elastic Reality. Thanks also to Steve Cherneff at Macromedia for Director and his valuable input. Thanks to Ed Lecuyer at Andover Advanced Technologies for North Coast Software Inc.'s PhotoMorph 2 and Access Softek Inc.'s Sound Track. We are grateful to Theresa Pulido at Creative Labs for letting us use an AWE32 audio card for creating and editing sound files and to Stacy Pearson at Turtle Beach Systems for Wave for Windows. Staffan Hillberg at Apple was extremely helpful by providing us with information on QuickTime for Windows. Thanks to Lauren Finkelman at S&S publications for Ulead Systems Media Studio, ImagePals and Morph Studio. Thanks also to

Maurice Hamoyat Inset for Hijaak Graphics Suite for Windows and Bill Hanlon at Inset who shared valuable information on working with graphics. Emma Rosen at Edelman was instrumental in supplying us with information on the MPEG decoder board ReelMagic, Rave and ReelMagic Producer. We also want to acknowledge Sean O'Tool at Xing Technology Corporation for his help on XingCD and MPEG compression in general.

Additionally we want to thank Pam Richardson, Angela Anderson, Patrick Berry and Tim Mattson at Ventana Press who helped in the production of this book. We want to thank Jessica Ryan, our editor, who offered valuable insight and guidance to help improve this book. Jessica went beyond the call of duty in order to help us keep the book as up to date as possible by making numerous last-minute changes.

Last but not least, we want to thank our wives Kim Merry and Eve Budnick for supporting us through this entire project.

Contents

Section III: Putting the Pieces Together

Section IV: Appendices

Introduction

Everyone wants to get published on the Internet, and why not? Publishing on the Internet is one of the most important and exciting happenings in computing since the launching of the PC revolution back in the early '80s. This book focuses on the most effective and by far the most popular Internet publishing method, publishing on the World Wide Web using HTML and HTTP.

Who Needs This Book?

Any Windows user that is interested in how to publish pages on the World Wide Web will find the answers in this guide. Even if you don't want to create the pages yourself, this book offers helpful information as to what you need to do to have someone publish Web pages for you. Knowing how Web publishing works can save you time and money. Many services charge between $100 to $200 an hour to create Web pages. So if you're interested in creating a presence for yourself or company on the Internet, this book will step you through the entire Web publishing process.

This book is written for the new user as well as the seasoned Net surfer. If you are already familiar with HTML, you'll find it includes numerous Web design tips, powerful Web publishing tools and a valuable HTML reference. If you're not familiar with the Web, the first part of the book gives a concise introduction to the Web and hypermedia publishing.

What's Inside?

The book is divided into four sections: The Elements of Hypermedia Design; Working With the Pieces; Putting the Pieces Together; and four appendices.

Chapter 1, "The World Wide Web & Hypermedia Publishing," introduces you to Internet jargon and provides a broad overview of publishing on the Internet.

Chapter 2, "HTML Editors & Convertors," helps familiarize you with the most popular HTML editors and converters that exist to create Web documents.

Chapter 3, "Structuring Information in Web Documents," provides a short introduction to structuring and designing effective hypertext documents.

Chapter 4, "Creating Your First Web Document," is a hands-on guide to creating a home page, the cornerstone of your Web site.

Chapter 5, "The Art of Linking," shows you how to exploit the power of links to publish complex Web documents and connect to files and other Web documents around the world.

Chapter 6, "Creating Your Text Appeal," introduces you to the many possibilities for creating and formatting text using HTML.

Chapter 7, "Getting Graphic With Images," explains the basic HTML tags for creating Web documents with hyperlinks and explains how to include images. Although the hands-on examples are centered around using HoTMetaL PRO, the standard HTML codes, called tags, are also included for anyone interested in using another HTML editor.

Chapter 8, "Adding Scintillating Sound & Vivid Video," takes a look at publishing multimedia files, both sound and video, on the Internet.

Chapter 9, "Forms, Databases & CGI," gives step-by-step instructions for creating forms and using the Common Gateway Interface to publish interactive documents.

Chapter 10, "Looking Good on the Net," shares examples of unique, professionally designed Web documents that you can use as design examples to help you look good on the Net.

Chapter 11, "Service Providers & Server Services," and Chapter 12, "Servers at Your Service," explain the different Web publishing alternatives, including using a service provider, server service or setting up a Web server and publishing Web documents from your own PC.

In the Appendices you'll find an annotated HTML reference section that includes HTML tags and Netscape extensions to HTML. Each HTML tag entry includes the standard syntax, an example and cross-references to similar or associated HTML tags and Netscape extensions. Also included is a comprehensive resource listing of Internet publishing–related programs and periodicals.

About the Online Companion

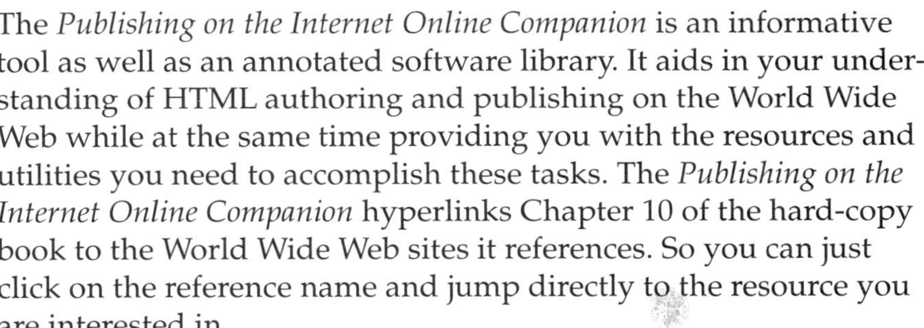

The *Publishing on the Internet Online Companion* is an informative tool as well as an annotated software library. It aids in your understanding of HTML authoring and publishing on the World Wide Web while at the same time providing you with the resources and utilities you need to accomplish these tasks. The *Publishing on the Internet Online Companion* hyperlinks Chapter 10 of the hard-copy book to the World Wide Web sites it references. So you can just click on the reference name and jump directly to the resource you are interested in.

Perhaps one of the most valuable features of the *Online Companion* is its Software Archive. Here, you'll find and be able to download the latest versions of all the freely available software mentioned in *Publishing on the Internet*. This software ranges from HTML editors, converters and templates, such as HotMetaL and Microsoft's Internet Assistant, to many of your essential publishing programs, such as MapEdit, a tool for making image maps, and GoldWave, an editor for audio files. To access the Online Companion, connect via the World Wide Web to http://www.vmedia.com/piw.html.

About the Companion CD-ROM

We are proud to include on the Companion CD-ROM the most highly acclaimed HTML editor, HoTMetaL PRO. This is the full commercial version of HoTMetaL PRO, which normally sells for around $200. To present Web document examples that can be applied to the real world, we used Canyon Software, a real software company, for most of the book's examples. Canyon Software is the creator of Drag And File, Drag And Zip, and Drag And View, three of the easiest-to-use Windows file management utilities available. The shareware version of these programs are also included on the Companion CD-ROM. By the way, we have no affiliation with Canyon Software other than being satisfied customers and are thankful that they've allowed us use their company for the examples.

Free voice technical support for *Publishing on the Internet* is offered but is limited to installation-related issues and is available for 30 days from the date you register your copy of the book. After the initial 30 days and for non–installation-related questions, please send all technical support questions via Internet e-mail to help@vmedia.com. Our technical support staff will research your question and respond promptly via e-mail.

What You Need

Other than an Internet connection, this book includes all you need to get started publishing on the World Wide Web. The Companion CD-ROM includes several of the Web-related applications and Web publishing tools explained in the book, including the newest commercial release of Netscape Navigator. Over twenty graphic image files and an assortment of graphic tools explained in Chapter 7 are also on the Companion CD-ROM. For example, we have created a Windows front-end for the giftool.exe program that lets you save graphics with a transparent background so the image appears to float on the Web page. The shareware version of the graphic editor Paint Shop Pro 3.0 is also included. On the multimedia front, we have included the shareware version of GoldWave, an impressive sound editor. To help you publish your documents, the CD also includes the two most popular shareware Windows Web server (HTTP) programs for publishing Web documents: Robert Denny's HTTPD server for Windows 3.1 and 3.11 and the EMWAC HTTPS for Windows NT. See Appendix B, "About the Companion CD-ROM," for a complete listing of the CD's contents.

The World Wide Web is moving at an incredibly fast pace. Netscape Communications, creator of the popular Netscape Navigator, which is quickly becoming the defacto standard Web browser, is continually adding powerful extensions to HTML. Many sections in this book were rewritten for the late-breaking Netscape extensions. At the rate things are changing on the Internet, it's nearly impossible to be provide information that is 100 percent up to date. If you find something we've missed or if you have any comments about this book, we would appreciate hearing from you. Please send us e-mail at either of the following addresses.

Brent Heslop
bheslop@isdn.bookware.com

Larry Budnick
lbudnick@mcs.com

SECTION I

The Elements of Hypermedia Design

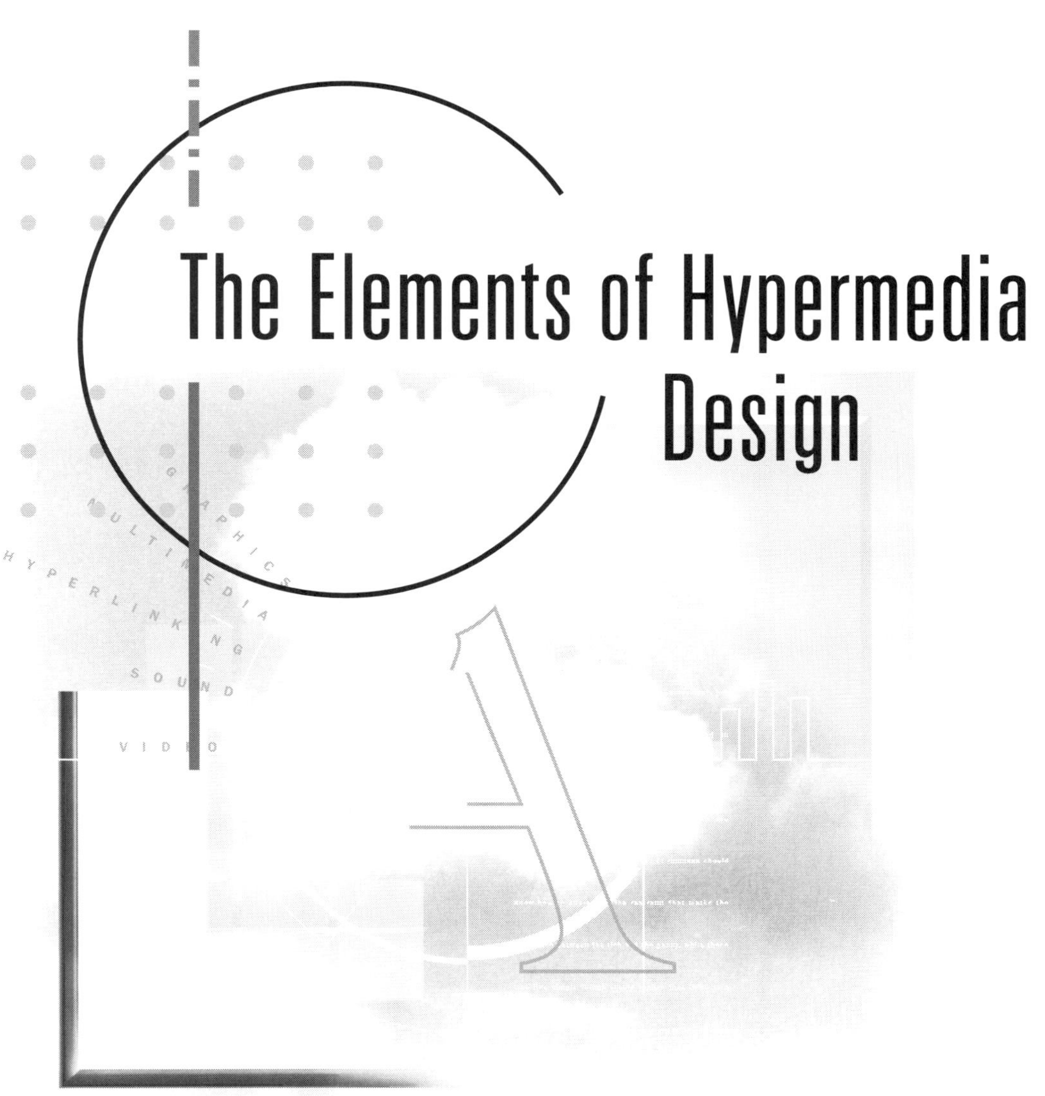

1 The World Wide Web & Hypermedia Publishing

Johannes Gutenberg's invention of the printing press advanced the economy and commerce, politics, society, literature and ideological changes that marked the beginning of the Renaissance. The World Wide Web is ushering in the next generation of publishing, bringing together hypertext, multimedia and global networking. The Web is growing at an astounding rate and is changing the publishing world by making it possible for anyone to publish information to people around the world.

In the fast-moving, global, competitive business environment, it is crucial that current information is available to the consumer who needs it. The World Wide Web lets you quickly publish marketing, customer service and research information from a central location. The Web is also a great forum for personal expression that lets you share ideas and topics of interest with others around the world. This chapter introduces the World Wide Web, explains how Web publishing works and gives an overview of Web publishing options.

What Is the World Wide Web?

The World Wide Web project was started in 1989 by Tim Berners-Lee at the CERN high-energy physics laboratory. The goal of the project was to find a way to share research and ideas with other employees and researchers scattered around the world. In its initial proposal, the Web was called "a hypertext project." *Hypertext* is a term coined by Ted Nelson back in the sixties that refers to text containing connections to other documents, so the reader can click a word or phrase to get additional information about a related topic. *Hypermedia* is a more inclusive term for documents that include information in multimedia formats, such as sound and video.

Technically speaking the World Wide Web refers to the abstract cyberspace of information. The Internet typically refers to the physical side of the network—that is, the hardware consisting of cables and computers. The foundation of the Internet and the World Wide Web is the use of *protocols*, the language and rules by which the computers communicate. For example, *TCP/IP* (Transmission Control Protocol and Internet Protocol) is a suite of networking protocols that lets different types of computers communicate and is the underlying protocol of the Internet. The World Wide Web is not just one type of protocol. Like a puzzle, the Web connects several protocols together, including FTP (File Transfer Protocol), telnet, WAIS (Wide-Area Information Servers) and more. Figure 1-1 shows the protocols that are used to share information. Because the World Wide Web uses the standard Internet protocols to transmit files and documents, the Web is often used synonymously for the Internet, referring to the collective network of computers as well as the body of information.

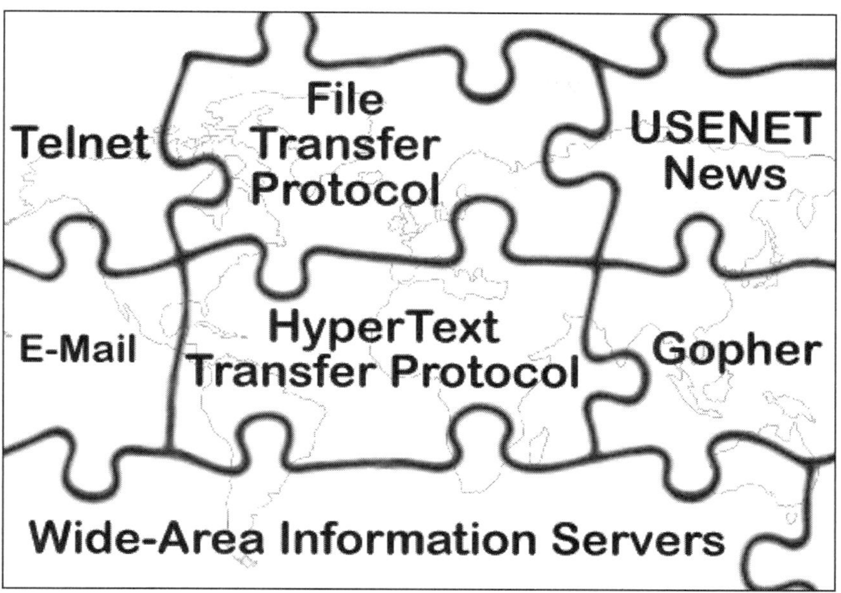

Figure 1-1: *The World Wide Web includes several Internet protocols, including FTP, telnet, WAIS and more.*

How Big Is the World Wide Web?

The release of the Mosaic Web browser by the National Center for Supercomputing (NCSA) in November 1992 marked the beginning of the Web's popularity. At the beginning of 1993, there were only 130 sites, less than half a year after the introduction of Mosaic, a Web client used to request and receive information from a Web server, there were over 10,000 servers. John Quarterman, who mailed out an Internet demographic survey to over 4,700 sites, estimates that, on the low side, there are more than three-and-a-half-million users.

How Web Publishing Works

Web publishing works under the client-server model. A *Web server* is a program running on a computer that is set up to serve documents to other computers that send requests for the documents. A *Web client* is a program that lets the user request documents from a server. Because the server only operates when a document is requested, it's an efficient way to share documents because it requires only a small amount of the server's resources. For example, a Windows NT server can serve up Web documents to over 200 clients connected at one time.

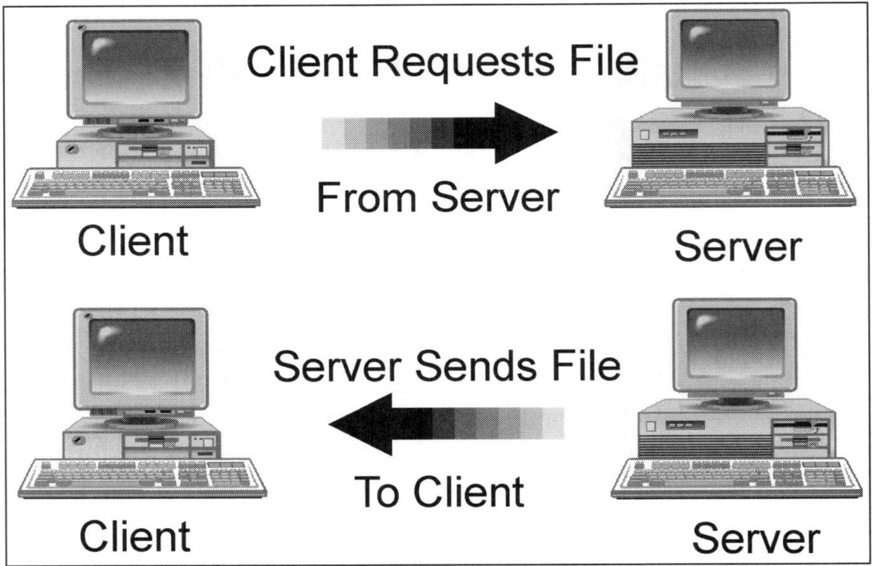

Figure 1-2: *The client and server connection.*

HTTP Servers

The language Web clients and servers use to communicate with each other is called the HyperText Transmission Protocol (HTTP). All Web clients and servers must be able to speak HTTP in order to send and receive hypermedia documents. The success of the

Web is due partly to HTTP's ability to handle multiple application protocols that allow users access to many Internet protocols, such as anonymous FTP, Gopher and WAIS data servers. HTTP also gives the system its multimedia capabilities, supporting the retrieval and display of text, graphics, animation and the playback of sound. Because the HTTP protocol is the foundation for most Web transactions, Web servers are often called HTTP servers.

Although World Wide Web servers are primarily run on UNIX servers, they are available for many platforms and environments, including Windows, Windows NT, Macintosh, VM and VMS. The domination of the Internet by UNIX servers is likely to change with the introduction of 32-bit platforms, such as Windows NT, the forthcoming Windows 95 and OS/2.

Which operating system and Web server you use to publish your Web documents depends largely on the audience you want to address. If you want to make your documents available to all the users on the Internet, you'll need to publish your Web documents on a multitasking operating system that can handle more than one user at a time, such as Windows NT or a UNIX operating system, such as BSD UNIX or Linux. Chapter 11 explains how to use a full-time connection offered by a service provider or a server service to publish Web documents. Chapter 12 gives hands on help for setting up your own server to publish Web documents.

Web Browsers

Running a Web client, usually called a *Web browser*, the client connects to a computer specified by a network address, called a Uniform Resource Locator (URL), which sends a request to that computer's Web server for the Web document. The server responds by sending the text and any other media referenced by a hyperlink in the text (pictures, sounds or movies) to the user's PC. The document the server sends is in the HTML (HyperText Markup Language) format. HTML documents, also called *Web documents*, let the reader click on a hypertext word or phrase to access files or jump to other HTML documents. These hypertext links between files and documents from servers around the world make the system work as if it were one huge web of information.

The best-known browsers are the NCSA Mosaic family of browsers, and the Netscape Communications family of Netscape browsers for UNIX, Windows and Macintosh computers. Text-based browsers, such as Lynx and Emacs-W3, are available for VT100 terminals.

Some companies give away a browser and then offer a more powerful version of the browser for sale. Many software vendors are purchasing licenses for browsers, such as Mosaic, and waiving the license fees for users to offer freeware implementations of browsers. The logic behind this is to create name recognition and to add value to other products. Netscape Navigator, for example, is licensed from Netscape Communications and is included on the Companion CD-ROM accompanying this book. Figure 1-3 shows Microsoft's main Web page, called a *home page*, using the Netscape Navigator browser.

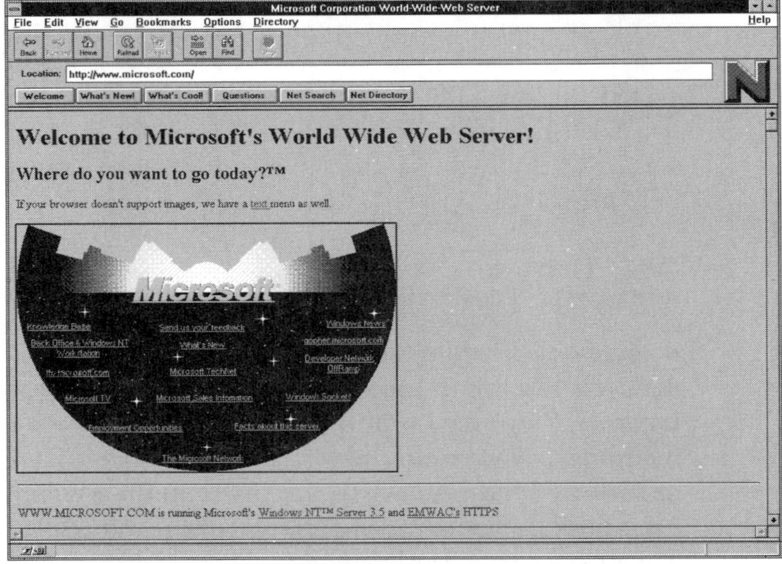

Figure 1-3: *Microsoft's home page in the Netscape Navigator Web browser.*

Some service providers offer software packages that include a proprietary browser. Proprietary browsers are somewhat limiting because many don't include or work using a standard WinSock program. *WinSock*, or Windows Socket, is a standard for implementing TCP/IP networking under Microsoft Windows. For example, Netcom's NetCruiser and Pipeline's Internaut programs let you view Web documents, but don't include standard WinSock software required to run other Web browsers, such as Mosaic and Netscape.

The appearance of a document will vary from one browser to the next according to the capabilities of each system and the user's preferences. Because there are different browsers, it's important to write and publish documents that will look good on any browser and not just the specific browser you have access to.

Uniform Resource Locators

Web browsers allow the user to specify a Uniform Resource Locator (URL) and connect to a document or resource. When selecting hypertext in a Web document, the user is actually sending a request to open a URL. It is possible to represent nearly any file or service on the Internet with a URL. A Web browser can also act as an FTP, Gopher and telnet client. Hyperlinks then can be made not only to other Web documents and media, but also to other network services. Users access different resources by using different types of URLs. Figure 1-4 shows the structure of a URL. Notice that the first part of the URL (before the two slashes) specifies the method of access. The second part is typically the address of the computer where the data or service is located. Further parts may specify the names of files, the port to connect to or the text to search for in a database. Table 1-1 lists some examples of URLs for accessing different resources.

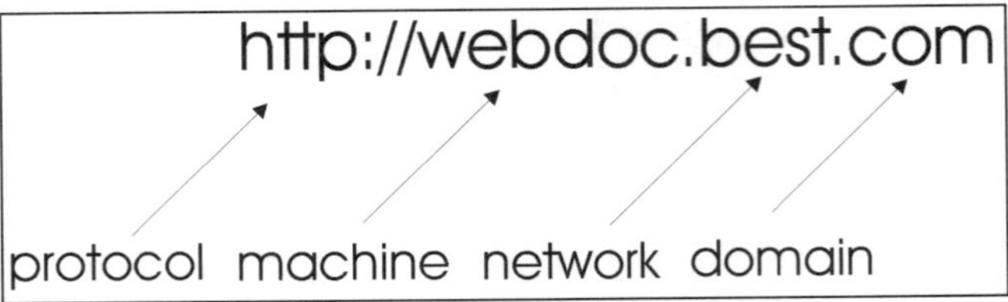

Figure 1-4: *The structure of a URL.*

Resource	URL
HTTP	http://akebono.stanford.edu/
FTP	ftp://oak.oakland.edu/pub3/win3/
Gopher	gopher://gopher.micro.umn.edu:70/1
telnet	telnet://rs.internic.net
USENET News	news:comp.infosystems.www.announce

Table 1-1: *URLs for Internet resources.*

Security & Authentication

Web servers are now including encryption and client authentication services so users can send and receive secure data. A secure server lets you be selective as to who can receive information to ensure that sensitive information is kept private. The advent of secure servers is sure to have a powerful impact on the number of commercial ventures on the Internet. Several companies are already setting up "pay-per-view" hypermedia Web sites. For example, users can subscribe to a service to access the *Encyclopedia Britannica* through the World Wide Web.

Dr. James H. Clark, the founder of Silicon Graphics Inc., and Marc Andreesen, who designed and developed the original Mosaic program, both joined forces to create Mosaic Communications. Shortly after introducing the Netscape Navigator browser and a lawsuit by the University of Illinois who owned the copyright to Mosaic, the company's name was changed to Netscape

Communications. Netscape Communications was the first company to introduce a secure server. In December 1994, Netscape Communications announced the Netsite server line, including the Netsite Commerce Server. This secure server is based on RSA Data Security Technology that incorporates Netscape's Communications Secure Sockets Layer (SSL). When combined with Netscape Navigator or other Internet browsers supporting SSL, the Netsite server lets users perform secure transactions to take advantage of commercial services, private online publications, financial services and online shopping. The Netsite Commerce Server was introduced at a whopping $5,000. A nonsecure server was also introduced at $1,495. Following the rule of supply and demand, the price for a secure server is sure to go down as more and more companies compete for the server market.

NCSA Mosaic isn't far behind. Version 2.0 of Mosaic, due out by early 1995, supports three types of security: basic authentication, enhanced authentication and secure HTTP. Basic authentication was developed by CERN/NCSA and is the least safe, allowing a password to travel unencrypted over the Net. Enhanced authentication uses Data Encryption Standard (DES) private-key encryption to let a business verify customers without sending passwords over the Net. A confirmation challenge is encoded along with the password to ensure that it was not captured from a previous message. Secure HTTP uses public-key technology from RSA Data Security, Inc. Secure HTTP is supplied by Terisa Systems. Terisa Systems is the most secure method, using a variety of public-key-based security schemes to encrypt data, such as a credit card number and expiration date, to perform secure, authenticated transactions. Several companies will be offering secure servers that work with these security standards in the near future. For example, Open Market (http://www.openmarket.com) has announced it will be selling secure servers by mid-1995, and First Virtual Holdings, Inc. (http://www.fv.com) lets you publish a page using a secure server for a nominal fee and small percentage of sales.

HTML, SGML & the Common Gateway Interface

The standard language the Web uses for creating and recognizing hypermedia documents is the HyperText Markup Language, commonly called HTML. Until the advent of Mosaic, the Internet was a multiplatform environment that made interchanging documents somewhat difficult. A special language called Standard Generalized Markup Language (SGML) was invented as a solution to the problems of sharing documents. SGML focuses on the elements in a document, so the recipient of information is freed from the proprietary choices of the originator.

SGML documents let you resize windows to make optimal use of your screen and let you print the documents so the printed document retains its layout. HTML was derived from SGML as a simple nonproprietary delivery format for global hypertext. Like SGML it provides a common method of authoring and format conversion.

HTML is fairly new and the language itself is easy to master. Web documents are typically written in HTML and are usually named with the extension ".html" or ".htm." These HTML documents are nothing more than standard ASCII files with formatting codes that contain information about layout, such as text styles, document titles, paragraphs, lists and hyperlinks.

The Three Versions of HTML & HTML Extensions

HTML is called a *markup language*, or simply *markup* for short. The description of the markup is called a "Document Type Definition," or DTD. The current HTML DTD supports basic hypermedia document creation and layout. There are three versions of HTML DTDs. HTML 1.0 was created primarily with specifications for creating hyperlinks. It has recently been replaced by HTML 2.0, the newly ratified standard by the Engineering Task Force. Version 2.0 specifications define features that let users display inline images and use interactive forms.

The Web moves fast, but most Web document authors are currently looking for new possibilities. Dave Raggett of the W3 Organization presented a set of HTML specifications in a white paper that have come to be known as HTML+. Some browser suppliers are adding their own extensions; for example Netscape is already implementing HTML+ and extensions that are specific to the Netscape browser. The next section takes a look at HTML and the emerging HTML 3.0 standard.

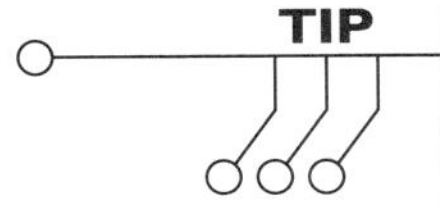

The annotated DTD for HTML 2.0 is available on the Web at http://info.cern.ch/hypertext/WWW/MarkUp/HTML.dtd.html

The Internet draft for HTML 3.0 is now available in ASCII text format via the Web at http://www.w3.org/hypertext/WWW/MarkUp/html3-dtd.txt

You can also get it at ftp://hplose.hpl.hp.com/pub/WWW/html3.dtd

HTML Markup

HTML is a fairly limited formatting language. HTML includes markup elements for headers, paragraphs, various types of character highlighting, inline images, hypertext links, lists, preformatted text and simple search facility.

Although HTML 3.0 is still in its final development stages, most browsers already support some HTML 3.0 features, such as tables. HTML 3.0 also supports e-mail URLs, so hyperlinks can be made to send e-mail automatically. For instance, selecting an e-mail address in a piece of hypertext would open a mail program, ready to send e-mail to that address. Additional layout and formatting options, such as text flow around floating figures, styles, figures, tables and mathematical equations are also quickly being added. HTML 3.0 also allows arbitrary nesting of the various kinds of lists, and lists items can now include horizontal rules. It also adds additional tags for Web information searching programs. Another interesting feature that is part of the HTML 3.0 specification is the ability to create text and graphics as objects. This will allow users to use icons to drag and drop text and graphics from the browser to another application.

The Common Gateway Interface

The unsung hero of Web publishing is the Common Gateway Interface (CGI). CGI is the interface that handles manipulating data generated by fill-in forms. It is also the basis for image mapping, which lets you define "hotspots" in images. Clicking a hotspot is the same as clicking a URL. Chapter 7, "Getting Graphic With Images" and Chapter 9, "Getting Interactive With Forms & Databases" give some examples of creating CGI scripts for creating interactive Web documents.

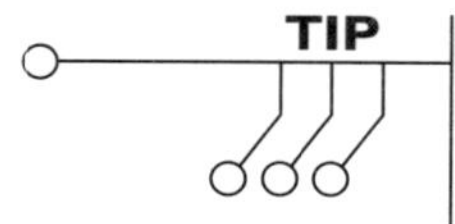

For an online introduction to CGI that includes a list of links to sample CGI programs, guides to creating and handling forms data and the common gateway interface specification, enter the URL: http://hoohoo.ncsa.uiuc.edu/cgi

Authoring & Publishing Tools

Several programs exist to help you create HTML documents or to convert existing documents into HTML format. Tools also exist that let you create interactive graphics with hotspots that the user can click to move to a specific location. The following section briefly introduces you to some of the authoring and publishing tools that help in the creation of HTML documents.

HTML Authoring & Conversion Tools

A variety of HTML authoring tools save you from having to enter HTML markup elements, called *tags*. An HTML editing program can also ensure that the resulting document complies with the HTML Document Type Definition (DTD). A few programs let you use macros or filters with common word processing packages, such as Microsoft Word, to convert formatted documents to

HTML. A few SGML tools let you convert SGML-based document formats to HTML documents. Chapter 2 takes a look at the HTML editors and converters.

Portable Document Programs

One of the hottest areas of publishing on the Internet is creating a portable multiplatform format standard that lets users view files no matter what type of computer they're using. Not everyone wants online information. Many users pay for online time. It makes sense to present large documents, such as detailed reports and online documentation, in a file that can be downloaded and read off-line. Because the Internet's roots are in UNIX, most files are stored in the PostScript format. With the advent of portable multiplatform document formats, however, this is beginning to change.

True to form each company is trying to create its own portable document standard. Adobe Acrobat is a suite of tools for creating and viewing documents in a Portable Document Format (PDF). Virtually any document can be converted into a PDF document. Apple is developing QuickDraw GX, but Apple is known for its proprietary formats and is not making the font format an open standard. Microsoft, the 800-pound gorilla, is developing TrueType Open. WordPerfect is currently shipping Envoy, a program that embeds a runtime viewer with the document. Farallon's Replica for Windows and the Macintosh also embeds a viewer and the document into a single file. BitStream, a formidable font company, has developed a technology called True Doc. The True Doc format is used in the next version of Common Ground, version 2.0, from No Hands Software, scheduled to be released early 1995. Common Ground 2.0 functions as a helper application, but it has the ability to load a mini-viewer on the fly to display documents, so you don't have to wait until the whole document is downloaded to start viewing it.

As of early 1995, Adobe's Portable Document Format is stealing the show with the ability to embed TrueType and Adobe Type 1 fonts, an Applications Program Interface (API) for plug-ins, and by offering the Adobe Acrobat Reader for free. Adobe Acrobat is one of the first applications to support the Mosaic Software development Interface (SDI) and Netscape's NCAPI, which are two-way interfaces that let other applications automatically work with the browser. This lets you include hyperlinks in a PDF document to a Web page. The biggest drawback to Acrobat is that it currently doesn't work with Windows NT, but this is likely to change.

Common Ground is the dark horse that is a little late out of the starting gate. The new version is not expected until mid '95, but the new version's ability to view a file on the fly is a marvelous feature. If, for example, you're downloading a 20-page document, you can see the first page within 30 seconds. The free mini-viewer is scaled down to only 200k so that it can be downloaded with a document. Common Ground version 2.0, like Acrobat Reader, supports Mosaic's SDI and Netscape's NCAPI, so you can also include hyperlinks in a Common Ground document to a Web page.

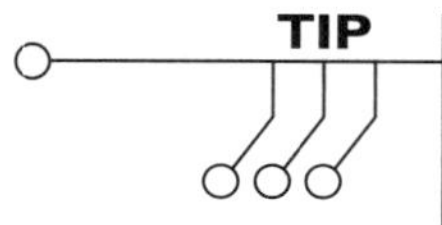

The Adobe Acrobat Reader and the Common Ground mini-viewer are included on the CD-ROM accompanying this book. The Adobe Acrobat Reader is also available for free at http://www.adobe.com

Web Publishing & Options

In order to publish a Web document, you need to make sure it is located on a server that is constantly available. Paying for a full-time connection is costly and publishing documents at modem speed is an unrealistic way to handle traffic. But relax, you don't have to have a Web server with a full-time connection in order to publish on the Internet.

Many service providers include special options for publishing Web documents as a part of their service or for a small fee. How much it costs to publish a Web document depends on the service you're using and what you want to publish. Costs can range from $10.00 a month for a simple home page to thousands of dollars a month for an interactive storefront.

Server Services & Web Design Services

You don't have to create a Web document on your own. Many server services and Web design services exist that will gladly do it for you—for a price. The resources section at the back of this book lists server services and Web design services that you can use to help you publish Web documents. The following section describes some of the types of Web documents you can publish.

From Home Pages to Virtual Storefronts

Web publishing can be broken down into three categories: a single page brochure, an information center and a virtual storefront. The main page that most users connect to is called a *home page*. The following types of documents can be published on the Web: advertising, brochures, database, demos, newsletters, press releases, customer support/FAQs (Frequently Asked Questions), interactive storefronts and magazines.

The Future of Web Publishing

Most Web browsers, such as Mosaic and Netscape, now support simple fill-out forms and tables.

SGML Web browsers and portable document viewers are beginning to address the limitations of HTML. SoftQuad has announced Panorama (freeware) and Panorama Pro (commercial version) to address the formatting features that are lacking in HTML. These SGML browsers work in conjunction with browsers, such as Netscape Navigator and NCSA Mosaic. Panorama opens automatically when the browser encounters an SGML file. The formatting features allow you to display interactive tables and basic mathematical equations. A powerful capability of Panorama is that it lets users choose from multiple DTDs to define styles for Web documents.

Styles for Web browsers are a hot topic. It is possible that styles could be identified as part of the document. Using styles, authors could specify aspects of Web documents, such as font families, text color and point size, and the use of white space around text and graphics. The use of images, colors and textures of the background offer further ways of creating a unique Web document. Inline images, images that appear in HTML documents, are currently limited to the GIF format. Work is already underway to support other inline image formats, such as JPEG images and MPEG video and QuickTime movie formats. This will allow images and videos to be displayed from within a document.

At the end of March '95 Adobe Systems and Netscape Communications took the next logical step for Web publishing. Adobe and Netscape announced they were teaming up to incorporate Acrobat into a future version of Netscape. The new Web browser would allow you to preserve the layout of the printed page. For example, you could display a two-column document with text that wrapped around an inline graphic in the center of the page. It will also make it possible to include sound and videos in Web documents that don't rely on external applications. Look for No Hands Software's Common Ground to either be integrated with an existing stand-alone browser or ultimately include the capability to browse the Web to display formatted documents.

HTML and HTTP are already extended to include workgroup features; for example, Lotus announced in early '95 the InterNotes Web Server. This server works with the HTTP protocol to publish Notes databases on the Net. Anyone can quickly convert an existing Lotus Notes database into an HTML document. This is only the beginning, it is quite possible that the Web could include integration with the telephone service for voice mail and video-telephone calls. As cable companies and high-speed transmission connections enter the scene, it's possible that Web browsers could also access radio and television channels.

Moving On

With a possible audience of millions the Web is becoming the new frontier of publishing. After browsing Web sites, you're bound to wonder what you need to publish your own Web documents. This book will guide you through the process providing hands-on examples you can easily modify to match your own publishing needs.

In order to publish on the Internet, you'll first want to take a look at the types of tools you have to work with. Although HTML is a fairly easy language to master, entering HTML commands can quickly become a tedious process. The next chapter gives you an overview of the editors and converters that can save you time when creating HTML documents.

2

HTML Editors & Converters

While it's possible to create even the most complex HTML documents with nothing more than a plain text editor, there are a number of programs that can save you time and effort in the process. If you are creating the content for your Web pages from scratch—and if the Web is the only place your work will be published—start with an HTML editor. HTML editors focus on the creation of new HTML documents.

If you're going to be working with an existing document, such as a brochure or press release, your best bet would be an HTML converter. An HTML converter is a program that translates your existing document from its current format (or a format your word processor can export) into a set of HTML pages. This means you can save yourself the trouble of starting over when you want to publish your work on the Web. There are some drawbacks to this method, however. HTML is still in its infancy and is far more limiting than existing page layout programs and word processors. A document that looks splendid when produced with a desktop publishing package will lose many of its endearing charms when shoehorned into the HTML format. For example, you could lose control of margins, indents, fonts and tables.

In this chapter we'll look at HTML editors and HTML converters. Before you rush into creating HTML pages, take a look at the benefits and limitations of these editors and converters and try both approaches to see which works best for you.

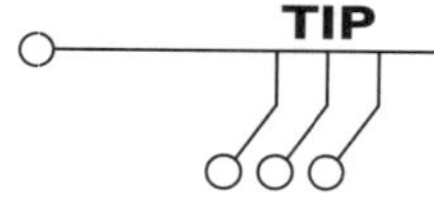

Don't worry if you don't understand what all the markups do right now. What you need to understand is the range of editor and converter programs available and how to choose the ones that best meet your needs.

HTML Editors

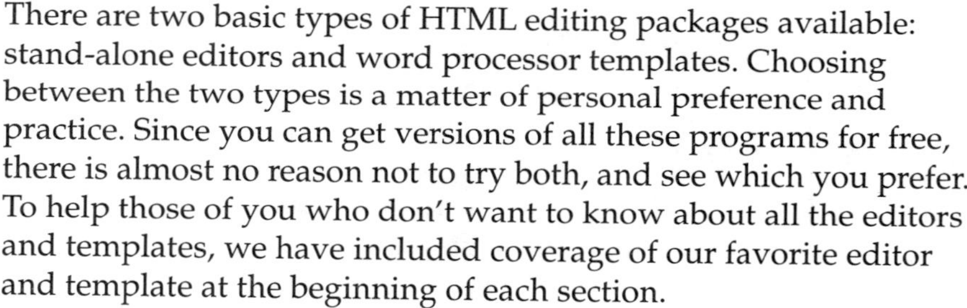

There are two basic types of HTML editing packages available: stand-alone editors and word processor templates. Choosing between the two types is a matter of personal preference and practice. Since you can get versions of all these programs for free, there is almost no reason not to try both, and see which you prefer. To help those of you who don't want to know about all the editors and templates, we have included coverage of our favorite editor and template at the beginning of each section.

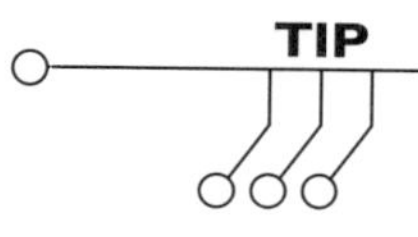

The fact that only Word for Windows templates are available at this time is due to coincidence rather than any inherent feature or capabilities in the Microsoft product, so if your word processor of choice is not Word for Windows, keep checking the Web for templates for your favorite word processor. Better yet, write your own and contribute them to the Internet community!

One feature you'll notice right away about every HTML editor for Windows is that when you create the HTML document, you will see the actual HTML markup—even if you don't want to. (You can, however, "hide tags" in HoTMetal PRO.) There is no such thing as true WYSIWYG (What You See Is What You Get) with publishing on the Web. Every Web browser, such as Netscape or Mosaic, has its own way of rendering the page, and the user has complete control over page size and font styles. So by forcing you to look at the HTML markup, you are reminded that you are merely creating a text document with hints to the viewer programs about what different parts of your document mean.

In this chapter, there are a few criticisms that can be leveled at each of the packages. Keep in mind that most of these editors are *free*, and the authors of these packages spent a lot of time on programs that may never bring them a dime. Some of the program creators are working on advanced versions of their programs that they can make money on, but for now they are offering their work to the public in the hope that someone will find them useful. This is indicative of the spirit of the Internet—sharing work and offering to help without expectation of compensation. Without authors like these, there would not be an Internet, or the World Wide Web, as we know it today.

Rules-based & Unchecked HTML Editors

HTML editors and templates fall within one of two categories: rules-based HTML editors and unchecked HTML editors. Rules-based editors require you to carefully follow HTML formatting conventions. You must insert the right tags in the right locations. The major benefit of using a rules-based editor is that it helps you create HTML documents correctly. If you try to open a document that includes nonstandard tags, the editor will typically display an error message when it tries to load the document. Unchecked HTML editors don't check the validity of the document—you can insert tags incorrectly and the editor will not let you know. The benefit of an unchecked editor is that you can use nonstandard tags.

Stand-alone Editors

Typically stand-alone editors don't require support from other software in order to work, although a few are written in Visual Basic and require a dynamic link library file named VBRUN300.DLL. This section explains the benefits and limitations of six popular stand-alone editors, including HoTMetaL and HoTMetaL PRO, HTML Assistant and HTML Assistant Pro, HTML Editor, HTML HyperEdit and HTML Writer. Two additional high-end commercial word processor/desktop publishing programs that promise to be powerful Web publishing tools are Frame's FrameMaker 5 for Windows and Interleaf's Cyberleaf. Both of these products include Web publishing features and are scheduled to ship in the second half of 1995. Unfortunately neither of these products were available at the writing of this book.

HoTMetaL PRO & HoTMetaL

Our favorite stand-alone HTML editors are HoTMetaL PRO and its shareware counterpart, HoTMetaL, from SoftQuad. The complete commercial version of HoTMetaL PRO is included on the CD-ROM accompanying this book. HoTMetaL PRO is a rule-based HTML editor that includes several features not available in shareware version that you'll find useful for heavy-duty HTML editing, including

- *Importing files through a filter*—This feature allows you to import files that are not correct HTML, but are close. The HoTMetaL shareware version simply refuses to open these files.
- *Spell-checking and thesaurus*—The addition of spell-checking and the thesaurus is an invaluable aid.
- *Additional editing flexibility*—The Pro version gives you fine control over editing and makes the creation process easier. It also provides additional HTML tag types not supported in the free version.
- *Macro language*—You can create, save, load and run keystroke sequences you define to speed your editing process—a handy feature.

- *Tables*—Although tables are not supported in HTML 2.0, some browsers have recently added table support based on future HTML version standards. HoTMetaL PRO allows you to insert tables into your HTML document.
- *Online documentation*—HoTMetaL PRO provides an extensive online help system that saves you from having to refer to the documentation for help.
- *Online tutorial*—An HTML document that guides you through the creation of an HTML document.

HoTMetaL PRO is based on SoftQuad's SGML editor, which makes moving from the HTML product to SoftQuad's SGML editor an easy transition.

SoftQuad is one of the founding members of *SGML Open,* "a non-profit, international consortium of providers of products and services, dedicated to accelerating the further adoption, application, and implementation of the Standard Generalized Markup Language, the international standard for open interchange of documents and structured information objects." If you're interested in learning more about this organization, check out the same open Web page at http://www.sgmlopen.org/sgml/docs/index.html.

Installing HoTMetaL PRO

In order to install HoTMetaL PRO, you must be using a PC with an 80486 or Pentium with 8mb or more memory. The optimal system is a Pentium with 12mb. To install HoTMetaL PRO, insert the CD-ROM into your CD drive, start Windows and from the Program Manager, and choose Run from the File menu. In the Run text box, enter **d:\sq\setup**. If you're using a CD-ROM drive other than d, replace the **d** with your CD drive indicator.

A dialog box appears asking you to enter the directory where you want to store HoTMetaL PRO. The default is c:\htmlpro. You can choose another drive and/or directory if you like. The setup program checks to make sure you have enough disk space. If you don't have enough space, the setup program prompts you to choose another location. Another dialog box appears that indicates the status of files being copied to your hard disk. Once the files have been copied, a dialog box appears asking you for the name of the program group where you want to store the HoTMetaL PRO icon. By default the setup program creates a new program group called SoftQuad HoTMetaL PRO. You can create a new group by entering that name in the text box. Be careful not to enter an existing program group name because the setup program will overwrite the existing group.

Configuring HoTMetaL PRO

Before you start HoTMetaL PRO, you need to make a few configuration changes in order to work with Netscape and Netscape's extensions to HTML by changing the browser and the rules setting. By default HoTMetaL PRO is set up to use the Mosaic browser. In order to start working with the Netscape browser that accompanies this book, you need to change the default setting in the sqhmpro.ini file. To do this, use a text editor, such as Windows Notepad, to edit the sqhmpro.ini file found in the HTMLPRO directory. Find the line that reads

```
html_browser     =d:\mosaic\mosaic.exe
```

Change the mosaic.exe setting to

```
html_browser     =d:\netscape\netscape.exe
```

Netscape Communications has added many extensions to overcome some of the layout limitations of HTML. Unless you plan on only entering strict HTML and not using Netscape extensions, you can leave the rules setting alone. Otherwise, in order to use the Netscape extensions, you need to change the default HTML rules setting in the sqhmpro.ini file. Changing the rules setting is similar to changing the browser setting. Using a text editor, edit the sqhmpro.ini file and find the line that reads

```
rules_file       = html.mtl
```

Change the html.mtl setting to

```
rules_file          = html-net.mtl
```

Getting Started With HoTMetaL PRO

To run HoTMetaL PRO, double-click its icon in the Program Manager. After an introductory copyright screen, you'll see a blank editing screen. Once you've gotten the program started, the simplest thing to do is to open one of the many template files SoftQuad has included. Samples range from a few simple paragraphs to a Web home page to a customer service forms–based page. If you find something similar to what you want, you're set. Even if you need to make modifications, using the template saves you the effort of figuring out how to create an HTML page from scratch.

By default, HoTMetaL PRO displays the HTML tags in a directed arrow format, as shown in Figure 2-1.

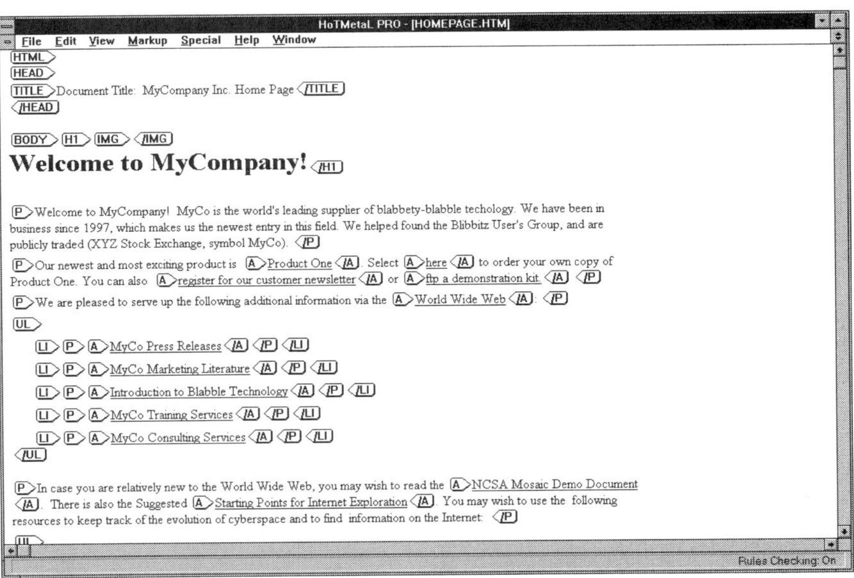

Figure 2-1: *Typical HoTMetaL PRO editing screen.*

You *can* turn the tags off and add text to existing parts of your page. As you can see in the preceding illustration, text is presented with varying font sizes to suggest how it may look when viewed with a Web browser.

Other features of HoTMetaL PRO include the ability to look at the structure of the HTML markup, enforce HTML structure, open existing HTML files, edit large files, preview images and have the program guide you through changing all the URL references from local references to network-name references.

Although you can open HTML pages created by other editors (or right off the Web), be aware that HoTMetaL PRO is a rules-based editor that checks for correct HTML syntax, so it will reject a good number of pages that seem to work okay on the Web. This is because most Web browsers are very accepting of bad HTML coding. You will be able to view HTML pages that bear little resemblance to properly structured HTML. HoTMetaL PRO is fussy and therefore is not the best choice for making a few small edits to an existing HTML page that isn't well coded.

Installing HoTMetaL

HoTMetaL PRO is not shareware or freeware. You can't copy it and give it away. SoftQuad's HoTMetaL program, however, is freeware and can be found at several locations on the Internet. SoftQuad isn't giving away the store. They believe that by giving away their basic product, they can convince you to upgrade to their professional edition. Also, by giving you a way to get started on HTML authoring for free, they are luring yet another writer into the larger field of SGML and electronic document publishing, a field in which SoftQuad is one of the leaders. To get the latest version of HoTMetaL check out the URL: ftp://ftp.ncsa.uiuc.edu/Web/html/hotmetal/Windows.

The file name of the shareware version is hotm1new.exe. This is a self-extracting file. You can find a list of other sites on the SoftQuad Web server at http://www.sq.com/hm-ftp.html. You can e-mail SoftQuad for more information at hotmetal@sq.com.

Move hotm1new.exe into a temporary directory for installing the program. In the File Manager, double-click on the file hotm1new.exe. This extracts the HoTMetaL installation files in the temporary directory. Double-click on the file hminst.exe to begin the installation. A welcome message appears. Click on the Continue button. Another dialog box appears, letting you specify the directory to install HoTMetaL. The default directory is c:\sqhm. Once the HoTMetaL files have been extracted, a dialog box appears with the name of the Windows program group that will be created. By default, the installation program will create a program group called SoftQuad HoTMetaL 1.0+. Once the group is created you can delete the temporary directory. HoTMetaL also comes with a sixty-page manual in PostScript format, which you can print on a PostScript printer or view with Ghostview. You can also download an ASCII version of the documentation at http://www10.w3.org/hypertext/WWW/Tools/ with the filename hotmetal.txt.

What's Ghostview?

This program works in conjunction with another free program named Ghostscript, a PostScript interpreter that runs on a variety of platforms, including Windows and Windows NT. If you want a way to read PostScript files without printing them, you should have Ghostscript and Ghostview. Ghostscript was written by Aladdin Enterprises, and commercial licenses are available. You can find Ghostscript and Ghostview on most anonymous FTP servers that have Windows programs. The most up-to-date version of Ghostscript can be found at ftp://ftp.cs.wisc.edu:/pub/ghost/aladdin/. The Windows file is named gs312win.zip. The Win32s program for 32-bit Windows is gs312w32.zip. The Ghostview file can be found at ftp://ftp.cs.wisc.edu:pub/ghost/rjl/. The compressed file for Ghostview is named gsvw113b.zip. Note that these file names will change to reflect new version numbers.

Getting Started With HoTMetaL

Once HoTMetaL is installed, simply create your own Program Manager icon as instructed in the README.TXT file. That's it. You start HoTMetaL exactly like HoTMetaL PRO—double-click its icon in the Program Manager.

All in all, the free version of HoTMetaL is an excellent HTML editing tool. It still suffers from an intolerance of incorrect HTML markup and insists on presenting the nitty gritty of the HTML markup, even when you'd rather be focusing on content and structure. If you run into problems using this version, you're on your own—SoftQuad offers no technical support for the free version.

HTML Assistant & HTML Assistant Pro

HTML Assistant and HTML Assistant Pro are designed for stand-alone editing of HTML pages. HTML Assistant is freeware and HTML Assistant Pro is the commercial version. The commercial version includes a printed manual and tutorial, file and URL search features, and formatting filters for creating readable documents from HTML files. Like HoTMetaL PRO, you can open existing HTML pages and edit them. Unlike HoTMetaL PRO, HTML Assistant lacks the ability to check the legality of the HTML markups. This is good if you are editing an existing page, and you're not worried that your HTML is correct. In fact, you can enter almost any markup, and the program won't complain. If you enter incorrect tags, however, the page will not display correctly. Also, there's no built-in preview mode to give you a sense of what the page will look like with a Web browser. However HTML Assistant does give you the ability to launch the Web browser of your choice to preview the documents you create. HTML Assistant also comes with a help system. One handy feature is the ability to create custom entries with a feature called User Tools. User Tools act like a macro, letting you repeatedly enter text you've defined with the click of a button. You can get a copy of HTML Assistant at ftp://ftp.cs.dal.ca/htmlasst with a file name of htmlasst.zip. HTML Assistant was written by Howard Harawitz, who can be reached at harawitz@brooknorth.bedford.ns.ca.

Installation

To install HTML Assistant, decompress the HTMLASST.ZIP file into a new directory. The compressed file contains the executable program, a number of information files, plus four support files that are required for the program to run. HTML Assistant was written in Visual Basic and uses three special Visual Basic files: CMDIALOG.VBX, THREED.VBX and VBRUN300.DLL. The VBRUN300.DLL is not distributed with HTML Assistant, but you can download it at ftp://ftp.cs.dal.ca/htmlasst/. The file name is vbrun300.zip. Before you download the VBRUN300.DLL file (vbrun300.zip), check your Windows directory. VBRUN300 and the other two files ending with the .VBX extension are common files, they may already be installed in your Windows directory. If these files are already on your system and the files ending with .VBX have file dates equal to or later than the versions supplied with HTML Assistant, you can delete these files from the HTML Assistant subdirectory. Otherwise, copy them to your Windows system directory so they will be available for HTML Assistant and any other Visual Basic programs you download. Once you have decompressed all the files, create an icon for the program and double-click the icon to start the editor. When you start up HTML Assistant, you'll see a title splash screen followed by the HTML Assistant screen. Figure 2-2 shows a typical HTML Assistant screen.

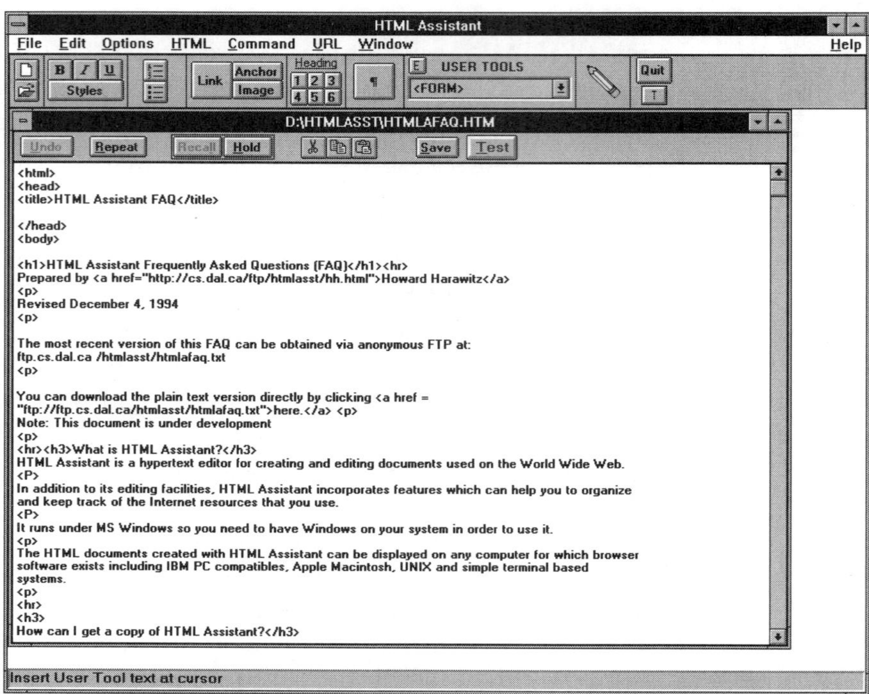

Figure 2-2: *A typical HTML Assistant editing screen.*

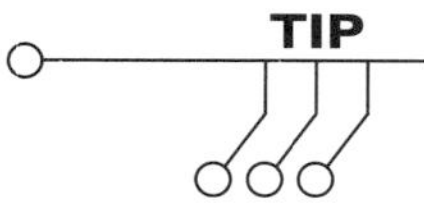

When you install HTML Assistant, you can leave the CMDIALOG.VBX and THREED.VBX files in the same directory with the HTML Assistant executable if you want to. The reason some instructions tell you to copy common files to the Windows or Windows system directory is to save hard disk space by allowing more than one program to share the same common files.

Getting Started

Using the HTML Assistant program is very simple: you select the markup you want from the toolbar at the top, and the program enters the markup for you. Text styles are entered by selecting the text you want to treat in a special way (such as bold, italic, etc.) and then selecting the Styles button. You can also create your own palette of tools in the User Tools dialog box, in case you want some short cuts to entering frequently used markups.

Once you get used to HTML editing, this program is an extremely handy way to quickly edit an HTML page. Very few keystrokes are needed for an HTML markup entry, but HTML Assistant doesn't check for incorrect format or structure.

A nifty feature of HTML Assistant is its integration with the Cello Web browser. If you use Cello, HTML Assistant will control it with Dynamic Data Exchange (DDE) messages. Cello will be automatically updated whenever you modify a page, and a button will appear in Cello to jump back into HTML Assistant for further editing.

One of the biggest disadvantages of HTML Assistant is that at the time of this writing, the program is limited to 32kbyte file sizes. While this size limit is inconsequential for most small home pages, it could prove to be a problem when creating more complex pages.

HTML Editor

HTML Editor is similar to HTML Assistant in that its focus is on simplifying the entry of HTML tags. It does not check for correct structure or format, so it is useful for quickly fixing an existing HTML document that is poorly constructed. HTML Editor adds easy entry of special characters via an optional floating toolbar. This can be important if you are editing in a language other than English. The program also makes a special effort to export to UNIX systems by including the correct end-of-line character combination. You can get an evaluation copy of HTML Editor from ftp://pringle.mta.ca/pub/HTMLed with a file name of htmed*xx*.zip, where *xx* is the version number. HTML Editor was written by Peter B. Crawshaw, who can be reached via e-mail at inettc@nbnet.nb.ca.

Installing HTML Editor

To install HTML Editor, decompress the program archive in a new subdirectory. The executable program named HTMLED.EXE appears along with a few text files. You can then create an icon for HTML Editor and click the icon to start it up. No additional support files are needed. Figure 2-3 shows the HTML Editor with a sample HTML page and all the standard floating toolbars active.

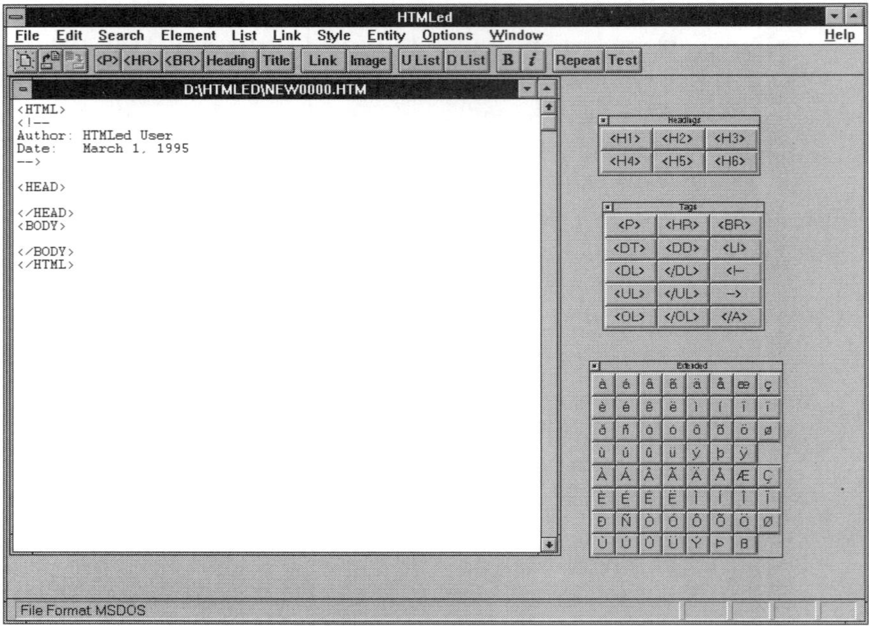

Figure 2-3: *A typical HTML Editor editing screen with floating toolbars active.*

Getting Started

One of the nicest features of this program is the floating toolbars, and the easy access to the "extended" character set used by most European languages. This is by far the easiest entry method of all the HTML editors covered in this chapter, and an essential feature if you plan to do any amount of editing in a non-English language.

This version of HTML Editor, like HTML Assistant, suffers from a limit on the file size, but a professional version is promised that will eliminate this problem. The professional edition will also have support for forms and colored syntax highlighting.

HTML HyperEdit

HTML HyperEdit is a slightly different kind of HTML editor. HTML HyperEdit is based on the Asymmetrix Toolbook runtime program, which means there are more files hanging around to make it all run, and it runs in a fixed-size edit window. It provides some interesting features not found in the other editors, such as a helpful search and replace function similar to most word processors. Another useful feature of HyperEdit is its training mode. In the training mode, HyperEdit walks you through the steps involved in creating a simple HTML document. This is the only package that does this, and for a new HTML author, it's a valuable aid. You can get a copy of this editor from ftp://ftp.curtin.edu.au/pub/internet/windows/hyperedit with a file name of htmledit.zip. The program was written by Stephen Hancock, who can be reached via e-mail at s.hancock@icarus.curtin.edu.au.

Installing HyperEdit

To install HTML HyperEdit, decompress the program archive into a new subdirectory on your hard disk. The directory contains a number of .DLL files, as well as the executable TBOOK.EXE. Create an icon and edit the command line using the File/Properties command to read as follows: **TBOOK.EXE HTMLEDIT.TBK**. Figure 2-4 shows the main HyperEdit screen.

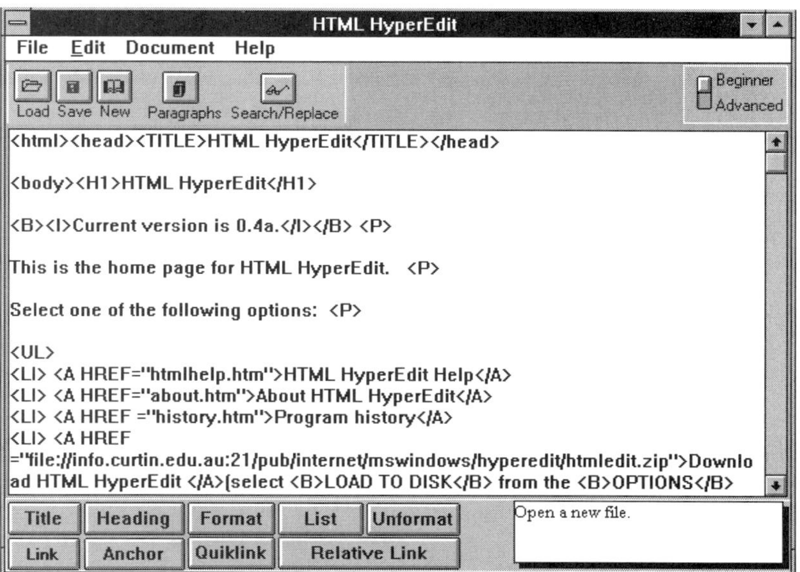

Figure 2-4: *HTML HyperEdit main screen.*

Getting Started

HTML HyperEdit is about halfway between a real HTML editor and an ASCII to HTML converter. One of the strengths of this program is the ability to quickly add HTML markups to an existing text-only document of moderate size (HyperEdit is limited to a 32k file size).

When in Beginner mode, the box in the lower right side is a help screen that changes whenever the mouse pointer crosses a different area of the screen. HyperEdit, unlike most Windows programs, doesn't include standard load, save and new options in the File menu. Instead you must use the toolbar commands.

When the Advanced option is selected, there are additional formatting commands available in the same location as the help text. You'll have to decide for yourself which is more important to you. When you open a new file, you have the opportunity to insert paragraph markers automatically wherever the program thinks one should go. Figure 2-5 shows HTML HyperEdit in its training mode.

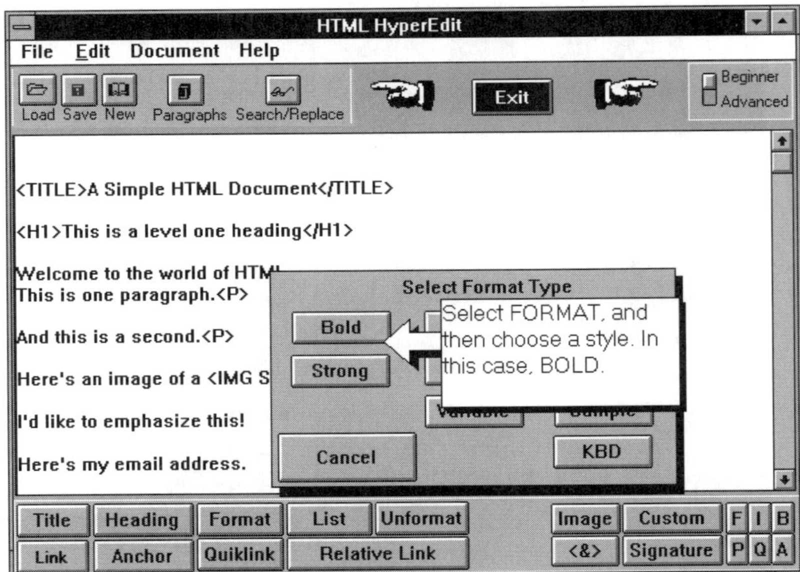

Figure 2-5: *HTML HyperEdit is the only editor that includes a training mode to step you through the process of creating an HTML document.*

HTML Writer

The HTML Writer is a basic tag entry program for HTML. It supports every HTML tag, but you need to know how to structure an HTML document, because there is no attempt to verify the correctness of your structure. HTML Writer comes with a very nice help file and the Test Using item in the Option menu lets you choose to launch Mosaic, Cello or Netscape as a Web browser to test your page. You can obtain a copy of HTML Writer at ftp://lal.cs.byu.edu/pub/www/tools. The file name of the latest official version is htmlwrit.zip. Occasionally you may find beta versions of the software under other names. HTML Writer was written by Kris Nosack, who can be reached via e-mail at html-writer@byu.edu.

Installing HTML Writer

To install HTML Writer, decompress the program archive into a new directory. The archive contains the executable program, a number of information files, plus four support files required for the program to run. HTML Writer was written in Visual Basic and uses four Visual Basic files that are included in the distribution: CMDIALOG.VBX, COMMDLG.DLL, EMEDIT.VBX and TOOLBARS.VBX. You also need a copy of VBRUN300.DLL in your Windows directories somewhere. Since these are common files, they may already be installed in your Windows directory. If these files are already on your system (and have file dates equal to or later than the versions supplied with HTML Writer), you can delete these files from the HTML Writer subdirectory. Otherwise, copy them to your Windows or Windows NT system directory. You can obtain a copy of VBRUN300.DLL at ftp://lal.cs.byu.edu/pub/www/tools/. The VBRUN300.DDL file is compressed and stored with the file name VBRUN300.ZIP.

Getting Started

When you want to add a markup to your document, you can either select the markup from the toolbar or from the HTML menu. The editor inserts a start and end tag (as appropriate) and you can then type the text in the correct spot. Alternately, you can type the text first (or paste from another application) and then select the element type. Adding jump destinations in links is made easier by the program with special dialog boxes you fill in with the desired information. The main screen for HTML Writer is shown in Figure 2-6.

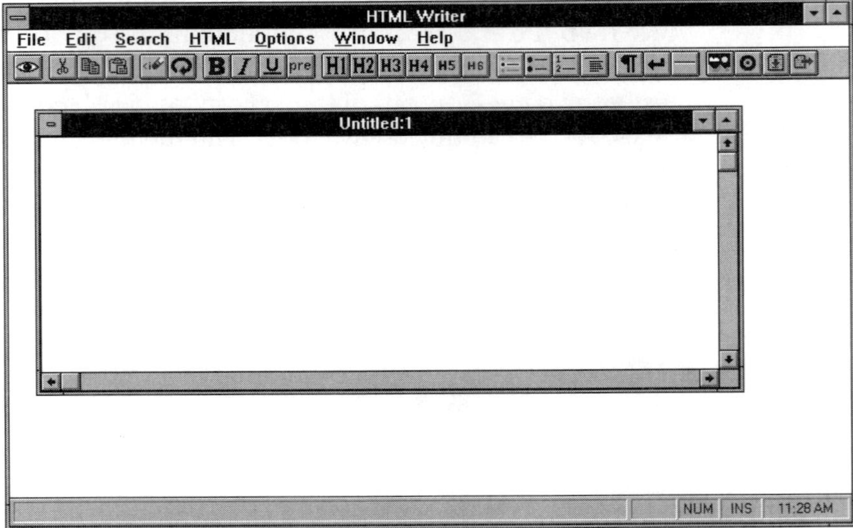

Figure 2-6: *HTML Writer's main screen.*

Microsoft Word Templates

As mentioned at the beginning of this chapter, all the templates that are available for Windows are created for Microsoft Word. While there is a great benefit of using a word processor you are already familiar with, there are some real limitations when using a Word template to create an HTML document. Depending on what you want to do you may find that you will want to use both a Word template and an HTML editor to create your Web documents.

None of the three simple template packages support all the special characters that are represented as HTML character entities (character entities are covered in Chapter 6, "Creating Your Text Appeal"). This means that certain characters, such as the copyright symbol or accented vowels are not properly generated in HTML using a template. You'll need to edit the HTML document and add the correct markup for these characters manually. Also, none of the templates support HTML parsing, which means you can insert incorrect codes into a document and not find out until you view them with a Web browser. Even then, some browsers may be more tolerant of bad HTML than others. You *could* check an edited document with HoTMetaL, but unless you're careful many documents will fail the stringent tests performed by HoTMetaL.

Installing Word Templates

Templates are installed with Word for Windows by copying the template files that end with the file extension .dot to the Templates directory (Word for Windows 6) or if you're using Word for Windows version 2, copy the file to the same directory as the executable program file (WINWORD.EXE). Once you've copied the template file, you may access the template by choosing File>>New from the menu and selecting the new template by name.

Microsoft's Internet Assistant for Word & Microsoft Word Viewer

Microsoft Internet Assistant is being published in conjunction with Microsoft Viewer and both are free. The Internet Assistant is a HTML converter, Web browser and authoring template for creating Web documents from within MS Word. The Internet browsing component for Microsoft's Internet Assistant (IA) is provided by InterNetworks, a product of Booklink Technologies. It includes OLE support, so it can be used with Microsoft Office applications to create hyperlinks between Word documents. Internet Assistant is the only single product that allows users to browse the Web and edit HTML documents from within a single, easy to use interface.

Microsoft Internet Assistant and Microsoft Viewer are posted under the "What's New" heading of the Microsoft Home Page on the World Wide Web. Microsoft's home page can be accessed at http://www.microsoft.com/. It will also be available on floppy disk directly from Microsoft at (800) 426-9400 for a $5.50 shipping and handling charge.

Installing Microsoft Internet Assistant adds a button to the toolbar and menu options that let you choose to work in HTML View or edit mode. The Browse Web menu item is added to the File menu, so you can use Word as a Web browser. Figure 2-7 shows Microsoft Word displayed in the Web browse view. One of Microsoft Internet Assistant's goals is to let users author Internet documents in Word's own file format and let Word automatically generate the hypertext markup. By offering the Internet Assistant and Microsoft Viewer, Microsoft hopes to give users the option of either automatically converting Word docs to HTML or creating Web documents in Word native format. Word native format supports multiple columns, fonts and headers, text that wraps around graphics and OLE 2.0 embedded objects. Word users view richly formatted documents on the Web that contain tables and spreadsheets.

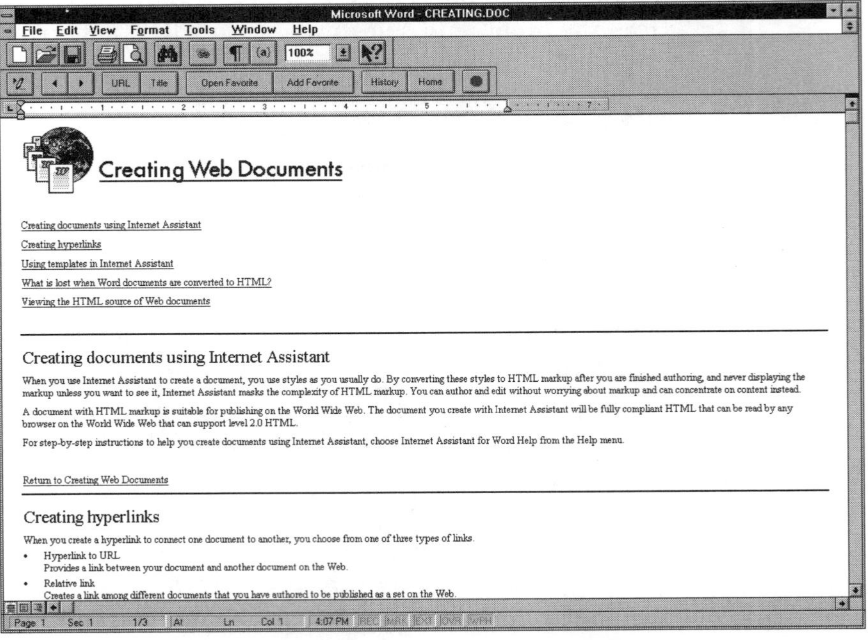

Figure 2-7: *Microsoft Internet Assistant lets you use Word as an HTML editor or as a Web browser.*

Quarterdeck's WebAuthor

Quarterdeck, the creators of the best-selling memory manager QEMM, released a commercial HTML authoring template system called Quarterdeck's WebAuthor. The introductory price for WebAuthor was $100 and after a limited time will go up to $149.95. Quarterdeck is also going to release a Web browser, called Quarterdeck's Mosaic, and a 16-bit server. It's likely that all these products will be sold as a bundle. WebAuthor is a document template system that was actually written by another company, Streetwise Software. Quarterdeck's WebAuthor Tools lets you create HTML files from within Word. It also lets you convert existing Word documents into HTML format or convert HTML into Word documents.

This well-designed editing tool is filled with features and includes excellent online help. One feature that is especially helpful is the use of dialog boxes to help step the author through the process of creating forms. Another slick feature is Print Preview, which lets you get a good idea of how the current HTML document will appear in a browser without leaving Word for Windows. Quarterdeck's WebAuthor can also validate your document to verify that you do not have any erroneous HTML tags.

Unlike other templates, Quarterdeck's WebAuthor comes with its own installation program. To install this template system, start Windows and from the Program Manager, choose Run from the File menu. In the Run text box, enter c:**install**. If you're using a hard disk drive other than c, replace the **c** with your hard disk drive indicator. The install program creates a program group that contains a Readme and a Help Icon.

Installing WebAuthor adds the option WebAuthor to Word's Tools menu. Unlike most Word template systems, you can create a new HTML document by simply choosing this option. Of course, you can use WebAuthor like any other Word template by choosing the HTML60 from the templates menu. When you create an HTML document WebAuthor removes Word's style menu. Instead, a Style button appears on the HTML authoring toolbar that you can use to apply HTML styles. Figure 2-8 shows the first screen that appears when you choose WebAuthor from the Tools menu.

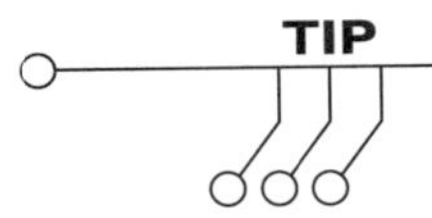

You can find more information regarding Quarterdeck WebAuthor, Quarterdeck Mosaic and the forthcoming server program by entering the URL: http://www.qdeck.com/.

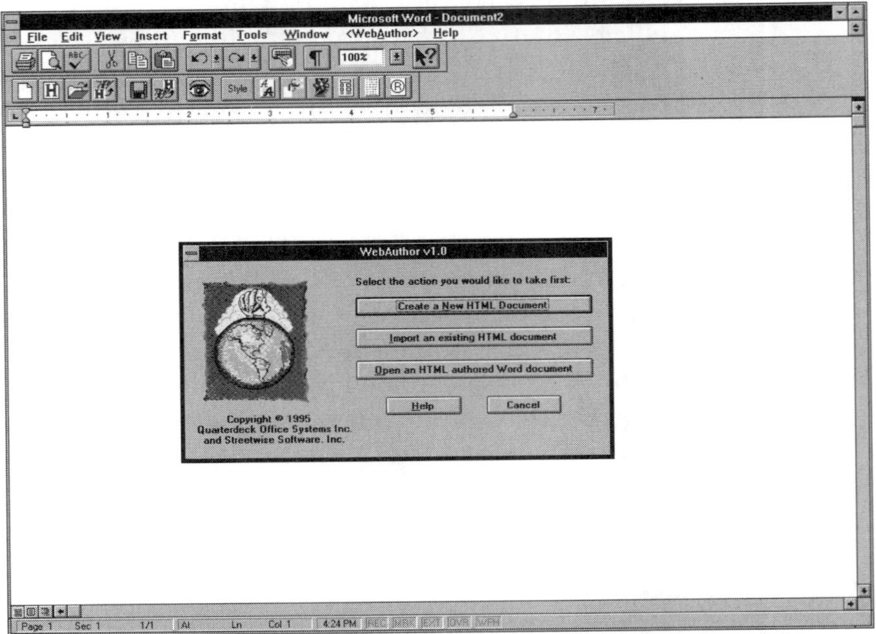

Figure 2-8: *WebAuthor displays a dialog box and a new toolbar for creating HTML documents.*

CU_HTML

The CU_HTML template for Word for Windows was written by Kenneth Wong and Anton Lam from The Chinese University of Hong Kong. You can get a copy of the template at ftp://ftp.cuhk.hk/pub/www/windows/util. The file name is cu_html.zip. The archive contains two templates: CU_HTML2.DOT and CU_HTML6.DOT, for use with Word for Windows 2.0 and 6.0, respectively. Choose the one you need, rename it CU_HTML.DOT and copy it to your template directory.

In addition to the template files, CU_HTML.DOT uses a dynamic link library (.DLL) file named CU_HTML.DLL. This file should be copied to your Windows system directory or the directory in which the Word for Windows executable file (winword.exe) is located.

CU_HTML is a well-executed template package. The basic method of operation is to create a new Word for Windows document using the CU_HTML.DOT template file. You can then add content, selecting either a paragraph style, or by adding special items, such as graphics, local links or remote links. The only noticeable change to the Word for Windows menus is the addition of five menu bar icons, and a menu selection for HTML, shown in Figure 2-9.

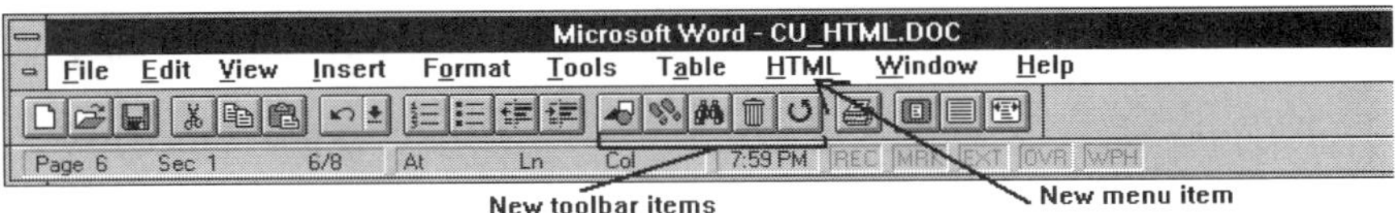

Figure 2-9: *New menu items are added when you use the CU_HTML.DOT template.*

During editing, you will select various styles for paragraphs, such as Heading 1, Heading 2, Numbered List, Unnum List, etc. These translate into HTML elements. The new toolbar icons allow you to insert graphics, add hyperlinks and produce HTML output. Using the CU_HTML template, you will always maintain a copy of the file in Word for Windows format, then export to an HTML file after saving the document. The template saves the special information needed for HTML export in Word document "fields."

You won't be able to open existing HTML files for editing with this template, since it is designed to operate on specially tagged Word documents, and is not a native HTML editor. The template doesn't translate tables at all, so don't use them. It also doesn't check for correct HTML syntax, and at this writing, the program created some incorrect syntax when creating nested lists, although Web browsers did read it without complaining. Depending on what is created with CU_HTML, you may or may not be able to open it in HoTMetaL.

CU_HTML does come with good installation and operating instructions, but has no online help. By leaving your documents in Word as their native format, you gain the advantage of being able to print paper copies, or use them in other formats besides HTML Web pages.

GT_HTML

Another Word template, GT_HTML, is from the Georgia Tech Research Institute (GTRI), and is available at ftp://ftp.gatech.edu/pub/www. The file name is gt_html.zip. Like CU_HTML, it is designed for the creation of new HTML documents and doesn't read existing HTML files. When editing a document with the GT_HTML template selected, modifications are made to the menu bar shown in Figure 2-10. The new menu items correspond to the commands shown in Figure 2-11.

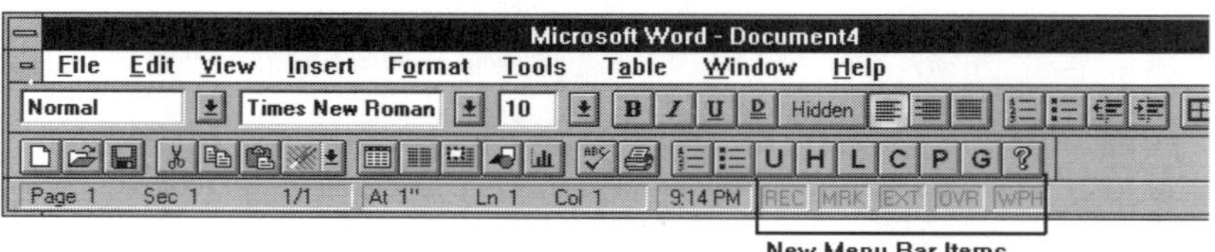

Figure 2-10: *Menu bar modifications with GT_HTML.*

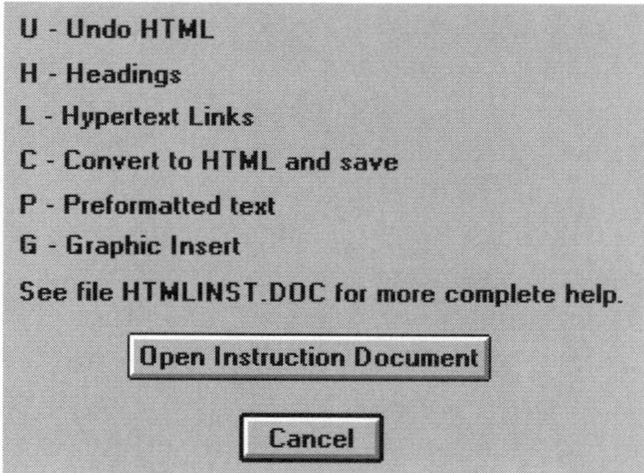

Figure 2-11: *New commands available with GT_HTML.*

You can see that headings, links, preformatted text regions and graphic inserts are done through this menu, as is exporting the document in HTML format. The document is also saved in Word format, and exported to HTML. When you are inserting links or graphics, the link-to text is manually edited after the insertion of the HTML markup.

GT_HTML comes with a short file for documentation that is adequate to cover the features provided. You should be familiar with HTML markup before editing with this package, since many of the tags must be changed manually. There is no syntax checking, and lists are not supported. Bold, italic and underline text is converted to HTML automatically when exporting.

ANT_HTML

Of the templates covered in this chapter, ANT is the most comprehensive template for creating and editing HTML files. There are two versions of ANT, one called ANT_HTML, and the other ANT_PLUS. ANT_PLUS is an enhanced commercial version of ANT_HTML that takes the basic capabilities of ANT_HTML and adds the nice feature of being able to read and format existing HTML documents so that they appear similar to the way they will look when displayed in a Web browser. Both templates can read and add to existing HTML documents. ANT and ANT_PLUS were written by Jill Swift, who can be reached via e-mail at jswift@freenet.fsu.edu. You can find the ANT_HTML template at ftp://ftp.einet.net/einet/pc in the ANT_DEMO.ZIP or ANT_HTML.ZIP file. The demonstration files include information about purchasing the nondemo versions of the templates. Unlike the preceding Word templates (CU_HTML and GT_HTML), ANT simply hides the codes it needs as hidden text.

When you first open a new document with the ANT template, or attach the template to an existing document, an entirely new toolbar is added at the top of the Word for Windows screen. Figure 2-12 shows the added toolbar.

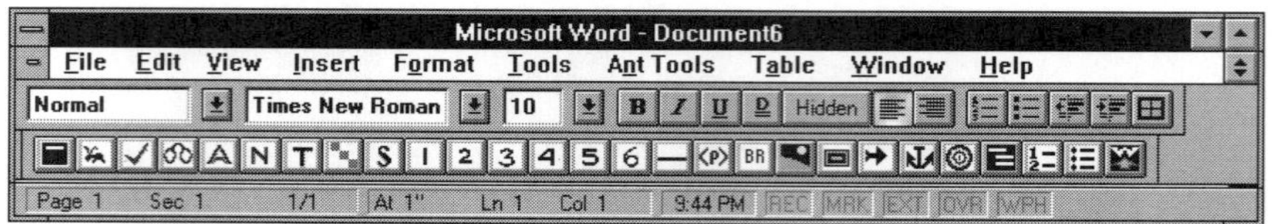

Figure 2-12: *The ANT_HTML template adds a toolbar to simplify adding HTML tags.*

You will also notice a new menu item called Ant Tools. One of the nicest features of this template is the ability to do things in more than one way. For example, if you want to create a Level 1 heading, you can do any one of the following:

- Type the text, select it and then click the "1."
- Click the "1." The cursor is positioned between the tags. Type the heading text.
- Type the text, and change the style to Heading 1 with the Word's Style selector. Click the checkmark tool to scan the document and add any HTML tags to paragraph formats that do not currently have them.
- Choose the Heading 1 style and type the heading.

Having more than one way to do things allows you to choose the way you like to work. If you are editing an existing ASCII document, selecting text and then selecting the element type is the fastest way, but if you are entering original text, it's faster to first select the style, and then start typing.

There are tools available for inserting each of the HTML elements. Online documentation is available in HTML format that allows you to load the file using your Web browser to read HTML documentation files provided with the template.

HTML TagWizard & SGML TagWizard

HTML TagWizard and SGML TagWizard are two products from NICE Technologies in France. HTML TagWizard is a Word for Windows 2.0 add-on and is available for free. SGML TagWizard is for Word 6, and is priced around $100. Both products focus on parsing HTML and SGML text you've entered. SGML TagWizard was, at the time of this writing, extremely slow, and is not a product that will help in the productive creation of HTML documents unless they are very small. Please check for newer, faster versions of SGML TagWizard, and ask around about current performance. Due to the quickly advancing state of the art in HTML and SGML editing, it's possible that the authors of this product will overcome the performance problems and produce a useful Word add-on product. For information about purchasing a copy of HTML TagWizard, see the appendix. Copies of the Word for Windows 2.0 version can be obtained at ftp://ftp.cica.indiana.edu/pub/pc/win3/winword. The file is named html.zip.

SGML TagWizard has the ability to import badly written HTML and point out where errors exist, as opposed to HoTMetaL, which simply refuses to read them. It also comes with an extensive manual in PostScript format. No online help is offered, and all tags must be entered manually, instead of being created automatically when a paragraph style is selected. Only documents well under 32k can be successfully imported.

HTML Converters

In the first part of this chapter you were introduced to a number of tools that made it easier for you to create new HTML documents, or to use Word for Windows templates to create documents with HTML markup. If you have a large set of existing documents you want to put on the Web, however, original authoring, or extensive modifications to existing documents may not be a viable option. The following sections explore HTML converters that let you create HTML documents from files in other formats. There are many converters and filters available, but most of them are created for the UNIX Operating System, where sophisticated filter tools are already available for other purposes. If you don't find what you want in this chapter, be sure to check the Web archives for new conversion tools.

The tools in the following sections are DOS-based converters that can run under Windows and Windows NT. At the time this book was written, there were no native Windows tools for document conversion to HTML.

RTF to HTML

This converter is the best we found. Almost all word processors can export documents in Rich Text Format (RTF). This program is a top-notch converter program with plenty of options to handle even the most uniquely formatted documents. As mentioned previously, this converter, along with all other HTML converters, is limited by what can be represented in HTML. If you're a programmer, one of the best features about the RTF to HTML converter is that the source code is available. You can get a copy of the converter at ftp://ftp.cray.com/src/WWWstuff/RTF/latest/binaries. The file name is dos.zip. The program is copyrighted by the Free Software Foundation, which gives liberal redistribution rights but insists that the programs stay free and may not be incorporated into commercial software.

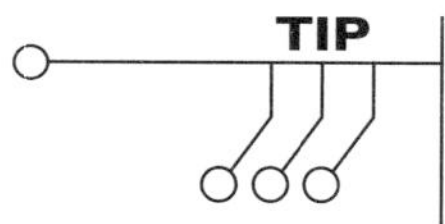

As a bonus, the CD-ROM that comes with this book contains a specially modified version of the converter that works as a Win-32 console application. It contains a special feature that interprets WinHelp-formatted RTF files, so you can convert your existing WinHelp RTF source files directly into HTML pages with all the hypertext jump information preserved. The source files are also included on the CD-ROM, so you can add your own extensions if you want to.

The main features of the RTF to HTML converter are:

- Bold, italic and underlined text art converted to HTML properly.
- Courier font text appears in HTML as the Teletype font.

- Tables will be converted to the "Pre-formatted Fixed Pitch Text" style, with the borders removed. (The current version of HTML does not directly support tables, although HTML 2.1 will.)
- Footnotes are placed into separate documents, and hypertext links are added.
- Table of contents entries and heading styles one to six are generated (as created with Microsoft Word for Windows). It will also generate a hypertext Table of Contents in a separate file. Each table of contents entry will link to the correct location in the main document.
- Document styles are directly supported through the use of either the html-tra (Windows 3.1) or the html-trans file (Windows NT and Windows 95), which comes predefined with many standard document styles as used in Word for Windows. If you use a style that is not in the html-trans file, you'll see a warning message. You can define your own styles in the "html-trans" file to support whatever document styles you use in your own work.
- Graphics that have been inserted into the RTF (for example, via the Insert Picture command in Word for Windows) will be written to individual files in one of the following formats, depending on the way it's stored in the RTF file: Windows MetaFile format, Macintosh PICT or Windows Bitmap. These formats must then be converted to the GIF format supported by most Web browsers. (See Chapter 7 for more information about graphics and graphics file formats.) The picture can appear in one of two ways: either as a text reference to the image or as an inline image. The option is chosen with a command-line setting when you do the conversion.
- Text that has been inserted into a document with a Copy/Paste/Link command will be connected via hypertext links.
- Headers, footers, tables of contents and indexes are ignored.

- You may manually embed HTML in a source RTF document and have the converter simply copy the HTML to the output HTML document.
- You may specify hypertext links in the RTF source that will be converted to HTML hypertext links.
- You may customize the converter to manage almost any special case of text conversion you encounter.
- The converter supports nested lists.
- Output files are created with the suffix HTML using Windows NT. (If you use the DOS version, the suffix will be HTM.) The name of the file is based on the name of the input RTF file.

As you can see from this list, the RTF to HTML converter is a very powerful tool for you to add to your HTML creation toolbox. Until the stand-alone HTML and SGML editors or Word add-on programs have fully matured, editing in your favorite word processor and then converting the RTF to HTML may be the best way to go for large documents.

There are a number of other converters available for UNIX-based systems, as well as for other operating systems. If you are interested, you can get additional information at http://info.cern.ch/hypertext/WWW/Tools/Filters.html and http://oneworld.wa.com/htmldev/devpage/dev-page.html.

PostScript to HTML

This program, which will accept a PostScript file from Windows 3.1 HP LaserJet IIP PostScript printer driver, is perhaps the most flexible program available. Except for the restriction that the PostScript file must come from a specific Windows 3.1 printer driver, there is virtually no limit on which program can create a file to be converted into HTML. For instance, there are no converters to create HTML files from Windows Write or AmiPro documents. But since both of these programs can print to a PostScript file, you can still create HTML pages from them. You can get a copy of the converter at ftp://ftp.area.fi.cnr.it/pub/dos/misc/

ps2html. The file is named ps2html.exe. The software was developed at Florence Research Area and Electromagnetic Research Institute of National Research Council in Florence, Italy, by Alessandro Agostini and Stefano Cerreti. The authors can be reached via e-mail at agostini@server.area.fi.cnr.it and ced@server.area.fi.cnr.it respectively.

Both authors of this program are currently working to enhance the functionality of the converter program, so be sure to check for the most current version. Because of the inherent limitations in HTML, you'll never be able to translate all the formatting from a word processor. Also, the program cannot create hypertext links for you. You will need to edit the resulting converted HTML document to manually add the links.

Moving On

Now that you've got a handle on the tools you can use to create HTML documents, it's time to explore the possibilities the Web brings to structuring information for publishing on the Web. If you're anxious to begin using HTML skip to Chapter 4, "Creating Your First Web Document," but be sure to come back to Chapter 3 for information about designing and creating nonlinear documents.

3

Structuring Information in Web Documents

At first glance publishing on the Internet may appear to be fairly easy. So easy, in fact, that the temptation exists to slap some words on a page, toss in some favorite hyperlinks, throw in a few images and put your creation on the Net for the world to see. Unfortunately, many Web authors have taken this approach by constructing documents that show little consideration for the reader. This chapter will help bring structure, efficiency and elegance to your documents by addressing the special needs and circumstances presented by the structure of the Web. It also offers some tried-and-true design principles from the world of "paper publishing" that apply to Web documents as well.

Linear vs. Hypermedia Documents

Typically when you pick up a book, you flip it open to the first page and start reading. Perhaps, you'll look at the Table of Contents to see what's there, and you skip around, awkwardly, by going to a particular chapter and skimming it until you find the reference or thought that aroused your interest in the first place.

The author has structured the information in a way that best presents the point he or she is trying to make, and you have little say in the way the author feels you should absorb information. This kind of a publication is called *linear*. You start at point A, and go to point B and so on. If the writer feels you should learn about birds before bees are discussed, that's the way it is going to be. If the process of gathering honey has captured your interest and you want to learn a bit about it before continuing on with the book, you have to wait until the author is ready to present this information before you can learn about it. You could shuffle through the book looking for references to the process. It is also possible, but not probable, that you could go to the library and get another book that discussed the honey-gathering process in detail to find the information you want. If you want to learn about something, you want it now. You don't want to have to wade through a lot of text that has little or no bearing on what you want to learn about.

That brings us to hypermedia. On the Web, *nonlinear* publications are the rule. Nonlinear publishing taps the power of the computer and the client/server model to let a reader follow almost any tangent he or she wants. (If the author provides the pathways, that is.) In the above example, if you wanted to learn about acquiring honey, and the path to that information had been presented in a Web document, you could simply position your cursor on the hyperlink, click and be transported to the beekeeping home page of the Entomology Department at a local university, or wherever the relevant information happened to be. When you got your fill of information on honey, and wanted to go back and learn something about birds, another click could zip you back from whence you came.

Structuring Your Web Document

The first decision you must make when creating a Web document is how to structure the information you want to present. Web documents most often contain a series of linked elements presented one idea or action at a time. If, for example, one part of your document included a customer survey or a large collection of

links to software, this would be a stand-alone element accessed by a link from other pages in your document.

These pages may also be visited directly from links that other authors have added to their documents at sites anywhere in the world. Keeping this one-at-a-time approach in mind, it becomes necessary to impose a structure on your document.

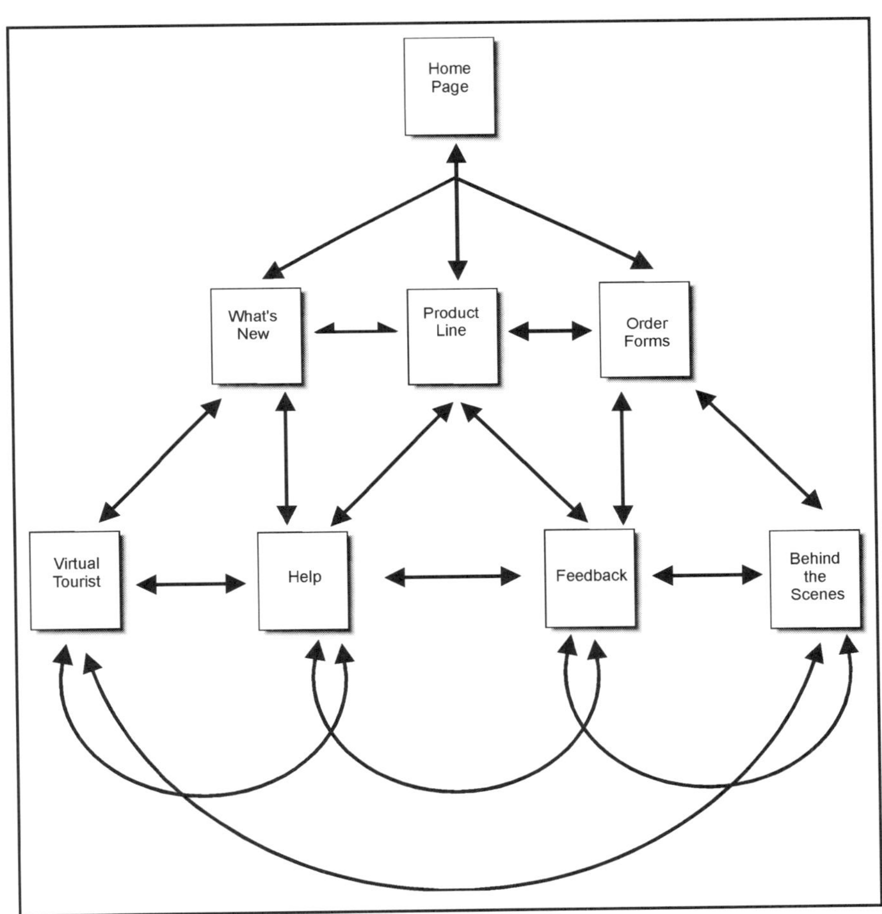

Figure 3-1: *It's a good idea to sketch out Web documents and links before creating your Web document.*

Establishing Hierarchies

The best way to initiate a structure is to create an outline. This helps you create a structured document and determines the links you need to create to documents or sites elsewhere on the Web, or within your own document. The following outline of Web pages and links uses a real world example from Canyon Software, a company that specializes in Windows utility software.

Home Page: Canyon Software's Home Page
  a. About Canyon Software
  b. What's New (link to page 2)
  c. Canyon Software's Product Line (link to page 3)
  d. Technical Support (link to page 4)
  e. Guides for the Virtual Tourist (link to page 5)
  f. Ordering (link to page 6)
  g. Feedback (link to page 7)
  h. Behind the Scenes (link to page 8)

Page 2: What's New
  a. Press Releases

Page 3: Canyon Software's Product Line
  a. Drag And File
  b. Drag And Zip
  c. Drag And View Gold

Page 4: Technical Support
  a. Frequently Asked Questions (FAQ)
  b. How to Get Technical Support

Page 5: Guides for the Virtual Tourist
  a. Our Favorite Hotlinks
  b. Test Your Viewers

Page 6: Order Forms
  a. Ordering the Commercial Versions
  b. Upgrade Policies
  c. Return Policies

Page 7: Feedback
  a. Customer Feedback
  b. Testimonials
  c. Customer Survey
  d. Client list

Page 8: Behind the Scenes
  a. Who's Who at Canyon Software

It's often beneficial to give each topic its own page. This makes updating easier and allows you to refer to the same page, like the Order Forms or Feedback page, over and over from various places within the document. The next item we need to consider is how to tie these documents together in a coherent way.

Determining Your Links

Once the Web documents have been outlined, you're ready to consider how you will link the various parts together. The actual process of linking will be covered in Chapter 5, "The Art of Linking," but you need to decide what you want to link early in the design process. It's a good idea to sketch out the structure of your Web pages. Make the home page the front door to your document so that visitors can move to other pages from the home page. Figure 3-1 shows the structure of Canyon Software's Web pages.

Be aware that the very nature of the Web allows visitors to enter in places other than the uppermost level. Readers can jump to a specific Web page by following a link that someone else established and find themselves on a page that is far removed from any introductory material. For this reason, one of your initial design considerations is to provide the visitor with an easy way to your home page, if they wish. This can be accomplished by providing a hyperlink to your home page on all of your Web pages. By creating a hyperlink to the home page, people can easily find the points of interest by the links established in the directing document (the home page). As well as providing links to your home page, you may also want to include links for readers to visit or return to other pages within the document. Figure 3-2 shows the bottom of *Interactive Age* magazine's Web page. Notice that there are several navigational icons and hyperlinks to aid the reader visiting the Web site.

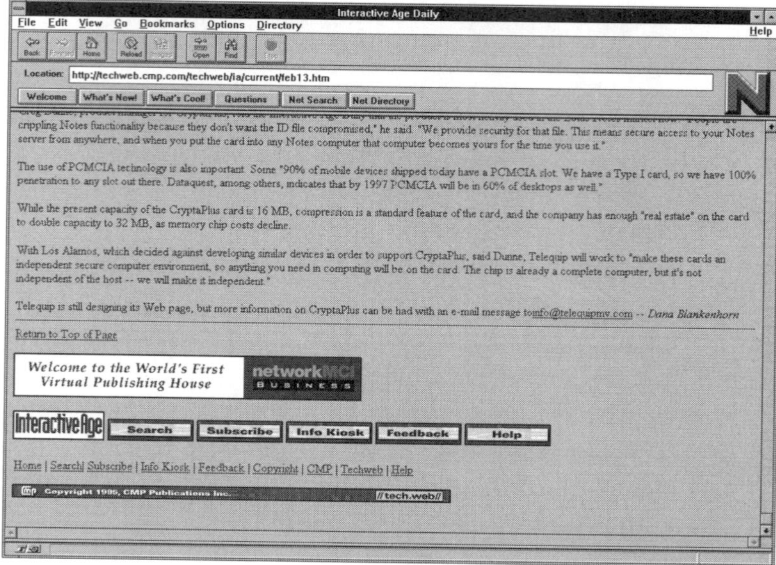

Figure 3-2: Interactive Age's *Web page is a good example of how to include navigational icons and hyperlinks, so people can easily move back to the home page or to another page.*

Designing Web Pages

Structuring and designing Web documents is not a simple job. Be prepared to make changes. It's a good strategy to plan it as if the home page will be the first page read. If you include a link on every page of your document that takes the reader to the first page, it really doesn't matter where the reader starts reading. The following sections examine determining your Web document's structure by defining your document's goals and designing your Web pages to capture the audience you want to address.

Defining Your Document's Goals

At the same time that you are creating an outline, you also need to articulate the document's goals, or purpose. A document that simply provides information can be successful by just including pointers to Web sites that have the information your reader wants to see. A corporate page, on the other hand, needs to provide a message of what the company is offering or trying to accomplish.

It may sound simplistic, but the most important thing you have to do is decide *what* you want to do. And, the best way to define this is often to ask yourself, "When a reader has finished reading my work, what do I want him or her to know?" Everything else you do will be judged by this standard. Keep focused and don't lose sight of your goal.

The bottom-line goal for Canyon Software is to generate sales by identifying the unique capabilities and key features of Canyon Software's software and making the shareware and commercial version of the software accessible. Therefore, the pages need to inform the reader of the benefits of dealing with Canyon Software, and let them acquire enough information to make them want to either download the shareware or place an order for the commercial version. Don't think that because this model is computer related that Web pages have to focus on computer products; the model could apply to a company like Acme Uniforms that sells sports uniforms.

Document Aesthetics

Even after the material you want to present has been selected, there are many other design elements yet to consider. Your publication will need a "look," it will also need a well-defined audience. It is also important, and prudent, to consider the limitations that your readers may have due to the browser and equipment they may be using, such as a 14,400bps modem or a high-speed ISDN connection.

Developing Your Look

Because readers will be jumping into, out of, or about within your Web pages, the importance of maintaining a consistent look throughout your work is not quite as important as if the work were to be published in print. However, it is still highly desirable to develop a look that will carry throughout your pages.

A consistent look accomplishes several purposes: first, you may decide to publish the document on paper sometime, and it will be ready to go; second, especially for commercial pages, readers should constantly be aware of who you are, and one good way to achieve this is through consistent visual cues—a logo on each page, for example. Third, and equally important, lack of consistency presents a scattered, unprofessional image you may not want to broadcast. Even if you're publishing an anarchistic newsletter, readers are more likely to keep reading when they are presented a consistent structure and design.

Capturing Your Audience

A considerable amount of thought should be devoted to defining the characteristics of your target audience. If you make your message too simple, or too complex, you will either insult or bore many of the people who visit your site. You are safe in assuming that anyone accessing your work through the Web is literate, and a possessor of sufficient resources to get into the Web in the first place. You are certainly sure that any reader has a curious bent of mind. This definition, however, includes the fourteen-year-old hacker, as well as the forty-year-old rocket scientist.

The trick then becomes how to structure your presentation and language to appeal to your ideal audience. Most of this selection process is accomplished by the style of writing you choose. For example, including puns, word games and hyperbole, or adding too lighthearted of a style could affect your credibility, causing others to view your site as a frivolous pastime, rather than presenting a serious professional image. This isn't to say you can't create a fun Web page, just be sure your writing style doesn't distract from the goal of your Web page.

It is also important to keep in mind the equipment that will be used to view your message—there are many differing hardware/software configurations and capabilities out there. Some machines just won't display graphics at all, and Chapter 4, "Creating Your First Web Document" discusses how to write for both graphic- and text-based Web browsers. However, even limiting our discussion to graphics-capable machines, there is still a wide diversity of possibilities. For example, there are many different Web browsers: NCSA Mosaic, Netscape Navigator, Enhanced Mosaic, etc., and each of these browsers displays your presentation differently.

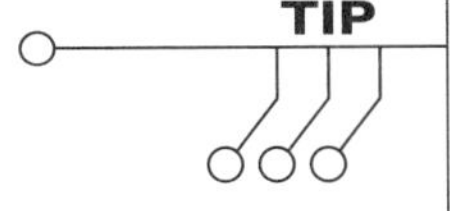

There has been a trend in some Web documents to include information about the browser that was used when testing the document, such as a message that goes something like: "Use Netscape to view this document at its highest quality." You might want to create a link to a formatted version designed specifically for the Netscape Navigator browser.

You should also consider the constraints placed on a reader by his or her hardware. There is probably someone out there who has figured out how to connect to the Net at 2400bps. You could also find someone who is trying to be "graphical" at a CGA resolution. You can be pretty safe in ignoring their needs. After all, making your presentation simple enough to be adequately viewed on equipment of this nature would detract from your message. (You would not be able to include any but the simplest graphics, since the download time would be unacceptable at 2400bps.)

What you do need to consider is the browser at SVGA 800 x 600 x 256 colors resolution or better. (Even though there are computers that will be looking at your page in a 640 x 480 x 16 color display mode—mostly notebooks—they can most often dither the colors to a visually pleasing display.) Also, the lowest modem connection you may want to test with is 9600bps.

Constructing Web Pages

Up to this point, we've talked about the collection of pages that, when assembled, make up your Web presence. Our consideration has also been directed toward the "big picture" design. Now, it's time to examine the process of constructing and designing individual pages. Each individual page in your document should contain certain elements: identity, look, links and information.

How to Let Them Know Who You Are

Remember that a reader does not, necessarily, use the front door (or your home page) to get into your document. Therefore, it's important for you to include some information that identifies yourself on each page. This can be a simple logo or some text that is linked to your home page or another page, where information about you can be found. Your purpose is to get your name and message out. You don't want the reader scratching his or her head wondering who you are.

How to Develop the Look You Want

The look of your presentation is very important. Consider how you look at your "snail" or postal mail. There are some publications you get that you know by sight. It could be a logo, a color, an envelope, or almost any unique identifier. You immediately know that this is a publication you want to read (or toss). You want your Web document to be read. Many of the same things that attract you to a mailed document can be used to make your Web publication stand out, too. The visual appeal of a page, the amount of white space, the depth of content and the ease of access all must be thought through.

Ask yourself, How you can make your pages artistically pleasing, given the limitations of your authoring tools? Can you stand back from the page, when it is displayed in a browser, and feel welcome? Everyone senses the artistic page on one level or another, however, and often this element above all others has an almost subconscious effect about how a reader perceives you and your organization. If you're not an artistic type, seek out someone who is and have them review your work. Several individuals and companies exist that provide Web design services. If you're interested in contacting a Web design service, check out the resources section at the back of this book for a list of some Web design service companies.

Another consideration is the size of your graphics. The amount of text on the screen at any given time should not be out of proportion to the size and placement of graphic elements. Don't clutter your page with too much text. Pages that contain a lot of text are often called *gray pages*. Not only does looking at gray pages make you feel intimidated by the amount of information they appear to contain, they look cluttered and unappealing.

You don't have any control over the *leading* (the space between lines of text) the *kerning* (the spacing between characters) or the font used. What you do have is absolute control over the number of words used in any paragraph. Most HTML editors insert extra space after a paragraph, use this as a design tool.

The depth of content is another major issue. The beauty of publishing on the Web is the ability to link elements within (and outside of) your document. Keep your pages short, concise and dedicated to one issue or topic. Include branches that lead to pages containing other ideas or issues. The reason for this is one of maintenance, as well as esthetics and ease of use. If all information about a topic is included in a known place, you only have to update it once.

Ease of access is another issue. While unfortunately ignored by many Web authors, a Web's ease of use probably leads to many instances of readers bailing out of publications without reading them. Even though most browsers give the reader the option of not loading graphics, not all readers are aware of this. If your pages contain large graphics, the process of downloading the graphic to the reader's browser can take so much time that the reader becomes impatient, and unreceptive to your message. If you want to include graphics (and you should), keep them small. You can offer the option of viewing a more complex version of the graphic by linking the smaller (thumbnail) version of it to the larger one.

Make sure all the links you add jump to other Web pages and all these sites work. All too often authors use links to sites that have changed. Surfing the Internet and encountering a dead link or a link to a site in which the URL has changed is frustrating. You should check your links and plan to recheck them regularly. Otherwise you're sending a subliminal message to the reader that not only is the link dead, but the information you are presenting is also out of date.

How to Design Your Home Page

A good design idea is to use the home page as a table of contents for the rest of your document. Figure 3-3 shows the home page of the Internet Business Center (http://www.tig.com/IBC/index.html). Notice that the page starts off with a graphic, the Center's logo. Following that is the identifying information, a very brief statement about what the center does. Three feature articles are then listed with links to their pages. (These pages are most likely more table of contents style pages that allow the reader to further refine what he or she wants to read.) Finally, a list of other sites is included in bullet-style. Even though the Netscape Navigator is set up to use a gray background, the page is still pleasing to view. The varying design elements (graphics, text and lists) make the page interesting and the appearance crisp and clean.

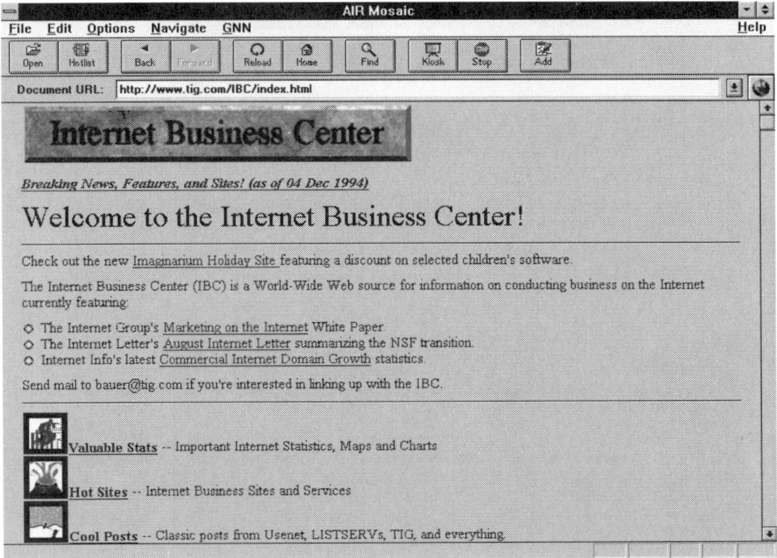

Figure 3-3: *The Internet Business Center's home page is an example of a simple uncluttered Web page.*

Another aspect of good design is to show sensitivity to all viewers. For example, you may want to present your pages in different formats: one for users that can handle large graphics and another for text browsers. If you are going to include browser specific features, it's also a good idea to give users a link to take them to a version of the document that has been optimized for the browser. Figure 3-4 shows the Ventana Media (http://www.vmedia.com) home page, which lets users choose between a rich-presentation format or a simple-presentation method.

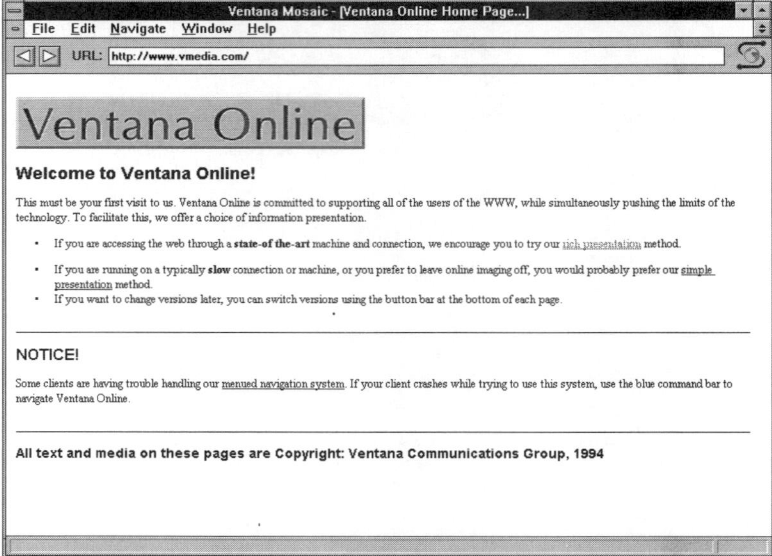

Figure 3-4: *Ventana Media lets users choose between a rich-presentation format or a simple-presentation method.*

How to Design Subsequent Pages

Many of the structure and design issues are the same for pages that are linked to your home page. The following are some general guidelines for creating subsequent Web pages.

An important design consideration is to include only one or two topics per page. Your readers came to this page expecting to see what they had selected on your home page, and little else. If you're going to include large Web documents, such as documentation or an online book, it is helpful to create a table of contents. A good example of a Web page that presents a table of contents can be found in The Magellan Venus Explorer's Guide at http://newproducts.jpl.nasa.gov/magellan/guide.html.

Figure 3-5 shows how a Web page can use links to create a table of contents that let the reader quickly move to information they want.

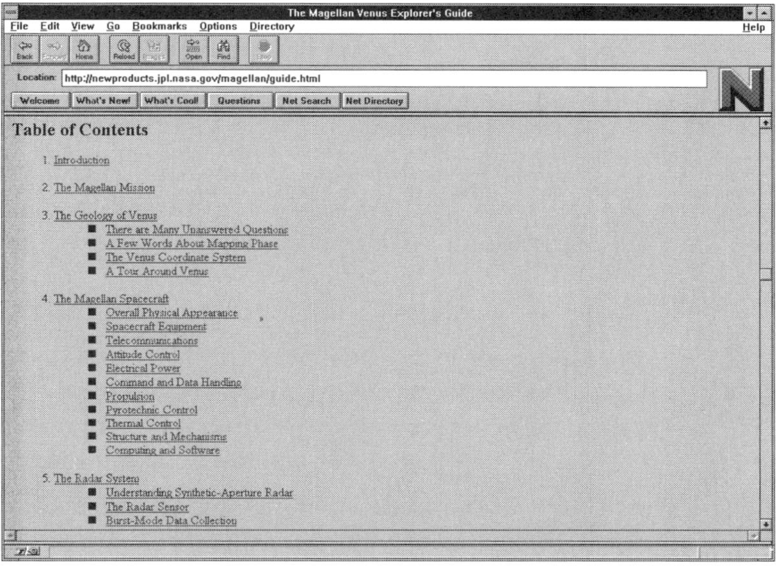

Figure 3-5: *The Magellan Venus Explorer's Guide is a good example of a linked table of contents.*

Some other items to keep in mind are

- Keep it simple. Pages that contain massive amounts of text are typically not read. A good rule of thumb is never to have more than 50 percent of the screen covered with anything. When you are viewing your page, step back from the monitor so you can't read any of the text, and look to see if the appearance of the gray (text-filled) areas and the rest of the screen is pleasing to the eye.
- Vary the text styles. Headings, body text and text attributes are discussed in Chapter 6, "Creating Your Text Appeal." Break your information down in such a way that you can use different levels of headings, when appropriate. Each level displays differently and gives your document eye-appeal. Include, when called for, text attributes that emphasize key points.

- Include a graphic or two. You will learn how to link images in Chapter 7, "Getting Graphic With Images." Use graphics as design elements to break up text or lend a little variety to your presentation.
- Be consistent. It is easy to view each document as a separate work, and in a sense you should do just that. Remember, though, that your readers will jump from page to page within your document. Be consistent with your usage of styles, graphics and other design elements.
- Give people a reason to return to your site. Many Web sites are one-shot wonders. Add value to your site to entice readers back by adding a hotlist page, tutorial, weekly comic, tips page or a page of links to interesting software.

The third, fourth and fifth level pages of a Web document do not differ a whole lot from the second page. Remember, however, to provide pathways for your readers to

1. Go back to the first, or home, page.
2. Go forward in your presentation to the next logical place.
3. Go directly to the Order Form, if you have one.
4. Go back and see what came before the current page.

Do's & Don'ts

We've covered a lot in this chapter. Much of it will be reinforced as you continue reading and using Web authoring tools. Below is a list of ten design issues you'll want to keep in mind when creating Web documents.

1. Decide what you want to do. If you don't know where you're going with your document, you will never get there. It is really difficult to keep yourself focused when you are writing any document, and the more structure you can bring to the process, the better the results.
2. Identify yourself. It's your turn on stage, take advantage of it. Each page should contain some kind of identifier, like a logo and a brief statement of purpose.

3. Know your audience. Design a publication that will be pleasing to view on a "normal" computer system. Structure your language, vocabulary and syntax to the audience you want to address. This can serve as a gatekeeper, welcoming in those you want and excluding those you don't. If you have high-quality graphics you want to include (pictures of your product, for example) consider creating a thumbnail of those images or linking those pictures to a page that individuals with slower modems can skip if they wish.
4. Keep your design simple. Allow linked documents to provide more in-depth information and keep all of your pages as simple and uncluttered as you can.
5. Vary your styles. Use the different levels of text (headings, etc.) as design elements to break up your page.
6. Include a graphic or two. Graphics are a great way to provide interest and style to your page. Keep inline graphics small, in bytes, and simple, in colors. They'll load faster.
7. Keep your design tight. There is no limit on the number of pages you can create. Keep the information presented highly focused on your goals. If you think a reader may want to go off on a tangent, provide a link instead of placing the extra verbiage on the current page.
8. There's no place like home. Be sure to provide links that will take readers back to where he or she may want to go—home or the previous page.
9. Be consistent. Try to develop your own style and carry it through the entire publication. People remember the feel and look of your publications, a consistent approach will gain you recognition much quicker than an inconsistent one.
10. Know your writing and artistic skills and get feedback. Publishing documents is a blend of art and craft. A publishing house employs designers, artists and page layout professionals in addition to the editors, marketers and accountants. If you're publishing Web pages on your own, ask other people their opinions about your finished document.

Moving On

Take the time to determine the goal of your site and design your Web pages to meet that goal—it will save you time in the long run. A site that has an efficient structure and a consistent, visually appealing design improves the chances that people will return to it. Designing a well-structured site is only the first step, it's time to begin learning how to use HTML and start creating your individual Web pages. The next chapter is a hands-on guide to creating a home page, the cornerstone of your Web site.

4

Creating Your First Web Document

There are a few ways you can start creating a Web document. You can begin with a template and modify it to meet your needs or download and modify the source code of an existing Web document off the Internet. Web browsers, such as Netscape Navigator and Mosaic, let you display a window containing the HTML codes and text used to create documents on the Web or save the HTML codes and text to a file. The problem with this method is that it is amazing how many Web documents break the basic rules of HTML. Just because you're viewing a home page for a large company is no guarantee that the page is created correctly.

This chapter takes a different approach. It discusses the basic elements used to create a simple home page and presents valid elements and procedures you can follow to construct your own HTML documents. References are made throughout this chapter to other areas in this book where you can obtain more detailed information about each subject. To help you create correct Web pages we'll focus in this chapter on inserting elements and verifying your document using HoTMetaL PRO, which is included on the Companion CD-ROM.

Adding Markup to HTML Documents

As mentioned in Chapter 1, "The World Wide Web & Hypermedia Publishing," the elements that specify how to display text are collectively called *markup*. Markup is the use of codes that tell the Web browser how to display your words. The document is composed of text that takes its cues from the markup.

Using markup is a lot like using parentheses in algebra or entering a formula into a spreadsheet. Instead of parentheses, HTML markup uses codes within angle brackets. Markup typically consists of a beginning code, commonly referred to as a *tag*, that specifies the effect, and an ending tag that includes a forward slash to identify the end of the markup. For example *<TITLE>* signifies the beginning and *</TITLE>* marks the end. The beginning and ending tags are sometimes referred to as *elements*. Each element has a name that corresponds with the tags, for example, <TITLE> </TITLE> specifies the title element. When text or data appears within a beginning and ending tag the entire element is sometimes called a *container*.

Not all elements demand a closing markup, and not all tags must contain text. Elements that don't contain text and don't require an end tag are sometimes referred to as *empty elements*. A few tags let you define *attributes* to the element specific to the element type. HoTMetaL PRO includes the Edit SGML Attributes command in the Markup menu to let you specify an attribute. For example, using an attribute you can define where text is placed next to an image or define alternative text to accommodate viewers that are unable to handle images.

If you choose to use a text editor or an HTML editor other than HoTMetaL PRO that doesn't automatically insert tags it's helpful to know that markup tags are not case sensitive; for example <title>, <TITLE> and <Title> all can be used for the title tag.

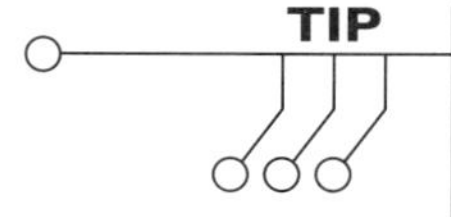

Because you don't know which browser will be used to view your documents, you should attempt to follow all the rules in the HTML language as closely as possible. Currently, using some HTML editors and templates you can get away with ignoring some elements and still produce a readable document. Keep in mind, however, that anyone can easily download your source code. If you don't follow HTML formatting rules, others may make judgments about you and your company from the quality of your documents.

Adding Markup With HoTMetaL PRO

HoTMetaL PRO is a rules-based editor that, unlike most HTML editors and text editors, protects you from making mistakes when inserting and editing markup tags. The process of inserting tags may take a little more time with HoTMetaL PRO than some HTML editors, but it saves validation time. HoTMetaL PRO automatically ensures that your document doesn't contain incorrect and unmatched tags. The Markup menu contains commands that let you add, split, join, change and remove markup tags and element attributes. Table 4-1 lists the most common operations found in the Markup menu.

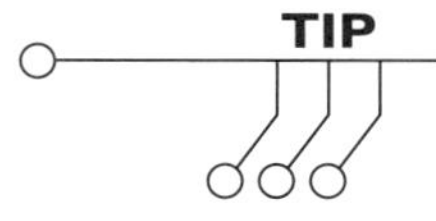

A unique feature of HoTMetaL PRO is that you can pin *frequently used dialog boxes. Pinning a dialog box allows it to remain open and saves you from having to continually choose menu commands to display the dialog box. To pin the Insert Element dialog box, press Ctrl-I, click the control menu of the Insert Element dialog box and choose the Pin menu item. HoTMetaL PRO is context sensitive, so only valid choices appear in the dialog box.*

Command	Description
Insert Element	Displays the Insert Element dialog box, so you can insert a new, empty element in which you can type text or insert other elements. The shortcut key for the Insert Element command is Ctrl-I.

Surround	Displays the Surround dialog box. The Surround command is only available when text is selected. If a portion of a document should be contained in a particular element, highlight the tags and text, and select this command to choose an element to surround the selected text. The shortcut key for the Surround command is Ctrl-U.
Change	Changes the markup. Select this command to get a list of valid elements to replace the current element. The shortcut key for the Change command is Ctrl-L.
Split	Splits the current element into two elements at the current insertion point or selection. The shortcut key for the Split command is Ctrl-P.
Join to Preceding	Joins the current element with the element preceding it, provided both are of the same type. The shortcut key for the Join to Preceding command is Ctrl-J.
Remove Tags	Removes the tag icons that delimit the current element, leaving the content unaltered. The shortcut key for the Remove Tags command is Ctrl-D.
Edit SGML Attributes	Displays the Attributes dialog box for changing the attributes of a selected element. The shortcut key for the Edit SGML Attributes command is F6.
Edit URL	Displays the Edit URL dialog box, which lets you add or edit the attributes of a selected URL. There is not a shortcut key for the Edit URL command.
Insert Character Entity	Displays a dialog box that lists special characters, such as symbols and foreign characters. The shortcut key for the Insert Character Entity command is Ctrl-E.

Table 4-1: *Markup menu commands.*

HoTMetaL PRO Editing Commands

HoTMetaL PRO's Edit menu includes standard editing commands, including Cut (Ctrl-X), Copy (Ctrl-C), Paste (Ctrl-V) and Delete (Del). At this point the one command you're bound to find most helpful is the Edit>>Undo command. The shortcut key for the Undo command is Ctrl-Z. It may take a little time to become familiar with how HoTMetaL PRO lets you select tags and text. HoTMetaL PRO only lets you select tags and text as groups. In other words, you can't edit a selection of text and an end tag. Instead you must select the text only, or you must select the beginning tag, the text and the closing tag.

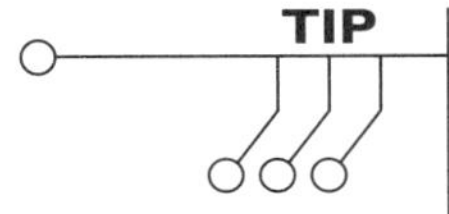

HoTMetaL PRO lets you paste raw HTML tags and text into an HTML document displayed in HoTMetaL PRO. The raw tags are replaced with HoTMetaL PRO tag icons. This lets you cut or copy tags consisting of text in a word processor, such as Microsoft Word, and paste the text directly in as tags in HoTMetaL PRO. Conversely, you can select and copy or cut HoTMetaL PRO tags and text and paste raw tags into Word.

Beginning Your HTML Document

A Web document is composed of two parts: the *head* and the *body*. Each document contains some common elements: a beginning HTML tag, a title, a body, some headings and an ending tag. To begin creating a home page, start HoTMetaL PRO. A window appears named scratch1.htm. This is the default window for creating a document. You can change the name to something other than scratch1.htm later when you save your document.

To start creating your page, choose Markup>>Insert Element or press Ctrl-I. The Insert Element dialog box appears, as shown in Figure 4-1. Make sure that the Include Required Elements check box is turned on. Double-click HTML in the list of elements, or, if this element is already highlighted, click the Insert Element button. This inserts three beginning and ending tags: <HTML>, <HEAD> and <TITLE>.

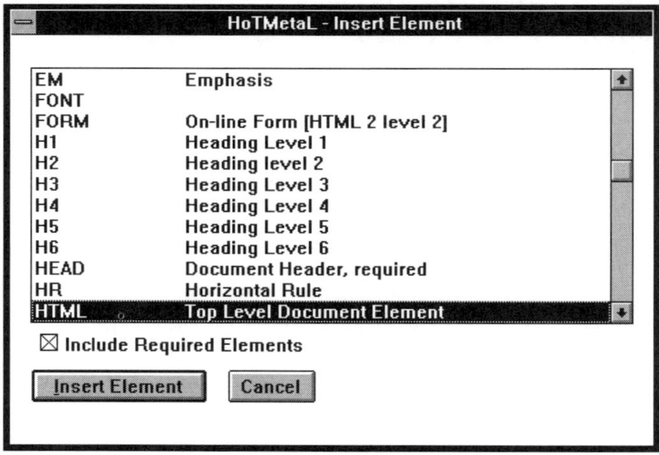

Figure 4-1: *The Insert Element dialog box.*

An HTML Comment
One element that can be included in the head or the body is the comment tag. Comments don't appear in the Web browser. HoTMetaL PRO doesn't support the comment tag, but you can include the comment tag using a text editor. The opening tag for a comment is <!— and the closing tag is —>. Because some Web browsers balk at multiple line comments, it is best to keep comments short or use the comment element for each line you want to add.

The Head Tags

Every HTML document starts with the markup tag <HTML>. The initial <HTML> tag informs the browser what kind of document it's looking at, so it can be displayed properly. This becomes more important as other documents, such as SGML documents for Panorama and other non-HTML browsers, start being used. The end tag </HTML> instructs the browser that the document is complete. It's included as the last tag in your document.

Immediately following the <HTML> tag is a tag called <HEAD>. The <HEAD> tag allows the HTTP server software to discover information about the document.

The next item that should be included is a document title. The title of a document, contrary to what you would expect, doesn't appear at the top of your document. Typically the title appears in the title bar of the window. The title is used for index information by Web searching programs, such as Web spiders and robots.

When you create a document using a HoTMetaL PRO, the words "Document Title" appear in the HoTMetaL PRO document window. This text only appears in the editing window display, it is not part of the text of the document.

The insertion point appears between the beginning and ending <TITLE> tags. Type a title for your sample document. Keep the title short yet descriptive. A descriptive title is important because many browsers will use this title if the reader saves your page as a bookmark or hotlist item. When you display this document in a browser, the contents of the title element will be displayed in the window's title bar. It is possible that the title will display in some browsers on a Document Title line. The following is a sample of the head tags.

```
<HTML> <HEAD> <TITLE> Canyon Software's Home Page
</TITLE> </HEAD> </HTML>
```

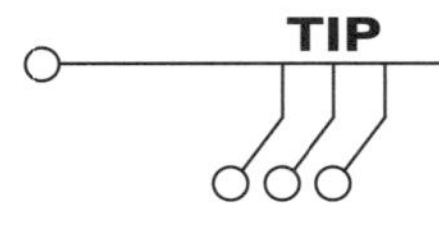

Other tags can appear in the head of a document, including the ISINDEX, BASE, LINK, NEXTID and META tags. For more information on these heading tags, see Appendix A, "An Illustrated HTML Reference."

The Body Tags

The main part of your document is the body, contained within the BODY element. Except for the ending </HTML> tag, everything from here on is a body element, including headings, paragraphs, special characters, lists, images, hyperlinks and so on. The following sections explain how to identify the beginning and the contents of the body of your Web page.

Identifying the Body of Your Document

To begin, move the insertion point to the right of the </HEAD> end tag. Choose the Markup>>Insert Element command. Only the BODY element appears in the Insert Element dialog box. HoTMetaL PRO is context sensitive; at this point, BODY is the only valid element. Either double-click the BODY Element or choose the Insert Element button to add the BODY tags. The

BODY tags are added directly before the closing </HTML> tag, as shown below:

<HTML> <HEAD> <TITLE> Canyon Software's Home Page </TITLE> </HEAD> <BODY> </BODY> </HTML>

Once the BODY tags are added, the Insert Element dialog box will present many additional element choices. Because you will frequently be inserting elements between the beginning and ending BODY tags, you may find it helpful to pin the Insert Element dialog box. To pin the Insert Element dialog box, press Ctrl-I, click the control menu of the Insert Element dialog box and choose the Pin menu item.

Organizing Your Document With Headers

Like any well organized document, it's a good idea to start with a heading. There are six possible heading tags, <H1> through <H6>. Each tag works just like a heading style in a word processing document, or levels in an outline, providing structure and division in your document. The type style and size of the heading changes depending on how the individual browser that is displaying your document is configured.

To create headers, select the <H1> element from the Insert Element dialog box. The insertion point appears between the starting and ending H1 tags. The following is a sample heading.

<H1>Welcome to Canyon Software's Home Page</H1>

Even though you can use up to six different levels of headings, it is best to stick to only four. Many browsers are not set up to display higher-level heads with font and character attributes that differ enough from each other to make them noticeable. Keep your headings structured like any outline. For example, you wouldn't put a lower-level heading before a higher-level heading in an outline. The same holds true for HTML headings.

If you're using an editor other than HoTMetaL PRO, don't try to combine the heading and title tags for the first level of a document. For example: <H1><TITLE>Canyon Software's Home Page </TITLE></H1> is incorrect. The TITLE tag can only ever appear inside the HEAD at the start of the document.

Inserting Paragraphs & Line Breaks

Unlike typical word processor documents, how lines wrap in your document has no effect on the how the HTML document displays in a browser. Pressing Enter may add line spaces to your HTML document, but the lines will not appear when displayed in a browser. Multiple spaces are also ignored. All spaces and multiple returns are collapsed to a single space. In order to specify a paragraph, you use the standard paragraph tag. The paragraph tag ends the current line and inserts additional spacing prior to the start of the next line.

Although the paragraph tag in version 2 of HTML doesn't require an ending counterpart, HTML version 3 does. This is partially to make HTML more compatible with SGML, but more important, it opens the way to include attribute information for the paragraph, such as centering or justification. HoTMetaL PRO automatically adds a starting and ending paragraph tag.

To start adding text, choose P from the Insert Elements dialog box. You can then enter the text you want between the beginning and ending paragraph tags. The following is the HTML source code for the first paragraph of Canyon Software's home page.

```
<P>Canyon Software is the creator of the easiest to use
Windows file and compression manager available. Canyon
has been in business since 1988. We were the first software
company to introduce a compression manager to work
seamlessly with World Wide Web browsers.</P>
```

The line-break tag <BR> lets you break a line without adding a space between the lines. The line-break tag is an empty element. It appears in HoTMetaL Pro with a starting and ending tag, although when displayed as raw HTML code the <BR> tag does not have an end tag. Line-break tags commonly are used with the address tags, which are explained later in this chapter.

Adding Horizontal Rules

The horizontal rule element is another way to divide your document into sections. The default rule is a shaded line that when viewed with a gray background looks like an inset 3D bar drawn across the width of the page. You may see some impressive horizontal rules in Web pages. Many people use inline graphic images in place of horizontal rules. To include a horizontal rule, choose HR from the Insert Elements dialog box.

<HR> </HR>

Netscape adds four proprietary extensions to the horizontal rule to let you specify the thickness, width, alignment and shading of horizontal rules. For example you could specify a rule that is a line 1/4" thick that appears centered and is 50 percent of the width of the document. Figure 4-2 shows the Edit Attributes dialog box for horizontal rules. Table 4-2 describes Netscape tag extensions that allow the document's author to describe how the horizontal rule should look.

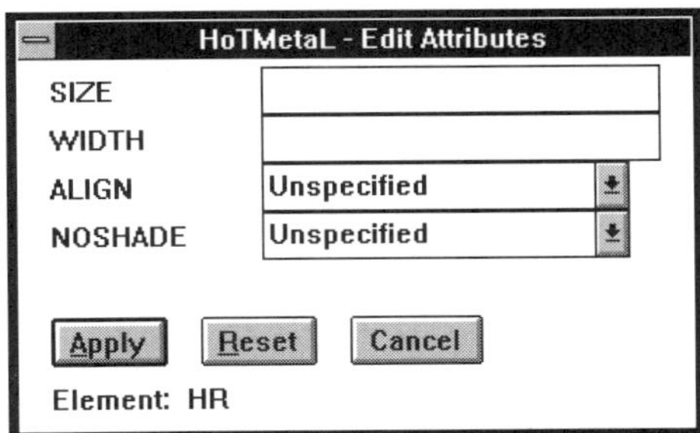

Figure 4-2: *The Edit Attributes dialog box for horizontal rules.*

Attribute	Description
<HR SIZE=*n*>	Specifies the thickness of the horizontal rule in pixels. The *n* stands for the number of pixels.
<HR WIDTH=*n*>	Specifies an exact width in pixels, or a relative width measured in percent of document width. The *n* stands for a number of pixels.
<HR ALIGN=*alignment*>	Specifies the alignment of the rule. The three choices are LEFT (left aligned), RIGHT (right aligned), or CENTER (centered).
<HR NOSHADE>	Specifies that you do not want any shading of your horizontal rule.

Table 4-2: *Attributes for horizontal rules.*

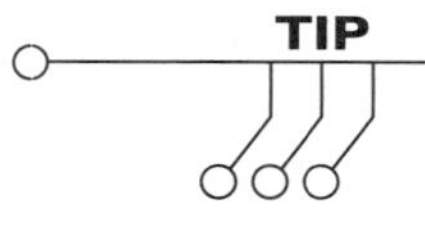

Just because something looks great in your browser doesn't mean it will look great when viewed in other browsers. Because we are creating a simple home page in this chapter, we recommend that you hold off on adding Netscape extensions. Once you have a handle on building pages, you can edit your pages to create a version that takes advantage of these extensions. Many of the features that the Netscape extensions bring to HTML will be available in HTML version 3.

Including Lists

There are four types of lists you can use in an HTML document: unordered lists, ordered lists, discursive lists and directory lists. An *unordered* list is another way of saying a bulleted list. An *ordered* list is a numbered list. A *discursive* or *definition* list is also called a *glossary* list. Discursive lists let you create two columns, one for terms and one for the description of the term. A *directory* list is a list of short items (less than 24 characters). Directory lists display a list of items with no bullets and without a hanging indent. Because lists are so common to HTML documents, we'll briefly cover these lists in this chapter. Many home pages, however, typically only include the unordered (bulleted) list.

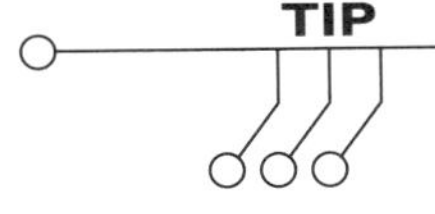

It's possible to nest lists in a Web document for an outline effect. Chapter 6, "Creating Your Text Appeal," explains creating nested lists.

Unordered (Bulleted) Lists

The unordered list tag, <UL>, is used to mark the beginning of a bulleted list. The unordered list uses the list item tag <LI> to indicate each separate list entry. This tag appears before the text used to denote the list item. The browser determines what character to use for a bullet. A DOS browser, for example, may use an asterisk or a dash. You can combine the paragraph tag to help add space around list items, as shown in the following example.

```
<UL>
<LI><P>Check out the 32-bit version of Drag And File.</P>
</LI>
<LI><P>View any file with Drag And View Gold.</P></LI>
<LI><P>The new version of Drag And Zip includes Zip View,
which lets you decompress files from any Web browser.
</P></LI>
</UL>
```

This would appear similar to Figure 4-3 in your document.

Our New 32-Bit Releases

- Check out the 32-bit version of Drag And File.
- View any file with Drag And View Gold.
- The new version of Drag and Zip includes Zip View, which lets you decompress files from any Web browser.

Figure 4-3: *An unordered list.*

A common mistake is to embed a heading within a list to make the list font larger. Doing this will lead to unpredictable results. It may look fine on your screen, but it will most likely cause problems when viewed with other browsers.

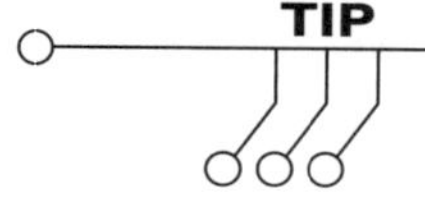

HTML version 3 adds a new TYPE attribute to the unordered list. The TYPE attribute lets you define one of three types of bullets: circle, disc or square.

Ordered (Numbered) Lists

The ordered list tag <OL> is used to mark the beginning of a numbered list. Like the unordered list, this tag must be followed by list item tags <LI> to denote the actual text used in the list. The end tag, </OL>, must be included at the end of the ordered list.

When the page is displayed the browser will automatically insert the numbers for each list item. This is convenient because it eliminates numbering errors. The following is an example of an ordered list:

```
<H2> License Agreement </H2>
<OL>
<LI><P> Grant of License </P></LI>
<LI><P> Copyright </P></LI>
<LI><P> Other Restrictions </P></LI>
```

This code would appear onscreen like Figure 4-4.

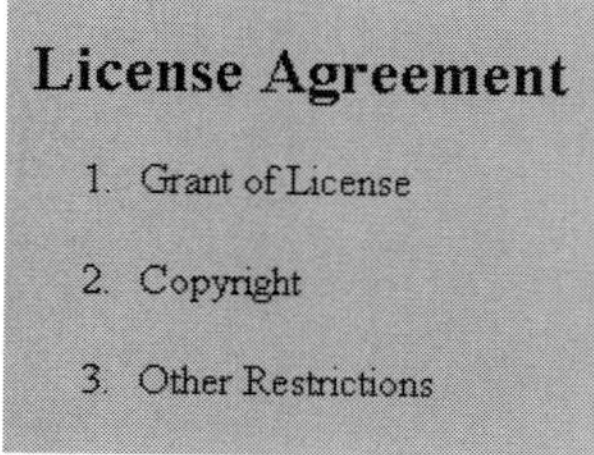

Figure 4-4: *An ordered list.*

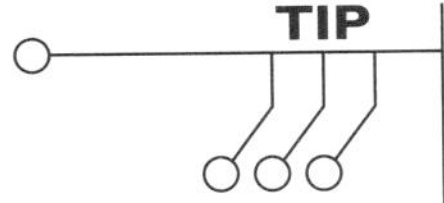

HTML version 3 adds a new TYPE attribute to ordered lists. The TYPE attribute lets you define the character used at each level of nesting. The number or the count can now be changed in the middle of a list. You also can specify to use uppercase roman numerals, lowercase roman numerals, uppercase letters or lowercase letters. For more information on the ordered list, see Appendix C, "An Illustrated HTML Reference."

Descriptive (Glossary) Lists

The descriptive list tag is used to construct a glossary-like entry. A descriptive list contains two elements: a descriptive title, <DT>, and its related list entry. Each description list entry is preceded by the markup descriptive definition <DD>. Descriptive lists can also include the <P> markup to include spaces between entries.

```
<DL>
<DT>Drag And File
<DD><P>Voted shareware product of the year by PC Maga-
zine, this incredibly easy-to-use, yet extremely powerful file
manager includes a fully customizable toolbar that works in
conjunction with Drag And View Gold and Drag And Zip.</P>
<DT>Drag And Zip
<DD><P>A Windows compression manager that works as a
stand-alone compression utility or in conjunction with
PKZIP. PKZIP is a DOS-based compression utility that has
become the defacto standard. Drag And Zip includes the
Zip View utility that lets you decompress files on the fly
from a Web browser.</P>
<DT>Drag And View Gold
<DD><P>A file viewer that lets you view the contents of
over 40 different types of files. Drag And View Gold will
view most word processing documents, spreadsheets,
databases, archives, bitmapped and vector graphics.</P>
</DL>
```

Inserting Inline Graphic Images

Most Web documents contain an inline graphic or two. This chapter contains an example of a logo added as an inline graphic. For this example the logo is kept on your local drive. In its simplest terms, a local inline graphic can be included in a document using raw HTML by including its source after the <IMG markup, in the form <IMG SRC= *"path/filename.gif"*>. When you use HoTMetaL PRO, choose Markup>> Insert Element and choose the IMG element from the Insert Elements dialog box. This displays the Edit URL dialog box. In the Name text box, specify the path to the image file with the back slash like you would any Windows path. When you view the URL in HoTMetaL PRO, however, the <IMG SRC displays the forward slash rather than the back slash. To view the URL in HoTMetaL PRO, choose View>>Hide Inline Images and choose View>>Show URLs, the URL for the inline image appears as <IMG SRC: path/filename.gif>. If you are storing the HTML document in the same directory as the graphic file, you can omit the path. For example, the raw HTML entry for an inline image without a path may appear as

```
<IMG SRC="cslogo.gif">
```

Not all browsers can display graphic images. To make sure that others viewing your page are not left in the dark, choose Markup>>Edit SGML Attribute. This displays the Edit Attribute dialog box as previously shown in Figure 4-2. Edit the ALT attribute field to specify text to display in place of the image. This lets a person viewing the page from a text-based browser, such as Lynx on a VT100 terminal, see the words "Canyon Software Logo" at the location of the logo.

```
<IMG SRC="cslogo.gif" ALT="Canyon Software Logo">
```

By default HoTMetaL PRO doesn't display the ALT attribute and text. There are two ways you can see the text that ALT attribute is set to display: choose the Markup>>Edit SGML Attribute or choose the View>>Show Link and Context View. In order to see the ALT attribute and text using the Show Link and Context, the insertion point must be in the line containing the URL for the image.

This adds the logo to the document, so it now looks like Figure 4-5. By default text is aligned with the bottom of the image. You can choose Markup>>Edit SGML Attribute to specify that the text is aligned at the top or the middle of an inline graphic.

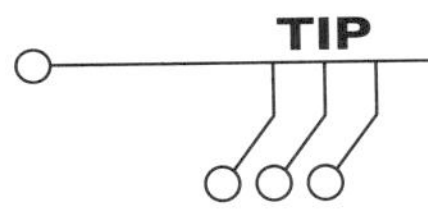

A complete discussion of inline and external graphics is the subject of Chapter 7, "Getting Graphic With Images."

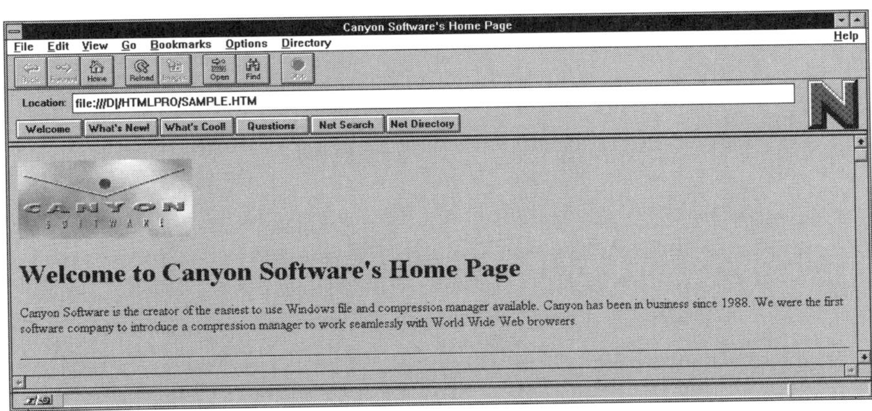

Figure 4-5: *The Canyon Software logo is added to the top of the Web document.*

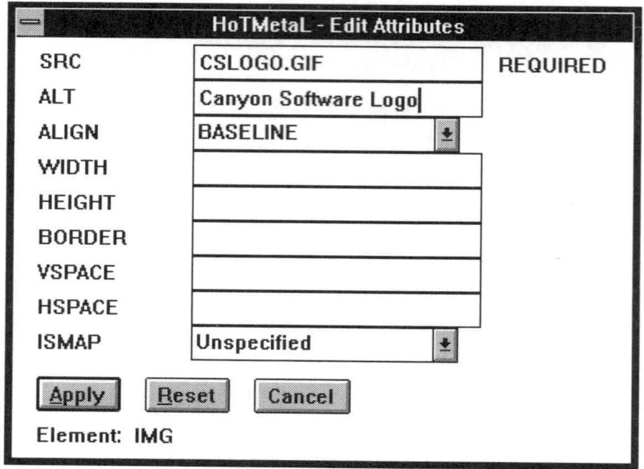

Figure 4-6: *The Edit Attribute dialog box lets you specify text for text-based Web browsers.*

Adding Links

A *hyperlink* is a term used to describe hypertext or an image in your document that acts as a pointer to another location or a file. The location could be another Web document on a remote system, another local Web document, or another part of the current document. The following section explains how to create a link to another location within the same Web document. Creating links to remote documents is discussed in-depth in Chapter 5. In order to create a link, you must identify the destination and create an anchor name that identifies the anchor's destination. The starting point and the destination points are referred to as anchors and appear between the <A> and </A> tags. Anchors can include one or more attributes, but each must have NAME and/or HREF attributes.

The HREF attribute specifies that the anchor is the start of a hypertext link and is followed by an equals sign (=) and the destination anchor or URL. The browser presents the text between the <A> and </A> tags as a hyperlink. The text after the <A> tag and immediately before the </A> shouldn't include any spaces, otherwise space characters will be highlighted. If the hyperlink text appears at the end of a sentence, it's good design to put the period directly outside the closing </A> tag. The path to the destination is established in the document by including the markup:

```
<P>Check out the 32-bit version of
<A HREF="#dragnfile">Drag And File</A>.
```

The NAME attribute specifies that the anchor is the destination of the link.

```
<P><A NAME="dragnfile"></A>Drag And File
</P>
```

In this example, #dragnfile label is used to specify the destination of the link. The words "Drag And File" appear in the document as the hyperlink text. If you click the "Drag And File" hypertext, you will be sent to the Anchor with the NAME="dragnfile" in the document.

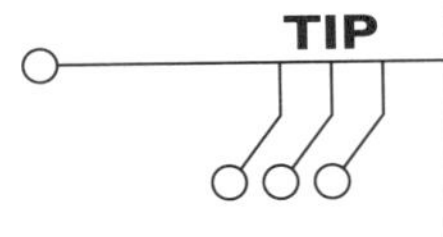

The above is a very simplistic execution of a link. To learn how to link to documents outside your system, or to get a deeper understanding of the linking process, refer to Chapter 5, "The Art of Linking."

Adding an Address

The <ADDRESS> tag is usually an e-mail address and is generally used to identify the author of a document or the Webmaster, thereby letting users contact the document's author. The output appears as italic text. In most cases you'll want to use the <BR> tag to provide line breaks for each part of the address.

```
<P>For additional information on Canyon Software's prod-
ucts and services, please send e-mail to
<B>info@canyonsw.com</B>, phone us at +1 415-382-7999,
or FAX your request to +1 415-453-6195. If you have prob-
lems or comments concerning our Web service, please
send e-mail to the following address:
</P>
```

```
<ADDRESS>webmaster@canyonsw.com</ADDRESS>
<P>You can also contact us via snail mail at</P>
<ADDRESS>
Canyon Software<BR>
1537 Fourth Street Suite 131<BR>
San Rafael, California 94901 USA<BR>
</ADDRESS>
```

A Sample Home Page

The following is the raw source for a page that includes most of the tags that have been introduced in this chapter. The graphic image file used as the logo in this sample is supplied on the Companion CD-ROM. The CD-ROM also includes the code for this example.

```
<HTML>
<HEAD>
<TITLE> Canyon Software's Home Page </TITLE> </HEAD>
<BODY>
<IMG SRC="images/cslogo.gif" ALT="Canyon Software
Logo">
<H1>Welcome to Canyon Software's Home Page</H1>
<P>Canyon Software is the creator of the easiest to use
Windows file and compression manager available. Canyon
has been in business since 1988. We were the first software
company to introduce a compression manager to work
seamlessly with World Wide Web browsers.</P>
<HR>
<H2>Our New 32-Bit Releases</H2>
<UL>
<LI><P>Check out the 32-bit version of
<A HREF="#dragnfile">Drag And File</A>.
</P></LI>
<LI><P>View any file fast with
<A HREF="#dragnview">Drag And View Gold</A>.
</P>
```

```
</LI>
<LI><P>The new version of <A HREF="#dragnzip">Drag
And Zip</A> works with any browser.</P>
</LI>
</UL>
<HR>
<H2>Canyon Software's Product Line</H2>
<DL>
<DT><A NAME="dragnfile"></A>Drag And File
<DD><P>Voted shareware product of the year by PC Maga-
zine, this incredibly easy-to-use, yet extremely powerful file
manager includes a fully customizable toolbar that works in
conjunction with Drag and View Gold and Drag And Zip.</
P>
<DT><A NAME="dragnzip"></A>Drag And Zip
<DD><P>A Windows compression manager that works as a
standalone compression utility or in conjunction with PKZIP.
PKZIP is a DOS-based compression utility that has become
the defacto standard. Drag And Zip includes the Zip View
utility that lets you decompress files on the fly from a Web
browser.</P>
<DT><A NAME="dragnview"></A>Drag And View Gold
<DD><P>A file viewer that lets you view the contents of
over 40 different types of files. Drag And View Gold will
view most word processing documents, spreadsheets,
databases, archives, bitmapped and vector graphics.</P>
</DL>
<HR>
<H2>How to Contact Canyon Software</H2>
<P>For additional information on Canyon Software's prod-
ucts and services, please send e-mail to
<B>info@canyonsw.com</B>, phone us at +1 415-382-7999,
or FAX your request to +1 415-453-6195. If you have prob-
lems or comments
concerning our Web service, please send e-mail to the
following address:
</P>
<ADDRESS>webmaster@canyonsw.com</ADDRESS>
<P>You can also contact us via snail mail at</P>
```

```
<ADDRESS>
Canyon Software<BR>
1537 Fourth Street Suite 131<BR>
San Rafael, California 94901 USA<BR>
</ADDRESS>
</BODY>
</HTML>
```

Validating Your Web Document

One simple but important final step you should take is to validate your document before publishing it. To validate your document with HoTMetaL PRO, choose the Special>>Validate Document command or use the shortcut key, F9. In addition to checking your entire document, HoTMetaL PRO lets you check an individual section of your document. If text in your Web document is selected, only the selection is checked, otherwise the entire document is checked. HoTMetaL PRO checks for all required beginning and ending elements and checks to make sure the attributes are in the correct form. If HoTMetaL PRO finds an error, a message box appears notifying you of the error and the insertion point moves to its location, so you can fix the error.

Publishing Your Web Document

When you get ready to publish your work on the Internet, you'll need to replace all the local references with URLs that point to your system as the network sees it. For example, during development, a local reference might be:

```
file://cl/mydoc/page1.htm
```

but the network reference might be:

```
http://www.mycompany.com/info/mydoc/page1.htm
```

HoTMetaL eases this transition by prompting you for the URL changes. To replace the local references, choose the File>>Publish command. HoTMetaL PRO displays the Publish dialog box, which lets you choose whether to find and replace the URLs on a one-by-one basis or replace all the local file references to network http references.

Moving On

Now you have an idea how easy it is to write a simple HTML document. You've only scratched the surface, however. Until you delve into the power of links, you really can't take advantage of the global publishing capabilities of the World Wide Web. The next chapter builds on the HTML tags you learned in this chapter to show you how to exploit the power of links to publish complex Web documents and connect to files and other Web documents around the world.

SECTION II

Working With the Pieces

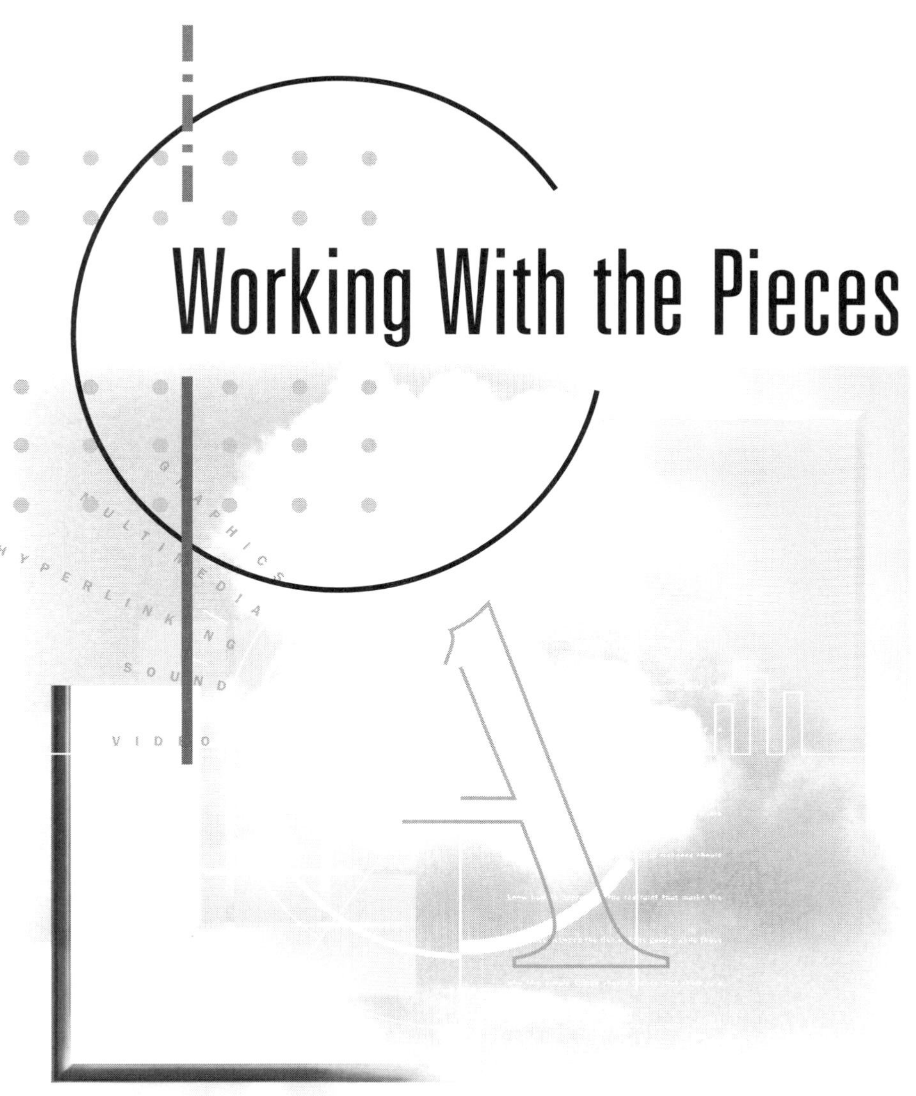

5

The Art of Linking

The last chapter took you through HTML basic training, showing you how to create a Web page and include a link to another part of the same page. A Web page with links only to the same page, however, is a little boring. This chapter lets you create more exciting interactive HTML pages by explaining how to create links that connect to additional pages on your own system and how to create links to connect to Web pages at other sites anywhere in the world.

An Introduction to Links

There are three types of links you can create: intra-page links, intra-system links and inter-system links. Intra-page links link to another place in the current page; intra-system links link to other pages on the current server; and inter-system links link to a page on another server.

The Anchor tag lets you create a link. Well-designed HTML pages have multiple links to produce easy-to-use, easy-to-read Web documents. The text examples in this chapter show the raw HTML source code, rather than the HTML tag icons which HoTMetaL PRO displays. A typical Anchor tag for a inter-system link in a raw HTML document looks similar to the following:

```
<A HREF="http://www.vmedia.com/">Ventana Online</A>
```

The opening <A> tag specifies the place you are linking to, that is, the destination URL or the name of a file. In this case, the destination is the URL http://www.vmedia.com/. Between the opening and closing tags is the text that will be highlighted on the page as the "hyperlink text," in this case, Ventana Online. The closing tag </A> indicates the end of the link text and hypertext reference.

How to Create a Link

There are two ways to create a link with HoTMetaL PRO. The most intuitive method is to first type the text you want, without inserting the hyperlinks. This keeps you focused on the information you want to convey, and helps you avoid the undistinguishing, wornout "click here" phrase that infests so many otherwise well-written pages. Select the text that will become the linked text, then use the Markup>>Surround command to add an Anchor tag. The shortcut key for the Surround command is Ctrl-U. Next, choose the Markup>>Edit SGML Attributes. The F6 key is the shortcut key for adding SGML attributes. This displays the Edit attributes dialog box for adding a link, as shown in Figure 5-1. Enter the file name or URL for the jump destination in the HREF field and choose the Apply button.

Alternatively, you can choose the Markup>>Insert Element command. This displays the Insert Element dialog box. Select Anchor, then select Markup>>Edit URL. Enter the link information and click the Apply button to add the hyperlink.

By default HoTMetaL PRO displays the hypertext reference next to the HREF anchor. If HoTMetaL PRO doesn't show the content of a link, choose View>>Show Link and Context View. This displays a window, shown in Figure 5-2, that shows the link information for the selected link.

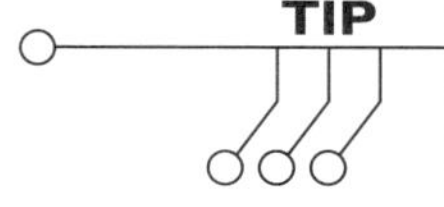

If you're not using HoTMetaL PRO, you can enter the text with an HTML editor or a text editor, such as Notepad. Windows 3.1 and Windows for Workgroups systems restricts you to the eight-letter name and three-letter extension naming scheme, which is why the files end with HTM instead of HTML. Windows NT and Windows '95 lift this file-name restriction, letting you name files with longer file names and extensions, provided the file name and extension doesn't exceed 256 characters.

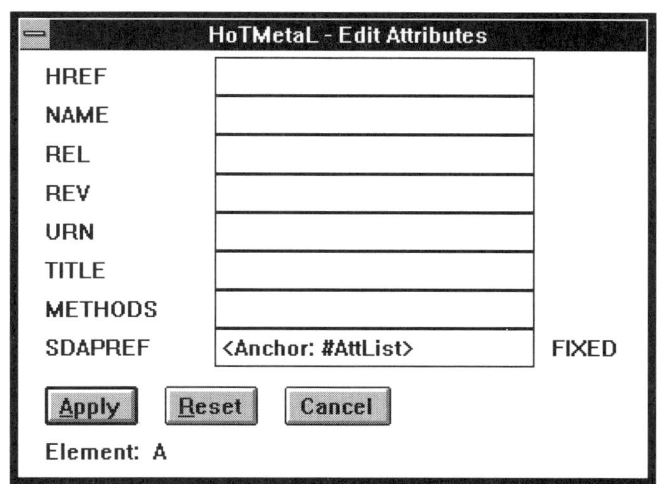

Figure 5-1: *The Edit Attributes dialog box lets you add a hypertext link.*

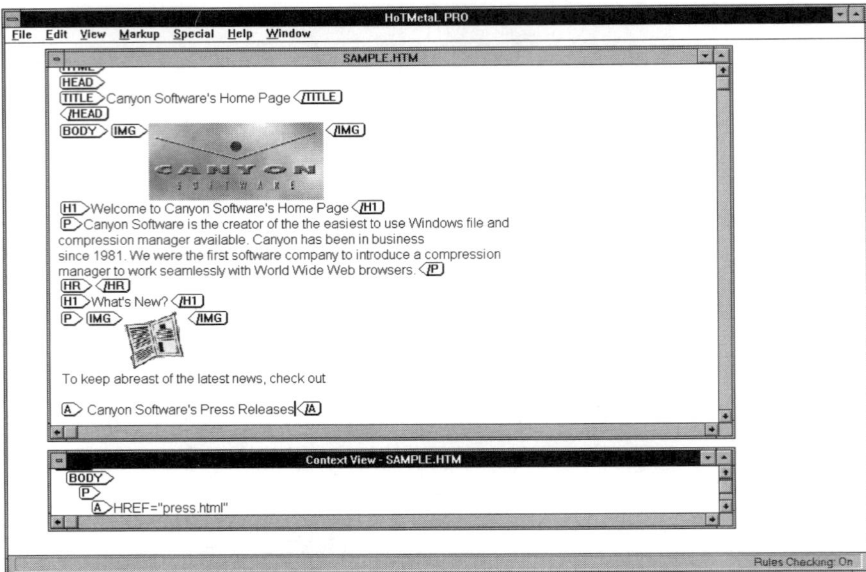

Figure 5-2: *The Context View window lets you see the information for the selected link.*

Creating a Link to a Local Page or File

When you're authoring for the Web, keep individual pages as short as is practical. This means you will wind up with a lot of inter-page links to individual pages. The following is a hands-on example that steps you through the process of creating two pages that point to each other with links using HoTMetaL PRO. Figure 5-3 shows the results of these two pages.

1. Start HoTMetaL PRO.
2. Choose Markup>>Insert Element or press Ctrl-I. The Insert Element dialog box appears. By default HTML is automatically highlighted.
3. Click the control box for the Insert Element dialog box. The control box is the hyphen-like icon to the left of the title bar. This displays the window menu for the dialog box. Choose Pin from the menu. This keeps the Element dialog

box open to save you from continually having to choose the Markup>>Insert Element or having to press Ctrl-I to insert elements.

4. Make sure the HTML element is highlighted and choose the Insert Element button. The insertion point appears after the phrase "Document Title:" between the TITLE and /TITLE tags. The phrase Document Title: is not a part of the document's title and will not display in a Web browser.
5. Click on the document's title bar. At the insertion point, type the title of the document **Link Sample Page 1**.
6. Move the insertion point between the /HEAD and /HTML tags. The Insert Element dialog box now displays only the BODY element. Choose the Insert Element button. This inserts the BODY and /BODY tags and the Element dialog box now displays available body tags.
7. Select the H1 element and choose the Insert Element button. The insertion point appears between the H1 and /H1 tags.
8. Click on the document's title bar. At the insertion point, type the heading **Link Sample Page 1**.
9. Move the insertion point between the /H1 and /BODY tag. Select the P (paragraph) element and choose the Insert Element button. The insertion point appears between the P and /P tags.
10. Click on the document's title bar. At the insertion point, type **This is a reference to page two**.
11. Select the text "page two," and then choose Markup>>Surround menu item or press Ctrl-U. By default the Anchor element is selected. Choose the Surround button.
12. Choose Markup>>Edit SGML Attributes. This displays the Edit Attributes dialog box. In the HREF field, type **page2.htm** as the link destination and choose the Apply button.

13. Choose File>>Save or press Ctrl-S and save the file as "page1.htm."
14. To create the second page, choose File>>Save As and enter **page2.htm** as the file name.
15. Change the "Page1" references to "Page2" and change the anchor references from "page one" to "page two."
16. Choose Markup>>Edit SGML Attributes or press F6. This displays the Edit Attributes dialog box. Replace the **page2.htm** with **page1.htm** for the link destination in the HREF field and choose the Apply button.
17. Choose File>>Save or press Ctrl-S to save your changes.
18. Close the Insert Element dialog box.
19. To test your sample link pages, choose File>>Preview. Alternatively you can open either page with the File>>Open File or the File>>Open Local File command on your Web browser.

The Link Sample Page 1 includes a link (page2.htm) that points to Link Sample Page 2. The Link Sample Page 2 includes a link (page1.htm) that points back to Link Sample Page 1. The source for the first page appears similar to the following:

```
<HTML><HEAD><TITLE>Link Sample Page 1. </TITLE></
HEAD>
<BODY><H1>Link Sample Page 1</H1>
<P>This is a reference to
<A HREF="page2.htm">page two</A>.
</P>
</BODY></HTML>
```

Page two appears similar to the following:

```
<HTML><HEAD><TITLE>Link Sample Page 2.</TITLE></
HEAD>
<BODY><H1>Link Sample Page 2</H1>
<P>This is a reference to
<A HREF="page1.htm">page one</A>.
</P>
</BODY></HTML>
```

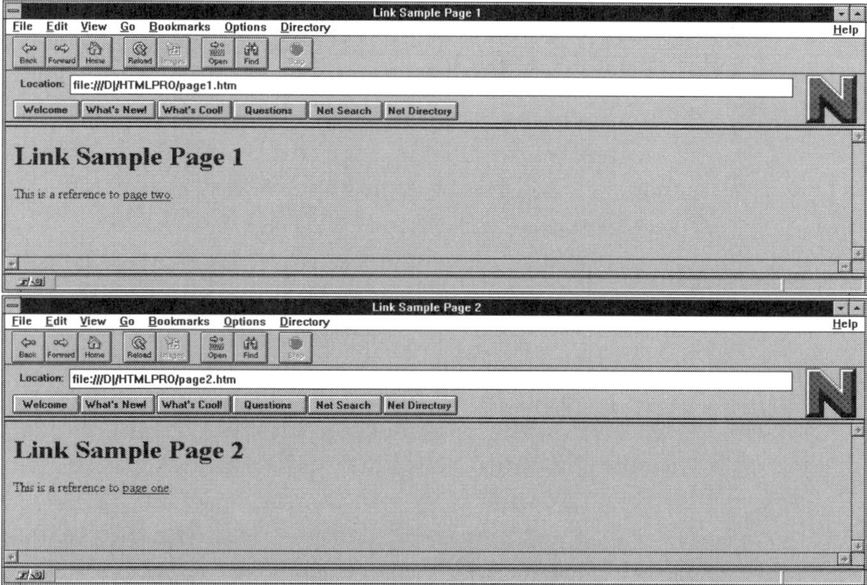

Figure 5-3: *How "page1.htm" and "page2.htm" appear in the Netscape Navigator browser.*

Relative Paths

In the previous example, the HREF attribute specifies only a file name. Notice there isn't a full URL prefix. This is allowed because your browser uses the HREF as a *relative* path. That is, if you opened the first file with the File>>Open command, the browser assumes that all HREFs that do not have a prefix specified, such as HTTP: or FILE:, are located in the same relative directory as the first file you opened. This is a handy feature, since you can move both files to another directory, and the links will still work. If you look at the "jump destination" in the status line of your browser (typically found at the bottom of the screen), you'll see the complete path to the file; for example,

```
file:///D|/html/page2.htm
```

The Importance of Local Links

It's important to use links that assist users when navigating through your pages in both directions. A common problem with many HTML pages on the Web today is the lack of good backward links.

Imagine for a moment you've navigated through the Web to a particularly interesting page. You add it to your bookmark list for future reference. Now, several days later, you call up the bookmark to look at that page again. At this point, you may wish to look at other pages on the same site, but unfortunately there are no links on the page you are viewing. At this point, you are effectively "lost in hyperspace," with little or no idea how to move around to other pages on the same server.

As a rule, you should *always* include a link from every HTML page back to your home page. From your home page you can create links to other pages or to other interesting places on the Web.

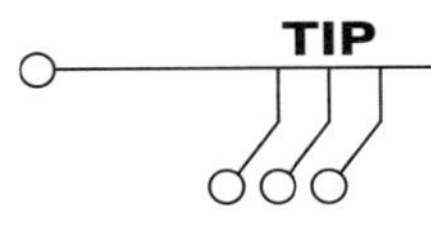

In addition to the text-based links discussed in this chapter, there are links that you can add to graphical images. For example, a common practice is to use a logo as a link to your home page. Making an inline graphic image a link is covered in detail in Chapter 7.

Creating a Link Within a Page

In most cases, it's a good idea to keep your Web pages short. This ensures that the text will fit in a screen or two on the reader's computer. There are cases, however, where this isn't practical or desired. For example, you may have a long price list or a FAQ (Frequently Asked Questions) you may want to keep together so people can easily print it out. When you have long pages, it's convenient to provide links between sections of the same page. This is done with *intra-page links*. There are a couple unique steps for creating intra-page links, specifically, establishing names or labels for the jump-to destinations in the page. Labels in pages are also created with the Anchor tag, using the NAME attribute of the Anchor tag to create the label. The following example steps you through the process of creating a link within a page.

1. Enter and select the text you want to make a hyperlink to jump to another specific part of your page.
2. Choose the Markup>>Surround command or press Ctrl-U. The Surround dialog box appears, as shown in Figure 5-4. Choose the Surround button to surround the selected text with Anchor tags.
3. Choose the Markup>>Edit URL. This displays the Edit URL dialog box.
4. Type a pound "#" sign and the text to match the label for the destination in the Name field and choose the Apply button. For example, Figure 5-5 shows "#help" added to the Name field to match the destination label named help in the same document.
5. Move to the destination you want to let users jump to in your document. Choose Markup>>Insert Element or press Ctrl-I. The Insert Element dialog box appears.
6. Make sure A (Anchor) is selected and choose the Insert Element button to add the anchor.
7. Choose the Markup>>Edit SGML Attributes or press F6. This displays the Edit Attributes dialog box.
8. Enter the jump destination in the Name field and choose the Apply button. This is almost the same as the text you entered in step 3. The only difference is you do *not* include the pound "#" sign.
9. Choose File>>Save or press Ctrl-S to save your changes.
10. Choose the File>>Preview command or press Ctrl-M to test the intra-page links.

In the previous chapter, we explained how to create a link to a specific part of the page using HoTMetaL PRO. This chapter shows a little different example that includes the label within a heading. In order for this to be a practical example, we included enough text so the link points to a section that isn't on the screen at the same time. Remember all the examples are included on the Companion CD-ROM, so you don't have to type in all the text.

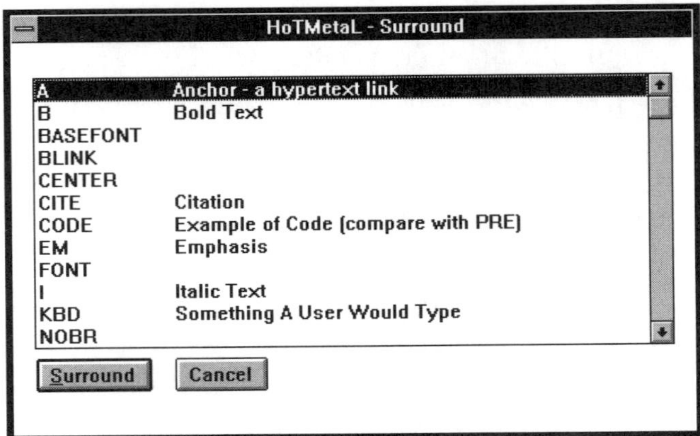

Figure 5-4: *The Surround dialog box.*

HoTMetaL - Edit URL
Attribute: HREF
Protocol: <name>
Host:
Port:
Name: #help
Choose File...
Apply
Cancel
A

Figure 5-5: *The Name field lets you label the jump destination.*

```
<HTML><HEAD><TITLE>Canyon Software's FAQ</TITLE>
</HEAD>
<BODY><H1>Canyon Software's FAQ</H1>
<P>This page includes answers to frequently asked ques-
tions about Canyon Software products.
</P>
```

```
<P>If you need help or technical support, you can move
directly to the section on
<A HREF="#help">Getting Help</A>.</P>
<HR>
<H1>What is Drag And Zip?</H1>
<P>Drag And Zip converts Windows File Manager into a Zip
file manager quickly and easily. To begin with, users drag
the files they want zipped to a zipper icon. Next, users give
a destination path and a name to the Zip file. At this point,
Drag And Zip will compress the files into a Zip file. This is
all done from within Windows with Drag And Zip's built-in
compression program (DynaZip) without the need for
PKZIP. Extracting files from a Zip file is also accomplished
by dragging it to the zipper icon or by double-clicking on it.
A viewer window showing the contents of the Zip file will
appear. From this viewer window, users can select files for
extracting, deleting, launching or viewing. Drag And Zip
can also be used as an interface to PKZIP (.zip), LHA (.lzh) or
GNU Zip (.z or .gz) programs. Some of Drag And Zip's most
notable features are that it</P>
<P></P>
<UL>
<LI>Works in conjunction with Internet World Wide Web
Browsers</LI>
<LI>Includes built-in compression and decompression</LI>
<LI>Includes built-in virus scanner</LI>
<LI>Works with files compressed with PKZIP, LHA and GNU
Zip Programs</LI></UL>
<HR>
<H1>How can I get a copy of Drag And Zip?</H1>
<P>Shareware versions can be found at the following FTP
sites</P>
<P></P>
<UL>
<LI>Canyon Software's FTP Site</LI>
<LI>SimTel Archive</LI>
<LI>Indiana University (CICA) Archive</LI>
</UL>
<P>Drag And Zip is also available on most online Services,
```

```
Bulletin Boards and Canyon's BBS at (415) 453-4289 or on
CompuServe at the WINAPG Forum, Section 4 (GO CAN-
YON).</P>
<HR>
<H1><A NAME="help"></A>Getting Help</H1>
<H2>Online Help</H2>
For help with Drag And Zip, click on the Help menu on the
menu bar in the main window. Context-sensitive help is
also available for most menus and dialog boxes. For infor-
mation and procedural help specific to a screen or menu,
click on the Help button.
<H2>Telephone Help</H2>
<P>Canyon Software is committed to producing software
that is useful and productive. To help users make full use of
Drag And File, Canyon Software maintains a technical help
line for registered users from 8:30 AM to 5:30 PM Pacific
Time.</P>
<UL>
<LI><P>Phone (415) 453-9779</P></LI>
<LI><P>Fax (415) 453-6195</P></LI>
<LI><P>BBS (415) 453-4289</P></LI>
</UL>
<H2>E-mail Help</H2>
<P>If you would like to contact Canyon Software via e-mail,
send a mail message to any of the following e-mail ad-
dresses.</P>
<UL>
<LI><P>Internet support@csoftware.com</P></LI>
<LI><P>CompuServe 71320,1277
</P></LI>
<LI><P>America On Line DanBCan</P>
</LI></UL>
<PRE>
</PRE>
</BODY>
</HTML>
```

In the above example, you can see the destination for the jump specified as a label in the same page, "help." The pound sign prefix in the parameter: HREF="#help" tells your viewer that the jump is internal to this page, to a place with the label "help." At the Getting Help section of the page, you see another Anchor tag, this time using the "NAME=help" attribute instead of the HREF= attribute. The NAME specifies the label to be used as a jump destination. If you create a file with this content, open the file in a browser and click the Getting Help hyperlink, the page jumps to the Getting Help section.

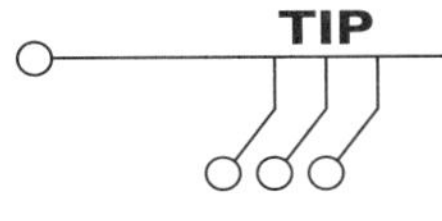

Anchor tags can be used for creating hypertext jumps and creating labels at the same time, if you use both HREF and NAME parameters. Also, you can combine inter-page jumps with jumps to specific labels so that you can jump from a particular point in one page to a particular point in another page. See the end of this chapter for a more complex example.

Creating a Link to a Page at Another Site

This is the most powerful type of Web link. It allows you to create a link from your page to any page anywhere on the Web. You need to be careful, however, to check the correctness of the link on a regular basis. Because you generally don't control the location of the destination page you are linking to, it's possible that the link may change. It is also possible that the network or host system you're linking to will be down at various times, making your link inoperative. Remember that since this is an actual inter-system link, you'll need to be connected to the Internet for it to work.

To create an inter-system link, you need to specify a full URL as the jump destination.

1. Enter and select the text you want to make a hyperlink to identify the place you want to let users jump to.
2. Choose the Markup>>Surround command or press Ctrl-U. The Surround dialog box appears. Choose the Surround button to surround the selected text with Anchor tags.

3. Choose the Markup>>Edit URL. This displays the Edit URL dialog box.
4. Click the arrow located to the right of the Protocol field. Choose the http option to indicate a Web server. If you want to connect to a host using a different protocol, such as an FTP or gopher site, choose the appropriate protocol from the list.
5. Enter the host address in the Host field. Because you specified the http protocol in the previous step, you don't need to enter the http:// prefix. For example to specify the URL for Ventana Online, enter **www.vmedia.com**. Choose the Apply button. If the link doesn't appear, you can choose the View>>Show Link and Context View to display the link.

Links in a Sample HTML Document

To help you better understand links, take a look at the following example. The following HTML sample document follows the structure set up in Chapter 3 and builds on the sample HTML page presented in the previous chapter. It includes local intra-page links and intra-system links, as well as an inter-system link to a page on another server.

Don't worry, the linked documents don't have to be created at this point. In fact, you don't even have to create the linked documents. Simply use the sample destination documents that we've included on the Companion CD-ROM. Later you can replace the text and images in these sample files with your own. As determined in this chapter, the Web documents that need links are as follows:

- What's New links to press.htm, which contains Canyon Software's press releases.
- Canyon Software's Product Line links to products.htm. The products page includes a complete listing of Canyon Software's products and three anchors for different products in the Products page: Drag And File (dragfile.htm), Drag And Zip software (dragzip.htm) and Drag And View Gold software (dragview.htm).

- Help links to faq.htm, which is Canyon Software's answers to Frequently Asked Questions. Sections cover different product and supply information on various methods of support, including the technical support phone number and a technical support e-mail address.
- Guides for the Virtual Tourist links to vtourist.htm, a page containing links to two helpful pages: a list of hotlinks and a viewer test page for testing helper applications with different file formats.
- Ordering links to an order form order.htm, a form for ordering any of Canyon Software's products.
- Feedback links to feedback.htm, which lists links to a client list and offers a customer satisfaction form for requests and comments to Canyon Software.
- Behind the Scenes links to behind.htm, which displays a look at Canyon Software, Inc. founder Dan Baumbach and key employees.

Figure 5-6 shows how this document appears when viewed in Netscape.

Because the content of a link is not obvious when viewing a HoTMetaL PRO document, the examples below show the source of the final HTML text, rather than HoTMetaL PRO. If you want to view the content of the links, open the sample document using HoTMetaL PRO and choose View>>Show Link and Context View. View>>Show URLs should show all the URLs inline in HOTMetaLPRO. When the cursor is next to an HREF, the content of the link will appear in the Show Link and Context View window.

```
<HTML>
<HEAD>
<TITLE>Canyon Software's Home Page</TITLE>
</HEAD>
<BODY><IMG SRC="CSLOGO.GIF">
<H1>Welcome to Canyon Software's Home Page</H1>
<P>Canyon Software is the creator of the easiest to use
Windows file and compression manager available. Canyon
has been in business since 1988. We were the first software
```

```
company to introduce a compression manager to work
seamlessly with World Wide Web browsers.</P>
<HR>
<H1>What's New?</H1>
<P><IMG SRC="NEWSLTR.GIF"> To keep abreast of the
latest news, check out
<A HREF="press.htm"> Canyon Software's Press Releases
</A>.
</P>
<HR>
<H1>Tear into Our New 32-bit Software</H1>
<P><IMG SRC="32-BIT.GIF"> Canyon Software has just
introduced new 32-bit shareware versions of Drag And File
and Drag And Zip. For more information on Canyon
Software's new releases, check out our
<A HREF="products.htm">Product Information</A>.
You can also download a copy of the any of our shareware
products at
<A HREF="ftp://ftp.canyonsw.com/pub/">Canyon Software's
FTP site</A>.
If you like what you see, the
<A HREF="order.htm">Virtual Order Desk</A>
lets you place an online order for any of Canyon Software's
products.</P>
<UL>
<LI><P>Check out the 32-bit version of
<A HREF="df.zip">Drag And File</A>.
</P></LI>
<LI><P>View any file with
<A HREF="dv.zip">Drag And View Gold</A>.
</P></LI>
<LI><P>The new version of
<A HREF="dz.zip">Drag And Zip</A>
includes Zip View which lets you decompress files from any
Web browser.</P></LI></UL>
<HR>
<H1>Guides for the Virtual Tourist</H1>
<P>
<IMG SRC="SUITCASE.GIF"> Fasten your seatbelt. Whether
```

```
you're a newbie or a seasoned World Wide Web traveler,
check out Canyon Software's
<A HREF="vtourist.htm">Virtual Tourist</A>
page, which includes links to our
<A HREF="hotlist.htm">Red Hot Links</A>
page and
<A HREF="viewtest.htm">Helper Application Test</A>
page. The Helper Application Test page includes hyperlinks
to over 20 files in different file formats to help you test your
viewers.</P>
<HR>
<H2>Comments or Problems</H2>
<P>
<IMG SRC="ASK_DAN.GIF"> Have a question or need
assistance? Check out Canyon Software's
<A HREF="faq.htm">FAQ</A>.
This FAQ includes several ways you can contact us for
<A HREF="faq.htm#help">help</A>
with any of our products. You can also drop us a line or
share your comments and requests by filling out our short
<A HREF="feedback">Customer Feedback form</A>.
</P>
<P>For additional information on Canyon Software's prod-
ucts and services, please send e-mail to
<B>info@canyonsw.com</B>, phone us at +1 415-382-7999,
or FAX your request to +1 415-453-6195. If you have prob-
lems or comments concerning our Web service, please
send e-mail to the following address:
<ADDRESS>webmaster@canyonsw.com</ADDRESS>
<P>You can also contact us via snail mail at</P>
<ADDRESS>
Canyon Software<BR>
1537 Fourth Street Suite 131<BR>
San Rafael, California 94901 USA<BR>
</ADDRESS>
<P>This page, and all contents, are Copyright (C) 1995 by
Canyon Software Inc., San Rafael, California, USA.
</P>
```

```
<HR>
<B>[
<A HREF="press.htm">Press Releases</A>
|
<A HREF="products.htm">Products</A>
|
<A HREF="order.htm">Order</A>
|
<A HREF="vtourist.htm" >Virtual Tourist</A>
|
<A HREF="faq.htm">Help</A>
|
<A HREF="feedback.htm">Feedback</A>
|
<A HREF="behind.htm">Behind the Scenes</A>
]</B>
</BODY>
</HTML>
```

All the anchors that include a hypertext reference following the form HREF=document.htm point to other HTML pages; for example, HREF=press.htm and HREF=products.htm reference HTML documents.

The third anchor's hypertext reference is HREF="ftp://ftp.canyonsw.com/pub. This example of an inter-system link points to the FTP site ftp.canyonsw.com. The /pub moves the reader directly to the /pub directory.

The fifth through seventh anchor's hypertext references point to local files with the HREF="df.zip,"HREF="dv.zip"and HREF="dz.zip."

The eleventh anchor's hypertext reference combines documents and labels. The second anchor's hypertext reference points to the document named faq.htm and the label help. Choosing this link lets the reader jump directly to the location labeled help in the faq.htm document.

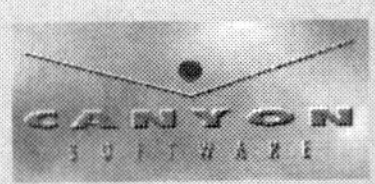

Welcome to Canyon Software's Home Page

Canyon Software is the creator of the easiest to use Windows file and compression manager available. Canyon has been in business since 1988. We were the first software company to introduce a compression manager to work seamlessly with World Wide Web browsers.

What's New?

To keep abreast of the latest news, check out Canyon Software's Press Releases.

Tear into Our New 32-bit Software

Canyon Software has just introduced new 32-bit shareware versions of Drag and File and Drag and Zip. For more information on Canyon Software's new releases, check out our Product Information. You can also download a copy of the any of our shareware products at Canyon Software's FTP site. If you like what you see, the Virtual Order Desk lets you place an online order for any of Canyon Software's products.

- Check out the 32-bit version of Drag And File.
- View any file with Drag and View Gold.
- The new version of Drag and Zip includes Zip View which lets you decompress files from any Web browser.

Guides for the Virtual Tourist

Fasten your seatbelt. Whether you're a newbie or a seasoned World Wide Web traveler, check out Canyon Software's Virtual Tourist page, which includes links to our Red Hot Links page and Helper Application Test page. The Helper Application Test page includes hyperlinks to over 20 files in different file formats to help you test your viewers.

Comments or Problems

Have a question or need assistance? Check out Canyon Software's FAQ. This FAQ includes several ways you can contact us for help with any of our products. You can also drop us a line or share your comments and requests by filling out our short Customer Feedback form.

For additional information on Canyon Software's products and services, please send e-mail to **info@canyonsw.com**, phone us at +1 415-382-7999, or FAX your request to +1 415-453-6195. If you have problems or comments concerning our Web service, please send e-mail to the following address:

webmaster@canyonsw.com

You can also contact us via snail mail at

Canyon Software
1537 Fourth Street Suite 131
San Rafael, California 94901 USA

This page, and all contents, are Copyright (C) 1995 by Canyon Software Inc., San Rafael, California, USA.

[Press Releases | Products | Order | Virtual Tourist | Help | Feedback | Behind the Scenes]

Figure 5-6: *The sample HTML document.*

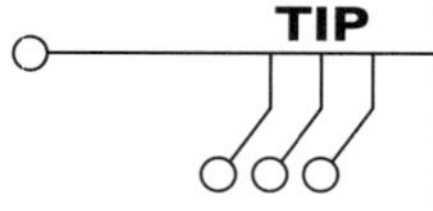

Normally, you will only use the HREF and/or the NAME Anchor tag attributes. As the Web evolves, however, use of other tags may become more prevalent. For more information on the different attributes that are available for links, see Appendix C, "An Illustrated HTML Reference."

Moving On

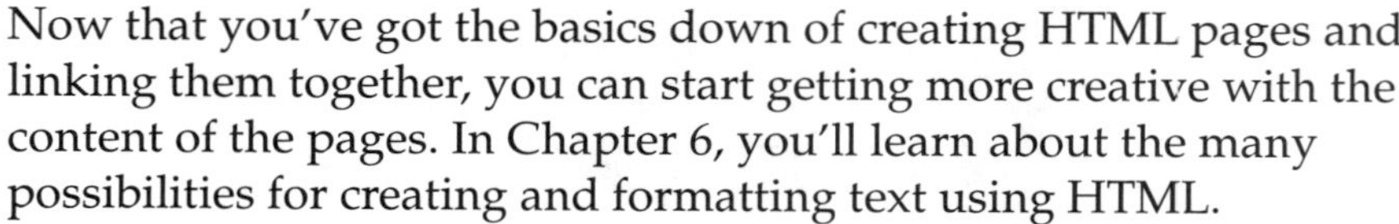

Now that you've got the basics down of creating HTML pages and linking them together, you can start getting more creative with the content of the pages. In Chapter 6, you'll learn about the many possibilities for creating and formatting text using HTML.

6

Creating Your Text Appeal

By now you can see the striking difference between how HTML documents are written and how documents are created with a word processor. Instead of focusing on a physical description of a page's margins, fonts and formatting, the tag structure of HTML focuses on the content of a document and what the various parts of a document mean. The focus of HTML markup is on the classification and content of a paragraph or group of words, instead of the look of the displayed or printed page. There are still a few tags that give explicit directions about rendering text, such as BOLD or ITALIC, but most are focused on the *logical* meaning instead of the *physical* rendering. In this chapter, you'll learn about the options you have as an author to describe the various parts of your page, and see how the different Web browsers will render that page.

Netscape's Extensions to HTML

Most of the tags described in this chapter are part of the HTML standard. A few, however, have been added by Netscape Communications. Use these extensions with care because a page created to look great on the Netscape browser using their extensions may look positively dreadful on another browser. You should always check your work with an assortment of browsers to make sure the rendering is acceptable on all of them.

Inserting Paragraph Elements & Attributes

Chapters 4 and 5 explained the two basic procedures to insert elements using HoTMetaL PRO. You can first type and select your text, then select the style in HoTMetaL PRO by choosing the Markup>>Surround menu items. This surrounds the selected text with the chosen tag. Alternatively, you can choose the Markup>>Insert Element and select the tag from the Insert Elements dialog box. If the tag acts as a container, you can then enter your text between the opening and closing tags. The most basic element is the paragraph. The paragraph element has changed from HTML 1.0 to HTML 3. HTML 1.0 specified only one tag at the end of the paragraph. HTML 3 requires a begining tag <P>, the text to be displayed, and an ending tag, </P>. The browser displays a single line space after an ending paragraph tag. It is a common mistake to include multiple paragraph marks for spacing, but if you add multiple paragraph elements, only one space will appear. The following sections describe additional methods of working with paragraphs.

Displaying Preformatted Paragraphs

If you want to create a block of text on a page and be sure that the style of text will not change when rendered by a Web browser, use the preformatted text element. This shows up as the PRE tag in HTML text. Web browsers use a fixed width font, like Courier, and break lines where they are broken in your source document. Preformatted text is useful when you want to create a computer listing, a table, insert a text file, like a USENET News article, or if you want to add white space to a document. Any white space you add between the opening PRE and closing /PRE tags displays when viewed in a browser. When you use the PRE tag you can add character styles and links, but not paragraph elements, such as headings. Keep your text between 60 to 80 characters when using the PRE tag. If you exceed 80 characters it's likely that the text will not display correctly.

Centering Paragraphs

One of the more exciting extensions to the HTML specification by Netscape is the CENTER paragraph tag. Note that this is an actual tag not just an attribute. The CENTER tag causes the paragraph or other element, such as a header or image, to be centered on the browser's screen. While this is a common feature in word processors, not all Web browsers support this nonstandard extension. Since a CENTER tag will generate a line break—as do all paragraph tags—if a browser ignores the CENTER tag, it will also leave out a line break you may have been expecting. For this reason, try to avoid using the CENTER tag for headings. Instead, use one of the standard heading tags. If you're creating a page especially for Netscape browsers, go ahead and use the CENTER tag to center elements. Figure 6-1 shows the logo and first heading centered on Canyon Software's home page.

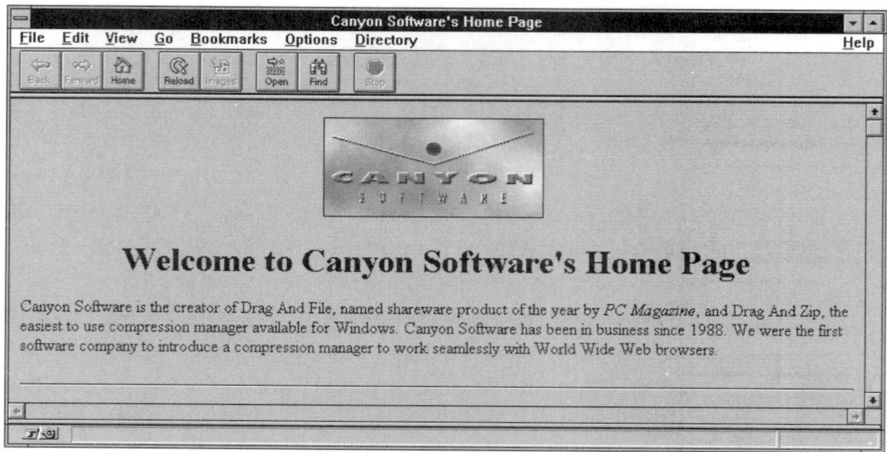

Figure 6-1: *The CENTER tag lets you center elements, such as images and headers.*

Adding a Quotation

The final paragraph style available is the BLOCKQUOTE style. This paragraph style should be used when you create text that is quoted from another source. Typically, Web browsers render this text as indented. Some Web browsers display block quotes in italics. Figure 6-2 shows examples of block quotes. In this example, the BR tag is used to place the name of the person quoted on a separate line, and the person's name, title and other information appears emphasized using the EM tag, discussed later in this chapter.

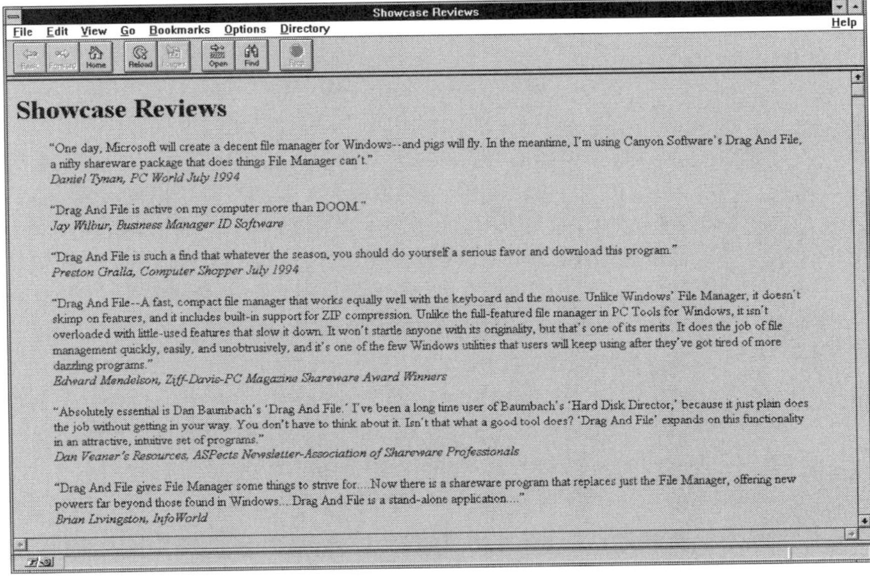

Figure 6-2: *The BLOCKQUOTE tag automatically indents quoted material.*

Using Lists

In Chapter 4 we introduced including lists in a Web page. The following sections include additional information on the four types of lists: unordered lists, ordered lists, directory lists and discursive lists (also called glossary lists). When you want to insert list items, move the insertion point before the end list item tag and use the Markup>>Split command or press Ctrl-P. This automatically places the insertion point between empty beginning and ending list item tags.

Creating Unordered Lists

The unordered list (UL) is also commonly called a bulleted list. Figure 6-3 shows how an unordered list appears in HoTMetaL PRO and Figure 6-4 shows how it appears rendered in Netscape. The standard handling for this list is to use bullets for various indent levels. The first indent level displays a disc, which appears as a round bullet. The second level displays a circle, which we found indiscernible from the disk. The third and last level displays a square bullet. An unordered list is started with the UL tag. Each entry in the list is created with an LI (List Item) tag. The list item may consist of more than one line. The menu list is another type of unordered list. Using the MENU tag instead of UL creates a more compact list than an unordered list. Each list item in a menu list should be no longer than one line.

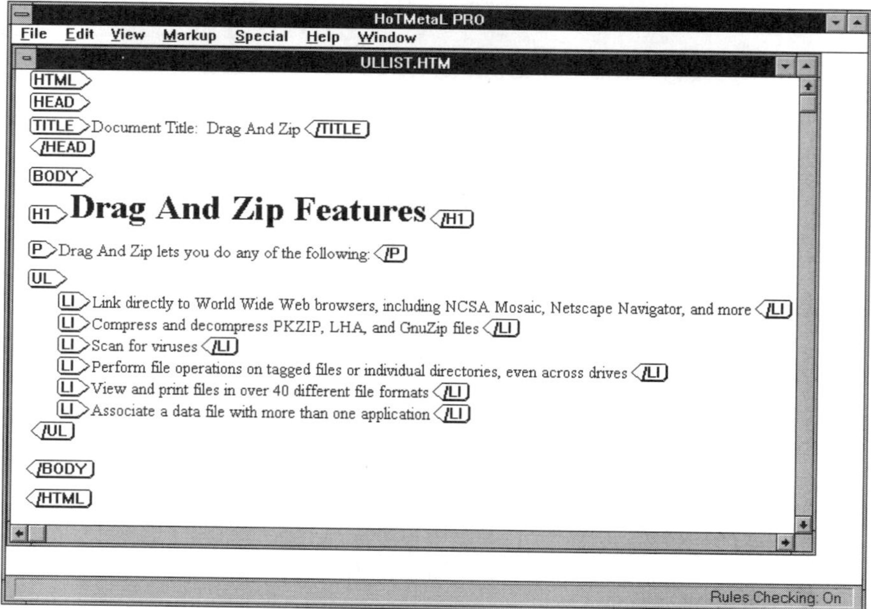

Figure 6-3: *An unordered (bulleted) list in HoTMetaL PRO.*

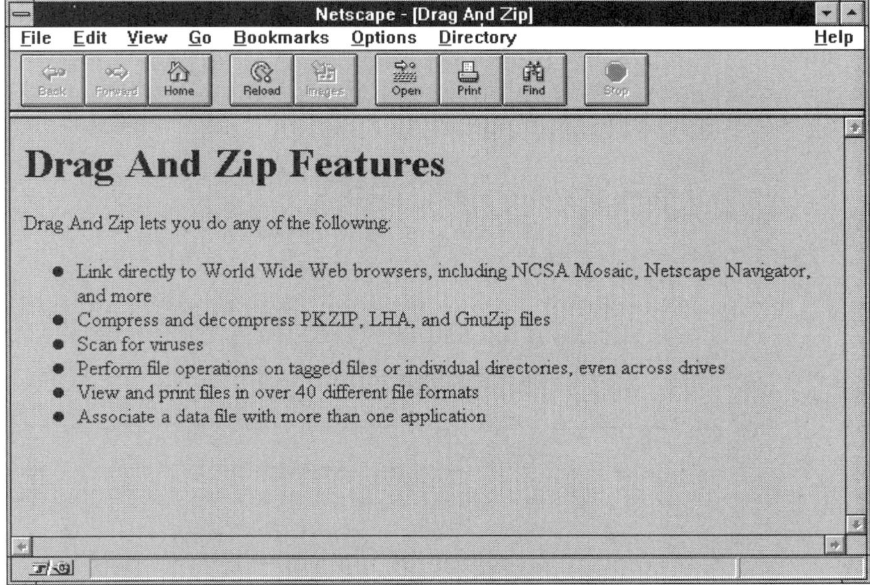

Figure 6-4: *An unordered (bulleted) list in Netscape Navigator.*

Netscape has added the TYPE extension to control the bullet type. To use this Netscape extension, move the cursor between the beginning and ending line-item tags for the item you want to change and choose Markup>>Edit SGML Attributes. This displays the Edit Attributes dialog box. In the TYPE attribute field, enter disc, circle or square. While there are three possible types, the only noticeable difference in Netscape for Windows occurs when you change from the disc to the square attribute.

This extension breaks from the preferred "logical style" concept into the "physical style" concept, since you control the actual bullet style, and browsers other than Netscape will not recognize the extension. For example, Mosaic will only display disc bullets.

Creating Ordered (Numbered) Lists

Ordered lists, or numbered lists, are lists that have numerals as the list-item bullet. By default, lists are ordered in ascending numerical order, 1, 2, 3, 4, etc. The numbering implies that the order of the elements in a list has special significance.

Netscape has added an extension so lists can be ordered in ways other than just 1, 2, 3, 4, etc. Netscape extensions also allow you to use capital letters, small letters, capital roman numerals and small roman numerals. Since non-Netscape browsers just default to numbers, be sure your text does not explicitly refer to "Item C" or "Item II."

To use a Netscape extension numbering scheme, move the cursor between the beginning and ending list item tags for the item you want to change and choose Markup>>Edit SGML Attributes. This displays the Edit Attributes dialog box. In the TYPE attribute field, enter one of the choices listed in Table 6-1.

Tag	Description
A	Specifies that the current list item and subsequent list items begin with capital letters.
a	Specifies that the current list item and subsequent list items begin with lowercase letters.
I	Specifies that the current list item and subsequent list items begin with uppercase roman numerals.
i	Specifies that the current list item and subsequent list items begin with lowercase roman numerals.
1	Specifies that the current list item and subsequent list items begin with numbers (the default setting).

Table 6-1: *TYPE attributes for lists.*

Another Netscape extension lets you start a list at a value other than 1. To enter a different value, you need to edit the START attribute field of the LI element, listed in the Edit Attributes dialog box. This Netscape extension changes the current list item value and acts as a starting value for subsequent list items. The START attribute has no effect on the TYPE setting; for example, entering 3 displays the current list item as "C" (TYPE=A), "c" (TYPE=a), "III" (TYPE=I), "iii" (TYPE=i) or "3" (TYPE=1). Figure 6-5 illustrates how an ordered list is entered in HoTMetaL PRO. Figure 6-6 shows how this looks when rendered with Netscape Navigator.

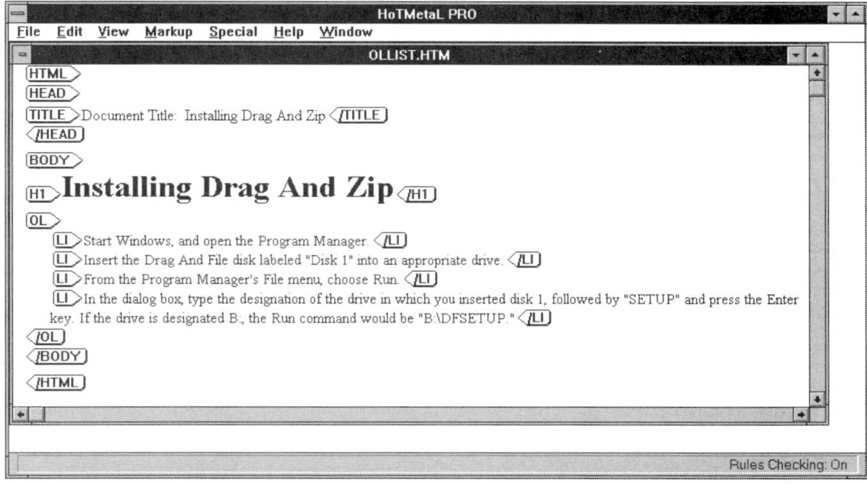

Figure 6-5: *An ordered (numbered) list in HoTMetaL PRO.*

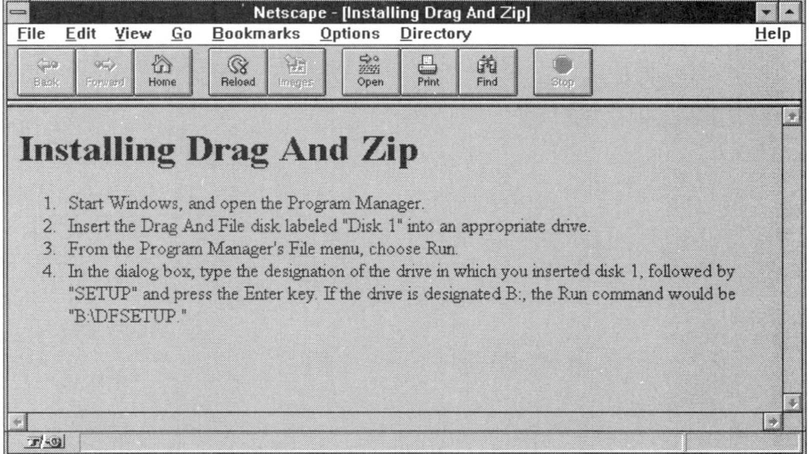

Figure 6-6: *An ordered (numbered) list in Netscape Navigator.*

Creating Directory Lists

A directory list is specified in the standard as a list of items that are less than 24 characters in length. Web browsers render this as a list of items with no bullets and no hanging indent, so while you can include items that are longer than 24 characters, if the line wraps around, there is no indication that it is part of a single list item.

Creating Discursive Lists

Discursive lists, also known as *definition lists* and *glossary lists*, are used to create lists in which each item also has a descriptive paragraph. Typical uses for discursive lists are for glossaries, and lists of definitions and their meanings. A discursive list is started with the DL tag. Each entry in the list is created with a single line *term* indicated by a DT tag, and a *definition* indicated by a DD tag. The definition may consist of more than one line. Figure 6-7 shows the HTML example of a directory and a discursive list in HoTMetaL PRO. Figure 6-8 shows how the directory and discursive lists appear in Netscape Navigator.

There is a "COMPACT" option for discursive lists that is specified in the standard, but at the time this was written, none of the Windows-based Web browsers tested did anything about it.

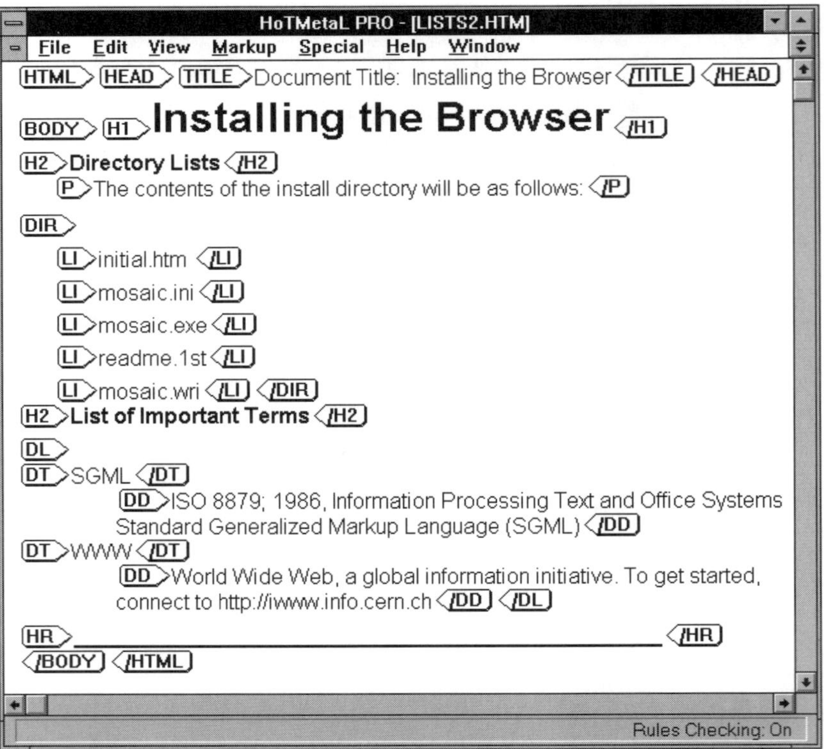

Figure 6-7: *HoTMetaL Window for directory and discursive lists.*

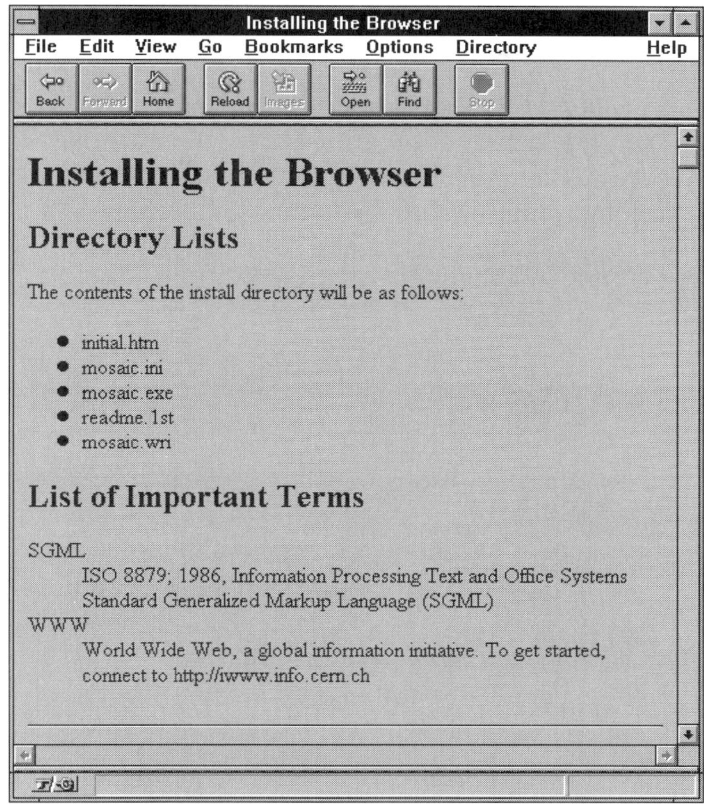

Figure 6-8: *Directory and discursive lists in Netscape Navigator.*

Creating Nested Lists

You can insert, or nest, a list within a list by inserting a list element, such as UL or OL, inside a list item (LI). We recommend that you don't nest lists deeper than three levels. Be aware that different browsers handle nested lists differently—just because the nested list appears with a round bullet in Netscape doesn't mean all browsers will use the same style bullet.

Adding an Address

The ADDRESS tag, as the name implies, is used to identify a block of text that contains an address. As with most HTML tags the address is rendered in a distinctive fashion by Web browsers. Although different browsers choose different styles, typically the address will appear in italics. As mentioned in Chapter 4, the ADDRESS tag is frequently used with the BR tag to separate each line of the address.

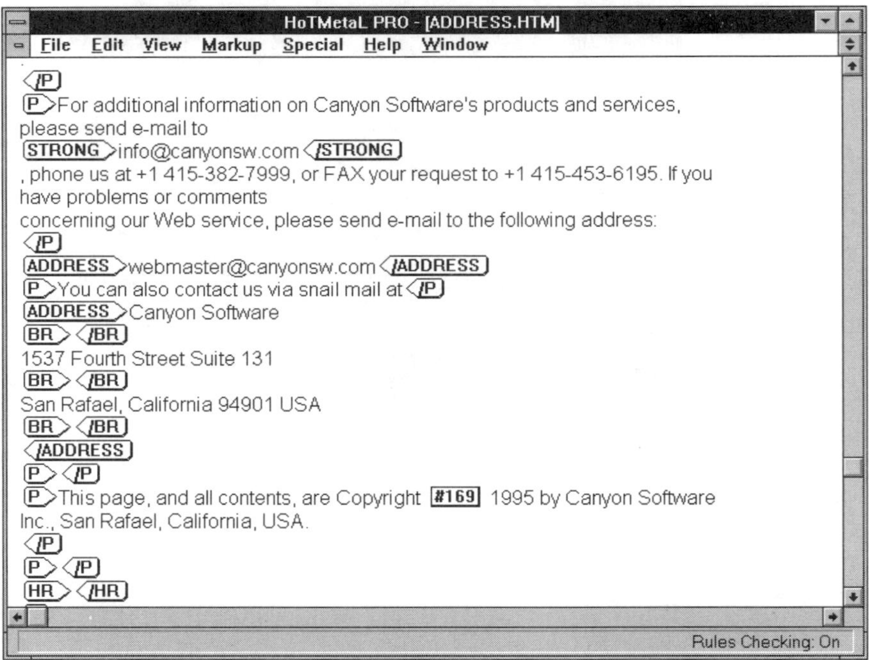

Figure 6-9: *An address style in HoTMetaL PRO.*

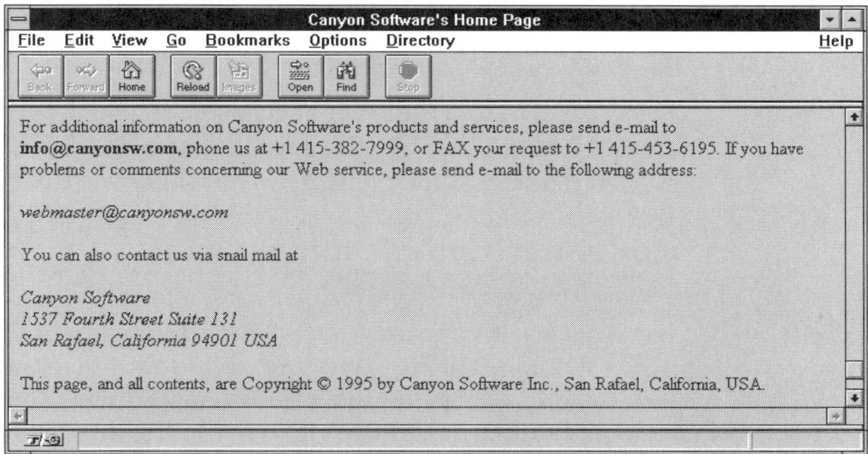

Figure 6-10: *An address style rendered by Netscape Navigator.*

Using Logical Styles to Format Characters

Logical styles tell the browser the kind of text to be presented and leave the rendering decisions to the browser. In general, you should use a logical representation instead of the physical representation whenever possible. Logical style tags are preferred over physical tags, because logical styles allow for more intelligent handling of text. Logical styles also give users more flexibility, allowing anyone to set up their browser however they see fit. The biggest limitation to logical styles is that you often find instances that have no corresponding logical style. For example, if you have text that is the "legalese" in a document, you may want it rendered in as small a font size as possible. This calls for a style to define small text, but such a style is not defined in HTML. This is handled in the electronic, multiplatform publishing world by using SGML with author-definable logical tags, but at the expense of great complexity, which has so far been spared in HTML. Suffice it to say that the use of logical styles versus physical styles is a subject of great contention within the Web community.

Emphasizing Text

There are two forms of emphasis used on an HTML page, EM for emphasis and STRONG for strong emphasis. Typically, EM is rendered as *italic*, and STRONG is rendered as **bold**.

Computer Code & Examples

For sections of your text that are computer code (or similar), use the CODE tag. This is usually rendered by a browser in Courier fixed-pitch font, and in most browsers, the size of the font is controlled separately from the size of other logical styles. If you have an entire paragraph of text that needs to be rendered in this fashion, use the PRE tag, which is a paragraph style. Do not use CODE—it is a character style, not a paragraph style, and, therefore, will not generate a line break.

Other logical styles include SAMP, which is defined in the standard as a sequence of literal characters; KBD, which would be text that a user would type on a keyboard; and VAR, which is used for variable names. It seems clear that the original designers of the HTML styles were computer users and programmers. The final logical style currently in the standard is the CITE style, which should be used when text on your page is a citation for a title or a reference. The citation text is typically displayed in italics.

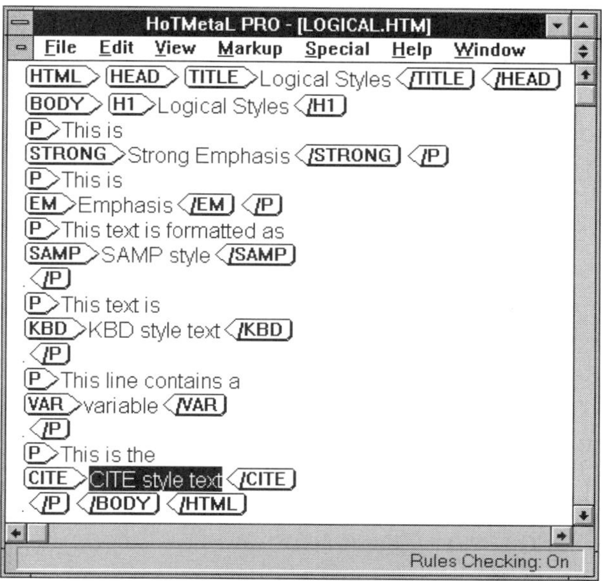

Figure 6-11: *Logical character styles in HoTMetaL PRO.*

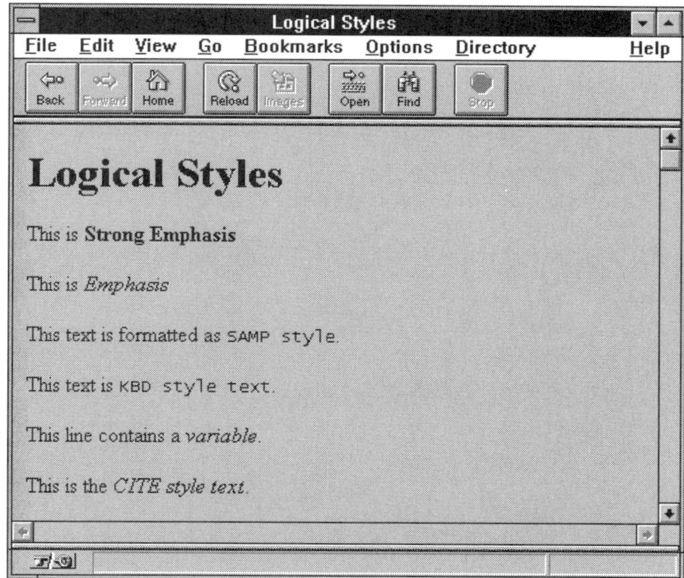

Figure 6-12: *Logical character styles rendered by Netscape.*

Using Physical Styles to Format Characters

The second category of styles for formatting characters is *physical styles*. Physical styles give an explicit direction to a Web browser about how to render a character. There are several physical styles, including bold, italic, underline, blink and fixed-width font. Examples of these styles (except the underline font) are shown in Figure 6-13 as HTML code and in Figure 6-14 rendered with Netscape Navigator.

Unlike the paragraph formatting tags, the character formatting tags do *not* cause a line break, and you can use multiple styles in the same sentence. Character formatting tags always *surround* the text that is to appear formatted; for example, emphasis text would start with EM and end with /EM.

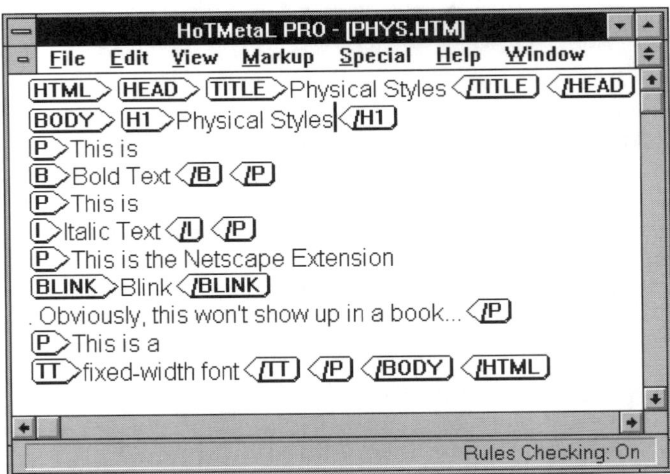

Figure 6-13: *Physical character styles in HoTMetaL PRO.*

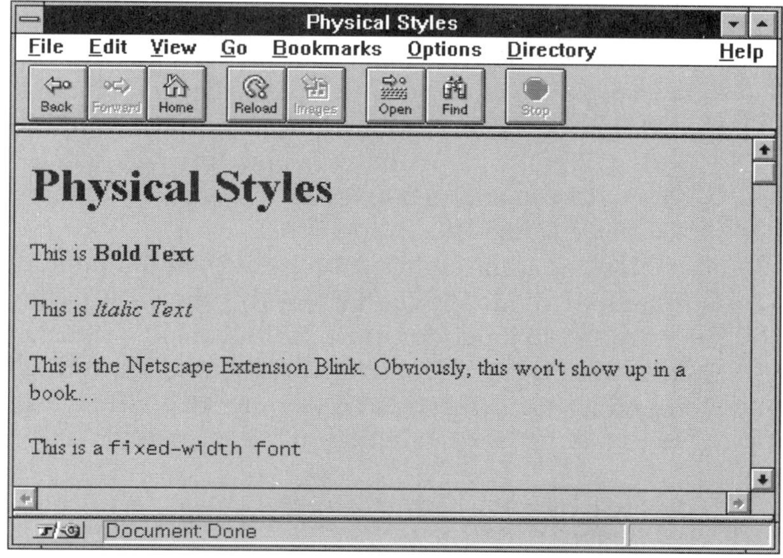

Figure 6-14: *Physical character styles rendered by Netscape Navigator.*

Adding Bold & Italics

Bold (B) and Italic (I) styles are the same as you would expect: bold text and italic text. As always, place the text you want treated with these styles between the opening and closing tags. With HoTMetaL PRO, you have the option to type away at your page, then go back later to add character formatting with the Markup>>Surround menu option. A particular advantage to formatting text after it's typed is that you avoid the overuse of formatting changes on a single page.

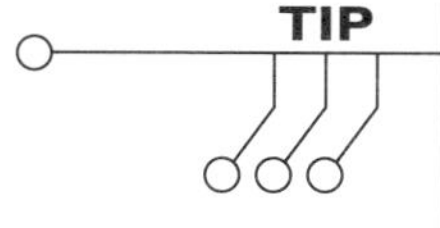

Use the STRONG tag instead of B wherever possible, unless you want to ensure that only a bold font is used. Use the EM emphasis tag instead of I wherever possible, unless you want to ensure that only an italic font is used. These two suggestions will keep your document as portable as possible.

You would need to specify physical rendering if you need to refer to the formatting explicitly in the text, such as: "The **bold** text is from the original document, and the *italic* text is from the first revision." Of course, some browsers cannot render bold or italic text, so include alternate ways of identifying specific areas of text, or provide an alternate page for browsers that don't support character-formatting properties.

The Underline style is a proposed standard and cannot be entered with HoTMetaL PRO at this time. Underlines are typically converted to italics for most professionally published documents. Instead of using the underline use italics. Underline has no corresponding logical style, so if you must underline text, you need to manually use the beginning <U> and ending </U> tags.

Including Blinking Text

An extension added by Netscape is the BLINK tag. The Blink style causes text to blink on and off on the viewer's screen. At first this may look like a nifty feature, but like using multiple exclamation points, it calls undue attention to itself. Just because it's new doesn't mean you have to use it. Looking at blinking letters can easily become a distraction and detract from your overall message. Use this extension sparingly, if at all. Since it is an extension to the HTML specification added by Netscape, you should not expect this to work on all browsers, but in general if the browser can't display the blinking text, the browser will ignore the BLINK tag and display the text.

Changing Fonts & Font Sizes

The control of the font point sizes in HTML is left to the discretion of the Web browser. Netscape, however, has decided that some control over the *relative* size of a font in a document is needed. Netscape has defined two tags for controlling font sizes, BASEFONT and FONT. The BASEFONT tag defines the relative size of the standard font for a portion of your text. You can use any number from 1 to 7 with 3 as the "middle" size to define the size. Size 3 is also the default. Netscape also lets you use the plus (+) and minus sign (-) to specify the font size relative to the basefont size. Figure 6-15 shows an example of the font size tags as they appear in HoTMetaL PRO. Figure 6-16 shows the resulting page in Netscape Navigator.

For specifying parts of paragraphs that use a fixed-width font, such as typewriter text, use the TT tag. Typically, the Web browser will use a Courier font. If you have an entire paragraph to be rendered in a fixed-width font, use the PRE paragraph style.

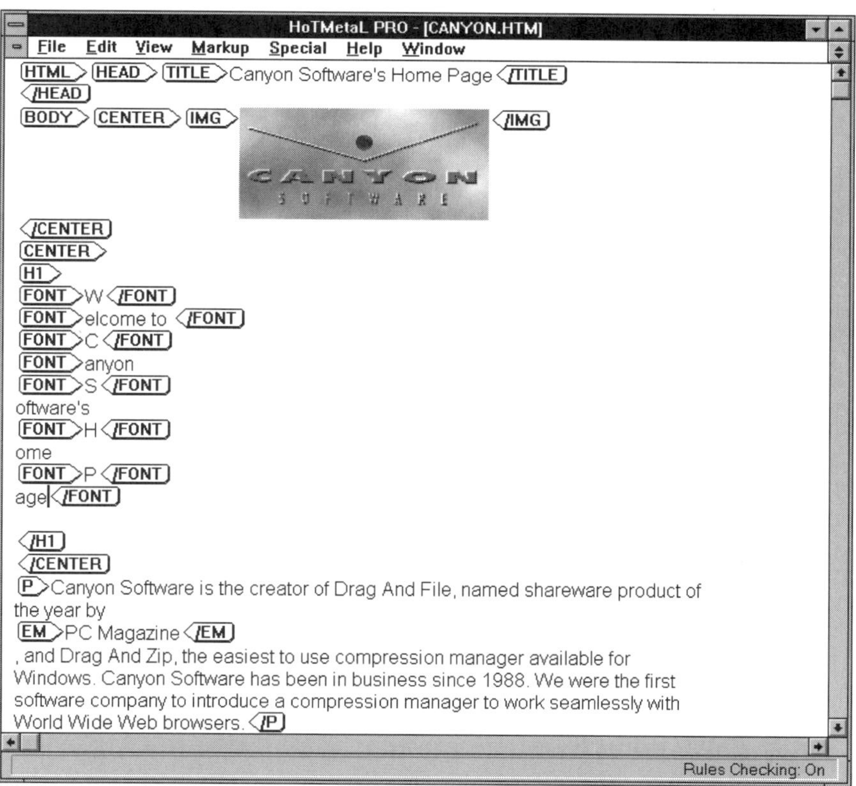

Figure 6-15: *An example of different font sizes in HoTMetaL PRO.*

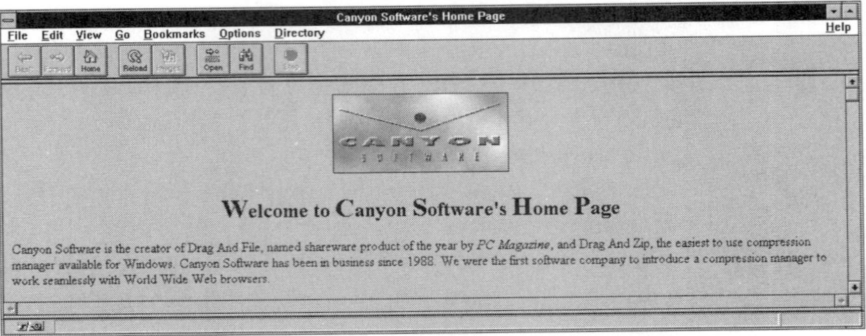

Figure 6-16: *An example of different font sizes in Netscape Navigator.*

Controlling Line Breaks

When the page you create is rendered on a computer screen with a Web browser, the size of the screen is entirely beyond your control. The browser itself flows your paragraphs to fit the width of the view screen (except for preformatted text, of course), so you can never tell where a line break is going to occur. There are instances, however, where you'll want to force a line break, or ensure that no line break occurs. To do this, use the break (BR) tag and the nobreak (NOBR) tag.

The BR tag inserts a line break at the point in the text that it occurs. The NOBR tag is used to surround text you don't want broken. This tag is a Netscape extension, so it may not work with all browsers. All text that appears between the starting and ending NOBR tag will not be broken on the screen. This is useful for long text strings with spaces that should not be broken across a line, such as a code example, or a line a user should enter in a computer program. Another place the NOBR tag is useful is in phone numbers, or the multiword links such as "Virtual Tourist" and "Red Hot Links" found on the Canyon Software home page. In addition to the NOBR tag, Netscape has added another tag called WBR, which stands for Word BReak. The WBR tag is inserted in strings of text where the text *could* be broken, if needed, for formatting.

Using Special Characters

HTML lets you include a large number of "special" characters that can be entered but are not normally found on a U.S. keyboard. The word "special" is in quotes, because for many writers of HTML pages these characters are simply part of the alphabet, but because of the limitations of the original definition of the 7-bit character set, we are now forced to take special measures to create these characters. In HTML parlance, these special characters are called *character entities*. Most of these characters are accented characters, currency marks and characters that have special meaning to the HTML language: such as the double quotation mark (") the greater than (>) and less than sign (<) and the ampersand (&).

What's Special & What's Not

Most characters that appear on a U.S.-style keyboard are regular characters that can be typed directly in an HTML document. This includes all alphabetic and numeric characters, and most commonly used punctuation. With HoTMetaL PRO, all you need to do is type these characters, and the corresponding HTML code will be inserted. If you're entering raw text, you need to identify that you're referring to a special character. HTML uses a special escape code to identify characters that have special meaning to HTML. The escape code begins with an ampersand (&) and ends with a semicolon, as shown in the following list of characters.

Character	Code
>	>
<	<
&	&
"	"

Users of Microsoft Word for Windows beware! If you plan on saving your work as RTF then converting to HTML, be sure to turn off the "Change Straight Quotes to Smart Quotes" option in the Auto-Correct menu. Smart Quotes are not properly converted by the RTF to HTML converter.

The special characters of HTML include all accented characters, plus special punctuation and currency marks. A complete list of these characters can be found in the "Illustrated HTML Reference" section at the end of this book. With HoTMetaL PRO, you can enter special characters by entering the keyboard sequence Alt-0*nnn* where *nnn* is replaced by a three-digit code for the character. If the character you've entered has a special representation in HTML, HoTMetaL PRO will enter that code. If there is no dedicated code, HoTMetaL PRO creates a general *entity tag* that inserts the character number you entered. The other way to enter special characters with HoTMetaL PRO is to use the Markup>>Insert Character Entity command. This brings up the Insert Entity dialog box, shown in Figure 6-17, from which you can choose the special character you want to insert.

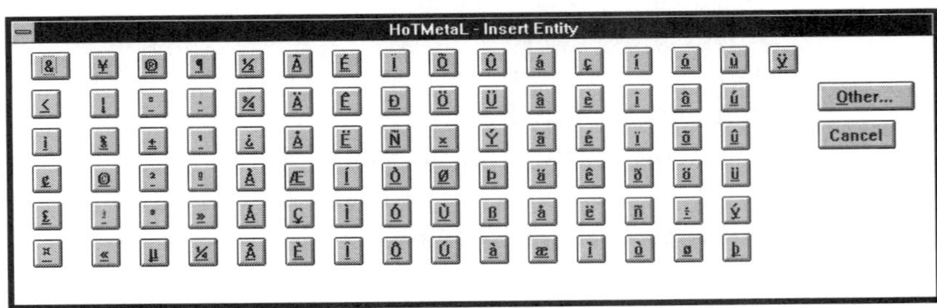

Figure 6-17: *The Insert Entity dialog box lets you insert special characters.*

Netscape includes two new entities: the registered trademark symbol (®) and the copyright symbol (©). The escape code for the registered trademark is ®. The code for the copyright symbol is ©.

As you create your Web document, keep in mind that the World Wide Web is a global network and for many of the people who can access your pages English is a second language. If you have the ability to author pages in more than one language, by all means do so. You'll help foster the globalization of the Web and attract an audience that might otherwise not have access to your site. Figure 6-18 helps show how special characters are used in an HTML

document. Figure 6-19 shows a portion of a page that includes special characters. For the complete page, take a look at http://www.sal.ists.ca/services/w3_can/qc.html.

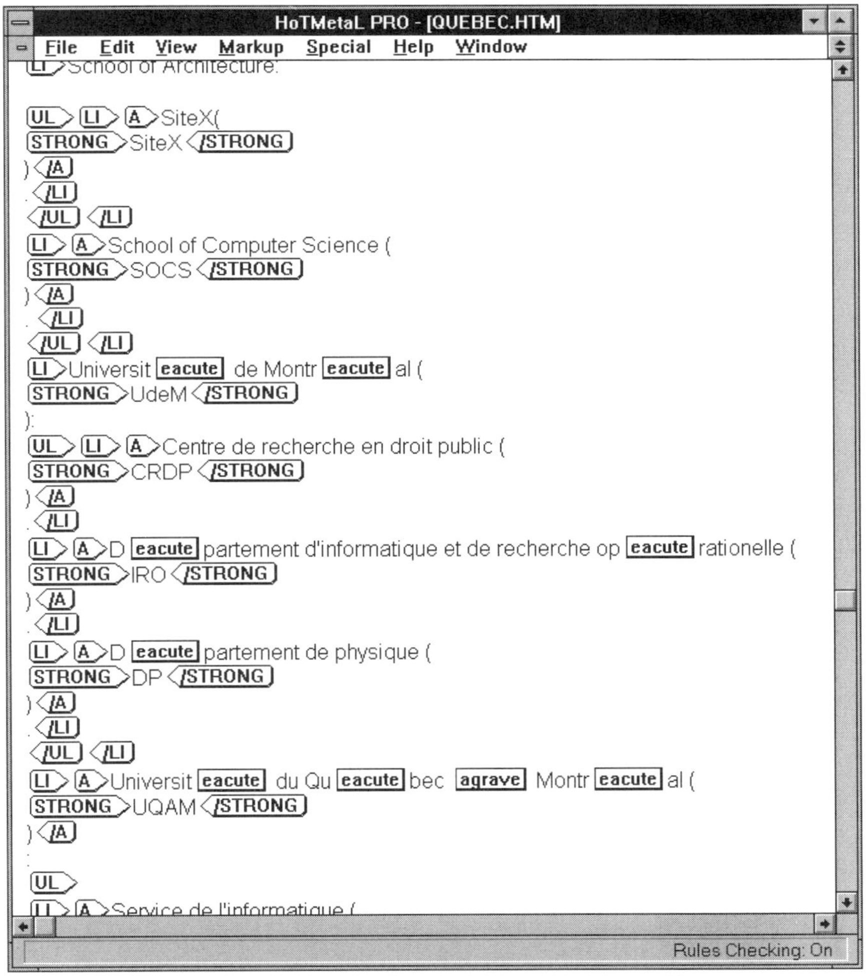

```
HoTMetaL PRO - [QUEBEC.HTM]
File  Edit  View  Markup  Special  Help  Window
LI>School of Architecture:

UL> LI> A>SiteX(
STRONG>SiteX</STRONG
)</A
.</LI
</UL </LI
LI> A>School of Computer Science (
STRONG>SOCS</STRONG
)</A
.</LI
</UL </LI
LI>Universit eacute de Montr eacute al (
STRONG>UdeM</STRONG
):
UL> LI> A>Centre de recherche en droit public (
STRONG>CRDP</STRONG
)</A
.</LI
LI> A>D eacute partement d'informatique et de recherche op eacute rationelle (
STRONG>IRO</STRONG
)</A
.</LI
LI> A>D eacute partement de physique (
STRONG>DP</STRONG
)</A
.</LI
</UL </LI
LI> A>Universit eacute du Qu eacute bec agrave Montr eacute al (
STRONG>UQAM</STRONG
)</A
:
UL>
LI> A>Service de l'informatique (
Rules Checking: On
```

Figure 6-18: *Fragment of a multilingual Web page in HoTMetaL PRO.*

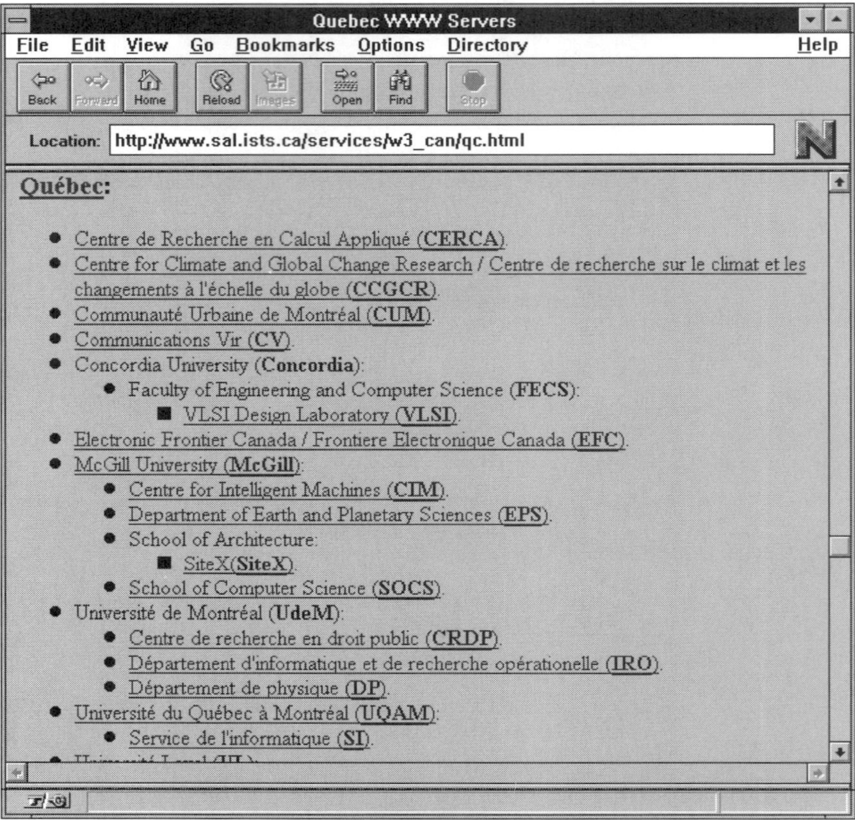

Figure 6-19: *Portion of a multilingual Web page.*

Using Horizontal Rules

The use of special elements, such as horizontal rules and repeating graphics, can add a special look to your pages, as well as provide the reader with visual cues as to the location of information on the page.

The horizontal rule, specified in HTML by HR, is used frequently to break up the page and separate elements on a page. This can be very useful to keep topics marked clearly, since you have very little other control over the formatting of a page. When converted to raw HTML, the horizontal rule is specified with the HR tag and *no* closing tag. (Note: HoTMetal PRO displays start and end tag icons for the HR tag, although only the start tag is saved as text.) In addition to the standard use of the horizontal rule, Netscape has defined the ability to specify the width of a rule as a percentage of the displayed page width. This can produce some very striking effects when using the Netscape browser, and some really ugly effects when viewed with any other viewer. Use the extensions carefully!

Although graphics are not specifically part of a chapter on text, it's worth noting here that some graphics can be used to provide a stronger presence to your pages. For example, the common horizontal rule could be replaced with a graphic element. This also gives the person reading your pages a hint as to how wide you really wanted the page to be. Use of common graphics is handy when you want to create a navigation bar at the top and/or the bottom of your pages. Check out Chapter 7 to find out about using graphics on your pages.

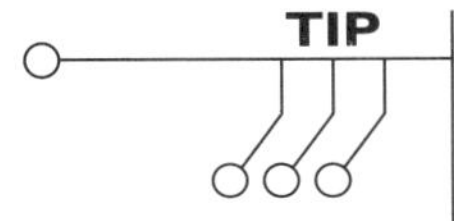

When a graphic is used as a control bar, you also need to tie your page in to the Common Gateway Interface (CGI), discussed in Chapters 7 and 9.

Netscape adds four Netscape HTML extensions to the horizontal rule to let you specify the size, width, alignment and shading of horizontal rules. For example a 1/4" rule that takes up 50 percent of the width of the document can appear centered. Just because something looks great in your browser doesn't mean it will appear the same in other browsers. Figure 6-20 shows the Edit Attributes dialog box for horizontal rules. Figure 6-21 shows an example of horizontal rules using Netscape extensions. Table 6-2 describes Netscape tag extensions that allow the document's author to describe how the horizontal rule should look. Although Netscape lets you use percentages to define the width, HoTMetaL PRO doesn't. Instead you must enter the number of pixels.

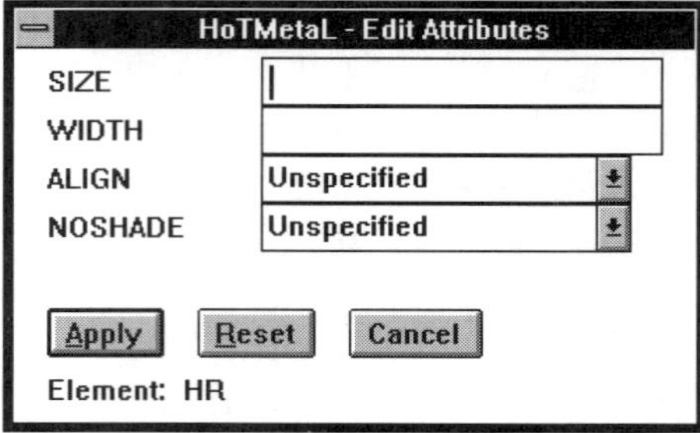

Figure 6-20: *The Edit Attributes dialog box for horizontal rules.*

Attribute	Description
<HR SIZE=*n*>	Specifies the thickness of the horizontal rule in pixels. The *n* stands for the number of pixels.
<HR WIDTH=*n*>	Specifies an exact width in pixels, or a relative width measured in percent of document width. The *n* stands for a number of pixels.
<HR ALIGN=*alignment*>	Specifies the alignment of the rule. The three choices for *alignment* are LEFT (left-aligned), RIGHT (right-aligned) or CENTER (centered).
<HR NOSHADE>	Specifies that you do not want any shading of your horizontal rule.

Table 6-2: *Attributes for horizontal rules.*

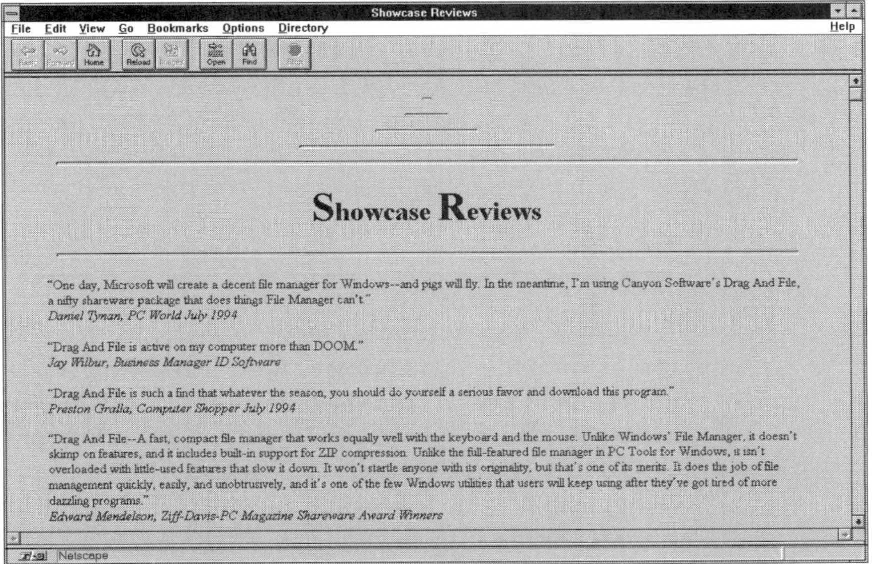

Figure 6-21: *Horizontal rules using Netscape extensions.*

Using Tables

Tables are a new addition to the HTML language and are not officially supported in the current version (HTML 2). They are in such demand, however, that you can already edit tables with HoTMetaL PRO and view them with Netscape Navigator and the NCSA Mosaic browser. Keep in mind that the table features are still experimental, and the table tag markups are still subject to modification. Naturally, the implementation of the tables can vary widely, so what you write in HoTMetaL PRO is not exactly what appears in a browser. This is not a flaw in HoTMetaL PRO or the browser—merely an illustration of the problems you'll face when working with not-quite-yet-standard features.

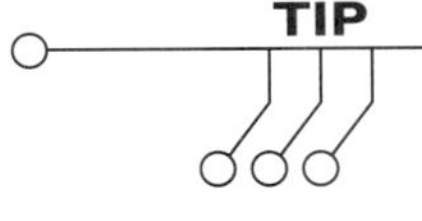

Netscape has added a few attributes for working with tables. In order to use Netscape extensions, you have to specify a special rules file in HoTMetaL PRO's initialization file (sqhmpro.ini). See Chapter 2 for information on how to specify Netscape rules in the sqhmpro.ini file.

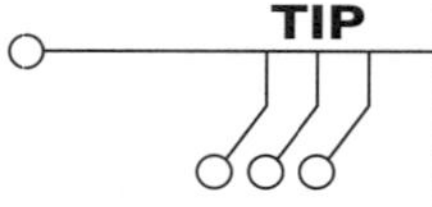

If you find you want to edit the initialization file frequently to switch between the standard HTML rules and Netscape rules, open the File Manager and drag the sqhtmlpro.ini file into a Program Manager group. You can then edit the file by double-clicking on the sqhmpro icon.

Adding a Table

Tables are an important element in many technical documents, and as such the availability of tables in HTML is a boon to those people trying to create HTML versions of existing technical documents. For the purposes of illustration, this chapter explains how to add table elements using HoTMetaL PRO and presents three sample tables. The following steps explain how to add a table with a border and a caption using HoTMetaL PRO.

1. In the body of your Web page, choose Markup>>Insert Element or press Ctrl-I. The Insert Element dialog box appears.
2. Highlight the Table element and choose the Insert Element button. The Insert Table dialog box is displayed, as shown in Figure 6-22.

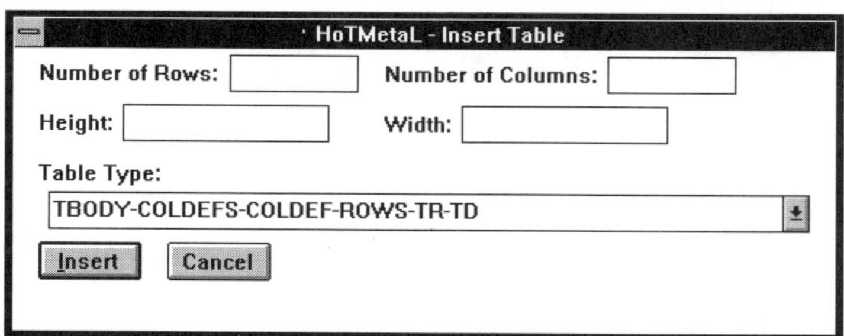

Figure 6-22: *The Insert Table dialog box.*

3. Specify the number of columns in the Number of Columns field and the number of rows in the Number of Rows field. Choose the Insert button. A grid appears, as shown in Figure 6-23.

4. Click to the right of the starting Table tag and choose the Markup>>Edit SGML Attributes or press F6. The Edit Attributes dialog box appears.
5. Enter a number in the Border field to specify the border size (number of pixels) you want for your table and choose the Apply button.
6. Choose Markup>>Insert Element or press Ctrl-I. The Insert Element dialog box appears.
7. Select the Caption element from the Insert Element dialog box and choose the Insert Element button. The insertion point appears between the starting and ending caption tags.
8. Enter the caption you want to appear above your table.

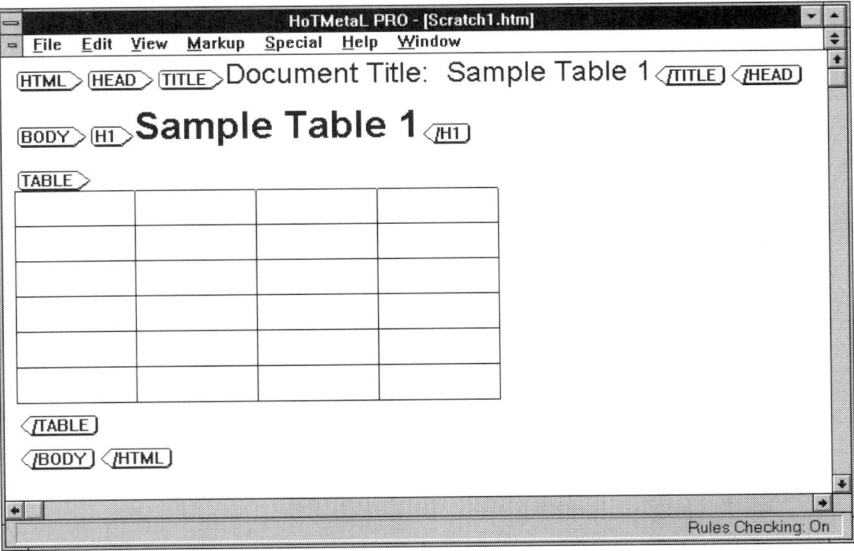

Figure 6-23: *When you insert a table a grid appears.*

Editing a Table

Once you've added a table and moved the insertion point in the table, the four table commands become active in the Markup menu, provided the insertion point is inside a table. Table 6-3 lists and describes the Markup menu options you can use to edit a table.

Option	Description
Table Properties	Displays the Table Properties dialog box, as shown in Figure 6-24. Any properties can be overridden by changes you make to individual rows, columns or cells using the Row-Column Properties menu. This dialog box is broken into three groups: Table Properties, Default Row Properties and Default Column Properties. Row and column separators include one line, two lines, three lines, a dashed line, a dotted line, a bold line, a blank or none. You can also choose one of four types of justification for the text in a column: flush left, both (left and right justified), centered and flush right.
Cell-Row-Column Properties	Displays the Edit Row/Column/Cell Properties dialog box, shown in Figure 6-25. The AC that appears as the default in many of the settings stands for *adopt current*. This means that the cell adopts the current style for the surrounding row or column element type.
Edit Table	Displays the Edit Table dialog box, as shown in Figure 6-26. This dialog box lets you choose buttons that let you insert rows above or below the current row or insert columns to the left or right of the current column. You can also choose to delete a row or column.
Cell Spans	Displays the Cell Span dialog box, as shown in Figure 6-27. Extends or contracts the boundary of the current cell by one grid cell in the direction of the arrow on the button in the dialog box.

Table 6-3: *Table editing options.*

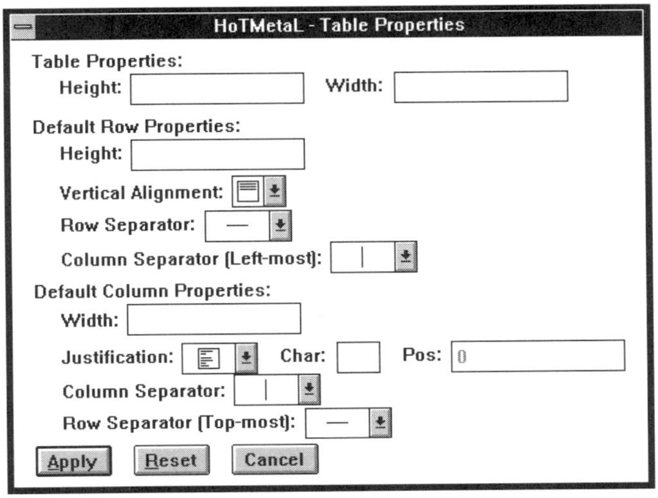

Figure 6-24: *The Table Properties dialog box.*

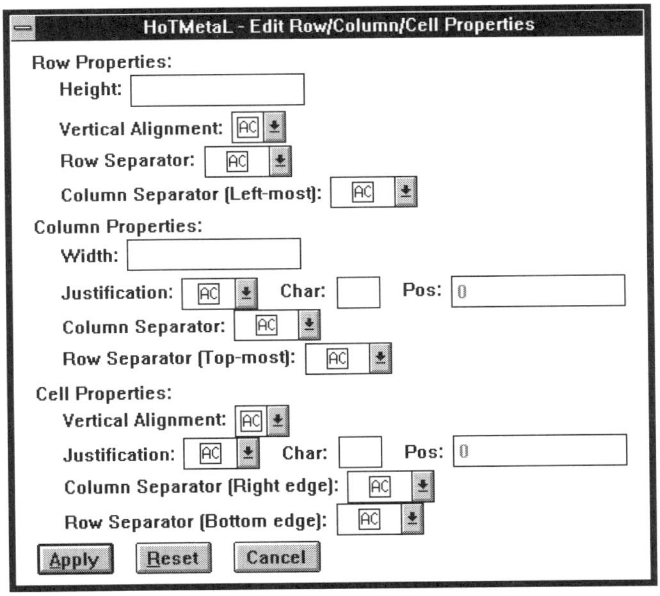

Figure 6-25: *The Edit Row/Column/Cell Properties dialog box.*

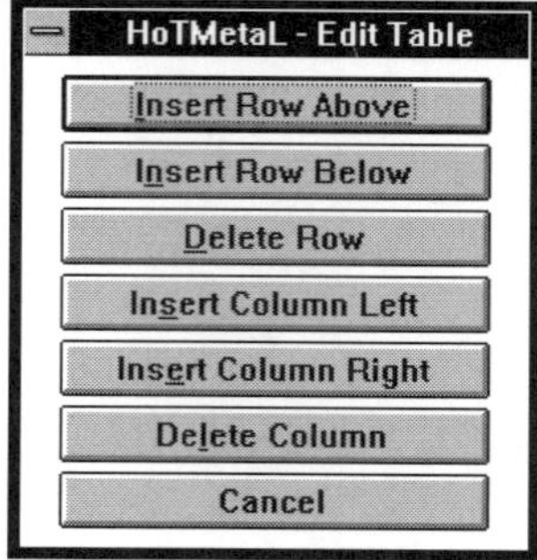

Figure 6-26: *The Edit Table dialog box.*

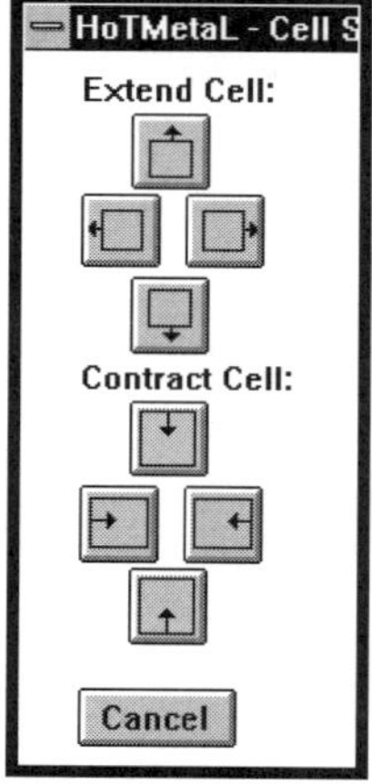

Figure 6-27: *The Cell Span dialog box.*

Sample Tables

Netscape and Mosaic browsers both support tables and can render tables with 3D borders. The following table takes advantage of HoTMetaL PRO's table tags. This code matches the results displayed in Figure 6-28. Table 6-4 on pages 155–157 lists and describes the tags used to create tables. Remember you can find the code for the tables presented in this chapter on the Companion CD-ROM.

In order for HoTMetaL PRO to display a visual grid for a table, it includes tags that specify column information and character positions (COLDEF, COLSTART and CHARPOS). These are not essential tags, but without them HoTMetaL PRO is unable to display a grid for a table. Because working with a visual table in HoTMetaL PRO is so much easier than working with straight HTML, we have included these tags in these examples. If you are not using HoTMetaL PRO, you can eliminate these tags from your HTML code.

```
<HTML><HEAD><TITLE>Table</TITLE></HEAD>
<BODY><H1>Sample Table 1</H1><TABLE BORDER="2">
<CAPTION>Sales Figures for 1995</CAPTION>
<TBODY><COLDEFS><COLDEF><COLDEF HALIGN="Right"
CHARPOS="0">
<COLDEF HALIGN="Right" CHARPOS="0"><COLDEF
HALIGN="Right" CHARPOS="0"></COLDEFS><ROWS>
<TR><TD COLSTART="1"></TD><TD
COLSTART="2">Eastern Region</TD><TD
COLSTART="3">Central Region</TD><TD
COLSTART="4">Western Region</TD></TR>
<TR><TD COLSTART="1" >January</TD><TD
COLSTART="2">2345.44</TD><TD COLSTART="3">
1120.33</TD><TD COLSTART="4"> 1436.33</TD></TR>
<TR><TD COLSTART="1">February</TD><TD
COLSTART="2">5300.00</TD><TD COLSTART="3">
1923.33</TD><TD COLSTART="4">1212.33</TD></TR>
<TR><TD COLSTART="1">March</TD><TD
COLSTART="2">2343.22</TD><TD
COLSTART="3">1232.10</TD><TD COLSTART="4">
1123.53</TD></TR>
<TR><TD COLSTART="1">April</TD><TD
COLSTART="2">2345.10</TD>
<TD COLSTART="3">1750.50</TD><TD COLSTART="4">
1565.35</TD></TR>
<TR><TD COLSTART="1">May</TD><TD
COLSTART="2">5434.22</TD><TD
COLSTART="3">1654.30</TD><TD COLSTART="4">
1110.40</TD></TR>
</ROWS></TBODY></TABLE></BODY></HTML>
```

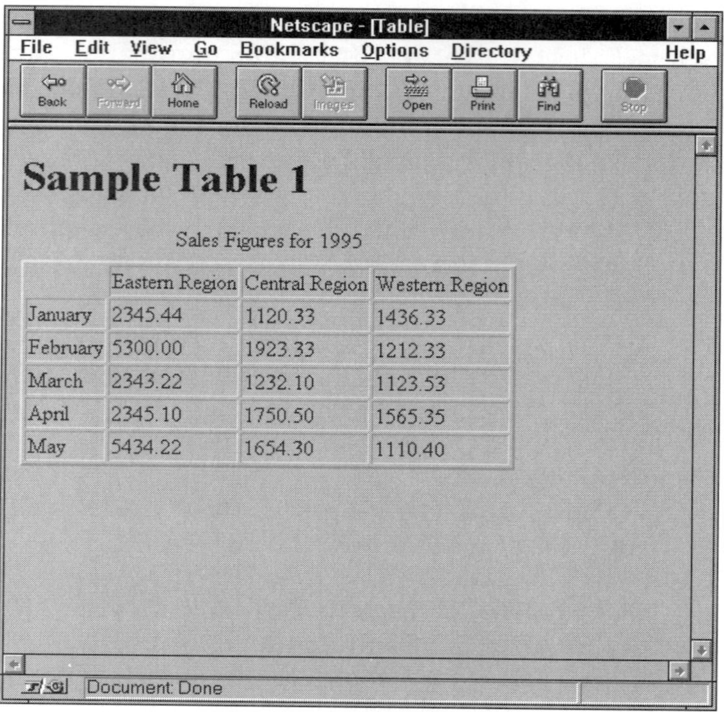

	Eastern Region	Central Region	Western Region
January	2345.44	1120.33	1436.33
February	5300.00	1923.33	1212.33
March	2343.22	1232.10	1123.53
April	2345.10	1750.50	1565.35
May	5434.22	1654.30	1110.40

Figure 6-28: *A simple table created using Netscape.*

The following is another example that is more complex. This table builds on the previous example by including row and column spanning. Figure 6-29 shows the results of the following HTML code.

```
<HTML><HEAD><TITLE>Table 2</TITLE></HEAD>
<BODY><H1>Sample Table 2</H1>
<TABLE BORDER="2">
<CAPTION>Sales Figures for 1995</CAPTION>
<TBODY>
<COLDEFS><COLDEF><COLDEF HALIGN="Right"
CHARPOS="0"><COLDEF HALIGN="Right"
CHARPOS="0"><COLDEF HALIGN="Right"
CHARPOS="0"><COLDEF HALIGN="Right"
CHARPOS="0"><COLDEF HALIGN="Right"
CHARPOS="0"><COLDEF HALIGN="Right" CHARPOS="0">
</COLDEFS>
```

```
<ROWS>
<TR><TD COLSTART="1" ROWSPAN="2"></TD><TD
COLSTART="2" COLSPAN="2">
Eastern Region</TD><TD COLSTART="4"
COLSPAN="2">Central Region</TD><TD COLSTART="6"
COLSPAN="2">Western Region</TD></TR>
<TR><TD COLSTART="2">Sales</TD><TD
COLSTART="3">Verified</TD><TD COLSTART="4">Sales
</TD><TD COLSTART="5">Verified</TD><TD COLSTART="6"
>Sales</TD><TD COLSTART="7">Verified</TD></TR>
<TR><TD COLSTART="1">January</TD><TD
COLSTART="2">2345.44</TD><TD COLSTART="3">No
</TD><TD COLSTART="4">1120.33</TD><TD
COLSTART="5">No</TD><TD COLSTART="6"> 1436.33
</TD><TD COLSTART="7">
No</TD></TR>
<TR><TD COLSTART="1">February</TD><TD
COLSTART="2">5300.00</TD><TD COLSTART="3">No
</TD><TD COLSTART="4"> 1923.33</TD><TD
COLSTART="5">No</TD><TD COLSTART="6">1212.33
</TD><TD COLSTART="7">No</TD></TR>
<TR><TD COLSTART="1">March</TD><TD
COLSTART="2">2343.22</TD><TD COLSTART="3">Yes
</TD><TD COLSTART="4">1232.10</TD><TD
COLSTART="5">Yes</TD><TD COLSTART="6"> 1123.53
</TD><TD COLSTART="7">Yes</TD></TR>
<TR><TD COLSTART="1">April</TD><TD
COLSTART="2">2345.10</TD><TD COLSTART="3">No
</TD><TD COLSTART="4"> 1750.50</TD><TD
COLSTART="5">Yes</TD><TD COLSTART="6"> 1565.35
</TD><TD COLSTART="7">Yes</TD></TR><TR><TD
COLSTART="1">May</TD><TD COLSTART="2">5434.22
</TD><TD COLSTART="3">Yes</TD><TD
COLSTART="4">1654.30</TD><TD COLSTART="5">Yes
</TD><TD COLSTART="6"> 1110.40</TD><TD
COLSTART="7">Yes</TD></TR>
</ROWS>
</TBODY>
</TABLE>
</BODY></HTML>
```

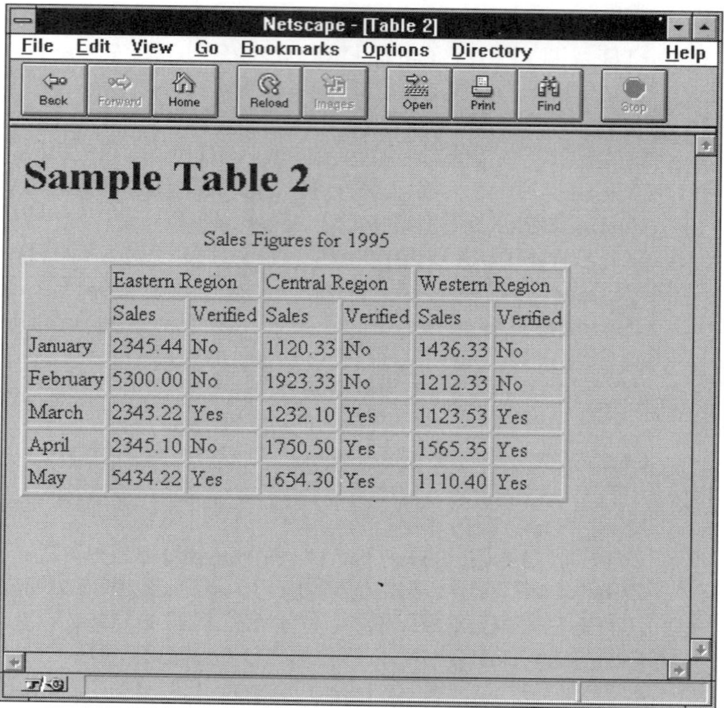

	Eastern Region		Central Region		Western Region	
	Sales	Verified	Sales	Verified	Sales	Verified
January	2345.44	No	1120.33	No	1436.33	No
February	5300.00	No	1923.33	No	1212.33	No
March	2343.22	Yes	1232.10	Yes	1123.53	Yes
April	2345.10	No	1750.50	Yes	1565.35	Yes
May	5434.22	Yes	1654.30	Yes	1110.40	Yes

Figure 6-29: *A sample table showing row and column spanning.*

The third and last example builds on the previous example, adding some finishing touches by centering the table, aligning the caption at the bottom of the table and including a larger border with cell padding and cell spacing. Figure 6-30 shows the results of the following HTML code.

```
<HTML><HEAD><TITLE>Table 3</TITLE></HEAD>
<BODY><H1>Sample Table 3</H1>
<CENTER>
<TABLE BORDER="8" CELLSPACING="4"
CELLPADDING="4">
<CAPTION ALIGN=BOTTOM>Sales Figures for 1995
</CAPTION>
<TBODY>
<COLDEFS COLSEP="VSingle" HALIGN="Center"
CHARPOS="0" TOPSEP="HSingle">
```

```
<COLDEF><COLDEF HALIGN="Right"
CHARPOS="0"><COLDEF HALIGN="Right"
CHARPOS="0"><COLDEF HALIGN="Right"
CHARPOS="0"><COLDEF HALIGN="Right"
CHARPOS="0"><COLDEF HALIGN="Right"
CHARPOS="0"><COLDEF HALIGN="Right" CHARPOS="0">
</COLDEFS><ROWS ROWSEP="HSingle" VALIGN="Top"
LEFTSEP="VSingle">
<TR><TD COLSTART="1" ROWSPAN="2"></TD><TD
HALIGN="Center" CHARPOS="0" COLSTART="2"
COLSPAN="2">Eastern Region</TD><TD HALIGN="Center"
CHARPOS="0" COLSTART="4" COLSPAN="2">Central Re-
gion</TD><TD HALIGN="Center" CHARPOS="0"
COLSTART="6" COLSPAN="2">Western Region</TD></TR>
<TR><TD HALIGN="Center" CHARPOS="0"
COLSTART="2">Sales</TD><TD HALIGN="Center"
CHARPOS="0" COLSTART="3">Verified</TD><TD
HALIGN="Center" CHARPOS="0" COLSTART="4">Sales
</TD><TD HALIGN="Center" CHARPOS="0"
COLSTART="5">Verified</TD><TD HALIGN="Center"
CHARPOS="0" COLSTART="6">Sales</TD><TD
HALIGN="Center" CHARPOS="0" COLSTART="7">Verified
</TD></TR>
<TR><TD COLSTART="1">January</TD><TD
COLSTART="2">2345.44</TD><TD HALIGN="Center"
CHARPOS="0" COLSTART="3">No</TD><TD
COLSTART="4"> 1120.33</TD><TD HALIGN="Center"
CHARPOS="0" COLSTART="5">No</TD><TD CHARPOS="0"
COLSTART="6">1436.33</TD><TD HALIGN="Center"
CHARPOS="0" COLSTART="7">No</TD></TR>
<TR><TD COLSTART="1">February</TD><TD
COLSTART="2">5300.00</TD><TD HALIGN="Center"
CHARPOS="0" COLSTART="3">No</TD><TD
COLSTART="4">1923.33</TD><TD HALIGN="Center"
CHARPOS="0" COLSTART="5"
>No</TD><TD COLSTART="6">1212.33</TD><TD
HALIGN="Center" CHARPOS="0" COLSTART="7">No
</TD></TR>
<TR><TD COLSTART="1">March</TD><TD
```

```
COLSTART="2">2343.22</TD><TD HALIGN="Center"
CHARPOS="0" COLSTART="3">Yes</TD><TD
COLSTART="4">1232.10</TD><TD HALIGN="Center"
CHARPOS="0" COLSTART="5"
>Yes</TD><TD COLSTART="6"> 1123.53</TD><TD
HALIGN="Center" CHARPOS="0" COLSTART="7">Yes
</TD></TR>
<TR><TD COLSTART="1">April</TD><TD
COLSTART="2">2345.10</TD><TD HALIGN="Center"
CHARPOS="0" COLSTART="3">No</TD><TD
COLSTART="4"> 1750.50</TD><TD HALIGN="Center"
CHARPOS="0" COLSTART="5">Yes</TD><TD
COLSTART="6">1565.35</TD><TD HALIGN="Center"
CHARPOS="0" COLSTART="7"
>Yes</TD></TR>
<TR><TD COLSTART="1">May</TD><TD
COLSTART="2">5434.22</TD><TD HALIGN="Center"
CHARPOS="0" COLSTART="3">Yes</TD><TD
COLSTART="4">1654.30</TD><TD HALIGN="Center"
CHARPOS="0" COLSTART="5">Yes</TD><TD
COLSTART="6">1110.40</TD><TD HALIGN="Center"
CHARPOS="0" COLSTART="7">Yes</TD></TR>
</ROWS>
</TBODY>
</TABLE>
</CENTER>
</BODY></HTML>
```

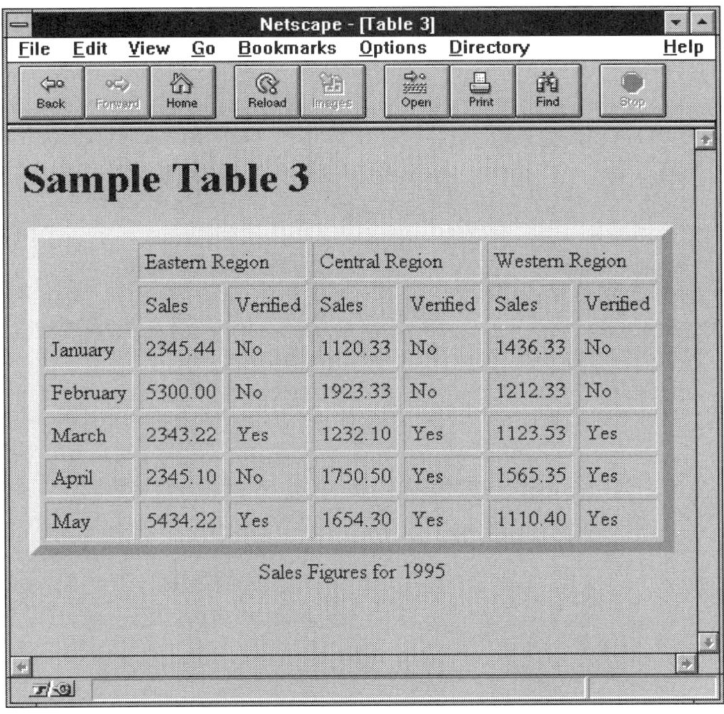

	Eastern Region		Central Region		Western Region	
	Sales	Verified	Sales	Verified	Sales	Verified
January	2345.44	No	1120.33	No	1436.33	No
February	5300.00	No	1923.33	No	1212.33	No
March	2343.22	Yes	1232.10	Yes	1123.53	Yes
April	2345.10	No	1750.50	Yes	1565.35	Yes
May	5434.22	Yes	1654.30	Yes	1110.40	Yes

Figure 6-30: *A table centered with a large border and cell spacing and cell padding.*

Tag	Description
<TABLE></TABLE>	Specifies the beginning (<TABLE>) and ending (</TABLE>) of the table. If the BORDER attribute is added, as it is in the previous examples, then Mosaic displays the table with a border. Netscape adds three attributes to the Table tag: CELLSPACING, CELLPADDING and WIDTH. The CELLSPACING attribute lets you specify the amount of space inserted between the cells in a table. The CELLPADDING attribute lets you specify the amount of space between the border of a cell and the contents of

	the cell. The WIDTH attribute lets you specify the width of the table in pixels. The WIDTH attribute can also be used with the TH and TD tags to specify the width of a cell.
<CAPTION></CAPTION>	Adds a caption or heading for the table. The caption for the sample Table 1 is "Sales Figures for 1995." The ALIGN=BOTTOM attribute lets you position the caption directly underneath the table.
<TR></TR>	Begins and ends a Table Row. Two attributes let you position the row. HALIGN determines the horizontal alignment and VALIGN determines the vertical alignment. The rows in the sample table are all set to HALIGN=RIGHT. The other HALIGN options are LEFT and CENTER. The VALIGN options are TOP, MIDDLE and BOTTOM.
<TH></TH>	Specifies the Table Header cell. You can specify the horizontal alignment (HALIGN) and the vertical alignment (VALIGN). The available alignment attribute settings are the same as the TR tag. In addition to the alignment attributes you can also specify the number of columns (COLSPAN=*n*) or rows (ROWSPAN=*n*) a cell spans. In order to specify the number of columns or rows to span, you need to use the Markup>>Cell Spans menu item. You can view the COLSPAN or ROWSPAN setting by choosing the View>>Show Link and Context View. You can manually edit the COLSPAN or ROWSPAN attribute settings by using the Markup>>Edit SGML Attributes. Another option that is not yet available from

	HoTMetaL PRO menus is to turn off word wrapping in a cell using the NOWRAP attribute. By default the table header cell's text is bold and centered. Attributes specified by the TH tag take precedence over the default alignment set in the TR (Table Row) tag. (Note: Be careful when editing tables. Changing COLSPAN or ROWSPAN could cause HoTMetal PRO to be unable to display the table in graphical form.
<TD> </TD>	Begins and ends each cell's table data. Table data can use all the alignment attributes available to the TH tag. By default text is left aligned and vertically centered. Attributes specified by the TD tag take precedence over the default alignment set in the TR (Table Row) tag.

Table 6-4: *Table tags.*

Entering Equations

Equations are not yet directly supported by the current version of HTML or by other widely used browsers. To put an equation in your text, you need to convert the equation to a bitmap and include it with your text as an inline image.

Entering equations is simplified when you use Word for Windows as your authoring tool. Whenever you want to use an equation, enter it with the Microsoft Equation Editor. Save the file as an RTF file, then use the RTF to HTML converter. The converter saves all the equations (as well as other images) as Windows Metafiles (.WMF) and inserts references to .GIF files in the text. Use a graphics program, such as Paint Shop Pro, to convert the .WMF graphics files into .GIF files. (Paint Shop Pro is a shareware package on the Companion CD.) The Web browser will pick up the GIF graphics files for all the equations. Check out Chapter 7 for more information about graphic programs files and conversions.

Moving On

You can create professional looking pages with the text elements you've learned about in this chapter. And with HoTMetaL PRO you have a jump start on getting the work done quickly. But to really capture your audience you'll want to mix text with images. The next chapter reveals how to effectively add images to the text components to create even more effective and more powerful Web pages.

7 Getting Graphic With Images

No matter how impressive your message, people respond to images. The reader's eye is naturally drawn to a picture before text and the choice and quality of the images you use will largely determine whether someone will take the time to read your Web page or pass it by. Much of the Web's success is due, in part, to its ability to include graphic images. Cliché as it may be, a picture *is* worth a thousand words. Because of the importance of images in publishing on the Internet, it's important to take the time to master the tags and graphic editing options necessary to include graphics.

Graphics is one of the richest fields of computing. Tools abound to help you create and present eye-catching images. This chapter covers creating and working with images in the GIF and JPEG graphic formats and points out the benefits and problems that these file formats present to a Web publisher. This chapter also covers one of the most important aspects of graphics on the Web: the ability to create interactive graphic images with image maps.

HoTMetaL PRO & Images

HoTMetaL PRO includes commands for previewing and working with images. Many of the commands that control viewing inline images can be found in HoTMetaL PRO's View menu. By default the View menu displays the Show Inline Images option. This option toggles to Hide Inline images, which only shows the IMG tag, which is the tag used to include inline images in your Web pages.

You can open a graphic file in an editor when previewing a page by setting up the configuration variable to point to a graphic editor program. This way you can easily display and edit the images in your HTML document. To view the picture from HoTMetaL PRO, choose View>>Show Image. This command only works if you've included the full path to the image.

By default, the variable setting in the sqhmpro.ini file, which is stored in your HoTMetaL PRO directory (the default is htmlpro), assigns the following values that point to the program for viewing images in the GIF and bitmap (.bmp) formats.

```
view_gif=c:\psp\psp.exe
view_bmp=c:\windows\pbrush.exe
```

The first line sets the GIF viewer to Paint Shop Pro. (This is a shareware program that is included on the Companion CD-ROM.) If you have a commercial editor, such as Image Pals 2, HiJaack Graphics Suite or Adobe Photoshop, you can enter the path to the program here. (Graphic editors are discussed later in this chapter.)

You can add variables of your choice by entering the program name, an underscore and the file extension of the file type you want to display (program_extension). For example, some browsers allow you to display JPEG inline images. To set up HoTMetaL PRO to view JPEG images for editing with Paint Shop Pro, enter the following line:

```
view_jpg=c:\psp\psp.exe
```

Graphic Formats

There is a world of graphic file formats, but to publish on the Internet you really only have to concentrate on two main types, Graphics Interchange Format (GIF) and Joint Photographic Experts Group (JPEG). It's easy for browsers to be set up to include other formats, such as Tagged Image File Format (TIFF) and Encapsulated PostScript (EPS), but most Web documents contain only GIF files and point to larger, high-resolution files in the JPEG format.

The Lowdown on the GIF Format

The GIF format was created by CompuServe to provide a way to quickly exchange graphic image files over phone lines. GIF files are stored in a compressed format so that the time to download the graphics files is minimal. GIF files support indexed color image types, as well as line art and grayscale images. A major benefit of GIF files is that they can be displayed on UNIX, Mac and Windows platforms.

There are two types of GIF file formats: GIF89a and GIF87a. GIF89a includes a transparency index that causes the background color of the display to remain unchanged for the color indexed as transparent. Interlaced images means the image can be progressively displayed. When an interlaced file is downloaded, it appears with a venetian blind effect. Interlaced files let the user begin viewing the rest of the document while the GIF image is downloading. Interlaced GIF files are supported by both NCSA Mosaic (version 2.0) and Netscape Navigator. Unfortunately some graphic editors don't support both GIF formats. Even Adobe Photoshop, powerhouse that it is, only produces GIF87a format.

The GIF LZW Controversy

In December of 1994 a controversy arose concerning the GIF file format. The controversy started because CompuServe and Unisys, the two companies that own the rights to the GIF file format, decided to start charging developers for products that include GIF support. Until this announcement the GIF format was treated as a public-domain standard—although it really wasn't. The GIF file format uses LZW compression. LZW comes from the names Lempel, Ziv and Welch. Lempel and Ziv were mathematicians who are originators of several compression schemes. Welch later added his input to Lempel and Ziv's compression algorithm. Unisys, a large networking and information management company, owns the patent for LZW and is requiring licensing for all software developers (*not* end-users) using the LZW compression. CompuServe Information Services has provided an optional licensing agreement that CompuServe-related software developers can enter into instead of dealing with Unisys directly. Software developers whose software is not "primarily for use with the CompuServe Information Service" will have to obtain a license from Unisys. CompuServe is licensing the usage of LZW in GIF products for 1.5 percent of the selling cost of the product. Of the 1.5 percent, 1 percent goes to Unisys. Unfortunately this has caused a lot of confusion and has been a stumbling block to many software vendors. If you want to follow up on this controversy, check out Unisys at http:/www.unisys.com/ and CompuServe's Web site at www.compuserve.com/ or Yahoo's collection of GIF links at http://www.yahoo.com/Computers/Software/Data_Formats/GIF/.

CompuServe has proposed a new standard called GIF24 as a successor to the GIF89a specification. GIF24 ups the ante on GIF by supporting 24-bit images. A file format named PNG is being used as the basis for GIF24. PNG uses a compression technology called "deflation" that is used in many freeware programs. It was developed to be a free and open standard. You can check the draft of the PNG specification at Thomas Boutell's Web server at http://sunsite.unc.edu/boutell/png.html.

The Lowdown on JPEG Format

JPEG is the standard of choice because of its high resolution and high compression. Many graphic editors, such as Adobe Photoshop, let you choose a quality setting for the compression. High quality is less compressed with a ratio of about 5:1 to 15:1. JPEG images are automatically decompressed when they are loaded in the browser. JPEG reduces image files to about 10 percent of their original size or smaller.

The JPEG algorithm is referred to as *lossy*, meaning that some data is lost. JPEG identifies and ignores pixels that are not essential to the overall quality of the image, such as a large area of a single color. Typically the absence of subtracted information is not noticeable. Once an image is compressed using JPEG, it loses some information so the image may appear indistinguishable from the original JPEG file and will be much smaller. Another advantage of JPEG is that it's supported in PostScript Level 2. PostScript has long been a standard on the Internet. When a JPEG compressed image is sent to a PostScript Level 2 printer, the file is sent to the printer then it is decompressed. Unlike GIF, JPEG supports 24-bit color. JPEG, unfortunately, doesn't support interlacing.

Including Inline Images

An inline image is an image that is displayed without the help of an external helper application. Netscape and Mosaic both support inline images in GIF and JPEG formats. The IMG tag <IMG> is used to insert graphic image files. Inserting an image in your document using HoTMetaL PRO is as easy as choosing Markup>>Insert Element and choosing the IMG element from the Insert Elements dialog box. There is no limit to the number of inline images you can use in a document.

Providing Alternative Text for an Image

Not everyone can view or chooses to view inline images. Many people who have modem connections turn off inline images to get information faster. To address people accessing your page using a text-based browser, such as Lynx, be sure to include alternative text to clue them in to what they can't see. To add alternative text, move the insertion point in the IMG tag and choose the Markup>>Edit SGML Attributes. This displays the Insert Attributes dialog box, shown in Figure 7-1, which includes the Alternative (ALT) attribute. In the ALT attribute field, enter the text you want displayed where the image occurs.

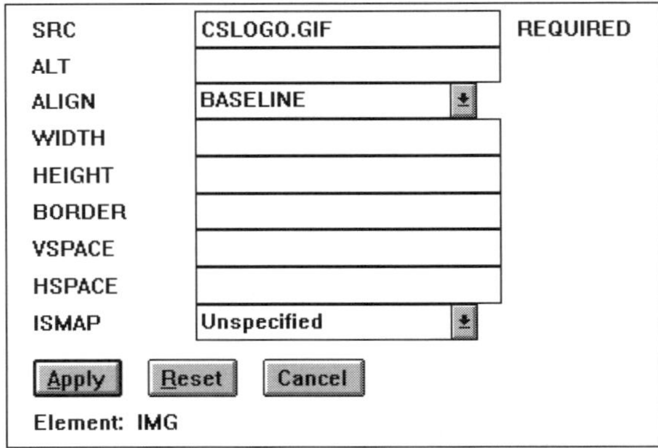

Figure 7-1: *The Edit Attributes dialog box includes the ALT field for specifying alternative text for text-based Web browsers.*

Making an Inline Image a Hyperlink

Any inline image can also be used as a hyperlink to another HTML document or file. When you insert an image tag in the hypertext part of the anchor, a border is displayed around the outside of the image. The following example displays an image named orderdsk.gif as a hyperlink:

```
<A HREF = "order.html"><IMG SRC = "orderdsk.gif"></A>
```

Clicking on the image lets the user jump to an HTML document named order.html. Figure 7-2 shows an inline image that's also a hyperlink.

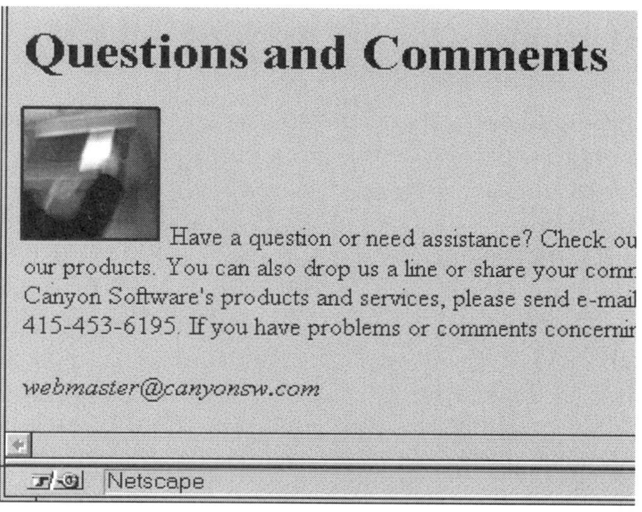

Figure 7-2: *An inline image can also be a hyperlink. Notice the outline around the image indicating it is a hyperlink.*

Acquiring Graphic Image Files

Adding images to your Web pages can give them a polished, professional look, thereby making a strong statement about you and your company. The biggest hurdle in creating a Web page, however, is acquiring and editing images to add to your page. If you are creating a Web site for your business, you may want to hire a desktop publisher to scan or create pictures for your page. Even if you have the graphic tools, there's a long learning curve to becoming a graphic artist.

In order to add an inline image, you'll need to either create a GIF image, which requires a bitmap editing program, such as Adobe Photoshop or Paint Shop Pro; to have access to an existing GIF image; or to use a scanner to acquire an image.

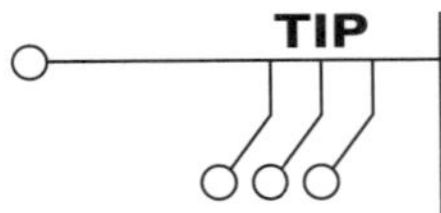

TIP

If you want to present a Web page for your business, consider using digitized photos rather than illustrations. Readers tend to show more trust in photographic images than in illustrations.

Professional Clip Art & Photo Images

Commercial clip art and photo images are everywhere. Clip art and photos seem to be the most popular add-on for most graphics and multimedia programs. Many packages include samples from different clip art and photo vendors. Corel DRAW! 5, for example, includes 22,000 clip-art images and symbols and 100 high-resolution photos. If that isn't enough, and believe it or not, it isn't, Corel also sells additional clip art and a photo library of another 200,000 photo images. Be aware, however, that the quality of clip art and photos can vary dramatically. Just because it's a commercial product doesn't mean that it belongs in the professional quality category.

Image Club is one company that has always stood out as a leader in the professional quality clip-art category. Image Club also offers affordable professional photo images. Another company that has impressive digital photos is CMCD, an offshoot of Clemont Mok's design firm. A trend in photo images is to use single everyday objects as metaphors. You can check out CMCD's latest releases of everyday objects at http://www.cmdesigns.com.

Keep in mind that there is not one standard format for clip art and photo files. Image Club's graphics are in EPS format. CMCD ships photos in Kodak's PhotoCD format. The accompanying CD contains image samples from Image Club and CMCD. Check the back of the book for other sources of clip art and photos.

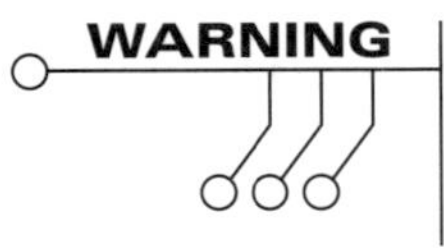

WARNING

Don't mix different types of graphic images. Black-and-white illustrations, color photos and clip art all have definite looks and moods. Choose images carefully so that the images complement your document's message. Using black-and-white illustrations and color photos on the same page may leave readers with a mixed message and will most likely leave readers cold.

Scanning Images

One way to acquire an image is to scan an existing picture or photo. Scanning images is dangerous. If you scan a photo from a magazine or other publication, most likely you're infringing on someone's copyright. It's much safer to create your own images or purchase royalty-free images. Many copy centers and service bureaus will scan your logos or pictures for a small fee. If you plan to have your own Web site, you might want to consider purchasing a color flatbed scanner, such as a Hewlett Packard LaserJet IIc.

If you would like more information on copyrights, Thomson & Thomson, a trademark and copyright research firm that provides some helpful resources on copyrights, is located at http://www.thomson.com/thomthom/resmain.html. A copyright FAQ is also available at http://www.cis.ohio-state.edu/hypertext/faq/usenet/Copyright-FAQ/top.html. You can also check the U. S. Copyright Office, a department of the Library of Congress at gopher://marvel.loc.gov/11/copyright.

Free Images at Web Sites

There are thousands of GIF files on the Internet. Several sites on the Web include free images you can use to create your Web documents. You can get collections of decorative elements, such as bullets, icons and line drawings that enhance the appearance of your Web document. You simply download the files to your system. Because GIF images are internally compressed, you don't need a decompression program. The viewer or paint program you display the image with will automatically decompress the GIF file. If you want to get collections of clip art, they may be stored in PKZip format. To help you expand compressed files, check out the version of Drag And Zip included on the Companion CD. Drag And Zip works with browsers to decompress PKZip files on the fly. Table 7-1 lists some sites that include graphic images, including bullets, icons and lines.

URL	Contents
http://www.yahoo.com/yahoo/computers/multimedia/pictures	A great inventory of picture files.
http://akebono.stanford.edu:80/users/www_server/Computers/World_Wide_Web/WWW_programming/Icons/	A huge listing of icons and clip-art links
http://colargol.edb.tih.no/~geirme/gizmos/gizmo.html	GIF images, icons, buttons, bullets and lines plus links to other resource archives.
http://inls.ucsd.edu/y/OhBoy/icons.html	GIF images, icons, bullets and lines.
http://ns2.rutgers.edu/doc-images/small_buttons/	Standard GIF icons.
http://white.nosc.mil/images.html	Space, travel, medical and other images plus links to other resource sites.
http://www-ns.rutgers.edu/doc-images/icons/	Standard GIF bullets.
http://www.cit.gu.edu.au/~anthony/icons/	Standard GIF icons.
http://www.cs.yale.edu/HTML/YALE/CS/HyPlans/loosemore-sandra/clipart.html	Pointers to archives filled with clip art.
http://www.di.unipi.it/test/new/icons/icons1-6.html	A large collection of icons.

Table 7-1: *URL's for image collections.*

Images & Copyrights

Publishing on the Web carries with it the same restrictions as traditional publishing. You're still subject to copyright and trademark laws. Be careful of what you use in your document. Many files are available that break copyright restrictions; just because they're available at a site doesn't mean you have the legal right to publish them in your document.

Image Editing Fundamentals

While graphic editors let you convert, trim, apply filters, adjust the number of colors, etc., be warned—mastering bitmap editing programs can be a time-consuming task. If you find a usable image, but it needs editing or is in the wrong format, you can use a graphics editor program to edit and save the file in the GIF format. If you want, you can also include other image files, such as JPEG images, that users can view using an external viewer. See the Resources section for information on GIF and JPEG bitmap editing programs.

Graphic Editors & Tools

Editing image files can be a tricky proposition. Several shareware and commercial graphic editors let you create and edit GIF and JPEG images. One of the most popular shareware editors is Paint Shop Pro. Paint Shop Pro is a product of JASC. Version 3.0 is included on the Companion CD-ROM. Figure 7-3 shows the Paint Shop Pro image editor. You can visit JASC's Web site to check for newer editions of Paint Shop Pro program by entering the URL: http://www.winternet.com/~jasc/pspscrn.html.

Figure 7-3: *The Paint Shop Pro image editor.*

A wide range of commercial graphic editors exist. In the low to mid range, we recommend Image Pals 2 and Hijaak Graphics Suite. Both of these packages let you convert almost any graphics format into a GIF or JPEG format. CorelDRAW! is an impressive suite of graphic tools that includes Corel Photo Paint for working with GIF and JPEG files. Anyone planning on working with graphics should also consider purchasing Adobe Photoshop. This is the best image editor we've ever used. While it is expensive, it includes just about every feature you could want in an image editor. Version 3.0 lets you work with layers and add lighting effects. Once you've tried Photoshop it's hard to go back.

One primary concern when publishing on the Web is that you want to create memorable graphics. Numerous graphic applications and utilities exist that go beyond simple graphic editing. One impressive graphics application is Fractal Design Painter. Painter lets you create images using tools that emulate traditional artist's tools, such as water colors, oil-based paints, charcoal, pastels and so on. We used Painter with the Kurta XGT graphic tablet to produce some marvelous images. Painter includes several other features for creating and editing animations and videos. 3D rendering applications, such as 3-D Studio, Visual Reality and trueSpace, are quite a bit more complex than graphic editors but they let you work with three-dimensional images to create eye-catching graphics that simulate and apply materials and textures, as well as change the lighting to create objects that reflect light and cast shadows. Most 3D rendering applications are also capable of creating and editing animations, which are discussed in the next chapter. Both graphics programs and 3D rendering applications let you use filter programs, also called *plug-ins*. Kai's Power Tools is probably the best known plug-in that works in conjunction with graphic editors, such as Adobe Photoshop and Corel Paint, to create unique special effects. Before you can effectively use a graphic editor and other graphic-related applications and tools, it's important that you understand the basic components of an image and the factors that affect the image's output when published on the Web.

Understanding Pixels & Color Palettes

A *pixel* is the smallest measurement of part of an image. The *pixel-depth* or *bit resolution* refers to a measurement of the number of bits of stored information per pixel. In other words each pixel is assigned a numeric value to represent a color. The greater the pixel depth the more colors you have available. GIF files have a color-depth of 8 bits per pixel for a possible 256 values. GIF files are indexed color images that use a color palette. A *color palette,* sometimes called a color look-up table (CLUT), is a mathematical table that defines the colors of pixels. Like a paint-by-numbers kit, each displayed pixel has a value that matches one of the indexed locations in a palette. For this reason a palette is sometimes referred to as an *indexed color system.*

Most graphic editors provide a palette tool for displaying available colors. Some image editors let you use a color picker to display or specify a particular color. As we mentioned, the GIF format uses a color palette with up to 256 colors. These colors can be 256 colors out of millions of possibilities. Only one combination of 256 colors can be used at one time. Windows itself reserves 20 colors for displaying windows. If you use a palette of 256 colors for one image and use another color palette that includes additional colors not in the other palette, the screen may flash strange colors on your screen while Windows creates a new palette and the old colors change to the new palette.

Using more than 256 colors can also cause distorted images. The colors are allocated as they are requested until 256 colors are used. Any additional graphics displayed onscreen can only use colors that are already allocated, unless a new color table is used. This is why some images may appear fine at the beginning of a Web page and subsequent images appear distorted. For example, if your page has two images that use more than 256 colors, when the browser displaying your page runs out of colors, the remaining colors will not be created. Instead, the closest colors of those already allocated will be used, which can distort your image.

The best way to keep from having images distort when displayed is to use the same palette for all images appearing on the same page. Graphic editors let you remap, optimize and customize palettes. JPEG files, on the other hand, support 24-bit color, which gives you up to 16.7 million colors. Using 16-bit and 24-bit images, you don't have to worry about palettes.

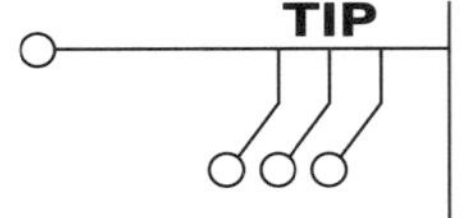

If you want to edit a color palette, you should convert the image to RGB (red, green, blue) mode. This gives you more editing options. After editing the graphic image, convert the file to an indexed image type.

Changing Resolutions, Cropping & Resizing Images

It's helpful to understand how resolution affects your image. First, it's important that you don't confuse the two types of resolution: image resolution and monitor resolution. *Image resolution* refers to the spacing of pixels in the image and is measured in pixels per inch (ppi). If the image has a resolution of 96 ppi, it contains 9,216 pixels per square inch (96 x 96 = 9,216). *Monitor resolution* is the number of dots per inch that your monitor uses to display an image. It determines how large and or how small images appear onscreen. Most monitors have a maximum resolution of 72 dpi for displaying graphics.

It's important to keep icons and buttons the same size. You may want to crop your graphic images to include only the image you want to show. Keeping images, such as icons and buttons, the same size gives your page a uniform and consistent feel.

Images can be distorted when you change image resolutions or resize an image. As we mentioned earlier, most clip art comes in high-resolution format. It is best to edit, resize and crop an image in its original high-resolution format before you convert the image to GIF format. You should also make sure that the pixels per inch don't change when saving a high-resolution image to a different format, otherwise the image will be saved with different dimensions. Be careful when enlarging images in GIF or JPEG format. This usually ends up giving your image the jaggies.

Dithering Images

After you've resized your image and reduced the color depth to 8 bits (256 colors), the next step is to select a dither type. *Dithering* is a process where the color value of a pixel is changed to the closest matching color value in the target palette. Dithering helps reduce the number of colors needed to display an image by simulating colors. Dithering places dots of color closer together, giving the appearance of more colors in an image than there really are. Another benefit of dithering is that it places similar colored pixels together, so they appear to blend. This creates a smooth transition between two different colors. Dithering options are built into most image editing programs. Using various dithers can improve the range of perceived colors. For example, diffusion dithering is a popular option available in most image editors that randomly positions pixels instead of using a set pattern. For instance, choosing the Error Diffusion Dither option in Paint Shop Pro can have a dramatic effect on how certain images appear when published.

Anti-aliasing Type

When you add text to images, the pixels can create text with jagged edges. These jagged edges are sometimes referred to as stairsteps or the jaggies. If you want to add text when using a graphic editor, make sure you choose the anti-aliasing option. The anti-alias option in image editors helps eliminate the jaggies by making the edges of text appear smooth and blend into the background.

Displaying Type as Graphic Images

HTML doesn't let you specify fonts in Web documents. If you want to present text in a decorative font, you need to use images to display the type. Some graphics editors, such as Adobe Photoshop and Paint Shop Pro, include the capability to add text and save the files as a GIF or JPEG graphic image.

Many drawing and paint graphics programs let you add special effects to text. For example, Adobe Photoshop lets you create layered, shadowed, recessed, embossed, glowing and translucent text. Several high-end products, such as trueSpace and 3d Studio exist to let you render text in different textures. Figure 7-4 shows a sample of text in the GIF format created using Adobe Photoshop.

Figure 7-4: *Text created using Adobe Photoshop.*

Converting GIFs to Transparent Interlaced Images

There are several methods you can use to create transparent images. A transparent image is sometimes referred to as a floating image because it appears to float on the Web page. Figure 7-5 shows a transparent image shown with a gray background.

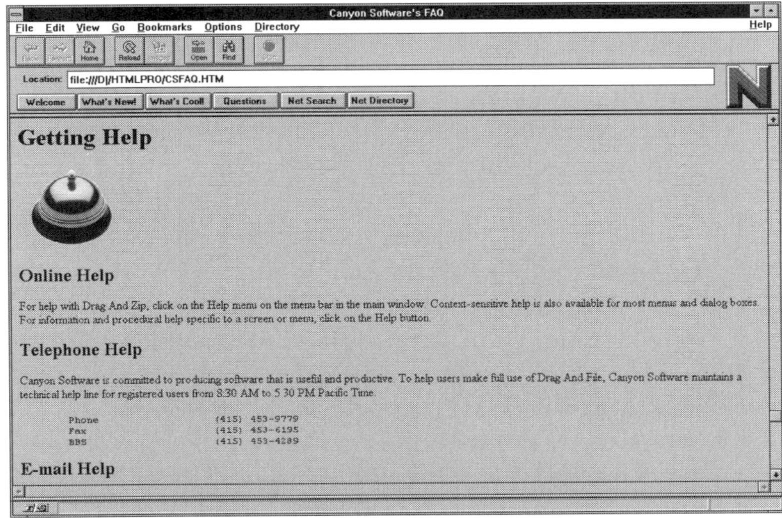

Figure 7-5: *A transparent image shown with a gray background.*

Most clip art and photos don't come in a format ready for Internet publishing. Luckily, converting an image into the GIF or JPEG format is as easy as saving a file. Most graphic editors let you use a Save As option to save files in GIF and JPEG formats. There are a couple of important conversion options you should consider: *interlacing* and *transparent backgrounds*.

There are several ways you can interlace GIF images. It's surprising that many graphic editors don't let you save GIF graphic files in the interlaced format. On the Companion CD-ROM there is a program called wgiftool.exe that automatically saves GIF files as interlaced image files and lets you define a transparent background color. The following sections explain how to determine the background color and describe different ways to create a transparent background and save files in a GIF89a format.

Determining the Background Color

If you don't know what the background is set to, you'll need to display the image and check the background color. You can use any graphic editor to find out the background color. In order to display the background color using Paint Shop Pro 3.0 that comes with this book, click the color picker (the eye dropper in the floating toolbox) on the background color. The index color appears next to the letter *I* in the middle of the status bar. The RGB (red, green, blue) values appear next to the index color.

The LView program is the default external image viewer for most browsers. While it's easier to determine the background color using Paint Shop Pro, LView Pro will also let you locate the background color. If you don't have LView Pro, you can get it at the following Web sites: ftp://oak.oakland.edu/pub3/win3/graphics and http://www.ncsa.uiuc.edu/SDG/Software/WinMosaic/viewers.html.

Once you have the downloaded and installed the program, you can view the background color by starting LView Pro and choosing File>>Open command to load your GIF image. Then choose Options>>Background Color. This displays the Select Color Palette Entry dialog box. To make sure you find the right background color, click the Mask selection using box, then click the white mask setting. This will cause your image to appear colored in with a white mask, so the entire window appears filled with the color white. If your background is white, choose the black mask setting. This will cause your image to be masked in black, so the entire window appears filled with the color black. Don't worry because the image is no longer displayed in the window; nothing is wrong. You can now click the palette entries you think match your background color. When you choose the right background color, the background displays and your image appears blocked out by the mask color you've chosen. This indicates you've found the right background color. The index and RGB settings for the background color appear at the bottom of the Select Color Palette Entry dialog box.

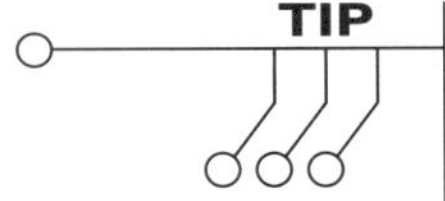

Make sure you use a unique color for the background of your image before changing the background or that portion of the picture will also be transparent. For example, if you have an image of a person and convert the picture of a face with a white background, the whites of the eyes and the teeth may become transparent, which will cause a problem when viewed on a gray background.

Creating a Transparent Interlaced Image Using Wgiftool

The giftool program, written by David Kobalas, is a command-line program that lets you change the background of an image so that it is transparent. To save you from having to enter long command lines to create a transparent background, we've included a Windows front-end to the giftool, called Wgiftool, that lets you define a transparent background and automatically saves the file in the interlaced format. Wgiftool only works with Windows NT and Windows 95. If you're using Windows you will have to use giftool.exe or giftrans.exe to create transparent images. The following steps explain how to use the Wgiftool program included on the Companion CD-ROM.

1. Open the File Manager and drag the wgiftool.exe file to the program group on which you want to store the wgiftool.exe icon. The Wgiftool icon appears in the program group.
2. Double-click the Wgiftool icon. The Wgiftool window appears as shown in Figure 7-6.

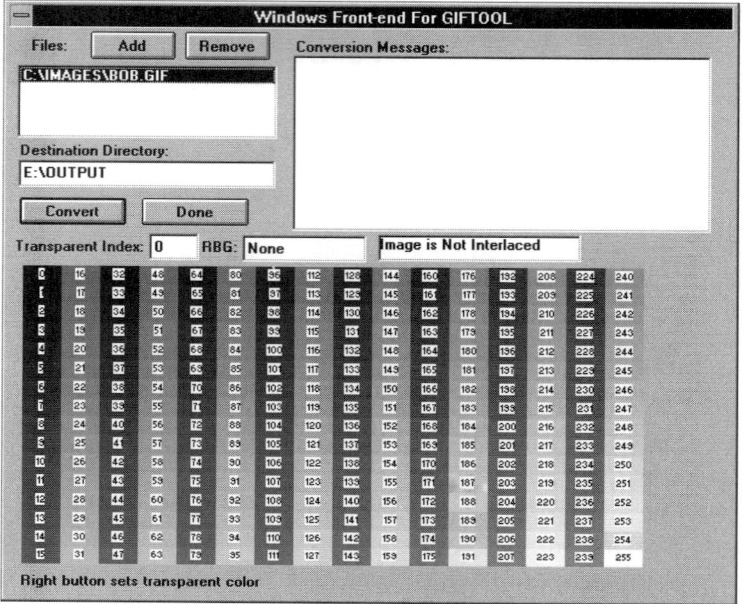

Figure 7-6: *The Wgiftool window.*

3. Click the Add button. The select a GIF file dialog box appears.
4. Choose the GIF file for which you want to specify a transparent background. You can select multiple files if you want, but you can only convert one file at a time.
5. Select the file you want to convert in the Files box. The color lookup table appears. The status box to the right of the RGB setting displays whether or not the image is interlaced.
6. Click your *right* mouse button on the background color you want to make transparent.
7. Enter the path and directory name where you want to store the converted file. You must choose a directory different than the directory where the original file is stored.
8. Choose the Convert button. Note the status box to the right of the RGB setting informs you the image is interlaced.
9. Click the Done button to close the window.

Creating a Transparent Interlaced Image Using LView Pro

You can also create an image with a transparent background using LView Pro. The following steps explain how to create a transparent interlaced image.

1. Start LView Pro and choose File>>Open and load your GIF image.
2. Choose Options>>Background Color.
3. Select mask selection using option from the Select Palette Entry dialog box.
4. Select the color that corresponds to the image's "background color" from the palette.
5. Choose the Options>>Save GIFs interlaced option.
6. Choose File>>Save As.
7. Select GIF89a from the list of file types.
8. Enter a new name for your file and choose OK.

Creating a Transparent Interlaced Image Using giftool

The Wgiftool program is nothing more than a Windows front-end for the command-line program giftool. Now that you're familiar with the LZW controversy it seems appropriate to point out that Wgiftool doesn't have anything to do with LZW compression, but lets the giftool program do the work. The giftool program is also included on the Companion CD-ROM accompanying this book. You can also pick up giftool at http://www.homepages.com/tools/.

The giftool program lets you convert a gif to an interlaced image with a transparent background. The following is an example of how to convert a noninterlaced GIF file to an interlaced GIF file:

```
giftool -i -o intrlace.gif original.gif
```

The -i tells giftool to interlace the specified file. The interlaced file name needs to be different than the original file. The -o lets you specify the output file name, which in this example is intrlace.gif.

If you want to also change the background color to transparent, enter a command similar to the following:

```
giftool -i -rgb 255,255,255 -o intrlace.gif original.gif
```

The -rgb 255,255,255 used to specify a white background is changed to the transparent pixel value. You can replace the 255,255,255 with the RGB values that you find for your background using Paint Shop Pro (explained earlier in this chapter). You can also use the index number by simply entering the index number after a dash. For example, the following specifies the index for the color white to be the transparent pixel value.

```
giftool -i -o intrlace.gif -0 original.gif
```

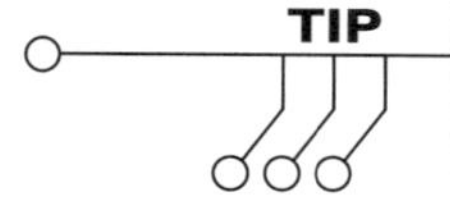

There are other options available for the giftool program. To list these options, enter giftool-help.

Creating a Transparent Image Using giftrans

Another command-line program that lets you create transparent images is giftrans.exe. The giftrans.exe program is also included on the Companion CD-ROM. You can also download the giftrans program at http://melmac.corp.harris.com/files/ or at http://sunsite.unc.edu/pub/packages/infosystems/WWW/tools/giftrans.

The giftrans program uses the following syntax:

giftrans -t*n* *original*.gif>*transparent*.gif.

The *n* refers to the index number of the background color that you want to make transparent. You can also use the RGB values to identify the background color. For example, entering 192,192,192 defines a shade of gray. The following example creates a transparent background for the indexed color white (0).

```
giftrans -t0 file1.gif>file2.gif
```

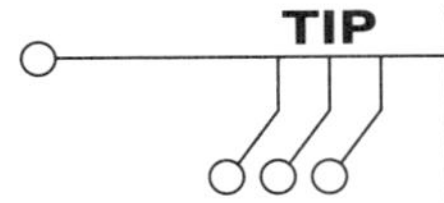

TIP

There are other options available for the giftrans program. To list these options, enter giftrans -?.

Saving Bandwidth by Using Thumbnails

An inline image can only be displayed in a 800 x 600 resolution whereas an external JPG image can be in 24-bit format. Say you have a killer 24-bit graphic you want to show off. Don't include the JPEG as an inline image. Instead present a thumbnail in the GIF format that links to the JPEG image. Clicking on the inline image hyperlink automatically opens the JPEG image file in a larger, higher resolution. Figure 7-7 shows a thumbnail image and Figure 7-8 shows the larger file it points to. To create a thumbnail image that is linked to a larger image, use the Anchor tag. The following is a raw HTML example of a GIF thumbnail file named small.gif linked to display a file named large.jpg:

```
<A>HREF=large.jpg><IMG SRC=small.gif></A>
```

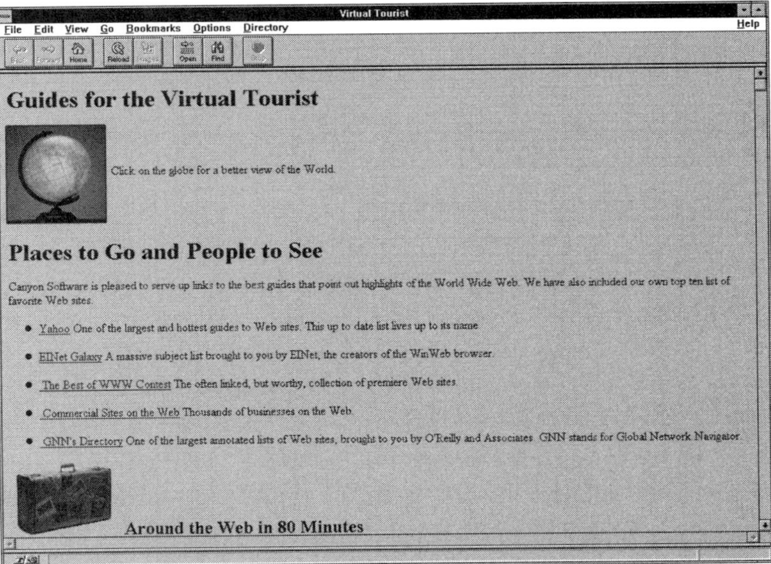

Figure 7-7: *A thumbnail of a globe in a Web page.*

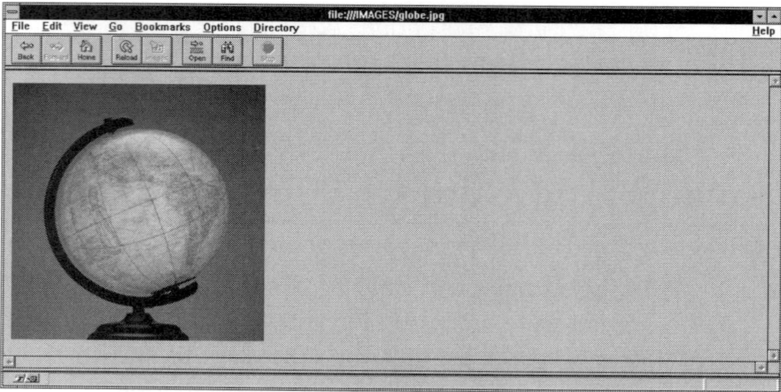

Figure 7-8: *The larger linked image of the globe.*

Positioning Images

Realizing the importance of graphics it's little wonder that of all the added Netscape tags, the image tag has the most extensions. Several extensions have been added to help you align text and images. Two powerful attribute additions are the "left" and "right" settings. These attribute settings let you align images that can float in margins. The rest of the align options correct what Marc Andreeson thought were "horrible errors" he made when first implementing the IMG tag.

To align an image using HoTMetaL PRO, move the insertion point between the starting and ending IMG tags and choose the Markup>>Edit SGML Attributes. The Edit Attributes dialog box appears, as shown in Figure 7-9. The raw HTML syntax for the alignment attribute is <IMG ALIGN=*postion*>. Table 7-2 explains the different alignment options.

In order to use Netscape extensions with HoTMetaL PRO you need to make sure the rules setting in the sqhmpro.ini file is set to the Netscape extensions rules file (html-net.mtl). Changing the rules setting from strict HTML to HTML with Netscape extensions is explained in the Installing HoTMetaL PRO section in Chapter 2.

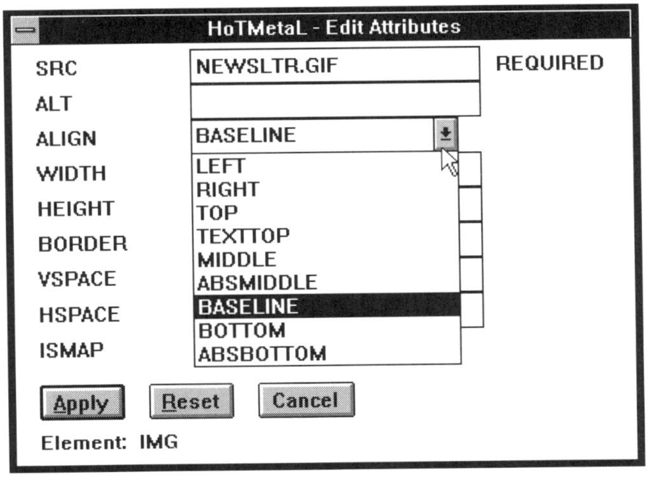

Figure 7-9: *The Edit Attributes dialog box for images.*

Position	Description
left	Aligns the image in the left margin. Subsequent text will wrap around the right-hand side of that image.
right	Aligns the image in the right margin. Subsequent text wraps around the right-hand side of that image.
top	Aligns the image with the top of the tallest item in the line.
texttop	Aligns the image with the top of the tallest text in the line. The texttop attribute is usually the same as the top attribute.
middle	Aligns the image so the baseline of the current line appears aligned with the middle of the image.
absmiddle	Aligns the middle of the current line with the middle of the image.
baseline	Aligns the bottom of the image with the baseline of the current line.
bottom	Aligns the bottom of the image with the baseline of the current line. This is the same as baseline.
absbottom	Aligns the bottom of the image with the bottom of the current line.

Table 7-2: *Position attributes for images.*

Adding Space Around an Image

Netscape includes two attributes for adding space around a floating image: <IMG VSPACE=*n* HSPACE=*n*>. Without these commands floating images could press up against the text wrapped around the image. The VSPACE attribute sets the vertical space above and below the image. The HSPACE attribute sets the horizontal space to the left and right of the image.

To help you better place images, Netscape added a CLEAR attribute to the BR tag. The CLEAR tag has three settings: left, right and all. CLEAR=left breaks the line, and moves vertically down until you have a clear left margin. CLEAR=right breaks the line and moves vertically down until you have a clear right margin. CLEAR=all moves down until both margins are clear of images.

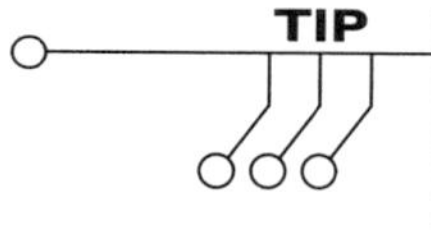

Transparent GIFs can be used as spacers to position images evenly or wherever you want them on the page. The best way to use a transparent GIF is to create a transparent GIF that is only a pixel high and however many pixels you need in width. This smaller the space the faster the image will download.

Adding Borders & Drop Shadows to an Image

A border can help accent an image, drawing the reader's eye to a graphic. Netscape has added the BORDER attribute to let you control the thickness of the border framing an image. In most cases, you don't really want to set a border for images that are also part of anchors. This can confuse people because they are used to having a colored border indicate that an image is an anchor.

To add the BORDER attribute to an image, choose Markup>>Edit SGML Attributes. This displays the Edit Attributes dialog box. In the Border field, enter the number of pixels you want to define as a border to your image. The raw HTML tag for adding a border appears as <IMG BORDER=*n*>, where *n* is the width in pixels of the border. Figure 7-10 shows an image with a two-pixel border.

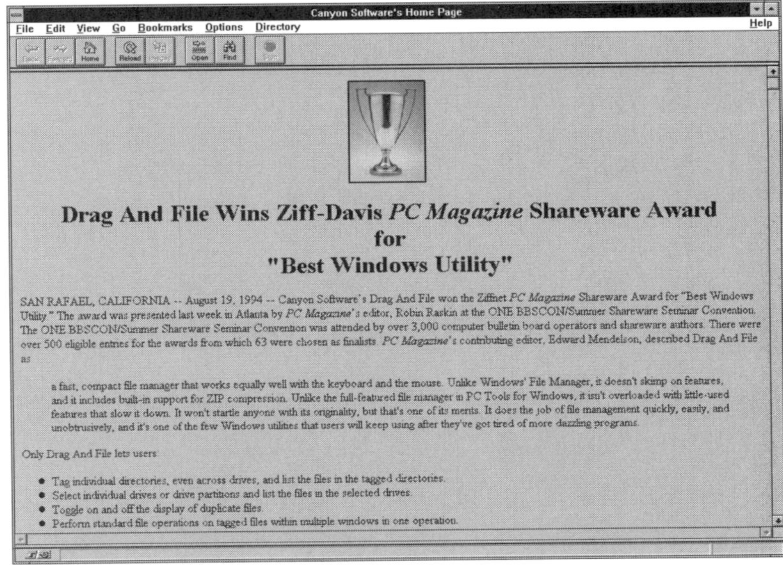

Figure 7-10: *An image with a two-pixel border.*

Another technique for calling attention to a graphic image is adding clip art as a border or including a drop shadow to the graphic. Adding a drop shadow is accomplished by editing the image and adding a dark border around a portion of the image. Drop shadows can be quite effective when you save the graphic with a transparent background. Figure 7-11 shows an image with a drop shadow and a transparent background.

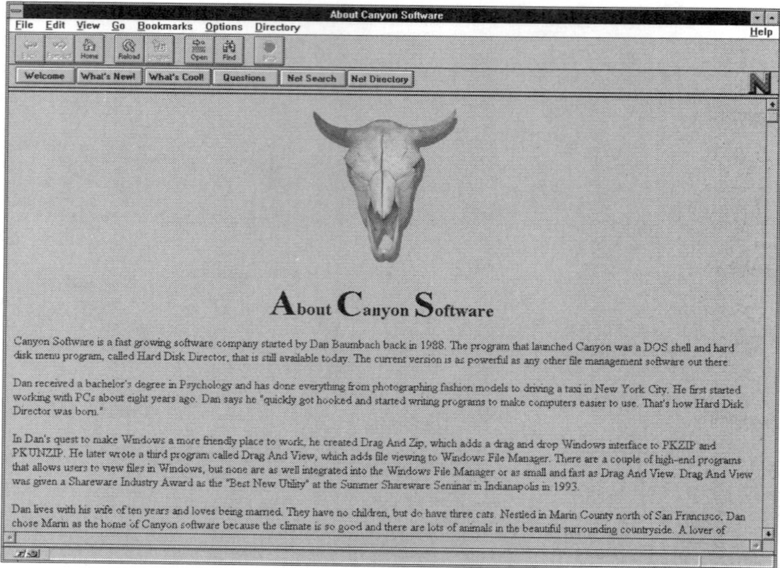

Figure 7-11: *An image with a drop shadow and a transparent background.*

Using an Inline Image as a Horizontal Rule

Horizontal rules are an effective way of visually breaking up your Web page. To enhance the separators in your Web documents, you can use colored lines or colored bars as horizontal rules. These are not created by using the <HR> tag, but instead are graphic inline images. Using inline images as horizontal rules is a great way to add color and pizzazz to your document. Many pages include rules that are made up of color gradients. Colored horizontal rules are a great way to accent the image colors in your document. Figure 7-12 shows inline images used as horizontal rules. You can pick up graphic files of horizontal rules by checking out some of the sites we listed earlier in this chapter.

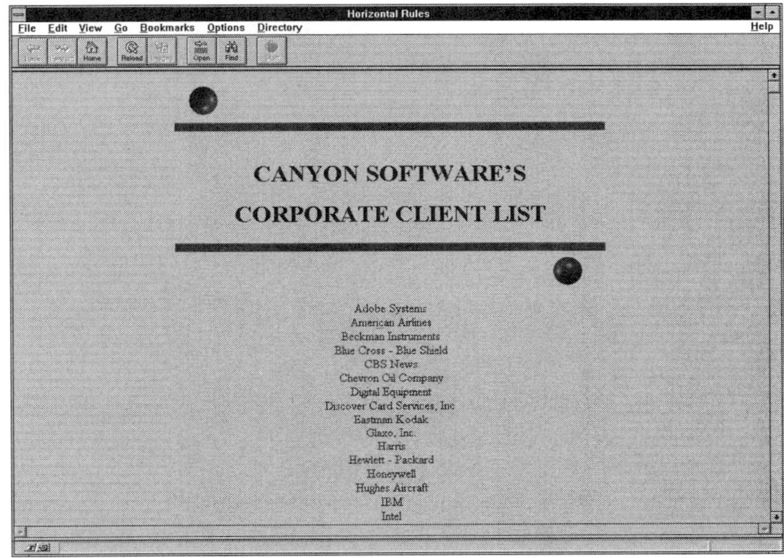

Figure 7-12: *Inline images used as horizontal rules.*

Using Inline Images as Bullets in a List

Besides using graphics for horizontal rules, you can also substitute graphics for bullets to create unnumbered lists. Many of the sites containing images that were listed earlier in this chapter used icons and images to replace bullets in lists. The following lines show how to create a list of hyperlinks using an image as a bullet instead of using the standard unordered list (<UL>) tag's bullets. Figure 7-13 shows an example of using a transparent image instead a bullet to present an unordered (bulleted) list.

```
<P>
<IMG SRC="duck.gif" ALT="Duck"><A HREF="http://
www.galcit.caltech.edu/~ta/cgi-bin/asylhome-ta">The
Asylum</A>
</P>
<P>
<IMG SRC="duck.gif" ALT="Duck"><A HREF="http://
sunsite.unc.edu/Dave/drfun.html">Dr. Fun</A>
</P>
```

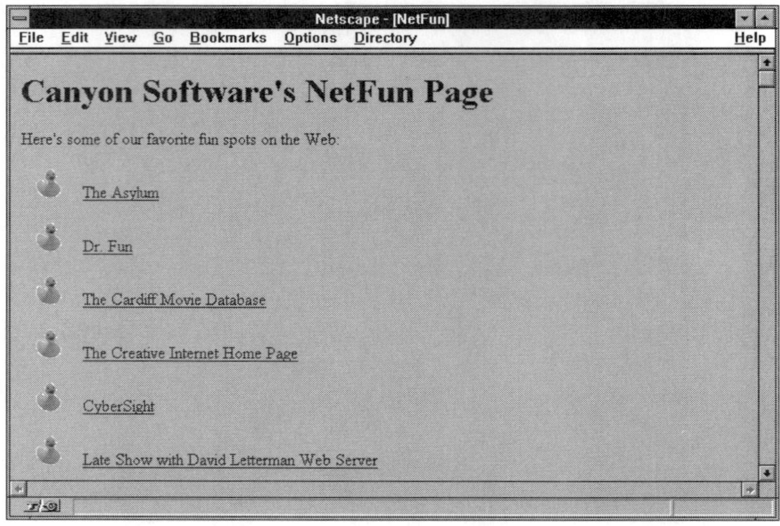

Figure 7-13: *Customized bullets in an unordered list.*

Specifying the Width & Height of an Image

Netscape also added the WIDTH and HEIGHT attributes to the IMG tag, primarily to help speed up display of the document. When Netscape encounters a new Web page it has to create an area for the image called a *bounding box*. Including the WIDTH and HEIGHT attributes saves the browser the time needed to calculate the size of the image. If a Web browser doesn't support the WIDTH and HEIGHT attributes, it ignores them. If you specify the wrong size for an image, it will be scaled to fit in the dimensions you specified.

You can find the width and height of your images using a graphic editor. Paint Shop Pro, for example, lists the width and height along with the number of colors in the first panel of the status bar. Like the other IMG attributes, you use the Markup>>Edit SGML Attributes to display the Edit Attributes dialog box. Fill in the Width and Height fields to specify the width and height in pixels of the image. The HTML tag appears similar to the following:

```
<IMG WIDTH=125 HEIGHT=125>
```

Fading in High-Resolution Images From Low-Resolution Images

Netscape has added yet another attribute to the IMG tag, called LOWSRC. This attribute is not supported by HoTMetaL PRO. The LOWSRC attribute is added to the IMG SRC tag to let you specify a low-resolution version of an image to load first and then load a higher-resolution version of the same image. You can include the LOWSRC attribute using any text editor or unchecked HTML editor. The high-resolution image fades in replacing the low-resolution graphic. The LOWSRC attribute instructs Netscape to load the image specified by the LOWSRC attribute on its first pass through the document. When all of the images are displayed in full, Netscape performs another pass and loads the image specified by the IMG SRC. Browsers that don't recognize the LOWSRC attribute load the image specified by IMG SRC. You can include both GIF and JPEG images using this method. If you also specify the width and height values, both the high-resolution and the low-resolution versions of the image will be scaled to fit. The following is an example of an IMG tag including the LOWSRC attribute.

```
<IMG SRC="high-res.gif" LOWSRC="low-res.jpg">
```

Changing the Window's Background & Foreground

With the introduction of Netscape Navigator 1.1, Netscape has included extensions that allow you to control the display of the background and foreground colors of browser's Netscape window. You can specify the color of the background or you can tile an image in the background, similar to using an image to Windows Wallpaper feature that you can set using the Desktop icon found in the Control panel. Keep in mind that right now this is a specific feature of Netscape, so users using a different browser will not see the background color or the background tiled image and the foreground colors. The following sections explain how to include these background and foreground extensions in your Web pages.

Specifying Colors

In order to specify a color, you need to choose a color and convert the RGB (red, green, blue) decimal settings to hexadecimal. As we mentioned earlier, Windows itself reserves 20 colors for displaying windows and each image uses a palette of 256 colors. If you use more than 256 colors, images will not display correctly. For this reason it is a good idea to stick with the standard Windows palette colors. This lessens the possibility that you will use a color that will affect the display of your inline graphics. To help save you the time of converting the RGB decimal settings to hexadecimal, Table 7-3 lists the hexadecimal settings for the standard Windows palette. Note that the table separates each red, green and blue setting with a comma, but you do not include commas when specifying a color.

Converting a decimal RGB color setting to hexadecimal is simple. Windows includes a calculator in the Accessories Group that can be used to automatically convert the decimal setting to hexadecimal. To use the calculator to convert decimal RGB settings to hexadecimal,

1. Start the calculator in the Accessories program group. The calculator window appears.
2. Choose View>>Scientific.
3. Enter the decimal setting for the red, green or blue color you want to display as hexadecimal. For example, the color hot pink has the RGB settings Red=255, Blue=153, Green=204, so first you would enter 255.
4. Click the Hex radio button and the hexadecimal equivalent appears. If you entered 255, for example, the hexadecimal number FF appears. Write the number down and click the decimal radio button.
5. Repeat steps 3 and 4 for the additional Blue and Green settings. You can then use the hexadecimal settings to specify the foreground or background color in the following sections.

Color	Hexadecimal RGB settings
Black	00,00,00
Dark Red	80,00,00
Dark Green	00,80,00
Dark Yellow	80,80,00
Dark Blue	00,00,80
Dark Magenta	80,00,80
Dark Cyan	00,80,80
Light Gray	C0,C0,C0
Grass Green	C0,DC,C0
Light Blue	A6,CA,F0
Medium Green	C0,DC,C0
Cream	FF,FB,F0
Medium Gray	A0,A0,A4
Dark Gray	80,80,80
Red	FF,00,00
Green	00,FF,00
Blue	00,00,FF
Yellow	FF,FF,00
Magenta	FF,00,FF
Cyan	00,FF,FF
White	FF,FF,FF

Table 7-3: *Hexadecimal codes for the standard Windows palette colors.*

Specifying the Netscape Window's Background Color

The Netscape extension BGCOLOR is not available in the current version of HoTMetaL PRO. The BGCOLOR is added as a BODY attribute. The syntax for specifying the background color is

<BODY BGCOLOR="#*rrggbb*"> Body text </BODY>

You must enter the red, green and blue color settings (rrggbb) in hexadecimal format. To enter a color, use Table 7-3 in the previous section to find the color you want or use the steps in the previous section to determine the hexadecimal setting for the color you want.

Using an Image for the Netscape Window's Background

One of the many additions to the specifications for HTML 3.0 is the addition of the BACKGROUND attribute to the BODY tag. The BACKGROUND attribute lets you specify a URL pointing to an image that is tiled to create a background of the Netscape window. The syntax for the using the BACKGROUND tag is

<BODY BACKGROUND="*path/image.gif*"> Body text</BODY>

The URL can point to any location. Netscape has supplied numerous background files, such as fabrics weaves, rocks, dots and water, that can be used. You can check out these backgrounds at http://home.netscape.com/home/. The following is an example of using a background stored at Netscape.

<BODY BACKGROUND="http://home.netscape.com/home/bg/water/raindrops_light.gif "> </BODY>

For example, Figure 7-14 shows a transparent image displayed using the Netscape raindrops_light.gif.

Figure 7-14: *An image displayed using a Netscape background.*

Changing the Foreground: Text & Links

In addition to changing the background colors, Netscape also lets you specify the color of text and links in a Web page. The TEXT attribute lets you specify the color of all the text other than links in your Web page. This syntax for the TEXT attribute is

```
<BODY TEXT="rrggbb">Body Text</BODY>
```

Like the background color, you specify the color in hexadecimal. You must enter the red, green and blue color settings (rrggbb) in hexadecimal format. To enter a color, use Table 7-3 in the previous section, "Specifying the Netscape Window's Background Color," to find the color you want or use the steps in the same section to determine the hexadecimal setting for the color you want.

Three attributes let you specify the color of links LINK, VLINK and ALINK. LINK refers to the links as they first appear on the page. The default color for links is blue. The V in VLINK stands for *visited*. VLINK changes the color of links that the user has chosen. The default color for visited links is purple. The A in ALINK stands for *active*. ALINK changes the color when the hyperlink is choosing. The default for active links is red. The following is an example that includes a dark cyan color for the background, white for text, yellow for links, medium gray for visited links and magenta for active links.

```
<BODY BGCOLOR="#000080" TEXT="#FFFFFF"
LINK="#FFFF00" VLINK="#A0A0A0" ALINK="#FF00FF">
Body Text goes here </BODY>
```

Creating an Image Map

The IMG element also lets you set up image maps. *Image maps* are graphic images that have defined "hot spots." Each hot spot is a link. Clicking on the graphic is the same as clicking on a hyperlink. The image lets the user jump to the URL that is defined for that region of the graphic. Image maps bring new ways to publish interactive Web pages. For example, a graphic can be a series of labeled buttons with each button image set to a different location.

Remember, if you use an image map, anyone using a text-based browser will not be able to see the image. If you use image maps, be sure you create a text-only version of the links for text-based browsers.

In order to create an image map, you first need to create an image that you want to include hot spots. You might want to use a motif or a metaphor for your images. For example, you might want to use an image of different buildings or an image of several planets, with each identifying a different link. Novell presents a bookshelf with each book labeled as a destination, such as "Service & Support" and "File Updates," as shown in Figure 7-15.

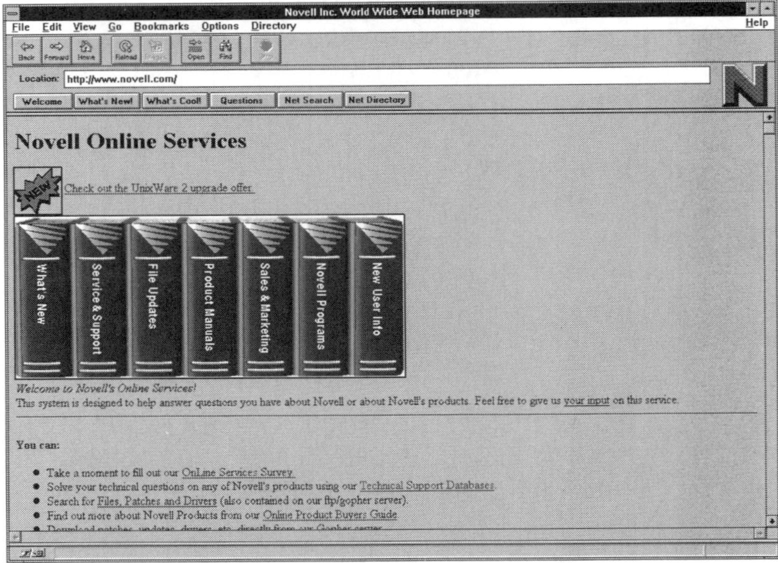

Figure 7-15: *Novell Web page displays a bookshelf with each book specifying a hyperlink.*

Specifying Hot Spots

There are different ways of identifying the parts of the image to specify a hot spot. You can manually enter the coordinates in a file and specify the URL you want to jump to, or you can use a image mapping program to create the file for you.

It's possible to identify the areas by noting the coordinates of the region you want to include, but there is an easier way. One of the biggest time savers for specifying hot spots is to use a program like Thomas Boutell's Mapedit. Mapedit is a utility that lets you draw rectangles, circles and arbitrary polygons and automatically adds the coordinates to an image map file. The Mapedit program is included on the Companion CD-ROM. You can check for updates at http://sunsite.unc.edu:80/pub/packages/infosystems/WWW/tools/mapedit/. The Mapedit file is named mapedit.zip.

Hot spots can be a variety of shapes, including a circle, rectangle or polygon. The most upper-left pixel is used as the beginning coordinate of an x axis, and the y axis begins at the upper left corner to the end of the right side of the image. This x and y grid lets you identify pixels you want to include as a hot spot. Most graphic editors use the same type of grid, allowing you to easily display specific coordinates. The next section explains how to use the Mapedit program to create a map file.

Using Mapedit to Create an Image Map

If the Mapedit program is not installed, create a directory and copy the mapedit.exe file to the directory. Open the File Manager and drag the mapedit.exe program to the program group of your choice. The following steps explain how to use Mapedit to create a map file.

1. Start the Mapedit program. The Mapedit window appears as shown in Figure 7-16.

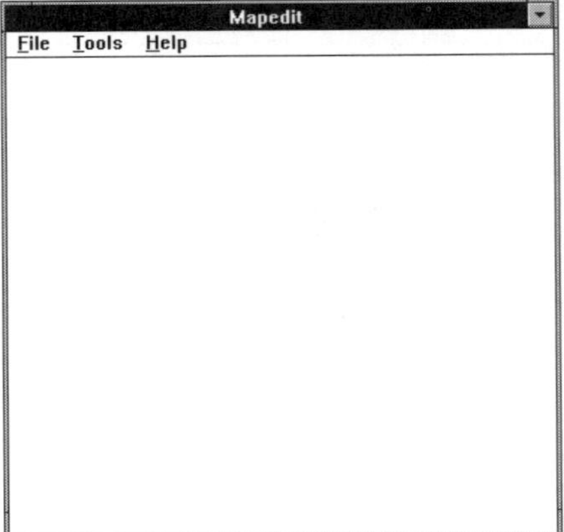

Figure 7-16: *The Mapedit window.*

2. Choose File>>Open/Create. The Open/Create dialog box appears, as shown in Figure 7-17.

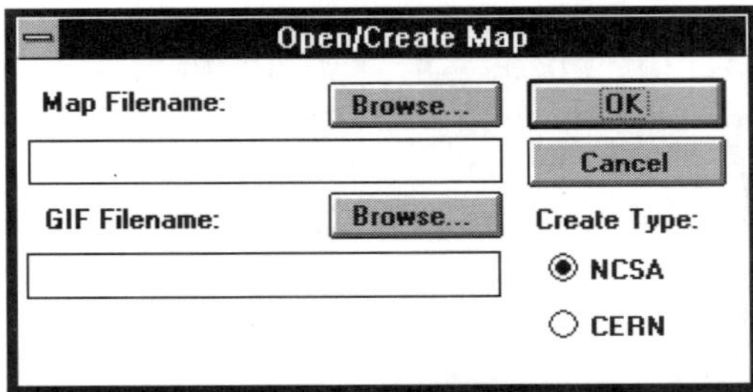

Figure 7-17: *The Mapedit Open/Create Map dialog box.*

3. Choose the NCSA radio button if you are using Robert Denny's 16-bit HTTPD server or the Cern radio button if you are using the EMWAC HTTPS server.
4. Enter the name you want to use for your map. This is the file that will store your hot spot coordinates. The default map files are stored in the httpd\conf\maps directory. It's important that you store your image map in this directory,

because this is where the image map script expects to find the map files. To have your map match the examples in the rest of this chapter, enter win3imap.map for the HTTPD server or enter ntimap.map for the EMWAC HTTPS server. If you have an existing map file, use the Browse button to locate and choose the existing map file.

5. Enter the name of the GIF file you want to use in the GIF Filename field. You can also use the Browse button to locate and choose the GIF file. For the examples in this chapter enter shapes.gif. The shapes.gif image file is included on the Companion CD-ROM.
6. Choose OK. Mapedit displays the message "Map file not found. Create it?" Choose OK. Mapedit loads your image for you to begin editing. Be patient, this may take a several seconds if the image is large. Figure 7-18 shows the sample image, shapes.gif, loaded in the Mapedit window. This image consists of a polygon, a circle and a rectangle. The shapes.gif image was created using the 3D graphics and animation trueSpace program.

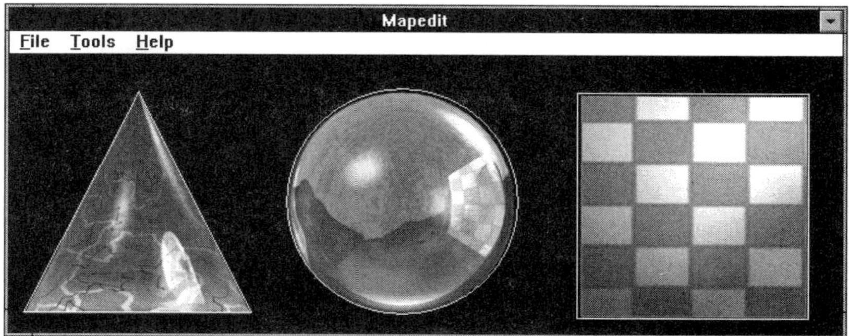

Figure 7-18: *The shapes.gif file loaded in the Mapedit window.*

7. Choose File>>Edit default URL. The default URL dialog box appears, as shown in Figure 7-19.

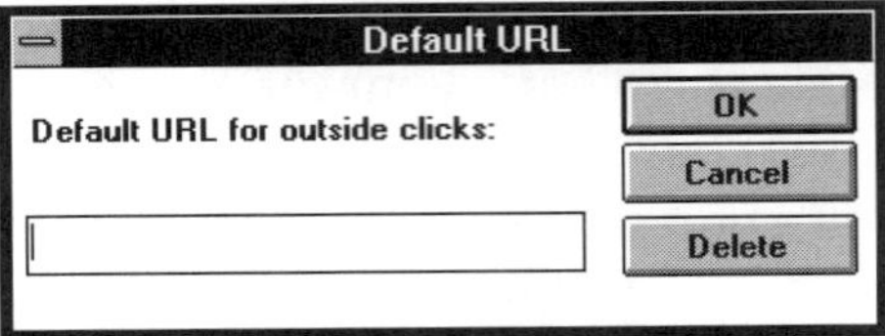

Figure 7-19: *The default URL dialog box.*

8. Enter the URL you want to default to for clicks outside the regions you are about to specify. If you want to point to a local file start with a forward slash. If you want to refer to a document on another server, enter the full URL. For this example, enter http://wings.buffalo.edu/contest/ and choose OK.
9. Click the Tools menu item and choose the item that specifies the shape you want to use to define a hot spot. The Tools menu includes your three choices: Polygon, Rectangle and Circle. The following explains how to define these regions. If two defined areas overlap, the first matching shape in the map file determines the URL which will be returned. If you don't like the region you selected, press the ESC key to cancel the marquee and start over. This example includes each of the three hot spots.

Polygon
Click the left mouse button at some point on the edge of an area of interest in the image. Move the mouse pointer to another point on the edge of the area of interest. Note that a line follows you from the point of the initial click. Click again at this second point. Continue clicking points until you have outlined all but the final connection back to the first point.

Rectangle
Click the left mouse button in one corner of a rectangular region of interest in the image. Now move the mouse pointer to the opposite corner, tracing out a rectangle.

Circle

Positions the mouse pointer in the center of the circle. Click the left mouse button and you can then move the mouse pointer to any point on the edge of the desired circle.

10. Click the right mouse button to accept the shape. The Object URL dialog box appears, as shown in Figure 7-20.

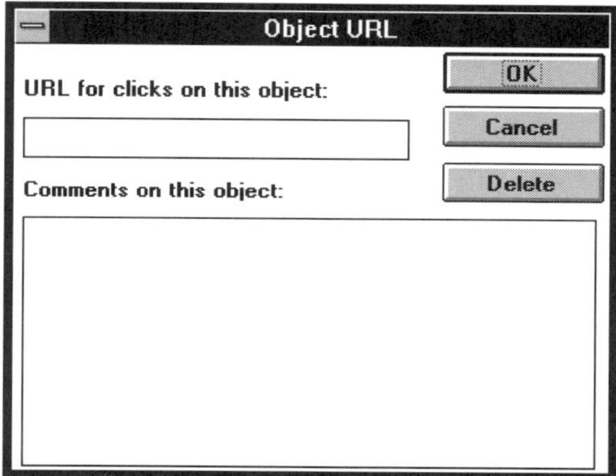

Figure 7-20: *The Object URL dialog box lets you specify the URL the object to link to.*

11. Enter the URL to link to. You can also add any comments in the Comments window. Choose OK when you're finished. For this chapter's examples, enter **http://www.yahoo.com/yahoo/** for the rectangle, **http://www.vmedia.com/** for the circle and **http://galaxy.einet.net/galaxy.html** for the triangle.
12. Choose the File>>Save command. If you open the image map file in a text editor, it will appear similar to Figure 7-21.

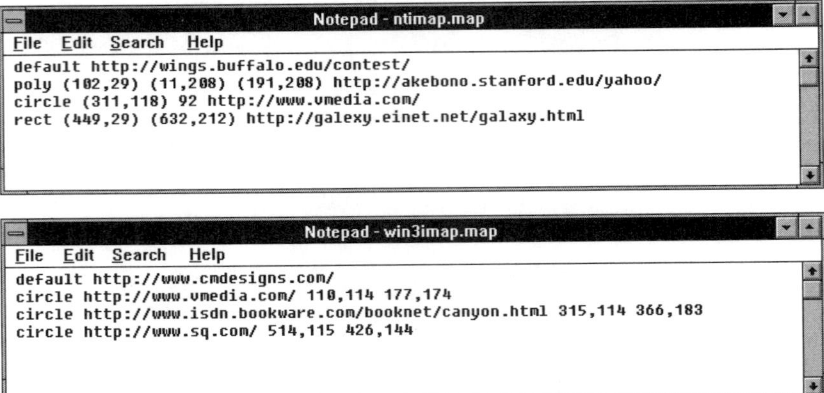

Figure 7-21: *A sample EMWAC HTTPS (ntimap.map) and a sample HTTPD (win3imap.map) image map file.*

Understanding the Map File

The settings that appear in the resulting map file depend on whether you chose the NCSA server or the EMWAC server. The map file is a text file consisting of definitions, comments and blank lines. You can edit the map file with any text editor. Map files end with the extension .map. The following section explains each type of entry in a map file.

The Default Setting

The HTTPS server lets you abbreviate default to def. The default setting defines the URL to jump to if the mouse click is outside a specified region. Both the HTTPS and HTTPD servers use the same syntax for the default URL: default URL. The following example shows an example default setting that points to the site listing the winners of the "Best of the Web Awards."

```
default http://wings.buffalo.edu/contest/
```

Polygons

The HTTPS sever lets you abbreviate the polygon setting to poly. The polygon is similar to a connect-the-dots puzzle. It defines a polygon with points at (x0,y0), (x1,y1), (x2,y2) and so on. The following is an example of a triangle defined for using the HTTPS server that points to the triangle.html.

```
poly (102,29) (11,208) (191,208) http://www.yahoo.com
```

The HTTPD sever lets you abbreviate the polygon setting to poly. The HTTPD server only lets you use 100 points to define a polygon.

The following is an example of an HTTPD setting for a rectangle defined to point to the Yahoo database of Web sites at Stanford University.

```
poly http://www.yahoo.com/yahoo/ 101,29 10,210 193,210
```

Circles

The circle setting for the HTTPS server defines a circle with center (*x*,*y*) and radius *r*, and the URL to jump to if the user clicks inside the circle. The HTTPS server defines the circle using the center point and the radius. The following is an example of a circle defined using an HTTPS server that points to Ventana Online, the publisher of this book.

```
circle (311,118) 92 http://www.vmedia.com/
```

The HTTPD server includes the URL between the circle setting and the coordinates defining the circle. The following is an example of a circle defined using the HTTPD server that points to Ventana Online, the publisher of this book.

```
circle http://www.vmedia.com/ 310,118 367,190
```

Rectangles

The HTTPS sever lets you abbreviate the rectangle setting to rect. It defines a rectangle with top left at (x0,y0) and bottom right at (x1,y1), and the URL to jump to if the user clicks inside the rectangle. The following is an example of a rectangle defined using the HTTPS server that points to the EINet Galaxy home page.

```
rect (449,29) (632,212) http://galaxy.einet.net/galaxy.html
```

The HTTPD server includes the URL before the definition of the rectangle. The following is an example of a rectangle that points to the EINet Galaxy home page.

```
rect http://galaxy.einet.net/galaxy.html 451,30 632,212
```

Using the ISMAP Tag

You identify an image map by the including the ISMAP attribute to the IMG element. The ISMAP attribute tells the browser to append the mouse coordinates to the URL and send it to the server. The anchor URL <A> must refer to an image map file on the HTTP server. The image map file is the file that contains the mapping of the hot spot coordinates so the user can just click the mouse to move to another URL. Without the ISMAP attribute, the mouse coordinates will not be sent.

To add the ISMAP attribute using HoTMetaL PRO, move the insertion point between the starting and ending IMG tags. Choose Markup>>Edit SGML Attributes. The Edit Attributes dialog box appears. Choose the ISMAP attribute. The raw HTML code for a real world example might appear as follows:

```
<IMG SRC="/images/shapes.gif" ISMAP>
```

The ISMAP attribute can also appear as

```
<IMG SRC="/images/shapes.gif" ISMAP="ISMAP">
```

The ISMAP attribute tells the browser that the image is an image map. The IMG element must be included in an anchor element to tell the browser where to send the request when the user clicks on the image. Clicking in the image causes the coordinates of the point on the image where the user clicks to be sent to the server, along with the URL specified in the anchor. An external image map processing program is usually started by the Web server to perform a mapping from the coordinates to another hypertext document.

Adding the Map to the HTTPD Configuration File

If you are using the HTTPD server, you need to add a setting to the image map configuration file (imagemap.cnf). This file is found in the httpd/conf directory. The imagemap.cnf file is a text file. You can add your map file to the existing map entries by using any text editor, such as Windows Notepad. The HTTPD image map program requires that your image map be included in the imagemap.cnf configuration file, or the image program will not work. The following example shows the addition of the map file, named win3imap.map, that we created using the mapedit program earlier in this chapter.

```
# Default imagemap.cnf
#
# -Casey Barton
#
imapdemo : c:\httpd\conf\maps\imapdemo.map
wizflow : c:\httpd\conf\maps\wizflow.map
win3imap: c:\httpd\conf\maps\win3imap.map
```

Surrounding the Image With the Anchor

Whether you're using the EMWAC HTTPS server or Robert Denny's HTTPD server, you need to insert the IMG tags inside an anchor. The HREF is going to be different for both these servers. If you're using the HTTPD server, you need to include the path to the image map program. Notice in the following example that after the imagemap.exe program there is a forward slash. A forward slash typically is used to identify a subdirectory. In this case, however, the *win3imap* is not really a subdirectory, but specifies to the image map program, which is the name of the map entry in the configuration file you want to use. Leave this out and the image map program will not know what to look for in the imagemap.cnf file.

```
<A HREF=/cgi-win/imagemap.exe/win3imap><IMG
SRC="images/3balls.gif" ISMAP></IMG></A>
```

The EMWAC HTTPS server doesn't require you to use a program and configuration file to identify the map file. Instead you specify the map file in the HREF attribute of the anchor surrounding the IMG tags. The following is an example of how to specify the location of the image map using the HTTPS server.

```
<A HREF="ntimap.map"><IMG SRC="shapes.gif"
ISMAP="ISMAP"></A>
```

In order for your image map to work, you must test it over the Net with the server started. You must use the URL for your site to test the image map, you cannot test an image map locally.

Moving On

Graphics can be powerful tools for conveying information about you and your company. But images are only one way of communicating. The upcoming Web wave is multimedia publishing. The next chapter takes a look at the multimedia possibilities the Web brings to publishing and ways you can catch the wave.

8

Adding Scintillating Sound & Vivid Video

If you want to show off your computer to your friends, most likely you'll pull up a sound or video file that takes full advantage of your PC's multimedia capabilities. It's little wonder then that many Web publishers are trying to impress their readers by pushing multimedia to the extreme. Many record labels, movie studios, TV and radio stations and bands have discovered the benefits of using the Web to gain exposure by including sound and video clips.

While multimedia is an enticing way to get noticed, it is not without its drawbacks. The biggest drawbacks are the size of the bandwidth and the disk space that are required by multimedia files. Limited bandwidth is a major problem that TV and telephone companies are fighting to overcome. Software publishers are investing lots of time and money to create powerful multimedia authoring tools. Many software publishers and hardware companies are creating and improving sound and video file formats so they can capture the multimedia publishing market. True multimedia on the Internet may be around the corner, but it's a big corner. This chapter explains the standard sound and video file formats found on the Web and provides solutions for creating and presenting sound and video files.

Publishing Sound Files

The low price of sound cards and the surge in multimedia-compatible computers has made the addition of sounds to Web documents commonplace. Web browsers, such as Netscape Navigator and Mosaic, can play some sound files directly off the Web and let users specify helper applications to play additional sound and video files. The latest version of Netscape Navigator, which is included on the Companion CD-ROM, comes bundled with a sound player.

While you can add a sound file that will be heard by most of your readers, digitizing sounds is still a fairly new technology. Downloading and playing large sound files can be a time-consuming, often awkward, and computer-intensive operation. Sound files can easily exceed one megabyte in size for each minute of playing time. If you include hyperlinks to sound files on your pages, be sure the sound clips are relevant to your mission. You may be asking a reader to devote a lot of time and hard disk space to get the sound, so don't disappoint them.

Sound File Formats

One of the issues surrounding any emerging technology is the flood of different formats. Seemingly, every hardware manufacturer has developed its own way to record and play sound files, and each of these needs its own software program to get the sound to the speaker. Fortunately, you don't need to become a master of formats to place sound files in your documents. The maze of standards has settled down a bit on the Internet. The following sections explain the most standard sound file formats on the Web, including Audio (AU), used by Sun workstations; AIFF, used by Macintoshes; and Microsoft's Waveform (WAV) format, used by PCs.

Occasionally you will come across files in other formats. For example, you may see files in .voc or .iff format. The .voc stands for voice and is the default format for the SoundBlaster card. The .iff file format typically refers to an Amiga sound file. These are not standard formats on the Internet and should be avoided. Converting .voc files is explained later in this chapter.

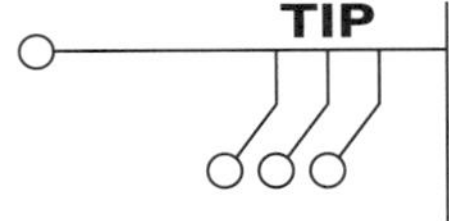

If you are interested in learning about sound file formats, compression schemes and other technical sound-related information, enter the URL: ftp://ftp.cwi.nl/pub/audio/AudioFormats/ and get the FAQ files titled Audio Formats.part1 and Audio Formats.part2. You can find the same information by entering the URL: ftp://rtfm.mit.edu/pub/usenet/news.answers/audio-fmts/.

The Sun Audio (AU) Sound Format

The most popular sound format and the only truly cross-platform sound format on the Web is the Sun Audio format. There are a couple of other names for this file format, specifically Ulaw, mUlaw, and Sun/NeXT. Sun Audio (AU) files end with the extension .au, but an AU file can sometimes be stored with the extension .snd. This is not to say that all files ending with .snd are AU files. In fact, a popular file format for Macintosh sound files also uses the .snd extension.

There are several types of encoding for AU files. Sun Audio files usually are 16-bit compressed files, but most sound files stored on the Internet are 8-bit Ulaw. Eight-bit sound files are the norm because they produce an acceptable audio quality and save bandwidth and disk space—important factors for publishing multimedia files on the Net. Most commercial Windows sound editors don't support the AU format, but many shareware sound editors do. GoldWave, which is included on the Companion CD-ROM, can play and edit files in the AU format.

The Waveform (WAV) Sound Format

Waveform is the standard sound file format for Microsoft Windows. Waveform files end with the .wav extension. Actually, Waveform is a subset of Microsoft's less popular Resource Interchange File Format (RIFF). This is why you see the Waveform format grouped with the RIFF file format option in some sound editors. Waveform files can be saved as stereo or mono in 8-bit or 16-bit audio files. If you publish files in the Waveform (WAV) format, it is likely that Windows users will be the only people listening. In most cases, you'll want to save or convert the file to the AU format (see "Converting Sound Files," later in this chapter for more information).

The Audio Interchange File Format (AIFF)

Developed by Apple, the Audio Interchange File Format (AIFF) and AIFC/MACE formats are Macintosh sound formats. The C in AIFC and MACE stands for compression. AIFF files end with the .aif extension or sometimes with .iff. The AIFF file format is also the sound standard for Silicon Graphics workstations, such as the SGI Indy. Many audio players for different platforms can play AIFF files. For example, most Windows shareware sound players and editors, such as GoldWave and WHAM (Waveform Hold And Modify), and PLAYANY (Windows Play Any File) can play AIFF files.

The MPEG Audio Format

MPEG stands for the Moving Pictures Experts Group, an organization that develops standards for digital video and audio compression. In simple terms, MPEG audio files are compressed using a *lossy* compression algorithm that removes frequencies that the human ear can't hear. This makes the file a lot smaller and easier to transport. The compression is about 6:1. MPEG audio files usually end with the extension .mp2. The quality of the sound file can be determined by the number of masked frequencies, and can

range from pitiful to high-quality CD sound. Recording and playing MPEG audio files requires an MPEG standards-compliant software program.

MPEG audio and video files are very different, and each requires its own player. See "The MPEG Video Format" in this chapter for information on the MPEG video standard.

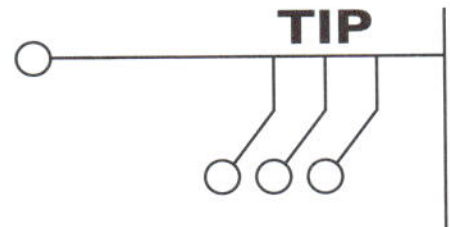

Shareware MPEG audio players are available, but MPEG audio recorders are most often distributed commercially. Xing Technologies has provided a shareware MPEG audio player, which is available from ftp://ftp.iuma.com/audio_utils/mpeg_players/Windows/. The file is named mpgaudio.exe.

Including Sound Files in a Web Page

To include a reference to a sound, use the same format you would use with any hyperlink text or image. The only difference is the extension of the file that you are pointing to. For example, a link to a sound file uses the following syntax:

```
<A HREF = URL/soundfile.au>hyperlink</A>
```

The URL would be the location of the file, including its full path. The soundfile.au is the name of the sound file. Here's an example of a hyperlink to a sound file that includes alternative text for a text-based browser:

```
<A HREF = http://sunsite.unc.edu/pub/multimedia/sun-
sounds/sound_effects/splat.au ALT="[SND]">splat</A>
```

It's best to publish sound files in the AU format, so others can play the file directly from the browser. If you use another file format, the file will have to be downloaded and loaded in an external helper application.

You may want to point to a sound file that is published at some other site, because of space limitations on your host or other reasons. A little caution should be exercised if you decide to do this, because external files may be changed without your knowledge. If you include the link, check occasionally to make sure the sound file is still available.

If you want to create an archive of sound files, be sure to identify the sound file with an icon that denotes a sound file, such as a speaker, a note or an ear. The following is an example of a local sound file in a directory named "sounds" identified by an icon named speaker.gif in the icons directory.

```
<IMG SRC="/icons/speaker.gif" ALT="[SND]"> <A HREF=
"/sounds/splat.au">splat.au</A>
```

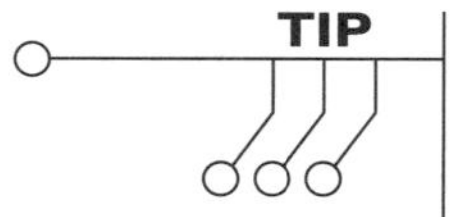

Make sure your intended audience has the necessary players. If there is a question as to whether or not your audience can listen to your sound files, refer them to the location of a player.

Acquiring Sound Files

Just as there are companies that sell clip art and digitized photos, there are also companies that sell sound files. Short, pre-edited sound clips that are designed for multimedia productions are sometimes called *bumpers*. The quality of sound files is sadly lacking in many sound-clip collections. Sound Choice from Cambium Development is a collection that provides quality bumpers and music files. Sound Choice offers CDs with 25 to 30 selections of music files in different styles, such as classical, jazz, Latin, new age and more. The files are stored in the Waveform, midi and CD audio formats. The selections are performed by accomplished studio musicians and mixed using state-of-the-art recording equipment. You can request a free sampler CD called Sound Choice Lite from Cambium (800-231-1779 or 914-472-6246), which includes 23 sound clips. Another quality sound-clip company is Prosonus, which sells MusicBytes, a CD with over a hundred sound and music files.

Multimedia program suites typically include numerous sample sound files. For example, Ulead's Media Studio and HSC InterActive are low cost (under $200) multimedia program suites that include a sound editor and come bundled with over a hundred sound clips.

Many sites on the Web include sound files. The problem is that many are poor quality clips and it's sometimes hard to tell which ones break copyright laws—use audio files from the Internet at your own risk. Of course, you can always create a link to a sound in an archive. The following is a list of sites that include sound clips on the Web. Just because we have listed these sites doesn't mean that you can publish them at your Web site. However, you may want to experiment with the sound files even if you don't add any of them to your Web pages.

URL	Description
http://ns2.rutgers.edu/sounds/	Bob Mende's collection of AU files. Sound files are organized into directories. Some of the sound files include music and quotes from movies, animal sounds, cartoons, Monty Python routines, telephone noises and sounds from *Star Trek* shows.
http://www.acm.uiuc.edu/rml/Sounds/	A large collection of AU sounds, many from movies and cartoons such as *Roger Rabbit, Ren and Stimpy, Beavis and Butthead*. The site includes other clips, such as computer sounds, dinosaur noises, Monty Python routines, music, quotes, Christmas sounds and other sound effects.
http://sunsite.unc.edu/pub/multimedia/sun-sounds/	The University of North Carolina at Chapel Hill has numerous sound files in the AU format, including bird calls, cartoons, comedy, commercials, computer sounds, Monty Python routines, movies, clips from *Star Trek* and *Star Trek the Next Generation*, sayings, screams, sound tracks, TV, whales and other sound effects. Some sounds in the Waveform format are stored in a directory named PC Sounds.

http://www.cmf.nrl.navy.mil/radio/byte_RTFM.html	A short sound bite is added to this site just about every day. Most are single words or short phrases. Many are computer related.
http://web.msu.edu/vincent/general.html	The MSU Vincent Voice Library collection of AU sound bites of famous individuals, such as Isaac Asimov, George Washington Carver, Amelia Earhart, Betty Ford, Will Rogers and Babe Ruth.
http://www.eecs.nwu.edu/~jmyers/sun_sounds/	Miscellaneous sound files in the AU format, such as a bark, bong, bubbles, birds chirping, cowbell, crash, cuckoo, doorbell, drip, flush, gong, laugh, ring, rooster, space music, splat and several telephone sounds.
http://155.187.10.12:80/sounds/	Assorted bird calls from a cockatoo to a spinebill.

Table 8-1: *URL's for sound files.*

You can also find sound files in a few newsgroups such as the newsgroup *alt.binaries.sound*. These sound files are often posted in a binary format, and will have to be decoded with a program similar to uudecode, before the clip can be played on a computer. The sound files posted in this newsgroup change daily. Most of the postings are multi-part files that have to be assembled before decoding. If you have a news reader that can put the parts together for you, such as the text-based tin newsreader program or WinVN, this is a simple operation. If you're not using one of these programs, prepare yourself for some aggravation and read the newsgroup's FAQ (Frequently Asked Questions) file.

Sound Editors & Tools

Recording digitized sounds is sometimes referred to as *sampling*. Sampling and editing sound files is a fairly straightforward process. Most sound cards, such as the highly rated MultiSound Monterey from Turtle Beach, the standard SoundBlaster from Creative Labs, and SoundBlaster compatible sound cards, such as Media Vision Pro Audio Studio, all come with software for creating and editing sound files. The better the card and the sound editing software, the better the results. On the low end, Windows comes with the Sound Recorder, which lets you create, mix and edit sound files with special effects, such as echo or reverse. The Sound Recorder only lets you record one minute at a time. You can cut and paste sound clips together, but you'll be much happier working with a high-end sound editor.

If you want to manipulate a sound file and don't have a sound editor, check out the GoldWave shareware sound editor that comes on the Companion CD-ROM. Figure 8-1 shows the GoldWave sound editor with a sound file loaded. You can check for updates at http://web.cs.mun.ca/~chris3/goldwave/.

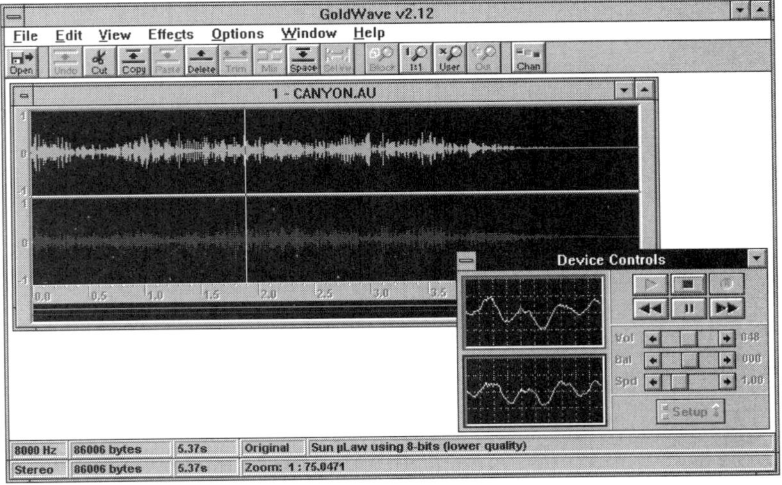

Figure 8-1: *The GoldWave sound editor lets you create and edit sound files in both the AU and WAV formats.*

Creating Sound Files

The ability to create a sound file, and the quality of that file once created, depends on the capabilities of your equipment. The sound file is recorded on a platform such as a PC using a virtual soundboard and one or more input devices, such as a microphone, tape deck or keyboard. It's safest to record the sound and use the Export or Save As feature to save the file in the Sun Audio (.au) format. Depending on your audience, you may want to use Microsoft's Waveform, Apple's AIFF format or the MPEG audio (.mp2) format. The following sections explain some terms and procedures related to sampling and editing sound files.

Sampling Rates

Most sound cards today are 16-bit or higher, but there is a huge installed base of 8-bit sound cards. The more bits, the better the audio quality. Eight-bit sampling lets you define 256 steps in the signal. Sixteen-bit sampling provides 65,536 steps. Some sites post sound files in two different formats (levels of quality), leaving the choice up to the reader. If the reader wants a high-quality sample, such as a 16-bit stereo file, it can be downloaded. If the reader does not have the time or the equipment to benefit from this quality, a much smaller rendering of the same file is often offered in a more compact format, such as an 8-bit mono sound file.

Sound editors let you choose a sampling rate. *Sampling rate* refers to the frequency at which the sound is recorded. Figure 8-2 shows the GoldWave sound editor's sample rates list box. The higher the sampling rate, the closer the sound file is to the original sound. The unit of measurement for the frequency of a sound is a *hertz* and is abbreviated Hz. Frequencies that can be heard by the human ear are typically in the range of 15 Hz to 20,000 Hz. If you're just including speech, you can keep the sampling rate to 4,000-8000 Hz. A sound can be in the range of 11,025 to 22,025 Hz. If you want to include music, you should use a sample rate of at least 22,025 Hz.

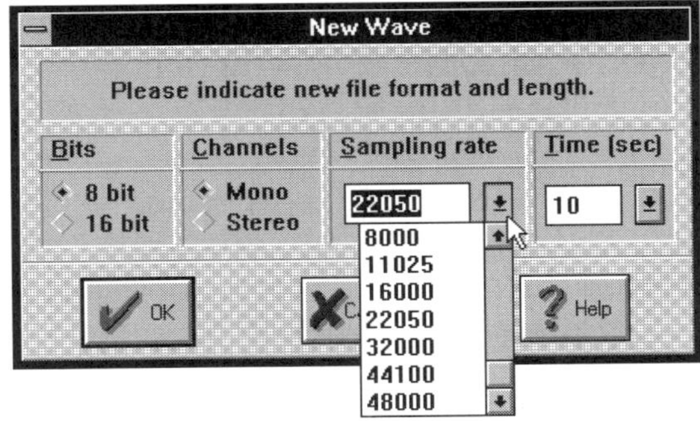

Figure 8-2: *GoldWave sound editor displays sample rates.*

Be careful when including sound files in your Web pages. If you record a file in stereo at a high sampling rate, the file can grow to an immense size, frustrating your readers when they download it. This is especially bad form if the sound file is not of a type that demands a high-quality recording, like a voice transcription. The converse is true as well. A poor-quality sound sample is a bad advertisement for you and your business.

Editing & Controlling Sound

Sound editors represent sound visually, so you can cut and paste portions of the visual representation of the sound or insert silence in your sound file. Just as you can use filters in a graphic editing package to achieve different results, there are sound filters that let you control sound output. Editing software uses digital signal processing (DSP) algorithms to present tools and filters for controlling sounds, such as fades, delays, reverb, blending and equalizing sounds, adding distortion and other special effects.

Editing sound files requires a great deal of precision. Some sound editors include an SMPTE time code. This is like the fast clocks that appear at the bottom of professional videos to help locate exact moments to cut. SMPTE time codes are extremely helpful when you are trying to synchronize two pieces of music.

You will most likely want additional features for working with sounds if you will be creating a video or animation. An advantage of some digital sound editors is that you can expand or compress the amount of time a sound file fills. This is a powerful feature when you have a video that is 15 seconds and your audio is 20 seconds long. For example, Wave for Windows, a Waveform sound editor from Turtle Beach Software lets you mark a block of audio output and compress or expand the marked block and choose one of three levels of accuracy. Figure 8-3 shows the time compression and expansion feature found in Wave for Windows.

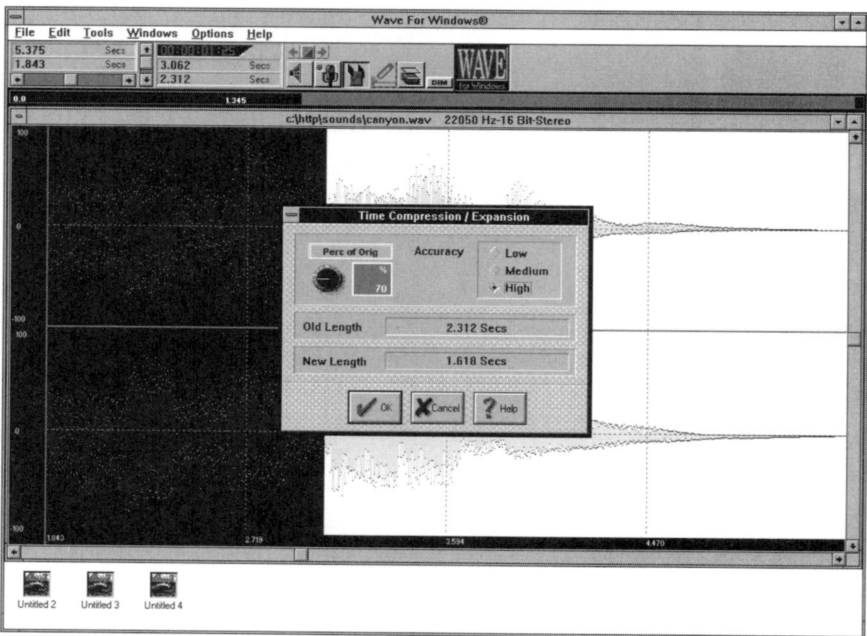

Figure 8-3: *Wave for Windows lets you compress or expand marked blocks of a sound file.*

What if you want to replace the sound in a video? Access Softek's Sound-Track is an AVI/WAV sound editing package that lets you remove, replace and mix WAV audio tracks in an AVI video file. The Sound-Track CD includes hundreds of sample AVI and WAV files and lists for less than $50. This is a great tool for adding sound-overs to a video.

Converting Sound Files

In order to convert a WAV file to the standard AU format, the file can be "translated" into the language of another sound format by using one of the many widely available shareware programs, such as GoldWave and WHAM. By saving or exporting the file in the AU format, you can be assured that everyone who has a computer with sound capability will be able to hear it. In most cases, you will want to use the sound editor's Export or Save As option to convert sound files from one format to another. Another less friendly conversion alternative is to use a DOS program called SOX (Sound Exchange). SOX lets you convert a sound file to a different audio format. You can pick up a PC version of SOX at ftp://ftp.cwi.nl/pub/audio/sox10dos.zip.

Creative Labs' SoundBlaster cards are the most popular sound cards for the PC. SoundBlaster has its own sound file format that ends with the extension .voc. If you have a SoundBlaster file you want to publish, you can convert it to the Sun AU format using a DOS-based program named sunvoc.exe. You can download the conversion program from Creative Labs' FTP site by entering the following URL: ftp://ftp.creaf.com/pub/creative/files/misc/sunvoc.exe.

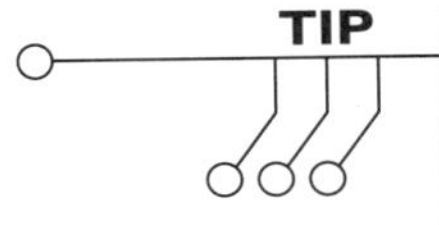

Shareware offerings change rapidly. To check for the latest shareware sound editor releases, use one of the following URLs: ftp://ftp.ncsa.uiuc.edu/PC/Windows/Mosaic/viewers/ or ftp://gatekeeper.dec.com/pub/micro/msdos/win3/sounds/.

Publishing Video

Video has had an accelerated childhood and is quickly entering adolescence. In its current state, video is going through serious growing pains. It's awkward and unruly, but there is a world of promise for video. The following sections take a look at the video compression/decompression and file format standards and explain what you need to create and publish video files at your Web site.

Video Codecs & File Format Standards

As you enter the realm of digital video, you will undoubtedly encounter the term *codec*, which stands for a compression/decompression algorithm used to compress and decompress video files. In order for a video to play smoothly, it needs to playback at 30 frames per second. A single frame of 24-bit video in its uncompressed state can require as much as a megabyte of disk space. That means that one second of uncompressed video is approximately 30 MB. There are solutions to this heavy data load, such as reducing the number of colors or the size of the video, or even removing frames from the video, but all of these methods diminish the quality of digital video. The need then is to find a standard codec that can compress the data to a manageable size so that it can be sent across the Internet without a noticeable loss in quality when decompressed and played back. Video files are the largest files you'll likely come across on the Internet. Some Web sites we've seen have published video files of over 12 MB.

MPEG and QuickTime are the two video file format standards on the Internet. As more and more PCs enter the Internet scene, it is likely that the standard Windows AVI file format will also squeeze in between these formats. The following sections explain the most popular codecs and video file formats that have become Internet standards.

The MPEG Video Format

MPEG gets its name from the Motion Picture Experts Group. One confusing point about the term MPEG is that while it is a codec, it is also used to refer to the file format. Actually, two types of MPEG codec standards exist: MPEG-1 and MPEG-2. MPEG-1 is the standard used on the Internet. MPEG-2 is a high-end broadcast-quality video standard. MPEG-1 videos use a resolution of 352 x 240 at 30 frames per second. In order to view an MPEG video at 30 frames per second, the person must be using a video board that includes a MPEG decoder chip. MPEG decoder chips are quickly being added to graphic boards. An MPEG file typically ends with the file-name extension .mpg. MPEG uses something called *predictive calculation* for compression. This method uses the current frame of video to predict what will be in the following frames. *This method of compression makes editing an MPEG video impossible.*

MPEG compresses and decompresses images and audio sounds at the same fast speed. It is the speed and ultra-high compression that have made MPEG the format of choice for video on the Internet. MPEG delivers decompressed data at 1.2 to 1.5 mb per second and compresses at a ratio of 50:1 or higher before you start to notice a degradation in video playback. Compression ratios as high as 200:1 are possible, but at compression rates this high, unless you are using high-quality hardware, the images are degraded. MPEG has the highest level of compression and delivers the best quality video when decompressed. It sounds great, so far, but this is only one frame of the MPEG video picture. MPEG is typically hardware-based compression. The biggest drawback is that the compression hardware is expensive. The cost of creating a video in the MPEG format is covered later in this chapter.

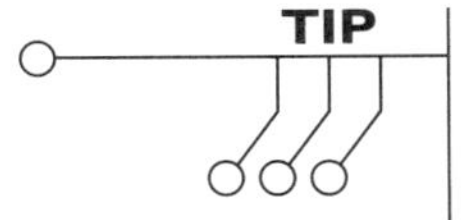

You can download an MPEG player (mpeg32wg.zip for the 32-bit version or mpgwin.zip for the 16-bit version) at the following site: ftp://gatekeeper.dec.com/pub/micro/msdos/win3/desktop/.

The QuickTime Format

Developed by the folks at Apple, QuickTime movies may contain any combination of video, sound, animation, audio, MIDI, text and even interactive commands. QuickTime is sometimes referred to as the movie format. Appropriately, QuickTime movie files typically end with the file-name extension .mov. Unlike files in the MPEG format, QuickTime files can be edited. QuickTime supports several codec schemes, including Photo (JPEG), Animation and Graphics, Apple Video, Cinepak, Indeo 3.2, MPEG, YUV, the Kodak Photo, CD and more. Each of these compressors is designed for a specific data type. Until recently you had to use a Macintosh to create QuickTime files, but now you can use programs like Adobe Premiere for Windows to create and edit video files in the QuickTime format. Autodesk Animator can also create QuickTime compatible animations.

QuickTime is a Macintosh file format, which consists of a different structure than PC files. The main issue for QuickTime files is that there are two file forks, a resource fork and a data fork, that must be combined into one file in order to be displayed and edited on the PC platform. The process of converting QuickTime files so they can be used on other platforms is called *flattening*. A cross-platform QuickTime file is sometimes referred to as a flattened QuickTime file. Flattening a QuickTime file consolidates the video and audio into a single file.

The newest version of Apple's QuickTime player for Windows (2.0) is not available on the Internet. The QuickTime player is commercial software, but that doesn't mean you can buy it as a standalone package. For now, Apple is making version 2.0 available by bundling it with third-party products that support QuickTime for Windows, such as movie clip libraries, and software applications, such as Adobe Premiere for Windows. QuickTime Version 2.0 is also available on the CompuServe network in the Apple Developer's Forum for less than $10. Another way you can get a version of QuickTime for Windows is by purchasing the QuickTime Development Kit for Windows. You can download the previous version 1.1 of QuickTime for Windows (qt11.zip) at http://www.ncsa.uiuc.edu/SDG/Software/WinMosaic/viewers/qt.htm.

The AVI Format

The Audio/Video Interleaved (AVI) format is Microsoft's format for video and audio. As the name of the format implies, the video data is interleaved with audio data within the same file, so the audio portion of the movie is synchronized with the video portion. AVI uses Intel's Indeo and the Cinepack codecs, which have been getting a lot of publicity lately. AVI files typically play at about 15 frames per second in a small window (320 x 240 pixels). With acceleration hardware or software, you can run AVI video sequences at 30 frames per second in a larger window or full screen. The AVI format accesses data from the hard disk without using great amounts of memory. It's quick loading and playing, because only a few frames of video and a portion of audio are accessed at a time. AVI files are also compressed to boost the quality of your video sequences and reduce their size.

While AVI format is the standard Windows video file format, it is rare to find AVI files on the Internet. This is likely to change as the user base changes to reflect the huge number of Windows users jacking into the Internet.

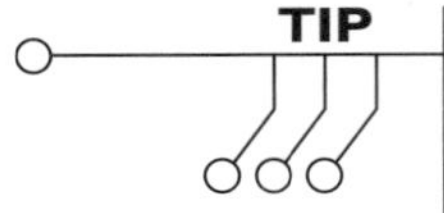

You can download a Video for Windows player (avivie42.zip) at ftp://gatekeeper.dec.com/pub/micro/msdos/win3/desktop/. The runtime version of MS Video For Windows (vfw11a.exe) is available at ftp://ftp.microsoft.com/developr/drg/multimedia/.

How Much Is That MPEG in the Window?

If you're excited by the prospect of including MPEG video clips at your site, you might want to brace yourself before reading the following. In order for you to produce a top-quality MPEG video clip, you'll need a hardware encoder that runs at least $4,000. Actually there is only one $4,000 MPEG encoder board, named the Producer, recently released by Sigma Designs. Sigma Designs also created the Reel Magic board, which was the first MPEG decoder board that can play back full screen MPEG video. Sigma was one of the first companies to offer a video card, named Rave, that includes an MPEG decoder chip. Sigma should be shipping the Producer as you read this.

Other MPEG encoder boards are much more expensive. MPEG Lab Pro from Optibase, for example, is around $19,000, and Prime View from Future Tel is around $14,000. This is too expensive for most Web publishers. The following sections present a couple of solutions that are much less expensive than purchasing an encoder board.

The Producer from Sigma Designs is more than an MPEG encoder. It takes a unique approach to make MPEG files editable. Sigma Designs worked with Microsoft to create an MPEG file format that can be edited with any AVI compatible video editor. The Producer adds a header to an MPEG file so that it can be read and edited as an AVI file by a video editing program like Adobe Premiere. The AVI Editable MPEG format can be edited only at certain places in the video called I-frames. Producer is bundled with a software video tape recorder controller (VTR), Adobe Premiere and the trueSpace 3D graphics and animation program. When you work with an AVI Editable MPEG file it can only be compressed to a 50:1 ratio. Once the file is ready for publication, it can be compressed using MPEG compression up to a 200:1 ratio.

The Service Bureau Solution

Some service bureaus will take a VHS/Beta videotape or a file in a format such as AVI or QuickTime and convert it to MPEG format for you. This price can range from $30 to $300 a minute. Most service bureaus are used to working with videotape. Converting files to the MPEG format is relatively new, so don't be surprised if the service bureau requires you to use videotape. Some service bureaus require a minimum order, usually around three minutes. It pays to shop around. To find a service bureau check the back of magazines like *DV Digital Video, PC Graphics and Video* or *New Media*. There are always ads for service bureaus that can encode MPEG files. The Resources section lists a few MPEG encoder services.

The Software Solution

Another way to use MPEG video clips at your site is to use a software encoder. For example, a company called Xing makes XingCD, a software encoder for Windows. Xing CD comes with an MPEG video and audio player. To use XingCD you need a video capture board. FAST's Movie Machine Pro, for example, is a video capture board that includes a bundled version of XingCD that is specific to the board.

After capturing your video, you can add effects with products such as Adobe Premiere or Ulead's Media Studio. You can also include still formats, such as BMP and TGA (Targa). Additionally, you can capture and edit audio in Waveform (WAV) or MPEG audio format. XingCD compresses the audio and video files and interleaves them to create an MPEG stream. Figure 8-4 shows the XingCD program.

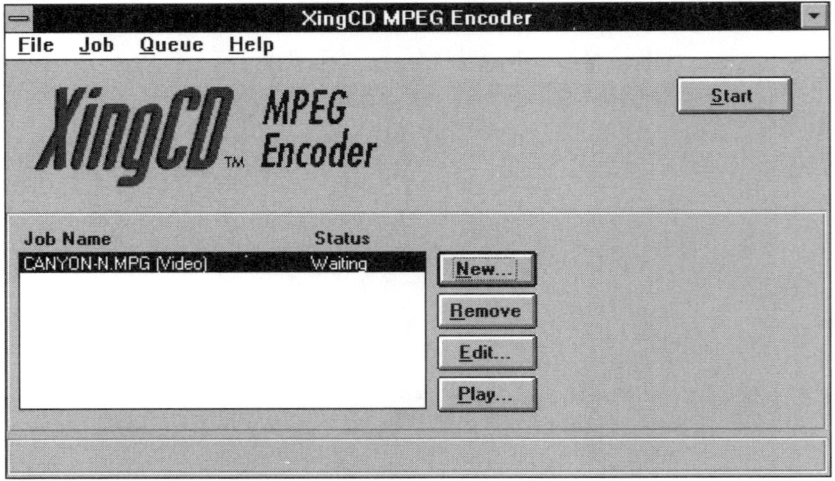

Figure 8-4: *XingCD is a software-based solution to MPEG encoding.*

If you plan on using XingCD to convert an AVI file, be sure to save the file at 30 frames per second in a 24-bit format. This requires at least a 486 PC and a state-of-the-art video capture board, such as FAST's Movie Machine Pro or Intel's Smart Video Recorder Pro. You also need to make sure you have optimized your memory and defragmented your hard disk. If you don't have enough memory or your disk drive is fragmented, you may get a freeze in the video stream. Be aware that using XingCD to encode a file to the MPEG format is a time-consuming process. An incredible amount of calculations have to be performed to compress the video. XingCD can take over one and a half hours to encode one minute of MPEG output using a video in the AVI file format as the source.

Acquiring Video Files

The safest way to present a video file at your site is to create one yourself or use a royalty-free video clip. First Light Productions and Four Palms are two companies that sell royalty-free video clips. Both of these companies are included in the Resource section at the back of this book. There are also lots of archives of videos on the Internet. As with audio files, some problems arise when using video files on the Internet. For one, many video files are of poor quality. Another problem is that it's sometimes hard to tell which videos break copyright laws. Use videos from the Internet at your own risk. Of course you can always create a link to a video in an archive. Table 8-2 lists and describes sites that include video clip files on the Web. As we mentioned in the section on sounds, just because we have listed these sites doesn't mean that you can publish them at your Web site. However, you may want to experiment with videos even if you don't add any of them to your Web pages. Working with an existing QuickTime or AVI video is a way to save time when you are becoming familiar with a video editing program.

URL	Contents
http://www.yahoo.com/yahoo/computers/multimedia/Movies/Archives	A listing of multimedia archives brought to you by Stanford University.
http://www.eeb.ele.tue.nl/mpeg/index.html	Lots of MPEG movies and animations. Several clips break copyright laws, such as videos of *The Simpsons* and popular movies. The list is broken into categories including supermodels, animations, music, space, racing and so on.
http://www.acm.uiuc.edu/rml/	Rob Malick's multimedia lab sponsored by the Association for Computing Machinery at University of Illinois includes lots of movie clips in FLI and QuickTime format.
http://tausq.resnet.cornell.edu/mmedia.html	Randolph Chung's archive of movie clips, including such copyright breakers as Disney's *Aladdin*, *The Lion King* and *StarTrek*.
http://ice.ucdavis.edu/whimsy/fun_stuff/fun_stuff_movies.html	Sample movie clips and links to Harvey Chinn's movie archive list.
http://mambo.ucsc.edu/psl/thant/thant.html	Thant Nyo's huge list of links to computer generated animations, visualizations, movies and interactive images.
www.univ-rennes1.fr/ASTRO/anim-e.html	Astronomy clips, such as planets, eclipses, rocket launches, astronauts in orbit and clips from science fiction films.
http://wwwzenger.informatik.tu-muenchen.de/persons/paula/mpeg/index.html	Andreas Paul's collection of various MPEG animations, such as a scene from Pink Floyd's *The Wall*, *Blade Runner* and *Psycho*. The site includes a disclaimer requesting the videos be used for personal use only.

Table 8-2: *URLs for video files.*

Including Video Files in a Web Page

To include a hyperlink to a video, use the same format you would use with a sound file. The only difference is the extension of the file that you are pointing to. For example, a link to a video file uses the following syntax:

```
<A HREF = URL/canyon.mov>hyperlink</A>
```

The URL is the location of the file, including its full path. The canyon.mov is the name of the video file. Here's an example of a hyperlink to an MPEG video file that includes alternative text for a text-based browser:

```
<A HREF = http://www.acm.uiuc.edu/rml/Mpeg/
simpsons1.mpg ALT="[MPEG]">Meet the Simpsons</A>
```

Publish video files in the QuickTime or MPEG format, so others can play the file directly from the browser. If you use another file format, the file will have to be downloaded and loaded in an external helper application.

You may want to point to a video file that is published at some other site, because of space limitations on your host or other reasons. A little caution should be exercised if you decide to do this, because external files may be changed without your knowledge. If you include the link, check occasionally to make sure the video file is still available.

If you want to create an archive of video files, be sure to identify the video file with an icon that denotes what type of file it is, such as a camera, a filmstrip or an eye. The following is an example of a local video file named canyon.mov in a directory named videos identified by an icon named camera.gif in the icons directory.

```
<IMG SRC="/icons/camera.gif" ALT="[GIF Logo]"> <A
HREF="/video/canyon.mov">Canyon Sofware's Logo</A>
```

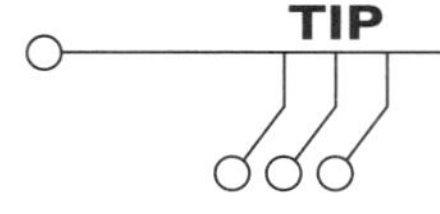

Make sure your intended audience has the necessary players. If there is a question as to whether or not your audience can view your video files, refer them to the location of a player.

Video Editors

There are several programs that let you edit video. If you want to work with video files in the AVI format, Microsoft's Video for Windows is a standard video editing program that is bundled with many Windows video capture boards. Make sure you're using Video for Windows 1.1. The previous version of Video for Windows was abominably slow. Version 1.1 will be the last version of Video for Windows. Microsoft has announced that the next version of Video for Windows will be built into the long-awaited release of Windows 95. Figure 8-5 shows the Video for Windows editor Video.

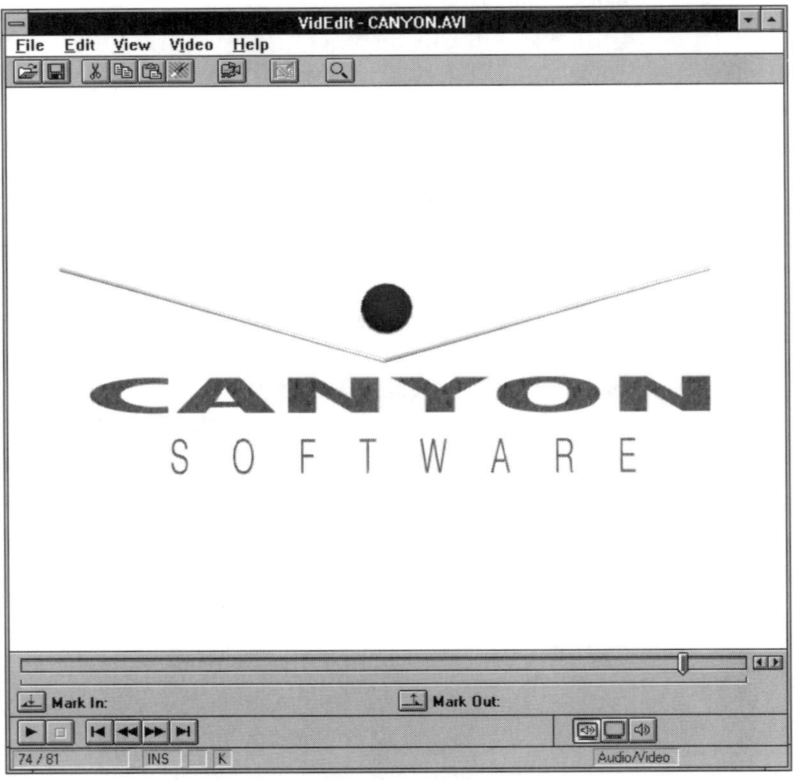

Figure 8-5: *The Video for Windows video editor.*

Macintosh users cannot view AVI files. In most cases, you will want to save your files in QuickTime format. If you want to work with QuickTime, and you should, check out Adobe Premiere. Adobe Premiere presents a construction window, so you can easily edit multiple video tracks and add audio tracks. Working with multiple tracks can be helpful especially when working with transitions between two video clips, which is commonly referred to as an *A/B roll*. Adobe Premiere lets you work with multiple AVI, QuickTime, video files and other file formats. Adobe Premiere includes numerous special effects, such as blends and transitions from one scene to another. It even includes *keying*, which lets you superimpose one video on top of another. Keying is the process used by your friendly TV weather reporter, who points out temperatures on a Chroma key weather map. Another powerful feature is *rotoscoping*, which lets you draw or paint on video frames to add animations to an existing video. You can also combine titles, sounds and graphic images. We have worked with Premiere 4.0 under Windows NT without any problems. Figure 8-6 shows an Adobe Premiere window for creating a QuickTime video.

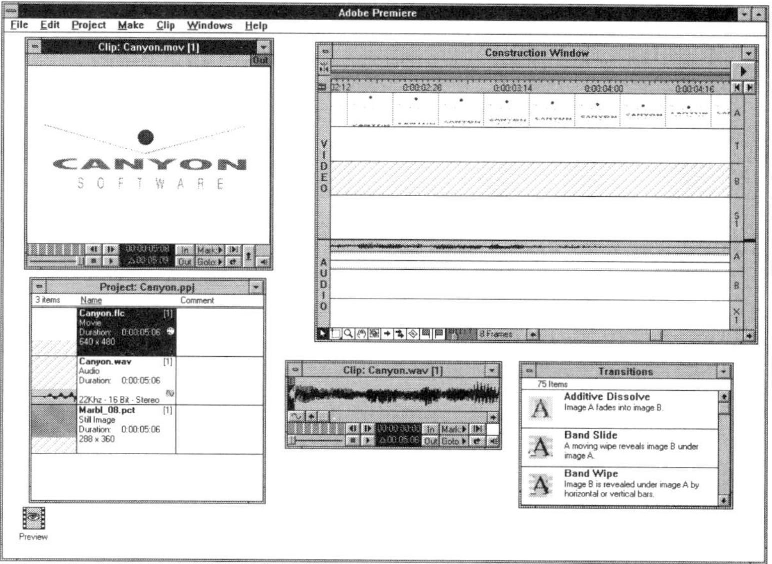

Figure 8-6: *Adobe Premiere lets you work with different file formats and can save files in the QuickTime format.*

Two less expensive programs that offer a lot of bang for the buck are Media Studio from Ulead Systems and InterActive from HSC. Each of these programs includes over 100 mb worth of video clips. Currently both programs are Windows 3.*x* programs that don't work under Windows NT.

Another video-related program that is receiving a lot of press and getting support on the Web is Director for Windows from Macromedia. This is an animation and multimedia program that has been fawned over by Macintosh multimedia authors for some time. Director is not a video editor; instead it is a multimedia authoring package that lets you create standalone programs for multimedia presentations. Director can work with both AVI videos and QuickTime movies. It uses a metaphor of a stage where you work with text, sound, graphics and video clips.

To add interactivity to a video, you use an English-like scripting language called Lingo. You can save your output as a video or a run-time module. There is no run-time royalty fee, although you need to let people know that it is a Macromedia file. It is recommended that if you create a video you save it in QuickTime format since Mac users will then be able to play your movie. A viewer for Windows Director files is available on the Internet. The Director Viewer, developed by Dave Walker, allows you to view Director files, just like an MPEG viewer, off the Net. This viewer doesn't work with Windows NT. You can pick up the viewer at http://www.portal.com/~dwalker/dirhome.html.

To visit a collection of Web pages devoted to Director, enter the URL: http://hakatai.mcli.dist.maricopa.edu/director/index.html.

Capturing Video

The process of digitizing video signals, like the process of capturing audio, is called *sampling*. In order to sample a video, you will need to get a video capture board. It is almost impossible to buy a video capture board that doesn't come with video recording and editing software. There are lots of video capture boards and video editing packages on the market, but only a few that produce quality results. Let us tell you up front that setting up a video capture board can be a daunting task. Many video capture boards require you to select one or more IRQ settings and unique memory addresses, which can be a time-consuming task.

The Movie Machine Pro from FAST is one of the best video bundles you're likely to find. It includes a TV tuner, audio support, and comes bundled with Adobe Premiere, Animator Pro, Video for Windows and XingCD. The bundle also includes an M-JPEG board that lets you capture and play back video at 30 frames per second (fps). This is a great collection of tools for capturing video and creating animation files. Most video capture boards, like the Movie Machine Pro, let you connect to a VCR so you can grab frames and edit to overlay images and titles. The only drawback is that the capture boards can be difficult to set up.

Another state-of-the-art video capture board is Intel's Smart Video Recorder Pro. This board excels at capturing video files in the AVI (Indeo and Cinepack codecs) format. It comes bundled with a recording program called DVP Capture and an editing program called Digital Video Producer. Producer lets you add audio transitions and special effects. One nice feature is that it also comes with an uninstall program. This is important because it changes the way the Windows Media Player works.

When setting up your capture board, be sure to select the NTSC setting before capturing your video. NTSC stands for the National Television Standards Committee, which defines the TV video signal standard for United States. NTSC videos consist of 30 frames per second. The UK standard is PAL (Phase Alternation Line), which is 25 frames per second.

If you plan to edit the video file, capture the video without compression. Different cards have different names for this. Some call it raw, come call it uncompressed. Some boards, such as Intel's Smart Video Recorder compress files automatically when they are captured, so this is not always a possible choice. After editing the file, you can save it using compression.

Conversion Programs

As you know by now, you will not find any options to save your video in the MPEG format. In most cases, you will capture the video in the AVI format and convert the file to a QuickTime format using a video editing program like Adobe Premiere. Another conversion program, available from Intel, is called SmartCap. The SmartCap conversion program translates an AVI video file into a flattened QuickTime file. Microsoft also has a developer tool that lets you convert AVI files to QuickTime.

If you want to convert a video file to MPEG, check with the service bureau to find out what format they recommend. Many service bureaus require that you deliver the video on tape, but this is changing with the advent of MPEG encoders that can process digital files, such as the Producer from Sigma Designs. When you use a service bureau to convert a video file to the MPEG format, you will most likely be asked to save the captured video file in the YUV format. When you save or capture a video using the YUV format, the file is actually split into three separate files: Y, U and V. The MPEG encoder accepts the separate Y, U and V files to produce the encoded MPEG file.

Animation

The most popular format for animation is the FLC and FLI file format. These are AutoDesk Animator files. The aaplay utility from AutoDesk is a freeware program that lets users play animation files. Figure 8-7 shows an animation in the aaplay viewer. There are several Web sites that include animation. Netscape and Mosaic require users to set up their browser with an external or helper application for viewing animation files.

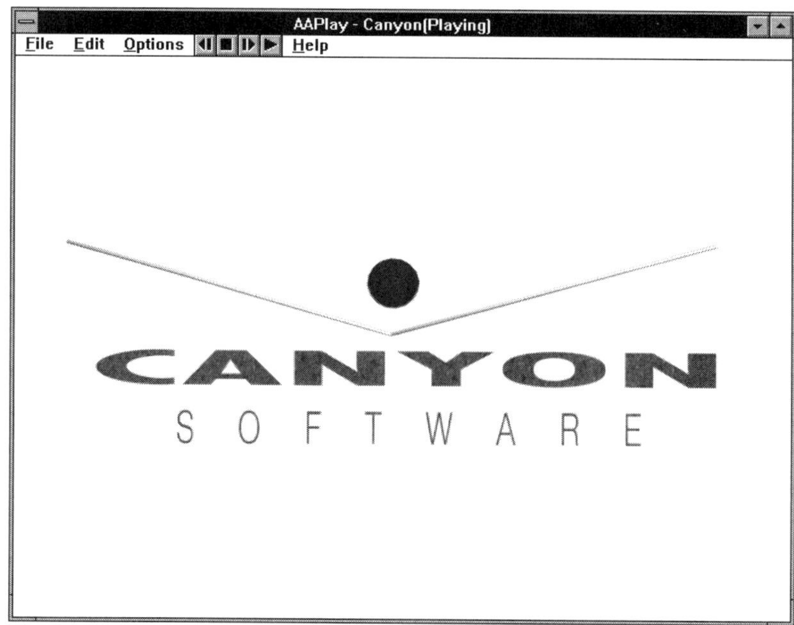

Figure 8-7: *The aaplay utility lets viewers play FLI and FLC animation files.*

When we think of animation, we usually think of hand-drawn art, such as a cartoon. But animations don't have to be illustrations; they can also be any series of video frames. Some video editing programs, such as Adobe Premiere, let you convert animation into an AVI or QuickTime file. For example, the short video of the Canyon Software logo that we included on the Companion CD-ROM was created using 3D Studio and saved as a FLC file. The file was then converted to a QuickTime file using Adobe Premiere.

Another video tool that shouldn't be overlooked is Fractal Design Painter 3. Painter 3 simplifies the formidable task of frame-by-frame editing by letting you edit a video frame by frame to animate and add special effects. You can paint and use filters to add spectacular special effects to a video. Masks can be assigned and applied to multiple frames. A truly impressive animation feature is the Image Hose, which lets you spray copies of an image on one or multiple frames.

Morphing

A hot trend in movies and advertising is *morphing*. Morphing lets you start with an image and create control points that determine how the picture will be transformed into another image. Because of the effects that morphing can produce, it is a unique way to present your logo or yourself on the Internet. Most morphing packages let you export files to the AVI format. From there you can convert them using a program like Adobe Premiere or a video converter. For example, we have included a video that transforms three of Canyon software's program icons into the Drag and File icon. This video was created using the impressive TransJammer program that comes with Elastic Reality, as shown in Figure 8-8. TransJammer includes over 50 editable transitions that you can use with your videos. Morphing programs like Elastic Reality also let you create professional animations and composite objects together. To morph two images, you identify the beginning shape of the image, the transitional shapes and the ending shape. Elastic Reality then uses key frames for *tweening*, creating frames between key frame positions. It can also create impressive warps, unique transitions and special effects; for example, Elastic Reality lets you create traveling mattes, so an image can appear to be moving in the background. If you are looking to enter the world of morphing and can't afford the E ticket for a $495, high-end program like

Elastic Reality, check out PhotoMorph 2, which lists for under $150. PhotoMorph 2 is more than just a morphing program; it includes features to create and edit animations, transitions, add titles and special effects, such as Chroma keying and warping images. It's a fairly easy program to use. Another even less expensive program is Ulead's Morph Studio, which lists for about $50. Ulead also includes Morph studio in its multimedia authoring suite of programs, named Media Studio.

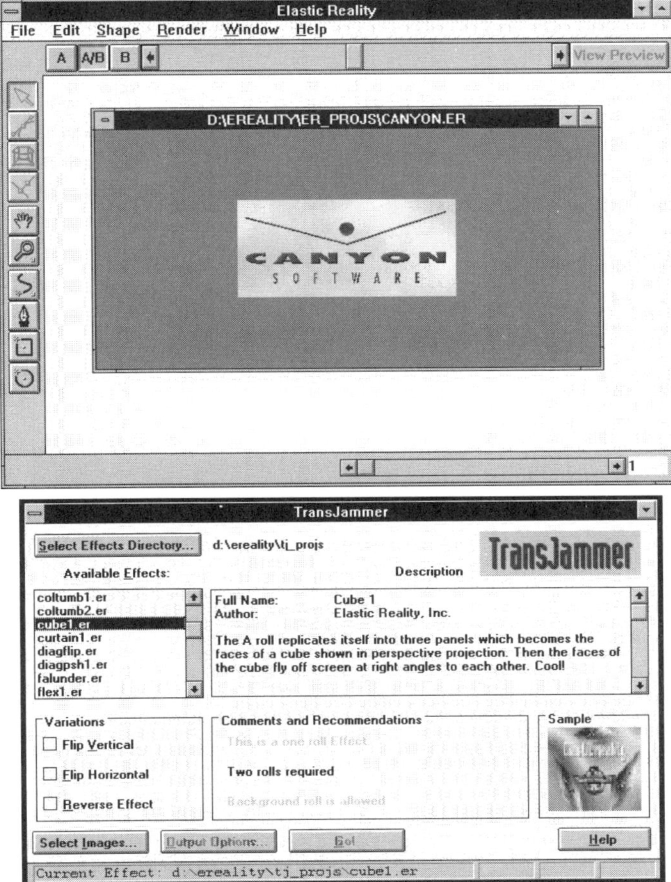

Figure 8-8: *Elastic Reality and the accompanying TransJammer program let you make impressive transformations.*

Moving On

Multimedia is a newly formed world, filled with fascinating possibilities. Because multimedia is such a hotbed of activity, you will need to keep up with the ways browsers add multimedia support and new multimedia authoring techniques. Several magazines, like *DV, New Media* and *PC Graphics and Video,* are great sources for keeping on top of new programs and following trends for publishing multimedia documents. Publishing multimedia files is a great way to entertain and involve your readers. The next chapter takes interactivity to another level by showing you how to create and publish interactive forms.

SECTION III

Putting the Pieces Together

9

Forms, Databases & CGI

Until now, you've been creating information for Web pages that go in one direction: from you to your reader. Through the use of forms, you can add two-way communication to your HTML pages. Forms allow a user to enter information, provide a method to supply that information to a "back-end" program of your choosing and creation, and return results to a user via regular HTML page construction. Forms were not part of the original HTML version 2 specification, but are so useful that most (if not all) Web broswers now support them. You can find many examples of forms on the Web. From these various examples you can pick and choose the features you want to use in your Web pages. In this chapter, you'll be introduced to the basics of form construction. We'll also learn more about the Common Gateway Interface (CGI), which was first introduced in Chapter 7, and the extensions to CGI, which were created by Robert Denny for his Windows-based HTML server. Last, we'll identify programs that can interact with these forms.

Using CGI With Your Web

Most HTML authoring is independent of the operating system running on the server. Once you venture into the realm of CGI and back-end processing, however, everything changes. Virtually anything you do relies heavily on the operating system and the HTTP server that you are running. In this book the discussion of forms is common across all operating systems. The CGI examples will focus on specific Windows or Windows NT HTTP servers, as indicated with each example. If you're using a UNIX-based server, the examples will illustrate the techniques you need to use, but the code will not be very portable.

Unlike most other examples presented in this book, *the examples in this chapter using CGI require you to be running server software if you want to try them*. There are two server programs on the Companion CD-ROM: the shareware version of Robert Denny's Windows 3.1-hosted server and the freeware version of the EMWAC Windows NT-hosted server. You can install either of these programs to get started. There are three other servers currently available for Windows and Windows NT: a 32-bit version of Robert Denny's server, which is included in a package from O'Reilly and Associates; a professional version of the EMWAC NT server from Process Software (http://www.process.com) and an NT server from Computer Software Manufaktur (http://www.csm.co.at/csm). For more information on servers, see Chapter 12.

One of the interesting capabilities of Robert Denny's servers is his addition of a Windows-based CGI extension. Because DOS and NT have such poor built-in batch-scripting capabilities, it's very difficult to write simple examples for CGI using batch programs, making the Windows-CGI proposed by Robert Denny an appealing alternative. The more complex examples in this chapter use this extended CGI. As opposed to the extensions offered by Netscape to the HTML standard, which create serious implications of incompatibility on the Web, these extensions affect only the server creators; users are completely unaware that the CGI back-end is different.

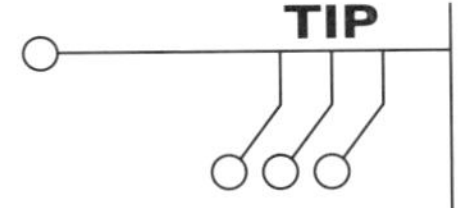

Perl users should be aware that there is a port of perl to NT, which offers a great deal of scripting power. So, if you currently use perl on UNIX, but want the simplicity of an NT-based HTTP server, you should get a copy of perl for your CGI back-ends.

There's a lot of discussion in the Web community about the precise syntax and extensions of the forms under HTML, so some things may change. The syntax is certainly going to change in HTML version 3, so stay tuned. Also, the *official* documentation for HTML version 2 is the Internet RFC. At the time of this writing, it was just being submitted to the IETF for consideration as a proposed standard.

Understanding How Forms Are Submitted

Every form contains at least one element. If there is only a single text field on a form, the form is submitted when the user presses Enter. On more complex forms there is a button or bitmap that triggers a submit operation. When a form is submitted, all the information entered in the fields is sent via HTTP to the server application. The information is sent in plain ASCII text, in a *name=value* format, with the name of the field sent first, followed by an equal sign, followed by the data that was entered in the field. Each *name=value* pair is separated with an ampersand (&). The way this information is sent to the server depends on the "method" used to send the form, which is described later in this chapter. The server application processes the information in some appropriate way, then returns a "results" page to the viewer. The results page can be anything you want, ranging from a simple "OK" to a complete database query result with multimedia elements. You can also create pages with CGI programs that are not related to specific database queries, but whose content (or address) changes on a regular basis.

As you look over the syntax for an HTML form you may wish to skip ahead to the "Common Gateway Interface" section to find out how the information entered by the user is processed.

Constructing a Form

In this chapter, you'll be creating elements that could make up a "Customer Comment" form to link to the Canyon Software home page constructed in the last few chapters. Figure 9-1 shows a comment form that illustrates all the elements you'll be working with in this chapter. Refer back to this figure to see how each element looks as rendered by Netscape.

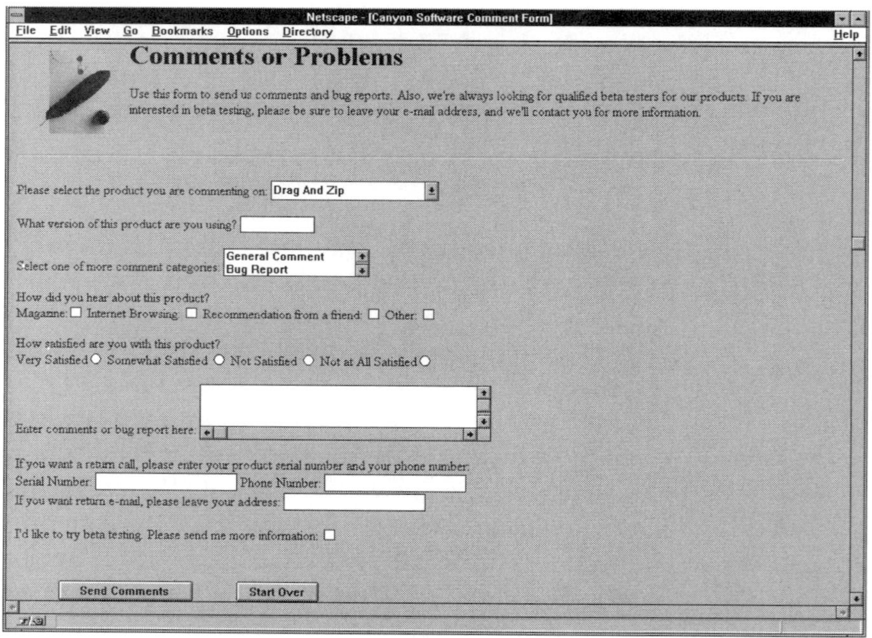

Netscape - [Canyon Software Comment Form]

File Edit View Go Bookmarks Options Directory Help

Comments or Problems

Use this form to send us comments and bug reports. Also, we're always looking for qualified beta testers for our products. If you are interested in beta testing, please be sure to leave your e-mail address, and we'll contact you for more information.

Please select the product you are commenting on: Drag And Zip

What version of this product are you using?

Select one of more comment categories: General Comment / Bug Report

How did you hear about this product?
Magazine: ☐ Internet Browsing: ☐ Recommendation from a friend: ☐ Other: ☐

How satisfied are you with this product?
Very Satisfied ○ Somewhat Satisfied ○ Not Satisfied ○ Not at All Satisfied ○

Enter comments or bug report here:

If you want a return call, please enter your product serial number and your phone number:
Serial Number: Phone Number:
If you want return e-mail, please leave your address:

I'd like to try beta testing. Please send me more information: ☐

Send Comments Start Over

Figure 9-1: *The Canyon Software comment form.*

A form is started and ended with the FORM tag and can contain a variety of fields and buttons. To get started, insert a FORM element, selecting from the HoTMetaL PRO Insert Element box. When you insert the FORM element, you will be prompted for an ACTION, METHOD and ENCTYPE. This is shown in Figure 9-2.

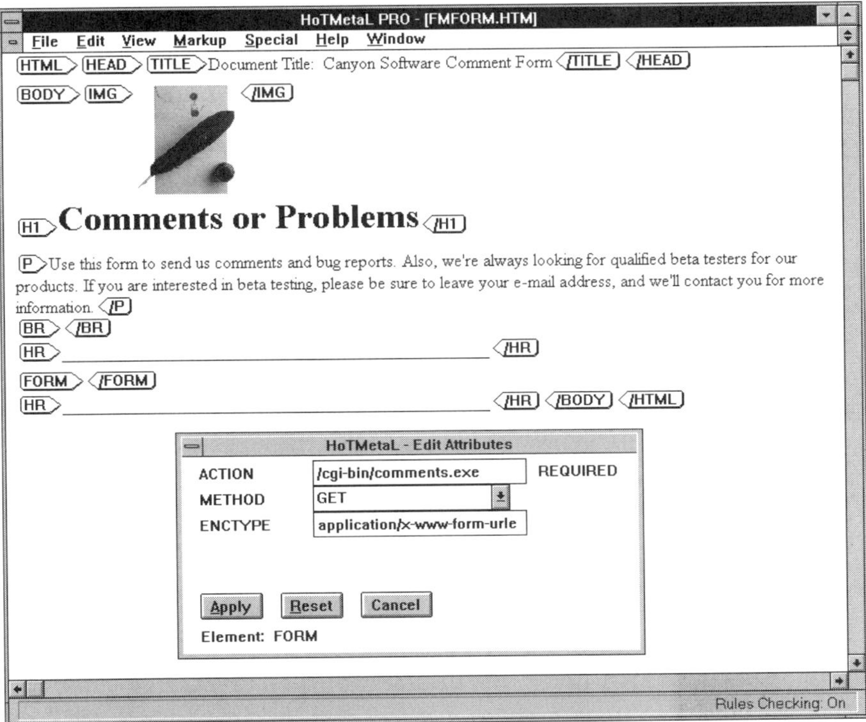

Figure 9-2: *Entering the FORM tag.*

For the ACTION attribute, enter **/cgi-bin/comments.exe**. This is the name of the program that will be executed when the form is submitted, and in this case the program *comments.exe* is located in a directory called *cgi-bin*. The name of the executable program directory you use for your own forms will depend on the server you are using. You could have entered a complete URL, host name and all. If you leave off the starting part of the URL, your Web browser will submit the form to the host that supplied the form. Since the ACTION attribute can be any URL, you could actually create a form that is submitted to a host besides your own.

For METHOD, you have two choices: GET and POST. The METHOD you choose when you create your own forms will depend on how your server supports the protocols. Enter **POST** for now, since this is the recommended protocol.

For standard CGI, the GET method puts the information submitted by your users at the end of the URL that is submitted to your server. Since forms can be very large, the GET method can create URLs that are huge. For this reason, the GET method is discouraged for newly created forms. With the POST method, the information from the user is put into the data stream of the HTTP protocol, and your back-end program can read the input via the "standard input" data stream. For Windows CGI, both methods put the information into disk files that your CGI program reads to obtain the data.

The last attribute, ENCTYPE, is always set to *application/x-www-form-urlencoded*. The HTML code for the form at this point might look like this:

```
<HTML><HEAD><TITLE>Canyon Software Comment
Form</TITLE></HEAD>
<BODY><H1>Comments or Problems</H1><P><IMG
SRC="file:///comment.gif">
Use this form to send us comments and bug reports. Also,
we're always looking for qualified beta testers for our
products. If you are interested in beta testing, please be
sure to leave your e-mail address, and we'll contact you for
more information.</P><HR>
<FORM ACTION="/cgi-bin/comments.exe"></FORM><HR>
</BODY></HTML>
```

Creating an Entry Field

Once the initial FORM tag is entered, you can start to enter the individual form elements. There are a variety of different form elements you can enter, including text fields, drop-down list boxes, scroll boxes, large text areas, buttons and boxes.

Creating a Drop-down List Box

A drop-down list box presents choices to a user. You have undoubtedly seen a drop-down list box in many Windows programs. The basic screen element is a box with a down arrow to the

right of it. When the user selects the down arrow, a list of choices is presented. The following steps explain how to include a drop-down list box in a form.

1. Insert a Paragraph tag and enter the text introducing the drop-down list box. For this example, enter **Please select the product you are commenting on.**
2. Insert a SELECT tag at the point in your page you want to position the list box. For this example, insert the SELECT tag between a beginning and ending paragraph tag. A dialog box appears asking if you want to stop and insert required elements.
3. Choose the Stop and Edit button. The Edit Attributes dialog box appears, as shown in Figure 9-3.

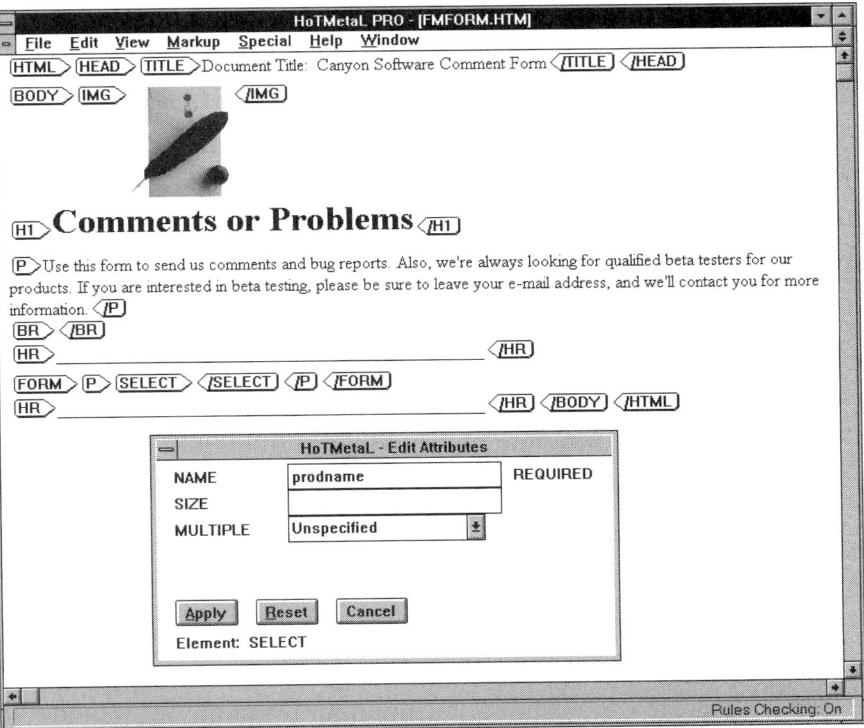

Figure 9-3: *Entering the SELECT tag.*

4. Enter a unique name in the NAME field. For this example, type **prodname**. Every item on a form has a different name associated with it, so that when the data is submitted, each piece of user data has a unique identifier. For your own forms, you can use any name you wish.
5. Choose the Apply button to add the element to your form. The insert point appears between the SELECT and /SELECT tags. Every item on a form has a different name associated with it, so that when the data is submitted, each piece of user data has a unique identifier. For your own forms, you can use any name you wish.
6. Insert an OPTION tag. The OPTION tag identifies each choice.
7. Type the text for the first option; for this example, type **Drag And Zip**. The insert point is now between the OPTION and /OPTION tags. Move the insert point to between the /OPTION and /SELECT tags.
8. Repeat steps 4 and 5 to enter all six options shown in Figure 9-4.

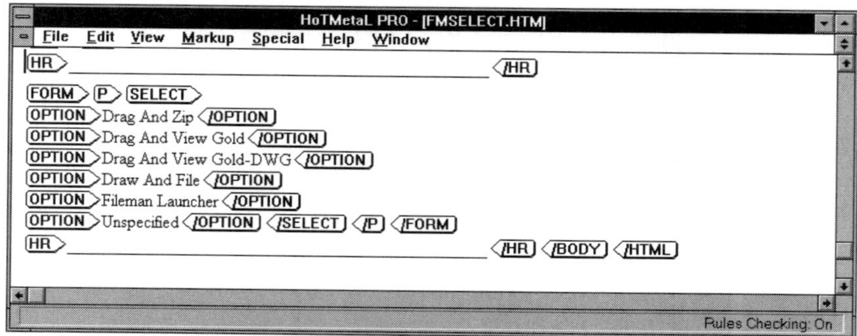

Figure 9-4: *Options for the SELECT field.*

The HTML code for the SELECT tag looks like this:

```
<P>Please select the product you are commenting on:
<SELECT NAME="prodname">
<OPTION>Drag And Zip</OPTION>
<OPTION>Drag And View Gold</OPTION>
<OPTION>Drag And View Gold-DWG</OPTION>
<OPTION>Draw And File</OPTION>
<OPTION>Fileman Launcher</OPTION>
<OPTION>Unspecified</OPTION></SELECT></P>
```

Creating a TEXT Field

A TEXT field gathers a single line of text from a user and is one of the most common fields used on a form. A TEXT field is created by using an INPUT tag and applying one of the many options for the INPUT tag. To create a TEXT field,

1. Insert a Paragraph tag after the previous example's ending paragraph tag and enter the text introducing the drop-down list box. For this example type **What version of this product are you using?**, as shown in Figure 9-5.

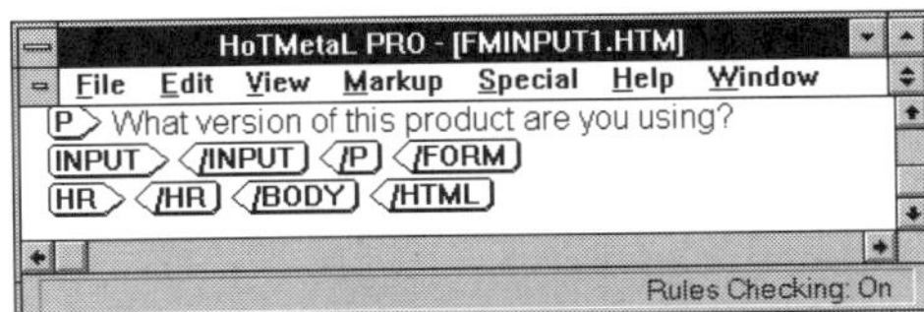

Figure 9-5: *A TEXT Field.*

2. Insert an INPUT tag at the point in your page you want to add a text field. The Input tags will appear with the insertion point positioned between the opening and closing tags.
3. Choose the Markup>>Edit SGML Attributes, or use the F6 shortcut key. Enter a unique name in the NAME field. For this example, type **"version"**. The TYPE attribute defaults to TEXT, so you don't need to change it. Leave all the other attributes empty.
4. Choose the Apply button to complete the TEXT field.

There are a number of other options for INPUT fields that are discussed later in this chapter.

The HTML code for the text field is shown here in:

```
<P>What version of this product are you using?<INPUT
NAME="version"></P>
```

Creating a Multiple Selection List Box

A multiple-selection list box is a variant on the drop-down list box. This type of list box allows the user to select more than one of the items on a list. The particular way a user selects the elements is dependent on the Web browser in use. The following steps explain how to include a multiple-selection drop-down list box in a form.

1. Insert a Paragraph tag after the previous example's ending paragraph tag and enter the text introducing the multiple-selection list box. For this example, enter Select one or more comment categories.
2. Insert a SELECT tag at the point in your page you want to position the list box. A dialog box appears asking if you want to stop and insert required elements.
3. Choose the Stop and Edit button. The Edit Attributes dialog box appears, as shown in Figure 9-6.

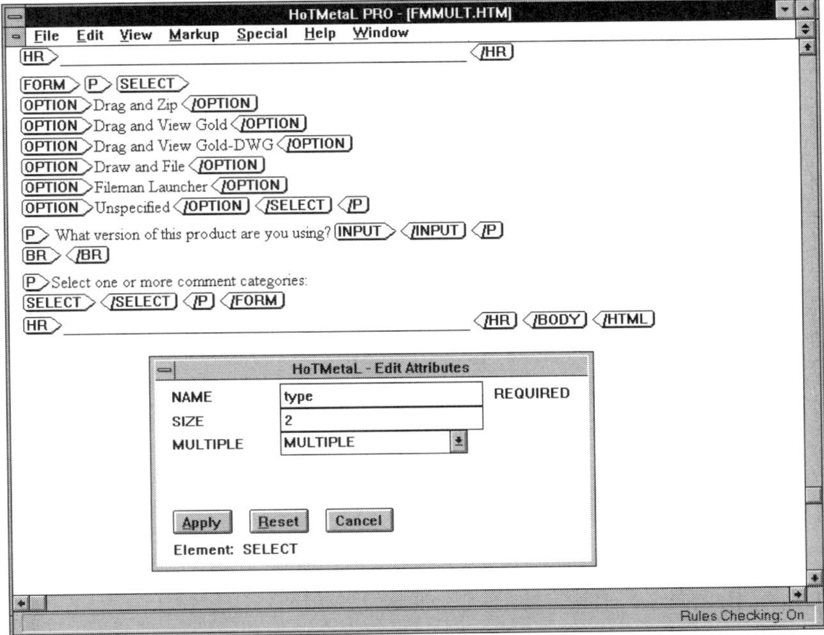

Figure 9-6: *Multiple Selection list box.*

4. Enter a unique name in the NAME field. For this example, type the name **type.**
5. Enter a SIZE of 2, and choose the MULTIPLE option for the MULTIPLE attribute.
6. Choose Apply to add the element to your form.
7. Insert an OPTION tag. The OPTION tag identifies each choice.
8. Choose Markup>>Edit SGML Attributes or press F6, enter a 1 for the first VALUE attribute and choose the Apply button. You will need to increment the VALUE attribute for each option you add. The OPTION tag attributes are shown in Figure 9-7.

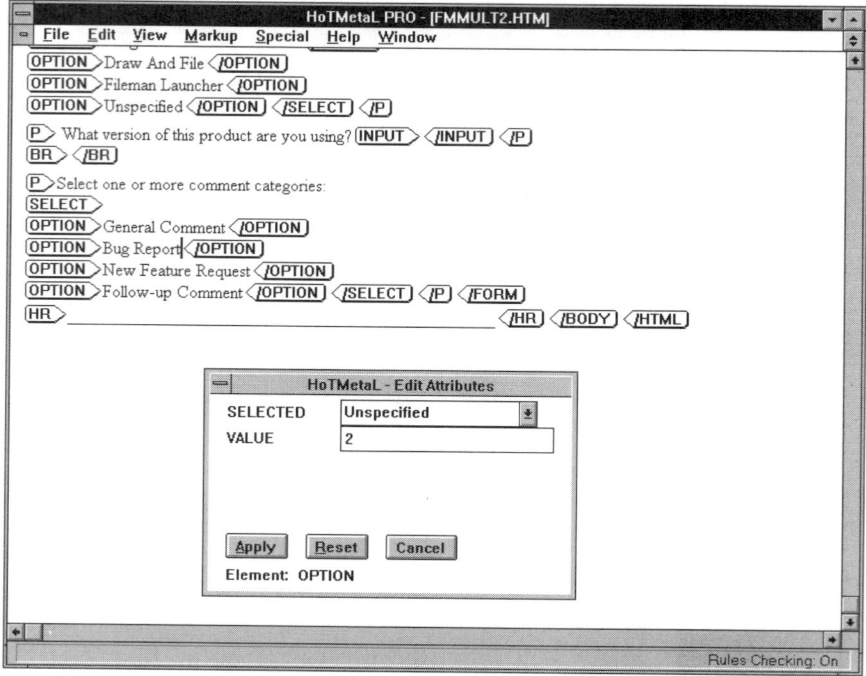

Figure 9-7: *Editing the OPTION tag.*

9. Type the text for the first option; for this example, type **General Comment**. The insert point is now between the OPTION and /OPTION tags. Move the insert point between the /OPTION and /SELECT tags.
10. Repeat steps 7, 8 and 9 to enter all four options shown in Figure 9-7.

There are a few new items in the SELECT element that you may have noticed. In step 5, you entered a SIZE of 2 and specified the MULTIPLE option instead of leaving it as Unspecified. The SIZE indicates how many elements are to be expected in the list box. If the actual number of elements exceeds the number specified, a scroll bar on the right of the list box becomes active so that the user can scroll up and down to the desired entry. When there are the same number as or fewer elements than the SIZE parameter, the scroll bar is inactive.

The MULTIPLE attribute specifies that more than one item in the list may be selected at a time. The user selects more than one element either by dragging with the mouse across multiple selections or holding down the Ctrl key while selecting. Figure 9-6 shows the screen for adding the Multiple Selection list box.

There was also a new element in the OPTION tag for this list box. In step 8, you entered a "1" for the VALUE instead of leaving it blank. This instructs a Web browser to use the "1" as the value of the field when it is submitted to your server *instead* of the text between the opening and closing option tags.

There are a few reasons you may want to do this. For starters, it may be more complex for a CGI program to parse out long text strings than shorter ones. Or, if you are creating a form in multiple languages, the content of the list box may vary while the meanings do not. The VALUE attribute comes in handy in such cases. The HTML code for a multiple SELECT list box is shown here:

```
<P>Select one of more comment categories:
<SELECT NAME="type" SIZE="2" MULTIPLE="MULTIPLE">
<OPTION VALUE="1">General Comment</OPTION>
<OPTION VALUE="2">Bug Report</OPTION>
<OPTION VALUE="3">New Feature Request</OPTION>
<OPTION VALUE="4">Follow-up Comment</OPTION>
</SELECT></P>
```

Creating Check Boxes & Radio Buttons

Check boxes and radio buttons are an alternative way to collect one or more choices from a list of options. When *check boxes* are used, the user can select any, all or none of the choices. With *radio buttons*, only one of the choices in a group can be selected, and one is always selected. (Some of us can actually remember car radios with mechanical push buttons!) Radio buttons are *grouped together* by using the same NAME for each button. The VALUE of the button is sent to the server to distinguish it from the others.

Check Boxes

To enter a check box,

1. Insert a Paragraph tag after the previous example's ending paragraph tag and enter the text introducing the multiple-

selection list box. For this example, enter **How did you hear about this product?**

2. Type the text that will identify the first check box at the point in your page you want to position the check box. In this example, enter **Magazine** before the area to display the first box.
3. Insert an INPUT element after the identifying text entered in step 1.
4. Choose Markup>>Edit SGML Attributes, or use the F6 shortcut key. Enter a unique name in the NAME field. For this example, fill in the name "Internet."
5. Select the value CHECKBOX for the TYPE attribute, and choose the Apply button. This is shown in Figure 9-8.

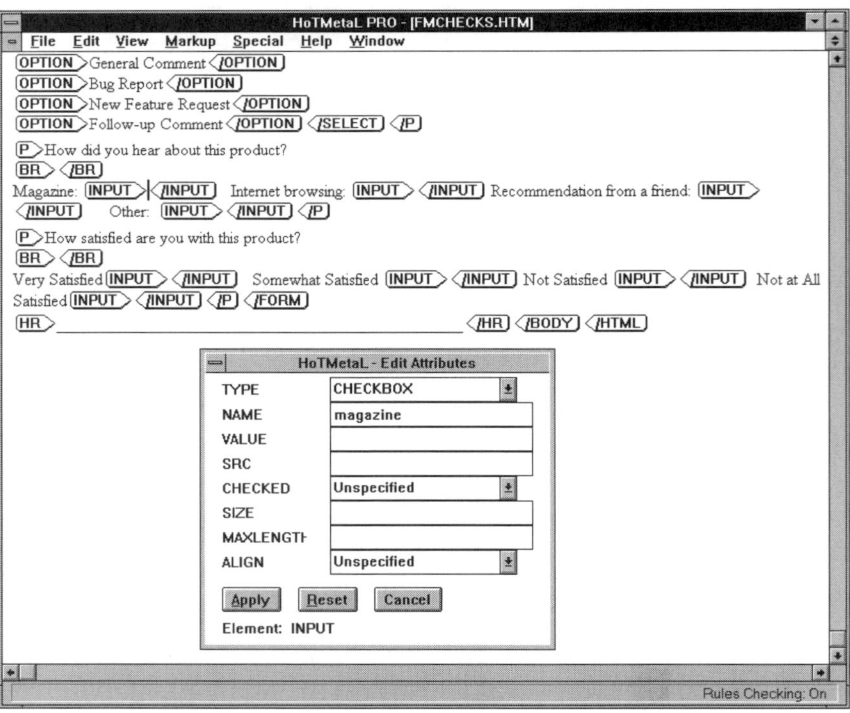

Figure 9-8: *CHECKBOX addition.*

6. Repeat steps 2 to 4 for every check box you wish to enter. For the example add three more checkboxes, as shown in Figure 9-8.

For check boxes, the VALUE attribute specifies the text that should be sent to the server when the box is checked. If you leave the VALUE blank as we did in this example, the default is the text "on," which is usually okay. Unchecked check boxes send *no data* to the server instead of a value of "no" or "off."

The HTML for a CHECKBOX looks like this:

```
<P> How did you hear about this product?
<BR>
Magazine: <INPUT TYPE="CHECKBOX" NAME="magazine">
Internet Browsing: <INPUT TYPE="CHECKBOX"
NAME="Internet">
Recommendation from a friend:
<INPUT TYPE="CHECKBOX" NAME="recommendation">
Other: <INPUT TYPE="CHECKBOX" NAME="other">
</P>
```

Radio Buttons

Radio buttons are very similar to check boxes, except each button in a group has the same name, instead of unique names. The following steps explain how to include a set of radio buttons in a form.

1. Insert a Paragraph tag after the previous example's ending paragraph tag and enter the text introducing the radio buttons. For this example, type **How satisfied are you with this product?** and insert a Break tag.
2. Type the text that will identify the first radio button at the point in your page you want to position the button. For the first radio button, type **Very Satisfied**.
3. Insert the INPUT element as you did for a check box.
4. Choose Markup>>Edit SGML Attribute and choose RADIO for the value of the TYPE attribute.
5. Enter the name of the push-button group in the NAME field in the Edit Attributes dialog box. For this example, type **howsat**.

6. Enter a unique value in the VALUE field.
7. For the button in the group that you want to appear as the default, specify the CHECKED option. This creates a default push-button selection.
8. Repeat steps 2 to 5 for the remaining push-buttons in the group, as shown in Figure 9-9. Enter the same value for the NAME field in each case. Enter a different value for the VALUE field in each case.

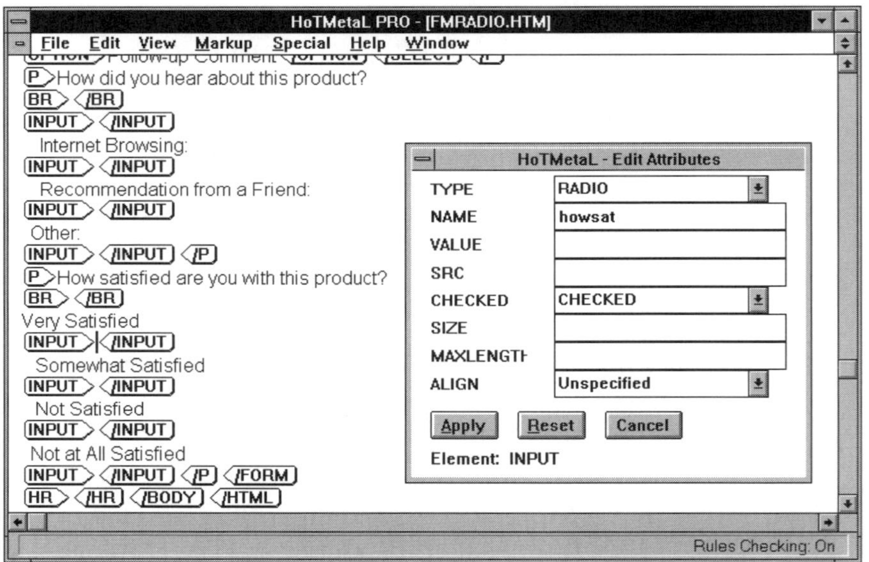

Figure 9-9: *RADIO button addition.*

You can have more than one radio button grouping on a form by using different names for the different groups. The HTML text for this radio button group looks like this:

```
<P>How satisfied are you with this product?
<BR>
Very Satisfied <INPUT TYPE="RADIO" NAME="howsat">
Somewhat Satisfied <INPUT TYPE="RADIO"
NAME="howsat">
```

```
Not Satisfied <INPUT TYPE="RADIO" NAME="howsat">
Not at All Satisfied <INPUT TYPE="RADIO"
NAME="howsat">
</P>
```

Creating Text Areas

Text areas are large "scratchpad" areas designed for free text entry that exceeds a single line. As the forms designer, you have the ability to choose the size of the text area by specifying the number of columns (of an average character width) and rows (lines) in the text area.

To create the text area,

1. Insert a Paragraph tag after the previous example's ending paragraph tag and enter the text introducing the text area. For this example, type **Enter comments or bug report here.**
2. Insert a TEXTAREA tag at the point in your page you want to position the text input area. You will be presented with a dialog box which prompts you for the Name and Size of the text area.
3. Enter **textcomment** as the NAME, **3** for the ROWS and **40** for the COLUMNS and choose the Apply button.

Because some Web browsers use variable pitch fonts in TEXTAREA fields, the number of COLUMNS is just an estimate of how many characters will fit across the field. The text field has both vertical and horizontal scroll bars, so the user can actually enter any amount of text in this kind of field, up to the internal limits set by the Web browser. The attributes for a TEXTAREA element are shown in Figure 9-10.

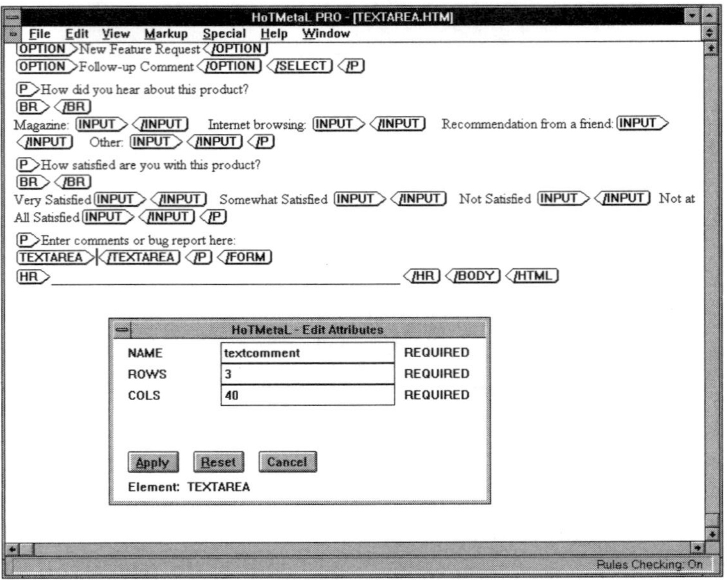

Figure 9-10: *TEXTAREA attributes.*

The HTML code for a TEXTAREA will look like this:

```
<P>Enter comments or bug report here:
TEXTAREA NAME="textcomment" ROWS="3"
COLS="40"></TEXTAREA></P>
```

Using Other INPUT Field Attributes

There are a few other attribute choices for an INPUT field in addition to the ones you have seen so far. On the sample form, there is an entry for a Serial Number as a PASSWORD field, and a *hidden field* that reports the revision level of the form. Last, but not least, the INPUT field is used to create the required SUBMIT button, special submission buttons created from images, plus a RESET button that lets the browser clear the fields in a form without submitting the form.

As a trick to create spacing on a form, use a transparent IMAGE file to provide white space between the buttons that would normally be right next to each other.

PASSWORD Fields

Use a PASSWORD field for text input areas that should be kept private. This is useful only for protection from "shoulder snoopers," because the text of the field is still sent across the network. On the Web browser's screen, asterisks appear instead of the text.

To create a PASSWORD field, enter the text that identifies the field, which in this case is "Serial Number," and an INPUT field with the TYPE attribute set to PASSWORD. Figure 9-11 shows how this appears in HoTMetaL PRO.

To create a PASSWORD field,

1. Insert a Paragraph tag after the previous example's ending paragraph tag and enter the text introducing the password field. For this example, type **If you want a return call, please enter your product serial number and your phone number** and insert a BREAK tag.
2. Enter the text that identifies the field, which in this case is **Serial Number**, and an INPUT field with the TYPE attribute set to PASSWORD.
3. Enter the text that identifies the phone number, which in this case is **Phone Number**, and an INPUT field with the TYPE attribute set to TEXT. Figure 9-11 shows how this appears in HoTMetaL PRO.
4. Enter the text that identifies the e-mail address, which in this example is to type, **If you want return e-mail, please leave your address** and in the INPUT field set the TYPE attribute to TEXT. Figure 9-11 shows how this appears in HoTMetaL PRO.

The HTML code for the PASSWORD field looks like this:

```
<P>If you want a return call, please enter your product
serial number and your phone number:
<BR>
Serial Number: <INPUT TYPE="PASSWORD" SIZE="20"
MAXLENGTH="16">Phone Number: <INPUT SIZE="20">
<BR>
If you want return e-mail, please leave your address:
<INPUT SIZE="20">
</P>
```

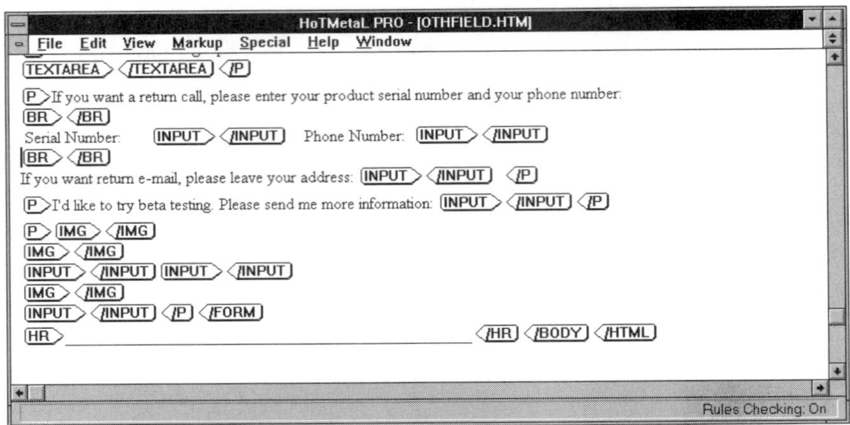

Figure 9-11: *The PASSWORD field.*

HIDDEN Fields

The HIDDEN type is useful for when you want to pre-load information in a field that will be sent to a server, but you would rather the user not see it. For example, if you have two forms identical in meaning but written in different languages, you may want to identify the language to the server when the form is sent. You could enter the language name (or some other identifier) in a HIDDEN field on the form, so the user is not distracted by it. Then when the form is sent to your server, the server program can identify the language of the form and possibly change how the form is processed.

On the sample comment form, the HIDDEN field type is used to create a "revision number" field. This revision number will be sent to the server so that the revision number of the input form can be tracked. To create a HIDDEN field, add a paragraph tag and insert an INPUT field with the TYPE attribute set to HIDDEN. Enter revision for the NAME attribute and set the VALUE to 1.0. This value setting is sent to the server when the form is submitted. The HTML code looks like this:

```
<P><INPUT TYPE="HIDDEN" NAME="revision"
VALUE="1.0"></P>
```

Images as Part of an INPUT Field

You can use images as input fields as well. When you specify an IMAGE as the TYPE for an INPUT field, you also specify a .gif file in the SRC field. The image of the .gif file is what will be displayed to the user instead of a box or button. When the user clicks on the image, the form is *submitted*, and the coordinates of the mouse pointer are sent in the form "name.x" and "name.y" where "name" is the NAME of the image field. Note that if there is also a SUBMIT button on the form, and the user selects the SUBMIT button, *no* information about the image is submitted.

One example of an image field is to use it to display a number of different models of some widget, so the user can select the model of widget they are commenting on or requesting information about.

Using Standard IMAGE Fields

In addition to images as part of an INPUT button, you can also include standard images on a form. Since GIF images can be made transparent, as you learned in Chapter 7, you can create an image with no visible content at all, and then insert the image on a form to force the Web browser to insert space between your input fields and buttons. The transparent image used in this example is ½-inch wide, and is used to create a ½-inch blank space between buttons. Figure 9-12 illustrates what the form would look like without the IMAGE spacers inserted.

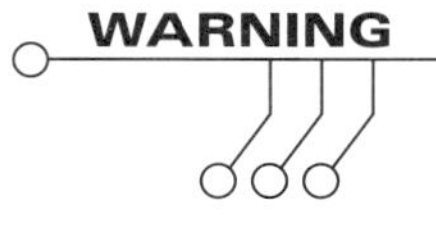

Be careful with this technique! If a Web browser has turned off inline images, the user will see the "default image" of the browser instead of your empty space.

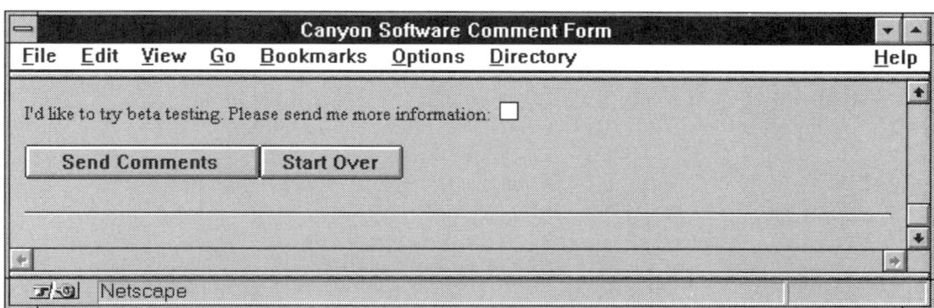

Figure 9-12: *Comment form without spacing.*

Images are entered as you learned in Chapter 7. As a review, the following steps show you how to enter a simple image.

1. Insert a Paragraph tag after the previous example's ending paragraph tag.
2. Insert an IMG tag at the point in your page you want to position the blank space. You are presented with an Edit URL dialog box.
3. Choose "file" as the PROTOCOL attribute. The PROTOCOL field specifies how the image reference will be inserted into the HTML code. When you eventually publish the form, this file reference will be replaced with a URL reference that includes your system name instead of the FILE type.
4. Leave the HOST and PORT attributes blank, since you specified "file" for the protocol. Again, when this form is published, you could optionally include a host that was not your own, and a port that is not the standard port 80. If you leave these fields blank, the default is to use the host system that supplied the form originally—which is a very reasonable default.
5. Enter the name of the .gif file to be included in the Name field. For the sample, enter **spacer.gif**. This is shown in Figure 9-13. You can use the Choose file button to search around on your system for an image if you don't know the complete file path name offhand.
6. Enter additional image fields if you want to insert additional space.

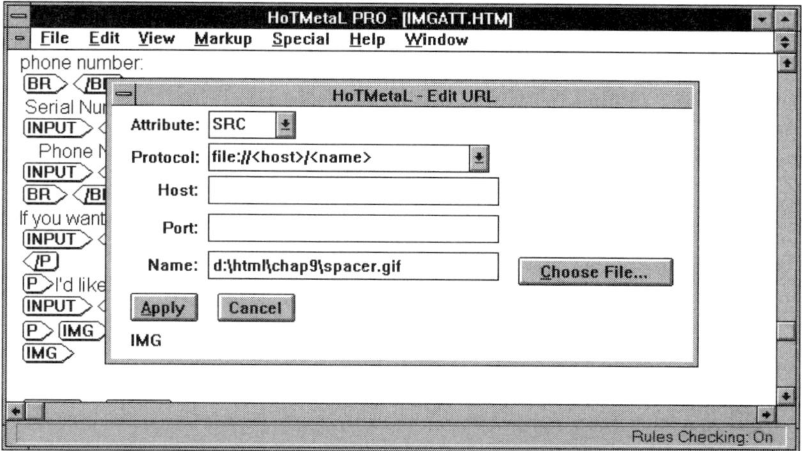

Figure 9-13: *URL dialog box for entering IMG elements.*

You can enter more than one IMG element if you want, for additional spacing.

```
<IMG SRC="file:///spacer.gif">
<IMG SRC="file:///spacer.gif">
```

Submit & Reset

Although last in this section, the final two possibilities for the TYPE attribute of an INPUT field are very important: SUBMIT and RESET. Every form that has more than one field *must* have a SUBMIT button. The default text for a SUBMIT button is "Submit Query." You can specify your own text for a SUBMIT button in the VALUE attribute. The resulting field on a form is a *push button* that is sized to the text you have specified. There is no NAME needed for a SUBMIT button, and when the SUBMIT button is selected, the contents of the form are transmitted to your server.

To add the SUBMIT button, enter an INPUT field with TYPE set to SUBMIT and the VALUE set to Send Comments.

The RESET button has a default text of "reset", and selecting a RESET button will only clear the fields on the local form. The form is not submitted, and no other action is taken.

To add the RESET button, enter an INPUT field with TYPE set to RESET and the VALUE set to Start Over. The HTML code for submit and reset buttons looks like this:

```
<INPUT TYPE="SUBMIT" VALUE="Send Comments">
<INPUT TYPE="RESET" VALUE="Start Over">
```

You can have more than one RESET and SUBMIT button on a form, but remember that in many cases the user will not see the entire form at one time, so it is customary to place only a single SUBMIT button at the bottom of the form to ensure that a user scrolls all the way to the end of a form before sending it to the server.

Wrapping Up

In this part of the chapter you have seen all the elements you can use when creating a form. It's likely that the forms you create for your Web pages will not include every form element—like this form does. This form looks busy and complicated, and is likely to discourage people from actually filling out the form. In the following sections, we'll discuss the Common Gateway Interface and use a simpler version of the comment form.

Common Gateway Interface

The Common Gateway Interface (CGI) is a standard for external gateway programs to interface with HTTP servers. It's a very flexible way to process data sent from a Web browser and passed through the server, and is easily portable across multiple operating systems. The CGI was originally designed with UNIX-based operating systems in mind, so much of the data passing in the standard relies on "standard in," "standard out" and environment variables.

To get a feel for how information flows with the CGI, take a look at Figure 9-14, which shows a standard CGI interface, and Figure 9-15, which shows the Windows CGI interface as currently defined by Robert Denny.

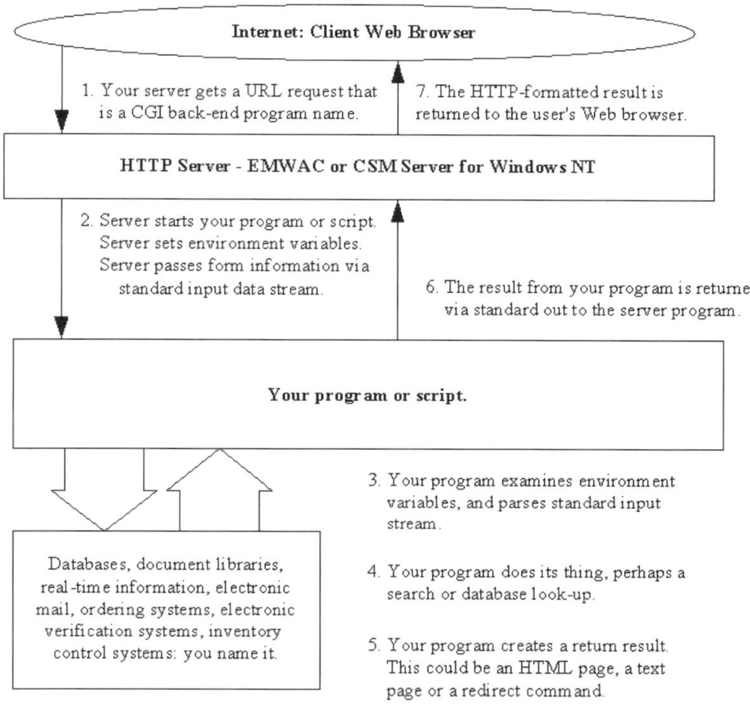

Figure 9-14: *CGI information flow.*

If you are working with a UNIX-based server, you'll find a broad variety of programs available to support development of CGI processing programs. (Check out the Web pages at http://hoohoo.ncsa.uiuc.edu/cgi/ for lots of great pointers.) Many of the same techniques can apply to the Windows and Windows NT environment, which is discussed later in this chapter. Due to the operating system–dependent nature of CGI processing, you should always check with the documentation that comes with your HTTP server to see how it handles CGI.

The most significant difference between how you use CGI on a UNIX system and how you use CGI on a Windows system is that with UNIX you would very likely use shell programming and a parser such as perl to process almost all CGI requests. When you write programs that handle CGI for Windows, you'll find it much easier to use Visual Basic or even C. This is because UNIX has several very powerful and flexible command-shell processors available, and a tremendous assortment of command-line–oriented programs for processing "standard in" data. Windows, on the other hand, is very much a graphically based system, with precious little flexibility at the command line. The most powerful tools, such as Visual Basic, are not command-line programs, and cannot be reached directly from the command prompt (the shell).

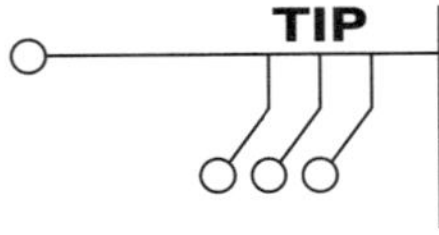

Even though the CGI interface is discussed in the chapter on forms, you can use CGI for anything you like! For example, you could have a hyperlink on a basic HTML page point to a CGI reference. The server will pass URL to the specified back-end program, and your program could generate the jumped-to HTML page in real time. This is useful for pages that change based on real-time data, or for pages that are completely generated from database references. Further, the CGI is also used with image maps, which were discussed in Chapter 7.

Processing CGI Data

Data passed from an HTTP server using the standard Common Gateway Interface is passed via two mechanisms: a stream data interface called "standard in" (when the POST method is used) and a set of environment variables. Because the Windows Server WinHTTPD has an alternate interface for Windows/DOS, which is far easier to use with Windows 3.1 than the standard CGI interface, this section will assume that you are using CGI with Windows NT and the EMWAC or CSM (ALIBABA) HTTP server. The next section on Windows CGI covers the use of WinHTTPD.

With Windows NT, you have command environment services very similar to those of UNIX. The standard CGI interface is used. With this interface, there is a set of Environment Variables that contain information about the information being passed from the user. The following table is a list of the standard environment variables supported by the EMWAC and CSM servers.

Variable	Definition
SERVER_SOFTWARE	The name and version of the information server software answering the request (and running the gateway). Format: name/version
SERVER_NAME	The server's hostname, DNS alias or IP address as it would appear in self-referencing URLs.
GATEWAY_INTERFACE	The revision of the CGI specification to which this server complies. Format: CGI/revision
SERVER_PROTOCOL	The name and revision of the information protocol this request came in with. Format: protocol/revision
SERVER_PORT	The port number to which the request was sent.
REQUEST_METHOD	The method with which the request was made. For HTTP, this is "GET," "HEAD," "POST," etc.
PATH_INFO	The extra path information, as given by the client. In other words, scripts can be accessed by their virtual pathname, followed by extra information at the end of this path. The extra information is sent as PATH_INFO. This information should be decoded by the server if it comes from a URL before it is passed to the CGI script.
SCRIPT_NAME	A virtual path to the script being executed, used for self-referencing URLs.
QUERY_STRING	When the GET method is used (or with the ISINDEX form type) this is information that follows the ? in the URL that referenced this script. This is the query information. It should not be decoded in any fashion. This variable should always be set when there is query information, regardless of command line decoding.
REMOTE_ADDR	The IP address of the remote host making the request.

CONTENT_TYPE	When the input method is POST, this is the content type of the data. At this time there is only one type: **x-www-form-urlencoded.**
CONTENT_LENGTH	This is the number of bytes of input data to read from the "standard in" stream when the POST method is used.
HTTP_ACCEPT	The MIME types which the client will accept, as given by HTTP headers. Other protocols may need to get this information from elsewhere. Each item in this list should be separated by commas as per the HTTP spec. Format: type/subtype, type/subtype

Table 9-1: *List of standard environment variables supported by the EMWAC and CSM servers.*

These variables are accessed by your CGI back-end program or script by a method that depends on the programming language you are using. For example, in C, the *getenv* function call is used to look up these parameters.

The way your back-end program collects data from the server depends on the method used to send the form. (Remember that you control the method when you set up your form, so you will know in advance which to expect.) With the POST method (the recommended method), the data from the form is sent to your application in the "standard in" stream. Your program knows how many bytes to read, as it is specified in the CONTENT_LENGTH environment variable. With the GET method, the data sent from the form will be in the QUERY_STRING environment variable. In either case the data sent will be in the format:

name1=data string 1&name2=data string 2&name3=data string 3

Each piece of data (each field on the form) is identified with the *name=* part of the data stream, and the actual user data follows that up to the ampersand. Your program will parse this data and take whatever action is appropriate, such as performing a search or a database lookup. To create the result, your program generates the data to be displayed on the user's screen. While this is typically an HTML form (Content-type: text/html), it can also be a

plain text display (Content-type: text/plain). The type of data returned is identified by your program to the server (and viewer) by the header information created by your program.

When returning the results page to the server, your program has the option of creating only the content of the return page, in which case the server adds HTTP headers, as shown in the following example.

```
Content-type: text/html
<HTML><HEAD><TITLE>Processed Return </TITLE>
</HEAD>
<BODY><H1>Processed Return</H1>
<P>This was processed by the server code to add HTTP
headers.</P>
</BODY></HTML>
```

Alternatively, your program can create the entire return message, including the HTTP headers, as shown in the following example.

```
HTTP/1.0 200 OK
Server: Server-version-here
MIME-Version: 1.0
Content-type: text/html
X-Script-name: Visual Basic CGI Test
<HTML><HEAD><TITLE>Transparent Return </TITLE>
</HEAD>
<BODY><H1>Transparent Return</H1>
<P>This was returned transparently.</P>
</BODY></HTML>
```

A third option for your program is to issue a two-line message that redirects the Web browser to yet another URL. The target URL could be any kind of document, including an HTML document or a plain text document. The two-line reply is shown in the following example:

```
Location: /mypath/my-document.html
[the second line is blank]
```

The document URL is typically another document on your own server, but could also be a full link to another site. This kind of a link can direct the Web browser to open a document that meets the criteria of a search, or direct a user to an instruction page if a query was done incorrectly.

Exploring the Windows CGI

When Robert Denny created his HTTP server for Windows 3.1, he realized that the CGI interface was clumsy in the Windows/DOS environment and that there were a number of "workarounds" needed to make standard CGI work. The DOS (and NT) batch processing language is very limited, and native Windows 3.1 programs do not have a concept of "standard in" or "standard out," so all the back-end processing needed to be done under DOS. While there are a number of DOS shell replacements available that ease this situation to some extent, the use of DOS still made many of the really powerful Windows tools unsuitable for handling CGI operations. So, in addition to supporting standard CGI operations (through a number of workarounds) for the Windows HTTP server, Denny invented an experimental Windows-based interface. To keep the spirit of the original CGI interface specification, the Windows interface does not use any Windows-unique features such as OLE or DDE. Instead, it relies on disk-based files to pass the information normally carried on the "standard in" and "standard out" streams. The server uses the WinExec program call to start your Windows-based back-end program, which can then open the input file, process the data and put the resulting HTML form or text in an output file. When the server detects that your program has completed its execution, it reads the output file and passes the data back to the user.

The most convenient programming language to use for creating Windows-based CGI processing programs is Visual Basic. With Visual Basic, you can access the broad spectrum of advanced data and information features available under Windows 3.1 and create these programs very quickly.

Processing Windows CGI Data

Figure 9-15 illustrates the information flow for the Windows CGI. Although the basic information flow is the same as that of the standard CGI illustrated in Figure 9-14, the Windows CGI uses an .INI file and temporary files to pass data between the server and your client program instead of using environment variables and "standard in" and "standard out" streams.

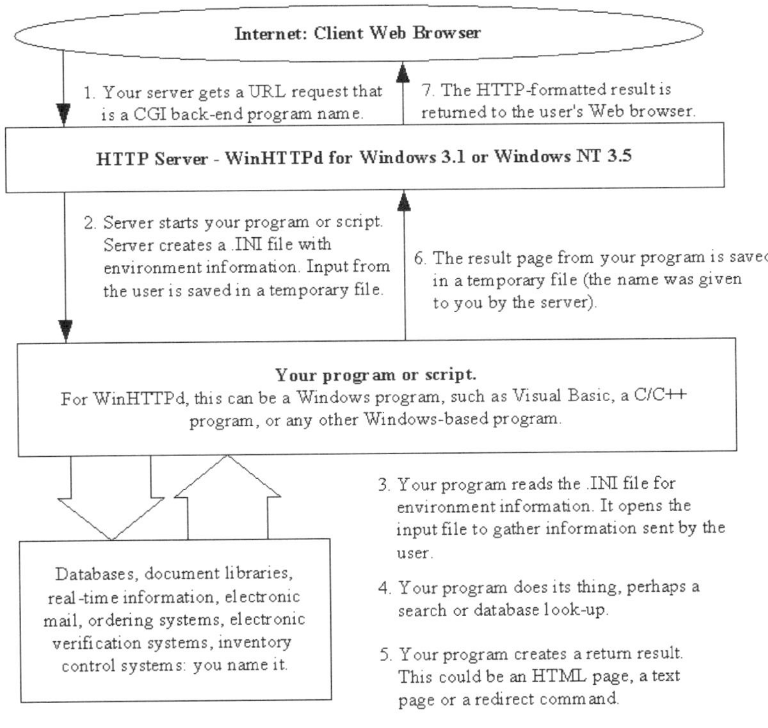

Figure 9-15: *Experimental Windows CGI information flow.*

Sample Program: Processing the Comments Form

In the first part of this chapter, you created a comments form that could be used to gather feedback from a user of your product or service. Now it's time to find out how to process that information at your server site. As already mentioned, the way that a CGI back-end program works and collects information relies on the specific operating system that is hosting the HTTP server. The example presented in this chapter is for Windows 3.1 using Robert Denny's WinHTTPD, which can be found on the Companion CD-ROM. The sample uses Visual Basic and the Windows MAPI interface to send Microsoft Mail to an administrator when someone fills out and submits the comments form. If you want to follow along with the example and build the sample yourself, you'll need a copy of Visual Basic installed on your computer.

The HTML for the form processed by this example is a simplified version of the comments form created at the beginning of this chapter. This code can be found on the Companion CD-ROM, so you don't need to type it all in. The following example shows the HTML code for the simplified form, and Figure 9-16 shows how it looks in Netscape. You must substitute the name of your own host system for "yourhost" in the IMG references in the example. Note that the ACTION attribute of the FORM specification points to "cgi-win/comment.exe." When you use the Windows CGI interface you should put the executable CGI programs in the cgi-win directory. If you specify the cgi-bin directory, the server will look in the cgi-dos directory.

```
<HTML><HEAD><TITLE>Canyon Software Comment
Form</TITLE></HEAD>
<BODY><H1>Comments or Problems</H1><P><IMG
SRC="http://yourhost/images/ask_dan.gif">
Use this form to send us comments and bug reports. Also,
we're always looking for qualified beta testers for our
products. If you are interested in beta testing, please be
sure to leave your e-mail address, and we'll contact you for
more information.</P><HR>
```

```
<FORM ACTION="cgi-win/comment.exe"
METHOD="POST"><P>Please select the product you are
commenting on: <SELECT NAME="prodname" SIZE="0">
<OPTION VALUE="1">Drag And Zip</OPTION>
<OPTION VALUE="2">Drag And View Gold</OPTION>
<OPTION VALUE="3">Drag And View Gold-DWG</OPTION>
<OPTION VALUE="4">Draw And File</OPTION>
<OPTION VALUE="5">Fileman Launcher</OPTION>
<OPTION VALUE="6">Unspecified</OPTION></SELECT>
</P>
  <P> What version of this product are you using? <INPUT
NAME="version" SIZE="10" MAXLENGTH="10">
</P><P>Select one or more comment categories:   <SELECT
NAME="type" SIZE="2" MULTIPLE="MULTIPLE">
<OPTION>General Comment</OPTION>
<OPTION>Bug Report</OPTION>
<OPTION>New Feature Request</OPTION>
<OPTION>Follow-up Comment</OPTION></SELECT>
</P><P>Enter comments or bug report here:   <TEXTAREA
NAME="textcomment" ROWS="3" COLS="40">
</TEXTAREA></P><P>If you want a return call, please enter
your product serial number and your phone number:  <BR>
Serial Number:      <INPUT TYPE="PASSWORD"
NAME="serialnumber" SIZE="20" MAXLENGTH="16">
Phone Number:  <INPUT NAME="phonenumber"
SIZE="20"><BR>If you want return e-mail, please leave your
address: <INPUT NAME="e-mail" SIZE="20">
</P><P>I'd like to try beta testing. Please send me more
information: <INPUT TYPE="CHECKBOX" NAME="beta">
</P><P><IMG SRC="http://yourhost/images/
spacer.gif"><IMG SRC="http://yourhost/images/spacer.gif">
<INPUT TYPE="SUBMIT" VALUE="Send
Comments"><INPUT TYPE="HIDDEN" NAME="revision"
VALUE="1.0">
<IMG SRC="http://yourhost/images/spacer.gif"><INPUT
TYPE="RESET" VALUE="Start Over">
</P></FORM><HR></BODY></HTML>
```

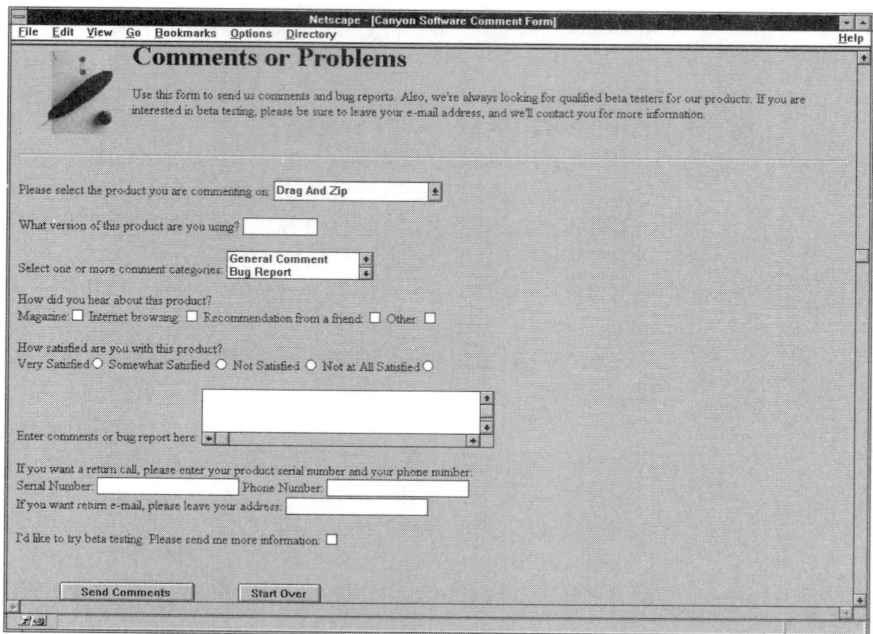

Figure 9-16: *How the comments form looks in Netscape.*

This form will submit up to nine fields of information to the sample back-end program, depending on how many fields are filled out. The source code for this example is located on the Companion CD-ROM, so if you have Visual Basic you can try it yourself.

Creating a MAPI-Based CGI Program

One way to handle comments from users is to mail the comment form to a system administrator. When using a Windows-based system, it's convenient to use the Microsoft Mail program that comes with each copy of Windows to act as the mail transport. Microsoft provides a programmer's interface called MAPI (Mail Application Programmer Interface) and a Visual Basic Control that allows Visual Basic programs to access the Mail functions of Windows. Denny provides a sample Visual Basic application with his server that handles all the basic processing of the CGI interface that would be common across all CGI programs. Between these two resources, we need to add very little code to produce a productive interface program. The additional code is shown in the example at the end of this section, which makes up the Visual Basic Module *CGIMAPI.BAS*.

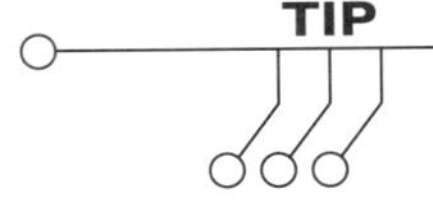

The entire program is available on the Companion CD-ROM in Visual Basic form as well as a text-only copy that you can print out and read. On the Companion CD-ROM the text-only file is called CGIMAPI.TXT.

The module CGI.BAS does the work of collecting the CGI data from the server. It puts the data you need in a number of data variables that you can use as you wish. Specifically, there are a number of variables that reflect the content of the environment variables described earlier in this chapter. There are also two arrays that contain all the information passed in from the form. These two variables are CGI_FormTuples(i).key and CGI_FormTuples(i).value. Both are string variables, and *.key* contains the name of the field as entered on the form, while *.value* contains the data the user entered in the corresponding field.

Most of the newly added module is shown on pages 274-276. The code in Section A sets up the MAPI session with Windows. The originator of the e-mail is the user "webdoc." In Section B, each incoming data field is examined. The fields are stored in the CGI_FormTuples array in the order they appear on the HTML form. For each recognized field, a line is printed in the output mail message. In Section C, the MAPI session is completed, and the mail message is sent off. Finally in Section D, a short message is composed, which is sent back to the Web browser saying the message was sent. After section D is an error-handling routine. For brevity, most of the error cases have been removed.

```
Sub CGI_Main ()
   Dim sel As String
   Dim buf As String
   Dim i As Integer
   Dim Msg As String
   Load Mapi1   ' This starts the Mail API Session by loading the FORM with the MAPI session
and message
   On Error GoTo handleerror
' ****** Section A ******
   Mapi1.MapiSession1.UserName = "webdoc"     ' The Web Page "user"
   Mapi1.MapiSession1.Password = "webdoc"
   Mapi1.MapiSession1.Action = SESSION_SIGNON
   Mapi1.Msg1.SessionID = Mapi1.MapiSession1.SessionID   ' Set up to send message
   Mapi1.Msg1.Action = MESSAGE_COMPOSE              ' Start creating the message
   Mapi1.Msg1.MsgIndex = -1                                   ' Message composition, not
reading
' ****** End of Section A ******
   If CGI_NumFormTuples > 2 Then ' Check to see that the processing is OK so far
      ' Now, assign the fields that are coming in from the Comments Form into a mail message
      ' You could also do other things here, such as store the info in a file, or a database
      ' We parse on the CGI_FormTuples(n).key, since when a field is not filled out on the
sending form
      ' the value is not included in the information sent here
      ' The possible values for the key, based on the form formsamp.hml are:
      ' prodname, version, type, textcomment, serialnumber, phonenumber, e-mail, beta and
revision
      Mapi1.Msg1.MsgNoteText = "Comment Form Submission: "
      For i = 0 To CGI_NumFormTuples - 1
' ****** Section B ******
         Select Case CGI_FormTuples(i).key
            Case "beta"
              Mapi1.Msg1.MsgNoteText = Mapi1.Msg1.MsgNoteText & "Beta Requested. "
            Case "prodname"
              Select Case CGI_FormTuples(i).value
                 ' Note here that we are using the VALUE parameter to select the correct product
                 Case "1": Mapi1.Msg1.MsgNoteText = Mapi1.Msg1.MsgNoteText & "For Product:
D&Z"
                 Case "2": Mapi1.Msg1.MsgNoteText = Mapi1.Msg1.MsgNoteText & "For Product:
D&VG"
                 Case "3": Mapi1.Msg1.MsgNoteText = Mapi1.Msg1.MsgNoteText & "For Product:
D&VG DWG"
                 Case "4": Mapi1.Msg1.MsgNoteText = Mapi1.Msg1.MsgNoteText & "For Product:
D&F"
                 Case "5": Mapi1.Msg1.MsgNoteText = Mapi1.Msg1.MsgNoteText & "For Product:
Fileman"
                 Case Else: Mapi1.Msg1.MsgNoteText = Mapi1.Msg1.MsgNoteText & "For
Unspecified Product"
              End Select
            Case "version"
              Mapi1.Msg1.MsgNoteText = Mapi1.Msg1.MsgNoteText & "Version Level: " &
CGI_FormTuples(i).value & ".  "
            Case "type"
              Mapi1.Msg1.MsgNoteText = Mapi1.Msg1.MsgNoteText & "Report Type: " &
CGI_FormTuples(i).value & "  "
```

```
            Case "type_1"   ' These cases are for multiple selections in the TYPE field
              Mapi1.Msg1.MsgNoteText = Mapi1.Msg1.MsgNoteText & "and " &
CGI_FormTuples(i).value & "  "
            Case "type_2"
              Mapi1.Msg1.MsgNoteText = Mapi1.Msg1.MsgNoteText & "and " &
CGI_FormTuples(i).value & "  "
            Case "type_3"
              Mapi1.Msg1.MsgNoteText = Mapi1.Msg1.MsgNoteText & "and " &
CGI_FormTuples(i).value & "  "
            Case "type_4"
              Mapi1.Msg1.MsgNoteText = Mapi1.Msg1.MsgNoteText & "and " &
CGI_FormTuples(i).value & "  "
            Case "revision"
              Mapi1.Msg1.MsgNoteText = Mapi1.Msg1.MsgNoteText & "Form Revision" &
CGI_FormTuples(i).value & "  "
            Case "textcomment"
              Mapi1.Msg1.MsgNoteText = Mapi1.Msg1.MsgNoteText & "Comment: " &
CGI_FormTuples(i).value & ".  "
            Case "serialnumber"
              Mapi1.Msg1.MsgNoteText = Mapi1.Msg1.MsgNoteText & "Serial Number: " &
CGI_FormTuples(i).value & ".  "
            Case "phonenumber"
              Mapi1.Msg1.MsgNoteText = Mapi1.Msg1.MsgNoteText & "Phone Number: " &
CGI_FormTuples(i).value & ".  "
            Case "e-mail"
              Mapi1.Msg1.MsgNoteText = Mapi1.Msg1.MsgNoteText & "e-mail Address: " &
CGI_FormTuples(i).value & ".  "
            Case Else
              Mapi1.Msg1.MsgNoteText = Mapi1.Msg1.MsgNoteText & CGI_FormTuples(i).key &
" = " & CGI_FormTuples(i).value & ". "
          End Select

          Mapi1.Msg1.MsgNoteText = Mapi1.Msg1.MsgNoteText & Chr(10)
      Next
    Mapi1.Msg1.MsgNoteText = Mapi1.Msg1.MsgNoteText & "End of Comment "
' ****** End of Section B ******
    Else
      Mapi1.Msg1.MsgNoteText = "Message Text Was Missing..."
    End If
' ****** Section C ******
    Mapi1.Msg1.MsgSubject = "From " & CGI_RemoteAddr
    Mapi1.Msg1.RecipDisplayName = "Comment User"
    Mapi1.Msg1.Action = MESSAGE_RESOLVENAME
    Mapi1.Msg1.Action = MESSAGE_SEND

    Unload Mapi1
' ****** End of Section C ******
' ****** Section D ******
    StartMailResp
    Send ("<H2>OK!</H2>")
    Send ("<P>Thanks for your input. Your comments have been recorded.</P>")
    GoTo Finishup
' ******End of Section D ******
 handleerror:
      Unload Mapi1
```

```
        StartMailResp
        Select Case Err
           Case MAPI_USER_ABORT:   Msg = "MAPI_USER_ABORT "
                        :
                        : More error handling
                        :
           Case CONTROL_E_NO_ATTACHMENTS: Msg = "CONTROL_E_NO_ATTACHMENTS "
           Case Else: Msg = "Error " & Err


        End Select
        Send ("<H2>Error:</H2>")
        Send ("<P>Due to a system error: " & Msg & ", this message could not be sent. We're
sorry..</P>")
        Resume Finishup

   ' Finish up with server admin's address. Return to complete HTTP.
   '
Finishup:
   Send ("<HR>")
   Send ("</A></BODY></HTML>")

   '****** RETURN, DON'T STOP! ******
End Sub
```

Trying Out the Sample Program

Even if you don't have Visual Basic, you can test the example program. You'll need to install Robert Denny's server on a Windows 3.1 (or Windows for Workgroups) system first. This is discussed in Chapter 12, "Servers at Your Service." Spend some time with the server to understand how it works, then come back here to test this program.

Copy the form SAMPFORM.HTM to the server's HTDOCS directory. Replace the place-holder "yourhost" in SAMPFORM.HTM with the name of your own server. Copy the program COMMENTS.EXE from the Companion CD-ROM to the *cgi-win* directory of the server directory tree. If you do not already have it in your Windows system directory, copy in the file MSMAPI.VBX. The Visual Basic file is VBRUN300.DLL and should be installed in your Windows System directory already—if you have tried out the samples that come with the Win-HTTPD server. Finally, copy the files comment.gif and spacer.gif to the *images* directory of the server.

You also need to have Microsoft Mail installed and working on your computer. Windows for Workgroups comes with MS Mail, but you may need to run it for the first time and create a post office on your PC if you have never run MS Mail before. Add two new "users" to the MS Mail post office: "WebDoc" and "Comment User." Set the password for the WebDoc user to webdoc. (Or change the VB code to match the user you want.)

Now open SAMPFORM.HTM with Netscape. You should see the form as illustrated in Figure 9-16. Enter text in the various fields and select the Send Comments button. After several seconds (about 15 seconds on a 386/18) you will see either an error message, if you did something wrong, or a "Thanks for your input" page as shown in Figure 9-17. Once this has succeeded, the "Comment User" MS Mail user can check for new mail. The new mail message from user "WebDoc" should look like Figure 9-18.

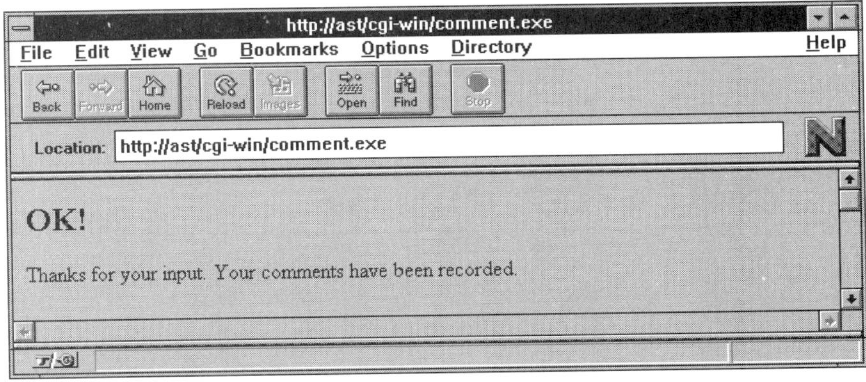

Figure 9-17: *Results page from the comment submission.*

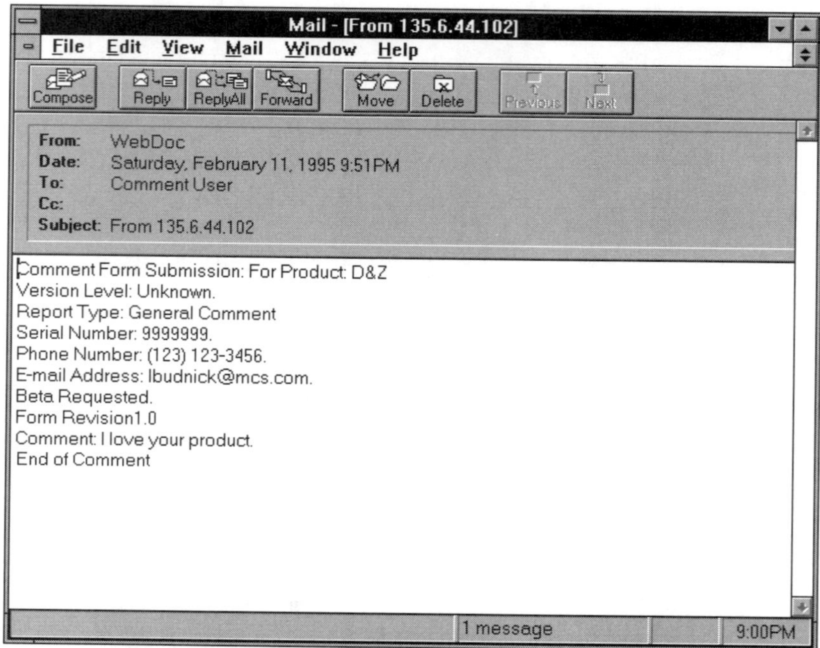

Figure 9-18: *The new mail message from the user named "WebDoc."*

Using an ISINDEX Tag

Using the ISINDEX tag is another way to gather input from a user. A page containing ISINDEX is generated by a CGI program so that when the user enters the information and presses Enter, the resulting URL is sent back to the same CGI processing program that created the page.

When the user enters text in an ISINDEX field and presses the Enter key, a special URL request is sent to the server. The URL is the original URL of the page, with the addition of a question mark and the text entered by the user. For example, if the URL of the HTML page with the ISINDEX tag were:

```
http://myhost.mycompany.com/cgi-bin/specialpage.exe
```

and the user entered:

```
aladdin lamp
```

then the resulting URL sent back to the server would be:

```
http://myhost.mycompany.com/cgi-bin/
specialpage.exe?aladdin+lamp
```

The server would send this command line to the program specialpage.exe, which would parse the data "aladdin+lamp" and return the appropriate information, which would typically be the result of a search of files or a database lookup. This is a frequently used technique with UNIX-based Web servers.

Real-Time Page Creation & Other Tricks

The ability to have a back-end program create text or HTML pages is not limited to responses to database queries and comment forms. Here are just a few ideas to get you started.

Page Content Based on Client Address

One of the pieces of information your CGI program gets when called is the address of the remote host. If you parse the remote host address, you could provide different information to different people. For instance, you may have a database of information that contains some sensitive information, so only certain users get the full information. Everyone in a group, however, should have access to the basic database information. Still others—not in the group—should be presented with a screen that invites them to subscribe to your database service. By reading the IP address that is requesting the information, you can create customized pages based on IP addresses.

Hackers almost always access their targets through systems that appear legal. You should only use this technique for systems that are secure, or isolated from the Internet. You could, however, combine this technique with the basic authentication provided by many of the servers to create an additional layer of security.

Master Pages That Point to Dynamic Addresses

The information on the World Wide Web is becoming increasingly commercial, and you may want to prevent others from linking to any page on your Web (or a part of your Web) other than your home page. For instance, you might want to have a significant copyright notice on your Web document, but not want to repeat it on every page. By making the "top" page of your document a CGI reference, you can have a CGI program generate your home page with internal links that change daily (or hourly) and have a coordinated program change the names of your internal pages at the same time. This way, if someone does establish a link directly to a subpage, the link won't be good for very long. Again, this is not a way to secure your server, but only to guide most users through a top page before accessing a lower-level page.

Creating a Game Web

You could create an entire Web page that's a game—with links that change randomly or according to what others are doing on your server at the same time. This is particularly interesting when used with image maps that just pass back the coordinates a user clicked. The CGI back-end could select different destinations at different times. Also, the images that are returned to a user could change, based on various factors.

Moving On

With the addition of forms and the CGI interface, your formal introduction to the pieces of HTML authoring is complete. Now it's time to move on to putting together what you've learned in a series of examples in Part 3, "Putting the Pieces Together." Additional examples of CGI interface programs for various Windows-based HTTP servers are provided in Chapter 12, "Servers at Your Service."

10

Looking Good on the Net

The Web is a unique new media venue that brings with it new ways to present information and marketing. The layout possibilities for an HTML document are fairly limited, but the Web is teeming with creativity. Looking good on the Net is its own reward. Unlike typical advertising, the Web is its own vehicle for publicity. If I like your Web page, I can, in turn, become a publicist for your site and include a link to your site in a list of sites that I recommend. And because the Web thrives on sharing information and recommendations, presenting a well-designed, good looking page will encourage others to promote your Web site. The cycle continues and soon your site is caught in the Web. This chapter shows different ways to present Web pages and shares some examples of sites that exploit the power of Web publishing.

Guidelines for Internet Publishing

In Chapter 3, we stressed the importance of structuring information and defining your document's goal to capture your audience. The following sections build on the skeletal outline of your Web site. The main concerns addressed are: making sure your Web documents match the reader's needs and creating pages that look good on the Net, regardless of who is accessing your site.

Present Content-Based Web Pages

Web publishing is an extension of other publishing media; it complements rather than replaces traditional publishing. The Web is still somewhat of a grassroots publishing movement centered around current, off-the-cuff information. For the most part, people searching the Web are looking for content-based information. They also may want to be entertained, but they don't want to be bombarded by advertising hype. The key to successful Web publishing is to take a unique approach to publishing visually appealing pages and presenting content-based messages that others will appreciate.

Look Beyond Web Browsers & Fast Connections

Anyone can access Web pages, how they access them can determine how well your Web pages appear onscreen. One reader may have an ISDN connection and another may connect using a 9600 baud modem. It's important to make the size of inline image files as small as possible, yet maintain a professional quality, or include two presentations of your site: one for graphics-based browsers and the other for text-based browsers. Whenever possible be sure to include the ALT attribute, to address people using text-based browsers.

If you want to make files available to the widest audience, you'll want to add other Internet services to capture Internet users that don't have access to the World Wide Web. FTP and Gopher are two text-based methods of sharing files and information that can also be accessed on the World Wide Web. Setting up an FTP server is a fairly simple operation. Most service providers, companies that sell Internet connections and provide server services, and server services, companies that sell space or Net publishing services, will set up an FTP site for a small charge. Setting up a Gopher site at a service provider or server service is usually a little more difficult and expensive. If you're publishing using a server of your own, Windows NT includes an FTP server. Many Windows 3.x TCP/IP packages, such as NetManage's Chameleon and Frontier Technologies's SuperTCP Pro, include FTP servers. Once you've set up an FTP site, you can add a link to the FTP site in your World Wide Web page.

Address Security Issues

Security is a major issue if you're selling a product or service online. If potential customers don't feel that ordering from your site is safe, you're not going to succeed. Some people are reluctant to use their credit card to place an order over the Internet, even if you're using a secure server. Therefore, it's important to give your readers an alternative to sending their credit card information over the Net, such as publishing an 800 number or including a fax order line. Some sites let users set up credit card accounts over the phone and then let users send in orders via e-mail. This ensures that the credit card information isn't intercepted over the Net.

If you're creating Web documents to be published on a UNIX-based server, you may want to search out a service provider or server service that provides a secure server. Netscape Communications and NCSA both offer secure servers and Web browsers. You also may want to check out some of the toolkits for conducting business on the Net. OpenMarket, for example, provides a StoreBuilder toolkit that works with existing Web clients and uses a payment URL that encodes the price and date in the information sent to the client program. You can find out about StoreBuilder and other OpenMarket products and services at http://www.openmarket.com/about/ProdBackground.html.

Terisa Systems, a joint venture between RSA Data Security and Enterprise Integration Technologies (EIT) has announced a suite of client and server tools called SecureWeb Toolkit that incorporates a variety of encryption schemes to enable you to perform secure transactions over the Net. Digital signatures, which can be used to verify the identity of someone over the Net, are also supported.

If you use a secure server, such as Netscape's commercial secure server, or an alternative method of security, inform your readers. Many people want to be reassured or will want to know just how safe your system is. The more comfortable a customer feels the more likely he or she is to purchase your product online.

Pretty Good Privacy (PGP)

If you want to share private documents with other users, check out PGP (Pretty Good Privacy). PGP is available as freeware for non-commercial users. Version 2.6.2 is the safest version. Version 2.3a is more popular, but there are some patent issues that have yet to be resolved. PGP lets you generate public and private keys for encrypting and decrypting documents. Some Web sites, such as CDnow! (http://cdnow.com/), use PGP to perform business transactions. If you want to buy a license for PGP, contact Via Crypt at (800) 536-2664.

Let Readers Respond

Be sure to include a link to a form for reader feedback. Many sites also include a guest book for readers to include comments. Letting readers respond shows that you care about what your readers have to say about your product, service or site. If you don't include a comments form, at the very least include an e-mail address. Publishing a Web document without an e-mail address connotes that the information is wanting, and will likely receive the same attention given an unsigned form letter. Not only does omitting an address frustrate readers, it also short circuits the power of the Web, cutting you off from individuals who may have valuable input.

Validate Your Web Document

HoTMetaL PRO is a rules-based HTML editor. If you create your document with HoTMetaL PRO, you can choose the Special>>Validate Document command to make sure that your document conforms to the standard HTML rules. Most Web browsers are very forgiving right now about bad HTML coding, but this is expected to change. The more HTML tools that enter the arena the greater the need to write HTML code that conforms to the HTML standard.

HTML validation services exist on the Web that can check the validity of an HTML document. Some can even point out common HTML authoring mistakes. For example, Weblint is a perl script written by Neil Bowers and is presented as a public service of UniPress. The Weblint form lets you enter your URL to check the validity of your Web document. It also checks for any anchor text that uses the word "here," a common Web publishing faux pas. The Weblint form is available at http://www.unipress.com/weblint/.

Another HTML validation site is available at HAL Computer Systems. Presented by Mark Gaither, this service lets you specify the level of HTML conformance, including Strict, Level 0 through Level 3, and a Mozilla option for testing HTML documents with Netscape extensions. To use the HTML Validation Service, enter http://www.hal.com/~markg/WebTechs/validation-form.html.

Provide Portable Document Alternatives

Not all information lends itself to short Web pages. In some cases, you may want to present a brochure that has high-quality images and extensive formatting, but you want to make them available to users of different platforms online. Some readers are paying for connection time and may want to download the document to save money and read the document off-line.

The answer to presenting a formatted document is to create a portable document using a program like Acrobat or Common Ground. This way you can have control over the output of the document. Adobe's Acrobat and No Hands Software's Common Ground are both trying to become the standard multi-platform publishing tool. Acrobat's PDF format supports hypertext links that start and load the Web page in your Web browser when you click a Web-based hyperlink. Both Acrobat and Common Ground viewers are free. Acrobat is the defacto standard. Common Ground 2.0 uses a proprietary format called Digital Paper. Digital Paper uses TrueDoc technology to convert TrueType and PostScript Type 1 fonts into compressed scaleable fonts.

Creating an Adobe Portable Document File requires that you purchase Acrobat Exchange, which includes the Acrobat PDF writer. To create a portable document, choose the Acrobat printer driver and print the document to a file. Creating a Digital Paper document is done in a similar manner. You purchase the Common Ground program and use a printer driver to print the file in the Digital Paper format. Common Ground also gives you the option of embedding the viewer and the document into a single executable file. So unlike Acrobat files, the reader does not have to have the Common Ground viewer to read the file. This is really a moot point since the Acrobat reader is free. It is also possible to print a document to a PostScript file and include a hyperlink to the PostScript file, but this is fast becoming an outdated method. Acrobat and Common Ground include many features, such as adding hypertext links, that can't be done with a PostScript file. Ultimately we will see a Web browser that includes the capability to read PDF or Digital Paper files.

The Acrobat Reader and Common Ground Viewer are both included on the Companion CD-ROM. As of this writing, Common Ground was not available on the Net. However the Acrobat is. If you like, you can include a link to Adobe's FTP site for users to download the Acrobat Reader. The URL for the Adobe Acrobat Reader is ftp://ftp.adobe.com/pub/adobe/Applications/Acrobat/Windows/acroread.exe.

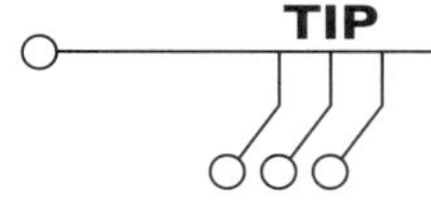

Adobe has done a great job of including a list of hyperlinks to sites that produce exemplary PDF documents. You can check out these PDF documents by visiting Adobe's site at http://www.adobe.com/.

Take a Unique Approach

One way to look good on the Net is to take a unique approach or offer a superior service to other Web sites. Just about anyone who has spent any amount of time surfing the Net has come across CyberSight. CyberSight's popularity is credited to its great graphics and unique interactive approach to presenting entertaining information. If you haven't seen CyberSight, enter the URL: http://cybersight.com/. Figure 10-1 shows CyberSight's home page. Taking an innovative approach to your site is sure to draw a crowd. The following sections include several examples of sites taking unique approaches to Web publishing.

Figure 10-1: *CyberSight is popular for having a sense of humor and its unique interactive approach.*

Offer Contests, Games & Freebies

Contests, games and freebies have long been a staple of TV and print advertising. One of the most impressive Net-based contests was written up in *Internet World* magazine by Andrew Kanto and Eric Berlin. Kanto and Berlin tell how Bill Powderly and his wife had bought a mansion in Hope, Pennsylvania, and began to renovate it. Later they decided to sell the mansion, but had little luck. After some thought, Bill decided to hold a contest on the Net to give away the mansion. For $100 a person, 14,999 people had a shot at winning a total of 98 prizes ranging in value from $500 to $50,000 plus the grand prize of either Powderly's 1.3 million dollar mansion or $500,000 in cash. In order to play you had to pay a $100 entry fee and download the contest software, which was a question-based game similar to Jeopardy.

Internet Marketing Inc., the same people that brought you CyberSight, created a site for Stolichnaya Vodka that includes an interactive puzzle, an interactive painting and a random Web site game. Figure 10-2 shows the interactive puzzle on the Stoli Cipher page. You can visit Stolichnaya's home page at http://www.stoli.com.

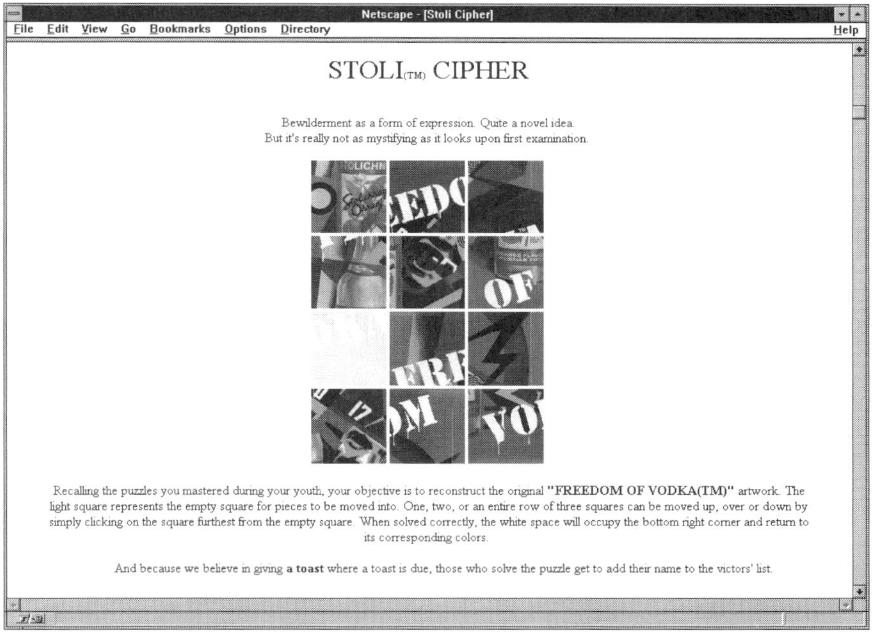

Figure 10-2: *Stolichnya presents Stoli Cipher, an interactive puzzle.*

Another way to catch readers' interest is to offer freebies, such as drawings for a free T-shirt. Some companies offer free items for anyone purchasing over a certain amount of merchandise. We looked up the word "contest" at Yahoo and found over 50 companies that offered free prizes for drawings or correct submissions that solved an online puzzle. While the idea of a drawing for a freebie is not unique, many sites add their own twist by presenting unique contests, for example one site offered prizes to the winner of a Web scavenger hunt.

Provide a Service

Some sites draw attention to themselves by offering a unique service. Depending on the type of service, this approach can sometimes require some programming expertise. Many large universities and companies have gained notoriety by offering searching services and subject listings. For example Stanford University, EINet, and O'Reilly and Associates, all have received accolades for their search facilities and well-organized subject listings of hyperlinks to Web sites. One of the most popular sites is Yahoo, which stands for Yet another hierarchical officious oracle. Figure 10-3 shows the Yahoo list of Web sites. You can visit Yahoo at http://www.yahoo.com/yahoo/.

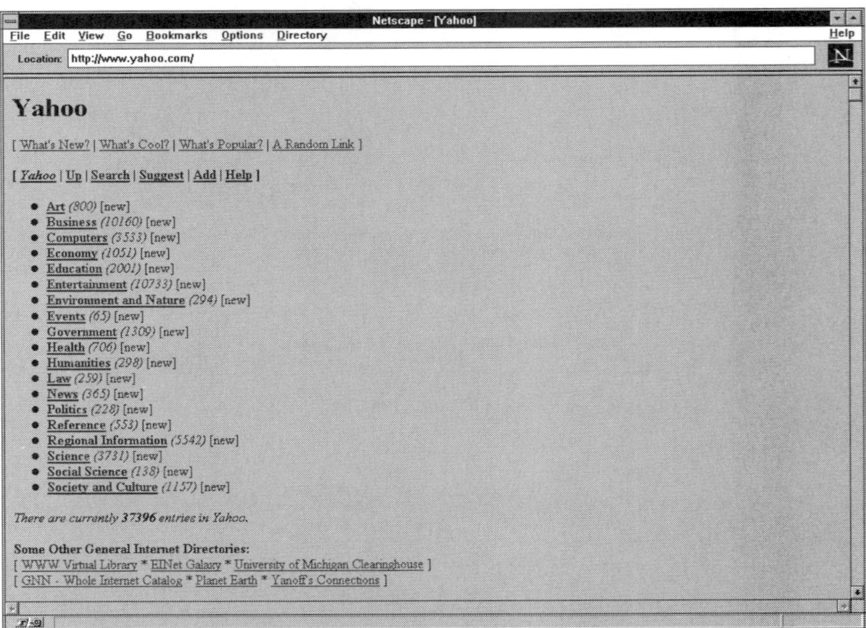

Figure 10-3: *Yahoo is a huge hierarchical listing of Web sites organized by subject.*

Computer Literacy is the largest computer bookstore in the world. A practical service Computer Literacy Bookshops brings to the Web is their database of computer books. Not only does this service provide information on computer related books, but obviously is helpful for their mail-order business. The search form lets you search for books by author, title, ISBN or subject. Figure 10-4 shows Computer Literacy Bookshops' database search form. You can visit the database page directly by entering the URL: http://www.clbooks.com/cgi-bin/browsedb.

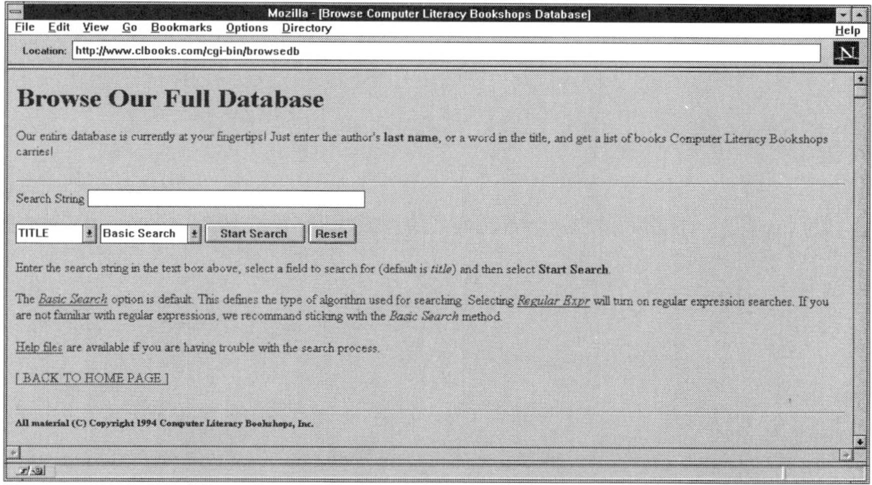

Figure 10-4: *Computer Literacy Bookshops' database lets readers look up books by author, title, ISBN or subject.*

David Koblas is well known for his Currency Converter Web page. This page is a part of O'Reilly and Associates Web site. It presents the value of a nation's currency relative to another nations. You can try out the Currency Converter at http://www.ora.com/cgi-bin/ora/currency. David is also the author of the command-line version of giftool, which is included on the Companion CD-ROM.

Taxing Times is a service provided by the S-Cubed Division of Maxwell Labs. The page presents U.S. and Canadian tax information. The primary service is an extensive archive of Federal and State tax forms and instructions in different formats, such as Adobe Acrobat's PDF format. You can even download the entire tax code. Many of the forms can be downloaded and legally used for submitting your taxes. Taxing Times resides at http://inept.scubed.com/tax/tax.html.

Kansas University Campus Internet Association came up with an innovative idea that has generated a lot of links and publicity. URouLette is a Web page that uses an image map of a roulette wheel to send visitors to a completely random Web site. Figure 10-5 shows the URouLette Web page. You can try out URouLette by entering http://kuhttp.cc.ukans.edu/cwis/organizations/kuica/uroulette/uroulette.html.

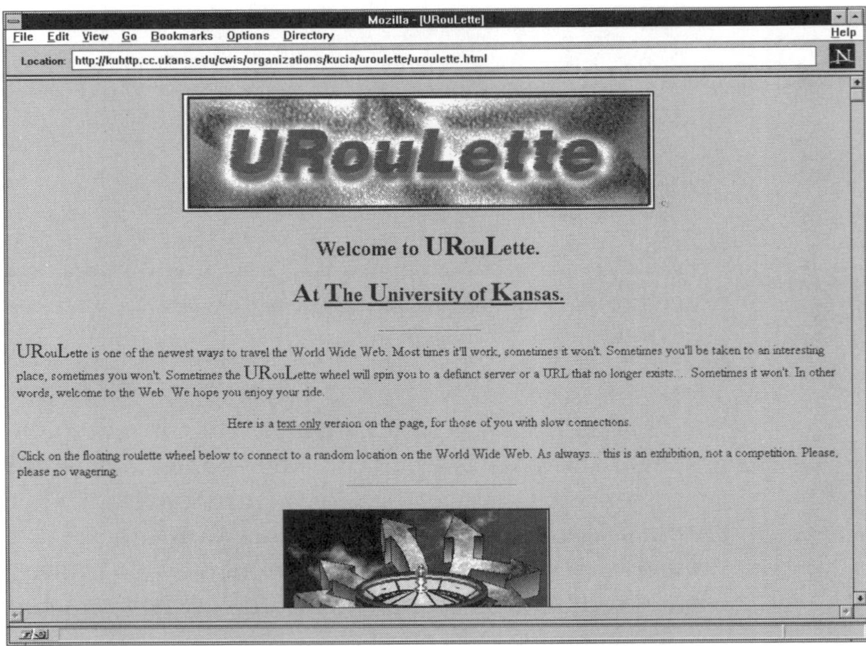

Figure 10-5: *The URouLette Web page presents an image map of a roulette wheel that when clicked sends visitors to a completely random Web site.*

Thomas Boutell is a savvy programmer who is responsible for the Mapedit program used for creating image maps. Mapedit is included on the Companion CD-ROM. Tom also came up with the idea to present an interactive form that tells you who was born on the current day's date. It also provides links to the person's home page. Figure 10-6 shows Thomas Boutell's birthday server. You can register your birthday and include your e-mail address so others can send you b-day e-mail. Boutell's Web is at http://sunsite.unc.edu/btbin/birthday.

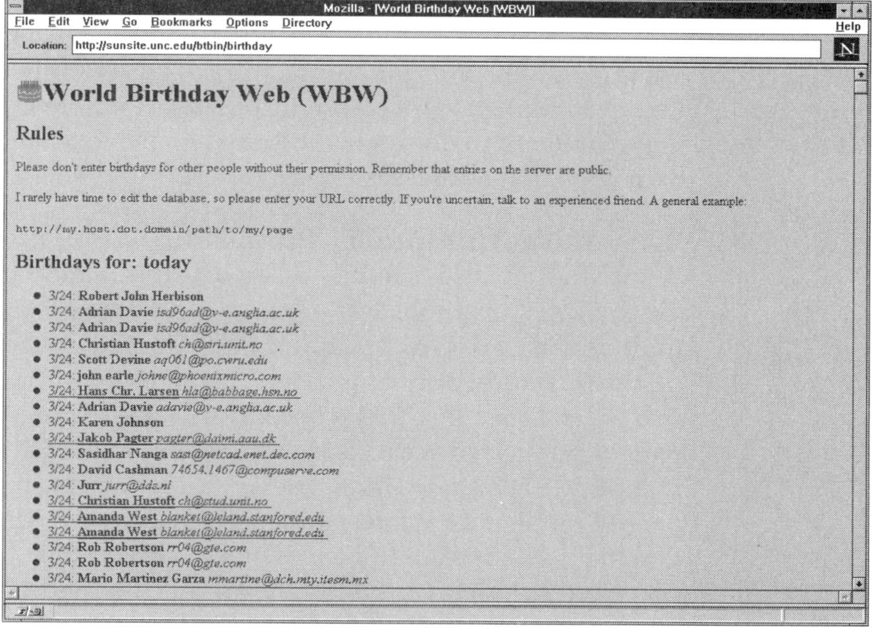

Figure 10-6: *Thomas Boutell's birthday server.*

Just about every appliance imaginable has been hooked up to the Internet and received Net coverage, including aquariums, coke machines, coffee pots, hot tubs, toasters and wine cellars. The latest trend is sites that let you remotely operate a robot's arm. You may want to be careful what object you connect to the Net or what you point your video camera at. One site that made the "Useless WWW Pages" list was a camera focused at one person's toilet.

Hey you can publish just about anything on the Net. If you want to take a look at interactive sites, check out Mark's list of Internet Interactivity at http://www.eia.brad.ac.uk/mark/fave-inter.html.

Another approach is to cover a subject you believe people are dying to know about. For example, at Christmastime many people use a Web searching facility using the keyword "Christmas" to locate sites offering Christmas related information. Centering a page around a seasonal holiday is a short lived attraction, but it does attract attention. At Christmastime, anyone who looked up the word "Christmas" was bound to come across the Cygnus Christmas tree, which presented an image of the company Christmas tree. A questionable service, but one that got a fair amount of attention on the Web and in the press. You certainly are not limited to a holiday. If you can't find a subject you're interested in, you may want to do some additional homework and create your own page that addresses the subject.

Interactive Multimedia Publishing

While the Net chokes a little when distributing large sound and video files, Web publishers get a lot of attention for presenting multimedia files. Carl Malamud has garnered quite a following by publishing audio files as a part of the Internet Multicasting Service and his Internet Talk Radio broadcasts. One feature that has been widely publicized is the "Geek of the Week," which is a weekly interview with a popular figure in the technical community. This type of publishing is fairly advanced and resource intensive, making it fall outside the realm of most Web publishers. You can check out the archives of interviews and Internet related news at http://www.ncsa.uiuc.edu/radio/radio.html.

Another multimedia centered Web site is the Internet Underground Music Archive (IUMA). IUMA is a well-designed, popular Web site that delivers a variety of free music. Rob Lord bills IUMA as "the Net's first free on-line music archive." Many of the pages include large, impressive inline images. The songs are high-quality (44.1kHz) and files are compressed and stored in the MPEG audio format. Readers can submit instant reviews and comments. An interactive form lets you set up a personalized view of the archive by choosing the artists and songs you're most interested in. Several record labels have home pages at IUMA, including Warner Brothers. Figure 10-7 shows the home page for IUMA. You can visit IUMA by entering http://www.iuma.com/.

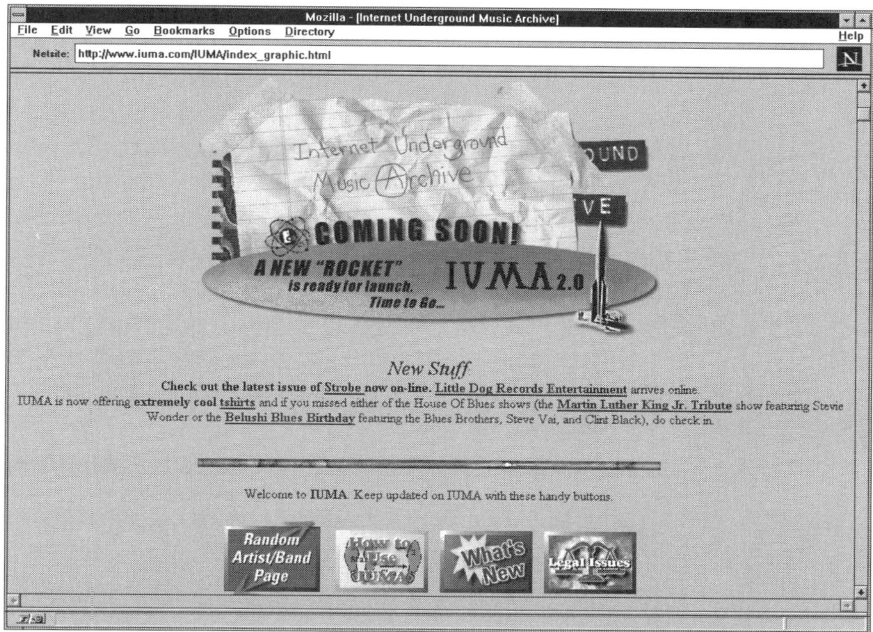

Figure 10-7: *IUMA is one of the most popular multimedia Web sites.*

Artist In Residence

Kaleidospace is an online gallery of independent artists. Artists provide samples of their works and Kaleidospace showcases them in a Web page. In order to look good on the Net and help promote the Web site, Kaleidospace employed a method of improving their recognition that has been used by many universities. They asked respected science fiction writer David Brin and graphic novelist P. Craig Russell to be artists in residence. This proved to be a great way to help promote the artists and the site. At the time we were writing this book, renowned horror author and film director Clive Barker was the artist in residence and was scheduled to share some of his original art. A behind-the-scenes interview with the cast and crew of the movie *Candyman* was also available along with a related QuickTime film clip. You can visit Kaleidospace at http://www.kspace.com.

Virtual Reality & Web Publishing

Virtual Reality environments are one of the newest trends in Web publishing. A language known as VRML (Virtual Reality Markup Language) is hovering on the horizon of Web publishing that will allow Web authors to create multi-dimensional documents. However, visitors of VRML Web sites will require a special browser. One of the first attempts at creating a virtual reality Web site using HTML is WAXweb. WAXweb marries David Blain's award-winning film, "WAX or Discovery of TV among the Bees," with the interactivity of a game, called a MOO (Multi-user Object-Oriented environments). The site embeds over a thousand images, hundreds of video clips and two thousand audio clips into the site. WAXweb lets readers interact by inserting comments and creating their own pages. Figure 10-8 shows the WAXweb home page. You can visit WAXweb at http://bug.village.virginia.edu.

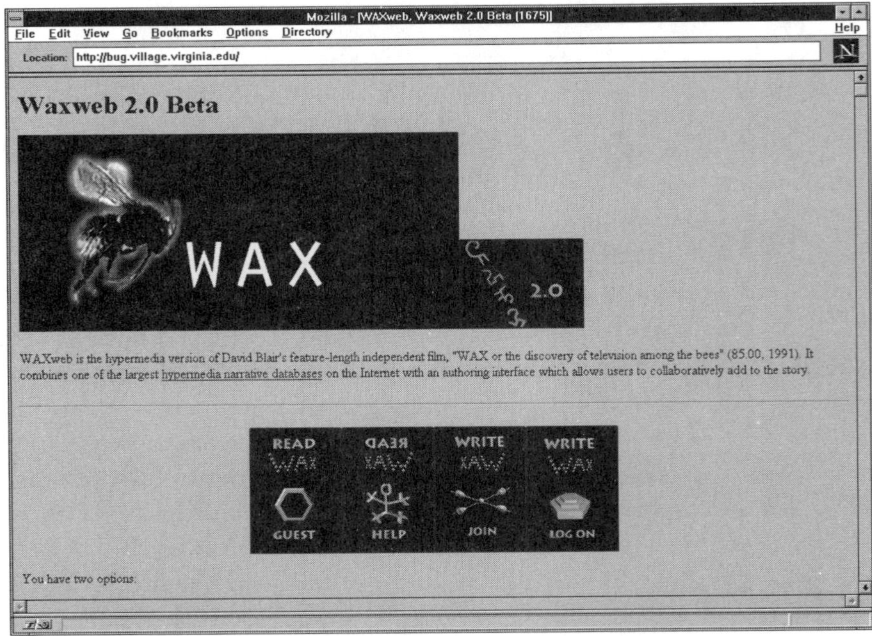

Figure 10-8: *WAXweb marries Web publishing with a MOO.*

Another multimedia MOO Web site that has received a lot of press is SenseMedia Publishing's ChibaMOO—The Sprawl. The Sprawl presents a virtual world that lets users interact and create objects and Web pages. Figure 10-9 shows the home page for the Sprawl. You can visit the Sprawl by entering http://sensemedia.net/sprawl.

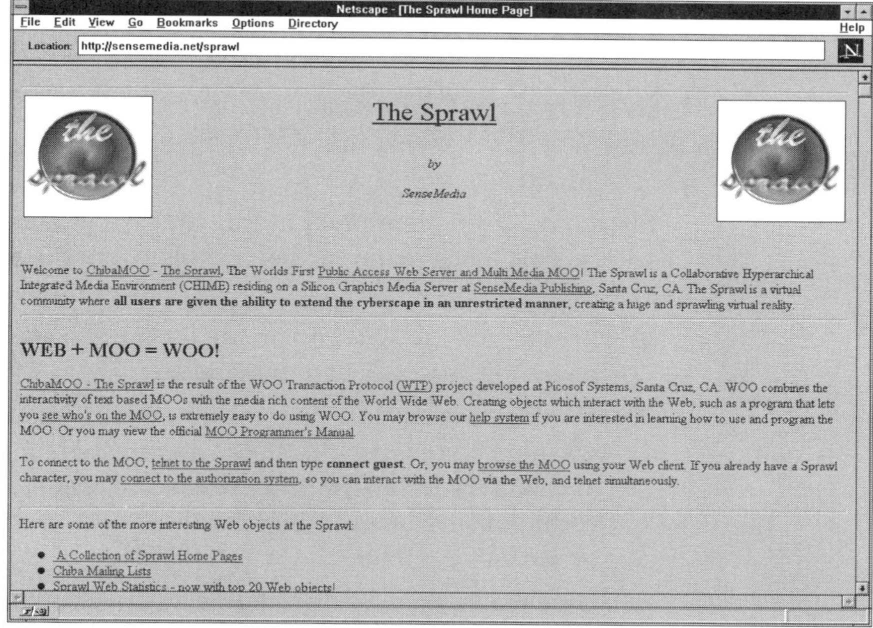

Figure 10-9: *SenseMedia Publishing's ChibaMOO—The Sprawl is an interactive cyberworld.*

Promote Your Site

In order to look good on the Net, people have to be able to find you. There are a few ways you can promote your site. You can announce your presence using other Web sites, such as NCSA's What's New page, the OpenMarket commercial sites index and the Net-Happenings mailing list and newsgroup. Some sites that include search facilities, such as Stanford University's Yahoo, are interactive and let you add your own home page to the list.

Wired, *Internet World*, *NetGuide*, *.net* and other Internet-related publications are always looking for well-designed Web pages that take a unique approach to delivering information. Ventana has two titles, *Internet Roadside Attractions* and *Walking the World Wide Web*, which list and describe interesting Web sites. These periodicals and books are only the tip of the iceberg. A more important resource, however, are the numerous Web sites, such as Netscape Communications, NCSA, GNN, and so on, that include lists of "new" and "cool" Web sites for people to visit.

Use a Design Checklist

Here are some pointers for designing a successful Web site. Some of these have been mentioned in this chapter and in previous chapters. This list is by no means complete, but it's a good place to start.

- Let readers know who you are. Be sure to sign your Web pages and provide an e-mail address.
- Use headings as headings. Don't use a heading for a note or warning just because of the formatting. New HTML tools and Web browsers promise to take advantage of HTML coding; using headers incorrectly would create an outline or table of contents that was unusable.
- Give readers a way to go home again. Every subsequent page should include a link back to the home page.
- Don't use the phrase click here. This not only insults the intelligence of your reader but it is a non-descriptive way of presenting information.
- Organize your pages so they are independent of each other. If you need to present a long document, such as documentation or a manual, include a link to the file in a portable document format.
- Copyedit and spell check your document. Grammatical errors and misspellings are annoying and can confuse your reader. Publishing a Web page filled with errors also affects your credibility.

- Don't use too many links and emphasis tags. This can make your page dark and difficult to read.
- Be consistent with the design of your Web pages. For example, don't mix two disparate types of images, such as color digital photos and black-and-white clip art.
- Inform your readers if you're using Netscape extensions. If you think that your readers will be confused include a link to the Netscape browser.
- Publish two presentations of your site if your site includes more than a couple of inline images. Create one that takes advantage of graphics for users with fast connections and the other that is primarily text-based. This way you address anyone using a text-based browser and the person who wants to get the information quickly without having to wait for the graphics to download.
- Interlace your inline images. This lets users start viewing your page quickly without having to wait for images to download.
- Keep in mind text-based browsers by including the Alternate text attribute and alternate text.
- Keep your images small—up to about 50k. Large images can be time-consuming to download and may frustrate readers with slow modem connections.
- Use thumbnails for large images. This lets readers decide which images they want to view in a larger size.
- Include the size of the file in the text if you include links to a large file, such as an image, sound or video file. This gives users some idea of how long it will take to download the file.
- Test your links to other Web pages. Many Web publishers have the best intentions when publishing a Web page, but don't take the time to ensure that the links work and are up to date.

- Provide access to a sample, rather than an actual product, you want to sell. Putting a product online at an unsecured site is one way to invite trouble. Some hackers may take this as a challenge.
- Include table of contents, indexes or cross references for long Web documents. You want readers to be able to go directly to the page or section that contains the information they want.
- Give readers a reason to come back. Present a service such as up-to-date information on a unique topic, an online comic, a contest or something that will give readers an incentive to return.
- Validate your Web pages before you publish them to make sure you haven't broken any HTML coding rules or overlooked any design mistakes.

Web Publishing Examples

Most Web documents fall into at least one of eight main categories: a home page, brochure, catalog, press release, zine, information center, virtual storefront or cybermall. The following are examples of well-designed Web pages from each of these categories. If you like, visit these sites and take a look at their source code. If you're using Netscape, choose the View>> Source command. If you want, you can use Netscape Navigator's File>>Save command to save the HTML source and modify portions of the HTML source code to meet your needs. Don't copy the site's code verbatim. Originality counts for a lot on the Web.

Home Pages

No matter what your goal, the place to start is your home page. First impressions count. If a person is not impressed with the home page, chances are they will not read on. We have chosen a couple of impressive personal home pages as examples. The first comes from Justin Hall, who publishes "Links from the Underground," an entertaining and enlightening information site that is a little on the edge. Justin is always improving his site by adding links and testing Netscape extensions. His home page shows off some of Netscape's newest extensions, such as the table's embossed border around links to the site's main attractions. If you visit, be sure to check his great hotlist. Figure 10-10 shows Justin's home page. You can visit Justin's "Links from the Underground" by entering http://www.scss.swarthmore.edu/jahall/index.html.

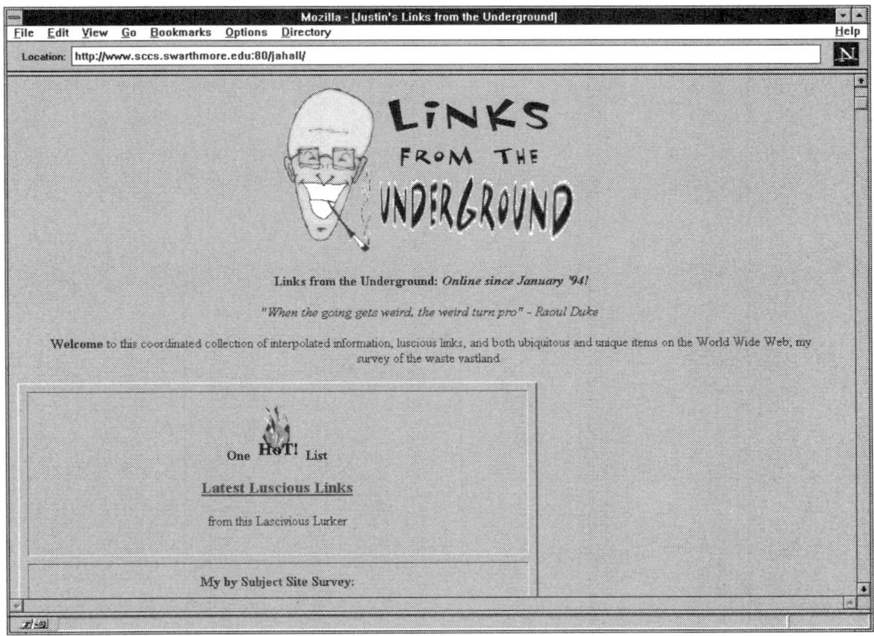

Figure 10-10: *Justin's "Links from the Underground" home page.*

Another well-designed personal Web page is brought to you by author and visionary Howard Rheingold. Figure 10-11 shows Howard Rheingold's home page. The page is fairly simple with eye-catching, transparent, interlaced graphic images strategically placed. The text is not overcrowded. The site is also divided into sections with graphic rainbow-colored horizontal rules. A few links point to pages that take advantage of the graphic and multimedia nature of the Web, including Rheingold's art, images of his painted shoes and an animation in the QuickTime format. The site also includes a link to a collection of Rheingold's popular "Tomorrow" column. This inviting home page is at once personal and professional. You can visit Howard Rheingold's home page at http://www.well.com:80/www/hlr.

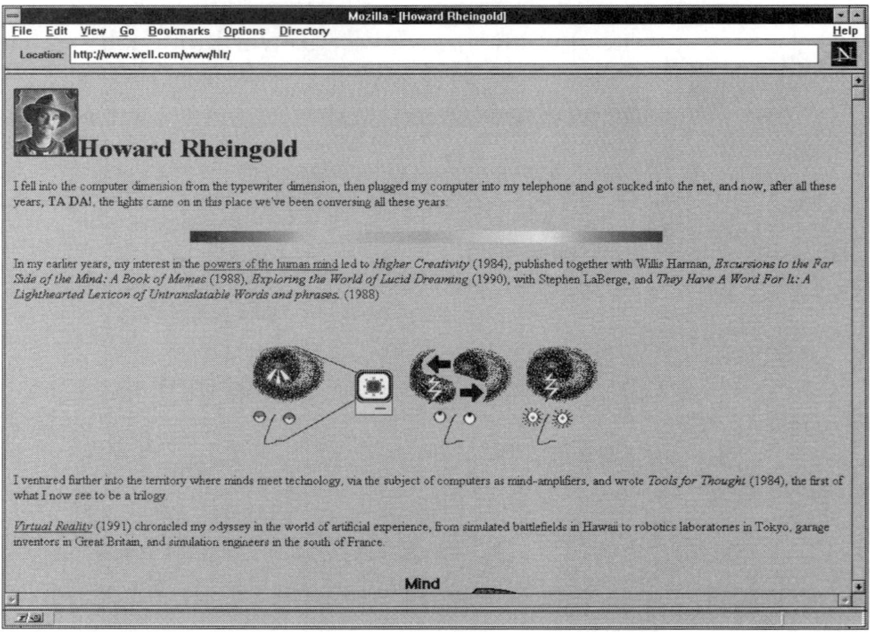

Figure 10-11: *Howard Rheingold's home page.*

Brochures

A brochure is used to describe a company's or individual's goals and are typically targeted to inform perspective customers about individual products or services. Brochures should be simple and concise. CyberSight publishes a good example of a simple Web brochure. Figure 10-12 shows some of the text used to describe CyberSight's services. You can view Internet Marketing Inc.'s brochure for creating Web sites by entering http://cybersight.com/cgi-bin/imi/s?main.gmml.

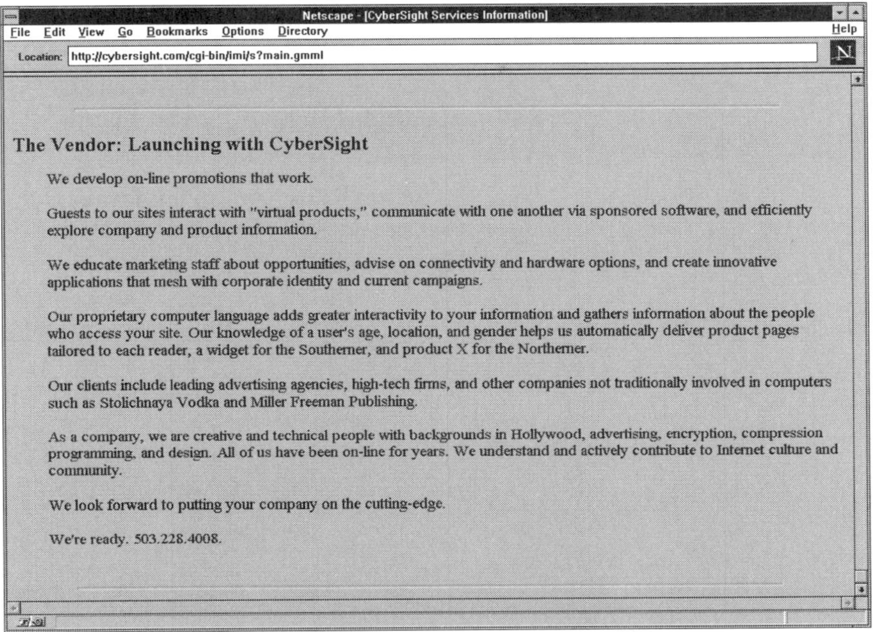

Figure 10-12: *CyberSights's brochure.*

Catalogs

A catalog is the next step beyond a brochure. Like a traditional catalog, an online catalog lists information about a product or service. Most Web catalogs include a link to an order form. A catalog may appear as a hypertext listing. One of the most comprehensive and impressive catalogs on the Net is CD*now!*'s listing of videos and compact disks. Figure 10-13 shows one screen of CD*now!*'s catalog of videos. You can visit CD*now!* at http://cdnow.com/.

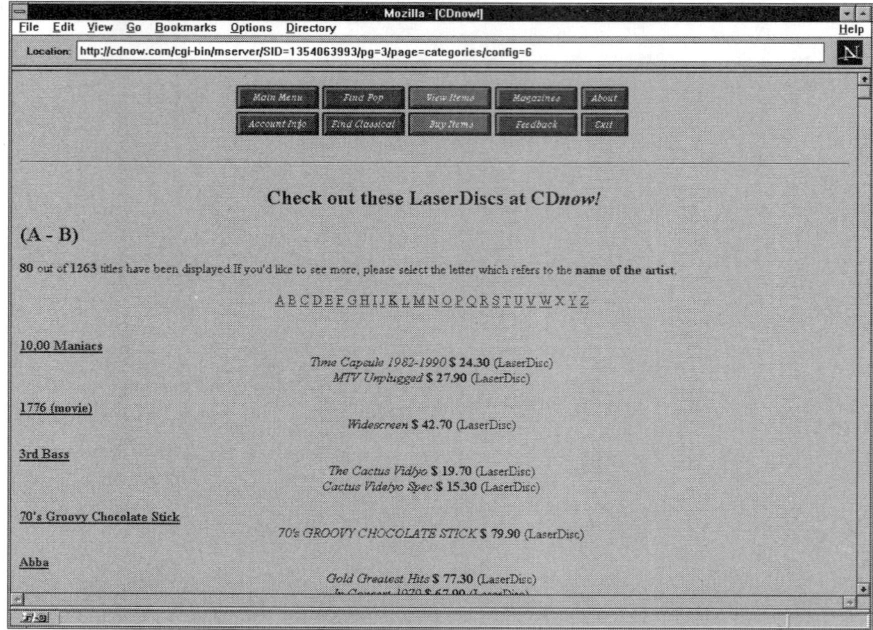

Figure 10-13: *CD*now! *includes an impressive catalog of compact disks and videos.*

Press Releases

Press releases follow the lead of their paper-based counterparts. In most cases, a press release appears exactly as it was sent out to the press. Currently only a few press releases include hyperlinks. Hyperlinks in press releases will become more prevalent as companies become more comfortable with the idea of hypermedia. Feel free to include a link at the bottom of the press release to an order form or back to the home page. Figure 10-14 show Netscape Communication's original press release for Netscape Navigator 1.1. You can display this press release by entering http://home.netscape.com/info/newsrelease16.html.

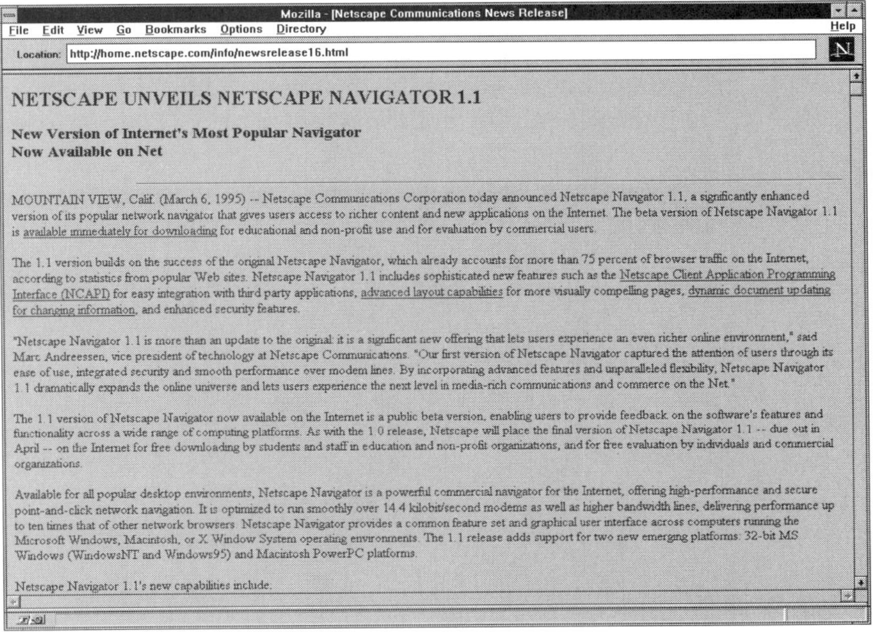

NETSCAPE UNVEILS NETSCAPE NAVIGATOR 1.1

New Version of Internet's Most Popular Navigator
Now Available on Net

MOUNTAIN VIEW, Calif. (March 6, 1995) -- Netscape Communications Corporation today announced Netscape Navigator 1.1, a significantly enhanced version of its popular network navigator that gives users access to richer content and new applications on the Internet. The beta version of Netscape Navigator 1.1 is available immediately for downloading for educational and non-profit use and for evaluation by commercial users.

The 1.1 version builds on the success of the original Netscape Navigator, which already accounts for more than 75 percent of browser traffic on the Internet, according to statistics from popular Web sites. Netscape Navigator 1.1 includes sophisticated new features such as the Netscape Client Application Programming Interface (NCAPI) for easy integration with third party applications, advanced layout capabilities for more visually compelling pages, dynamic document updating for changing information, and enhanced security features.

"Netscape Navigator 1.1 is more than an update to the original: it is a significant new offering that lets users experience an even richer online environment," said Marc Andreessen, vice president of technology at Netscape Communications. "Our first version of Netscape Navigator captured the attention of users through its ease of use, integrated security and smooth performance over modem lines. By incorporating advanced features and unparalleled flexibility, Netscape Navigator 1.1 dramatically expands the online universe and lets users experience the next level in media-rich communications and commerce on the Net."

The 1.1 version of Netscape Navigator now available on the Internet is a public beta version, enabling users to provide feedback on the software's features and functionality across a wide range of computing platforms. As with the 1.0 release, Netscape will place the final version of Netscape Navigator 1.1 -- due out in April -- on the Internet for free downloading by students and staff in education and non-profit organizations, and for free evaluation by individuals and commercial organizations.

Available for all popular desktop environments, Netscape Navigator is a powerful commercial navigator for the Internet, offering high-performance and secure point-and-click network navigation. It is optimized to run smoothly over 14.4 kilobit/second modems as well as higher bandwidth lines, delivering performance up to ten times that of other network browsers. Netscape Navigator provides a common feature set and graphical user interface across computers running the Microsoft Windows, Macintosh, or X Window System operating environments. The 1.1 release adds support for two new emerging platforms: 32-bit MS Windows (WindowsNT and Windows95) and Macintosh PowerPC platforms.

Netscape Navigator 1.1's new capabilities include:

Figure 10-14: *Netscape Communications press release for Netscape Navigator 1.1.*

Hypermedia Zines

Zines are electronic magazines and are a popular forum for self-expression on the Net. A zine can come in many different formats, such as ASCII text, hypertext, PostScript or Adobe's Portable Document Format. Hypermedia zines include many elements that are found in traditional magazines such as a masthead, table of contents and list of contributors.

One exemplary hypermedia zine is *Urban Desires: A Magazine of Metropolitan Passion*. It is an online culture magazine covering topics such as art, film, music, food and erotica. *Urban Desires* takes a highly interactive approach. For example, one Web page titled "Pocketful of Posies" includes a "Replant" button that when clicked rearranges the images on the page. It also includes pages that take advantage of Netscape's background and table extensions. *Urban Desires* is brought to you by a group of talented Web authors at agency.com, who are also responsible for *Vibe Online*, another zine. Figure 10-15 shows the front page of *Urban Desires*. To check out *Urban Desires*, enter http://desires.com/.

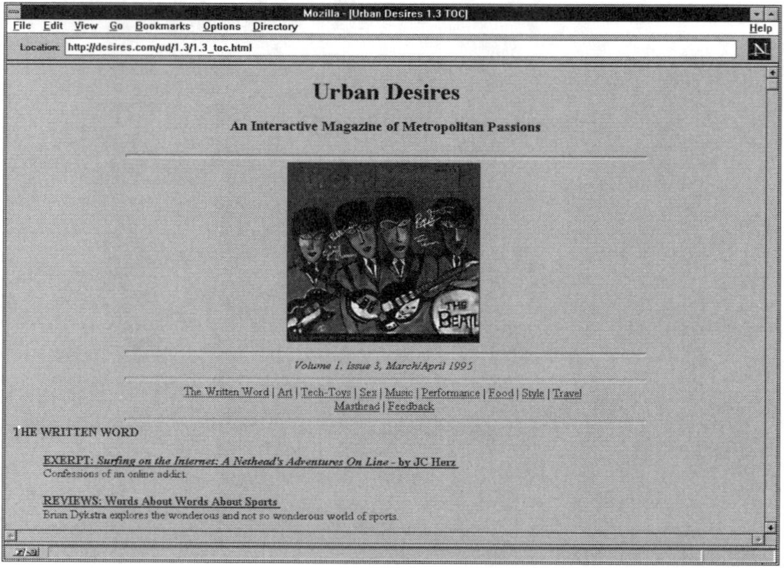

Figure 10-15: Urban Desires:An Interactive Magazine of Metropolitan Passion *is a well-laid out interactive culture zine.*

Melvin is the zine brainchild of Matt Nolker at New Media. It has been chosen by several sites, including Netscape Communications, as one of the best zines on the Net. This irreverent, humorous zine is strongly reminiscent of *National Lampoon*'s glory days, back when Doug Kenny, Michael O'Donohue, Tony Hendra, Gerald Sussman and John Hughes were writing. *Melvin* takes a unique design approach. It delivers some formatted pages as inline GIFs. This looks gorgeous, but it does have the drawback of possibly losing readers with slow connections. The images are created with a couple of Macintosh graphic programs and a UNIX layout program. It's possible to create a similar type of image file using a program such as CorelDRAW! or Adobe Illustrator to format the text and loading the file in an graphics editor program like Corel Paint or Adobe Photoshop to add and edit the images. Only a few of the pages use inline graphics to present formatted text, but many pages do include large inline images. The final production is very slick. Figure 10-16 shows the feature story presented as an inline image. You can out check out *Melvin* at http://www.melvin.com.

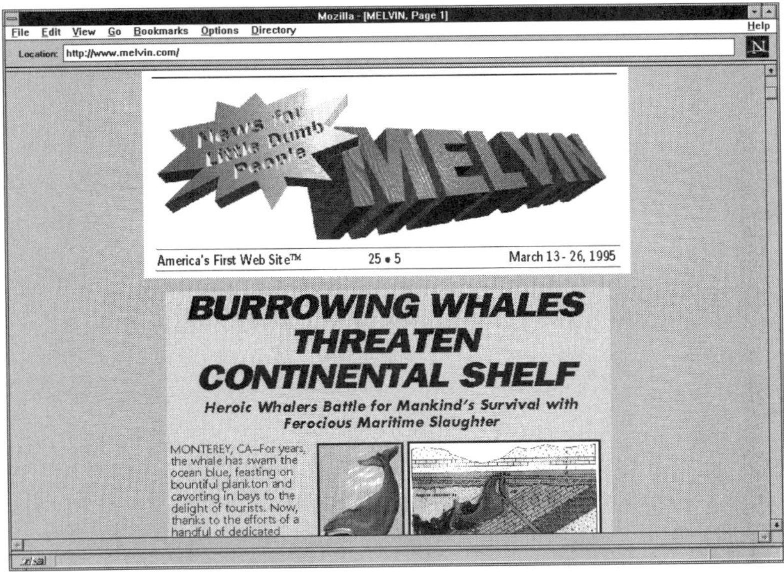

Figure 10-16: Melvin *takes a unique approach using GIFs to present two column text and graphics.*

Urban Desires and *Melvin* are two unique Web zines, but there are several other sites that are Web counterparts to traditional magazine publishing. HotWired is *Wired* magazine's foray into the Web zine scene and is one of the most popular zines on the Net. HotWired takes advantage of the Web medium to add interactive capabilities that Web publishing brings, rather than just trying to convert the text from the current issues of *Wired* magazine. You can visit HotWired at http:/www.hotwired.com. Figure 10-17 shows HotWired's home page.

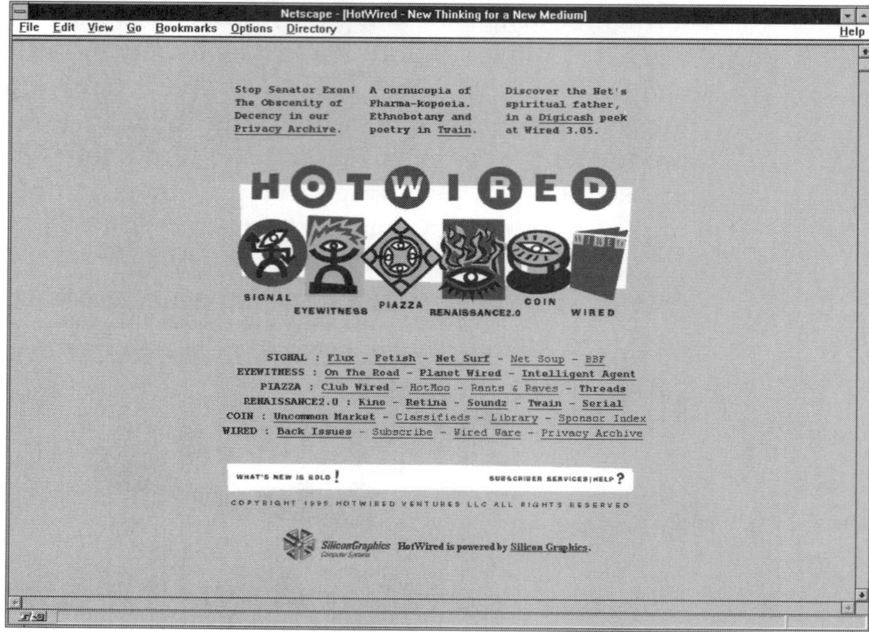

Figure 10-17: *HotWired's home page.*

Some magazines simply mirror portions of their paper-based counterparts; for example Time Warner has a site that includes links to *Time* and *People* magazine (http://www.pathfinder.com/) and Ziff Davis has a site, named Ziff Net (http://www.ziff.com), that includes links to online versions of *PC Magazine, PC Computing, Windows Sources, Computer Shopper* and more. In addition to magazines, newspapers are also appearing on the Web. One example of a newspaper on the Web that is exceptionally well designed is the San Jose Mercury News. You can read the San Jose Mercury News by entering http://www.sjmercury.com.

Information Centers

An information center is the closest type of Web site to a virtual storefront. The only difference is that an information center doesn't take orders online from the Web site. Information centers can be set up to accept orders by phone or fax. Many companies set up accounts over the phone and then accept orders via e-mail. The majority of businesses on the Net are information centers. For example, Adobe, Microsoft and Compaq are all business sites that currently fall into this category. Figure 10-18 shows Compaq's home page, which is made up of a large image map. You can visit Compaq at http://www.compaq.com.

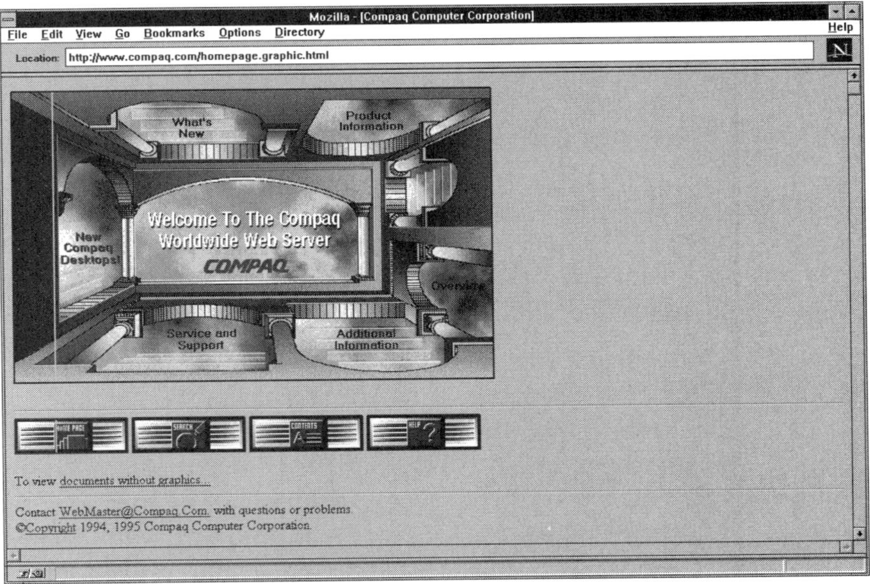

Figure 10-18: *Compaq is an example of an information center.*

To contrast two information centers, take a look at Adobe's Web site, shown in Figure 10-19. Notice that the icons are consistently designed and are fairly small in size. You can visit Adobe directly at http://www.adobe.com.

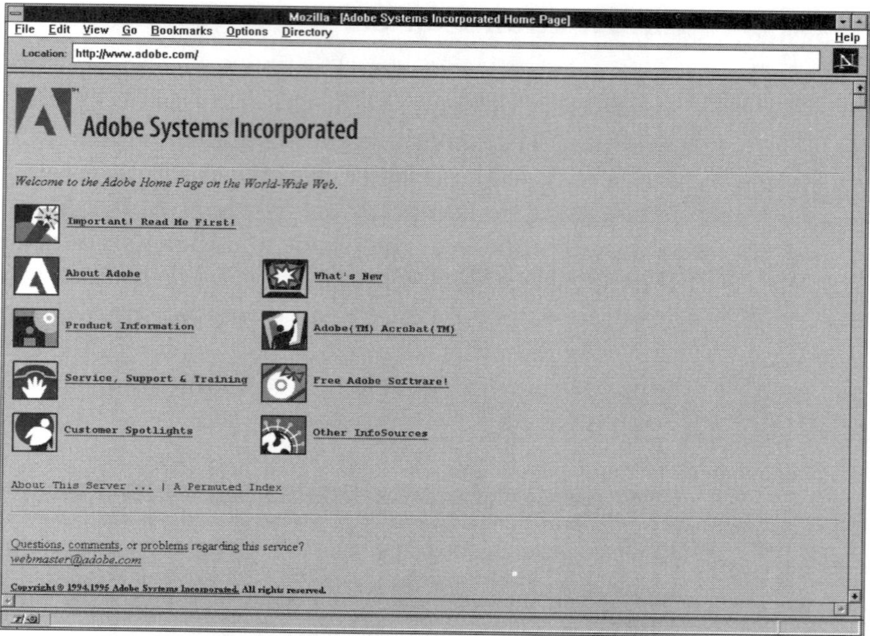

Figure 10-19: *Adobe Systems is another example of an information center.*

Virtual Storefronts & Cybermalls

A virtual storefront can be a part of a cybermall or stand alone on a server by itself. A virtual storefront, like an information center, presents products and services, but is also set up to accept credit cards online. A good example of a virtual storefront is software.net. This exceptionally well-presented site sells and ships shrink-wrapped software in addition to selling selected software programs online. The use of consistent graphics is pleasing to the eye and helps meet the site's objective. It includes all the Web pages required to inform the reader about the products and services and make the customer feel secure about ordering. This site includes the right mix of Web pages, such as a what's new page, a catalog of products indexed by subject or company, a customer support page and an online forum for sending feedback. It also has several draws, including the full text of *PC World* magazine, giveaways (at the time the site was offering free tickets to Internet World) and a drawing for a free T-shirt for readers from the pool of readers that leave feedback. Software.net is the one site that others should look to as the premiere example of a virtual storefront. Figure 10-20 shows the home page for software.net. To visit software.net enter https://www.software.net.

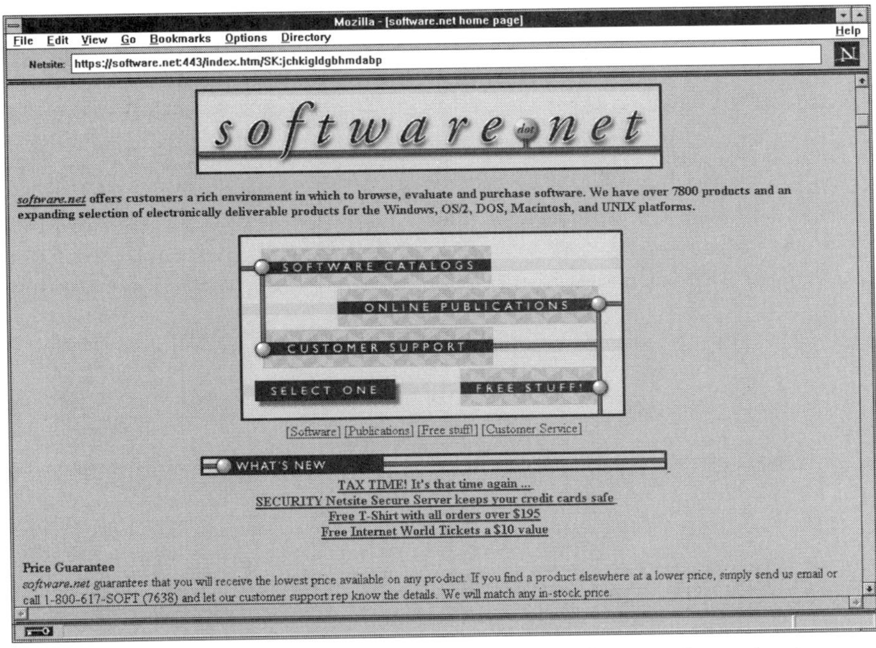

Figure 10-20: *Software.net is the premiere example of a virtual storefront.*

Another exceptional example of a virtual storefront is the Internet Shopping Network (ISN). ISN started as a part of Commerce Net, a non-profit consortium funded in part by a grant from the U.S. government's Technology Reinvestment Project. ISN was recently purchased by the Home Shopping Network. Like the Home Shopping Network, ISN presents numerous companies' products and makes it possible to order them online. ISN presents both a text-based and graphics-based version of the site. It includes one of the best online catalogs on the Web, including over 10,000 software- and electronic-based products. Pages can present products sorted either by subject or company. There is also a search facility. Figure 10-21 shows a page that allows users to take a guided tour of the Internet Shopping Network. As a draw, ISN includes online issues of *InfoWorld* and *Computer Currents* magazine for registered users. You can take a tour on your own by entering http://www.internet.net/.

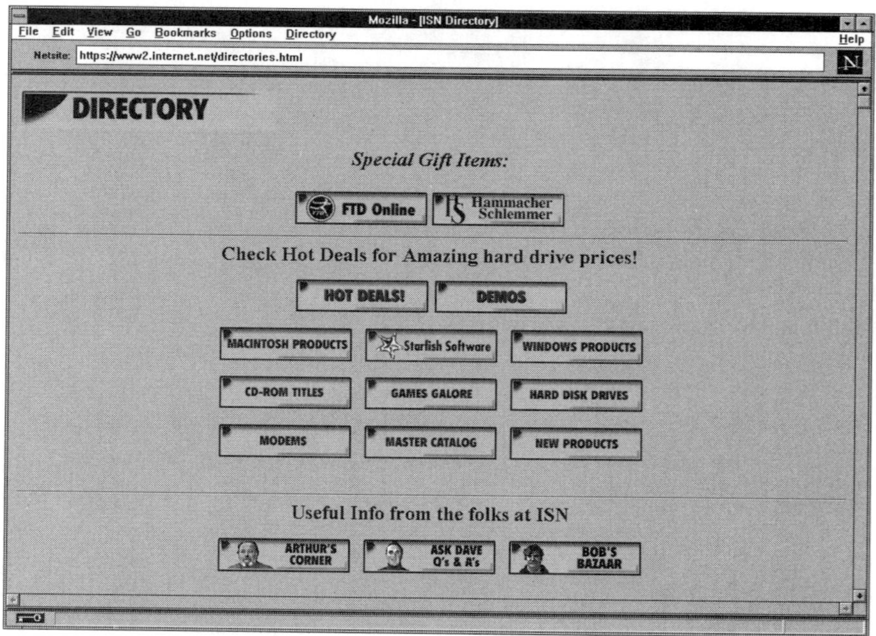

Figure 10-21: *The Internet Shopping Network.*

Recently ISN included two companies at its site. ISN is slowly making the transition from virtual storefront to cybermall. A cybermall is a Web site that includes a collection of virtual storefronts. Cybermalls are typically presented by server services, companies that sell space or Net publishing services. Some service providers, companies that sell Internet connections, also provide server services. InterNex, for example, is both a service provider and a server service. Typically the Web documents that make up the virtual storefronts are stored at the server service's or service provider's site, but they can also be links to other sites. An exceptional cybermall is Branch Mall, located at https://www.branch.com. The brainchild of Jon Zeeff, Branch Mall was one of the first, if not the first, cybermall on the Net. Figure 10-22 shows Branch Mall's home page.

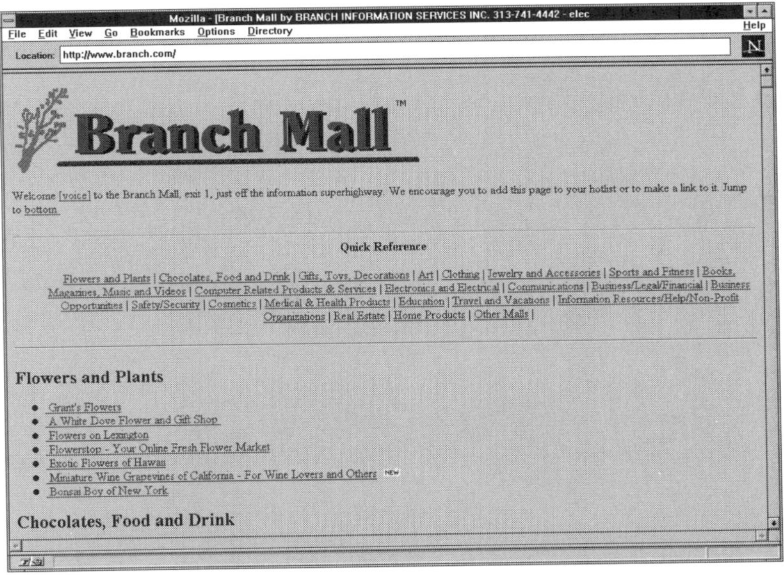

Figure 10-22: *Branch Mall was one of the first cybermalls on the Net.*

Moving On

Looking good on the Net means effectively communicating with your reader. If the reader is put off by your presentation or if you fail to meet his or her needs, the communication is lost. If the reader connects, chances are he or she will return. This chapter presented several techniques for connecting with readers and gave examples of different types of Web documents. The following two chapters take the next step by giving you the information you need to publish Web pages using a service provider, server service or setting up an HTTP server and publishing on your own.

11

Service Providers & Server Services

Now that you've created your HTML-based Web masterpiece, the only remaining question is how to bring your work to the international Internet. For some, this may not be an issue—particularly if you're developing an internal corporate server and already have a network set up. For many, however, the issue of getting a server onto the Internet is a big decision: Should I run my own server and have my own connection to the Internet, or should I rent space on someone else's server and just look like I have a direct connection?

This chapter provides the information you need to weigh the options of sharing space on a server service—a service that provides Internet publishing services such as Web servers, FTP servers and virtual storefronts; services dedicated to commercial trade; or sharing space on a multipurpose host at a service provider. Service providers typically provide dial-up Internet access in addition to Web services.Which option you choose depends to a large degree on what you're trying to accomplish.

Understanding the Services Available

Before you choose your commercial service provider, you need to define the services you want to provide to the readers of your Web pages. A broad range of services is available. The most basic Web server might just deliver your HTML pages with no additional services, no CGI and no image maps. On the other hand, the most sophisticated Internet shopping center server might support secure transactions, credit cards, advertising and perhaps provide you with your own unique URL. Although the range of options is fairly continuous from the simple to the sophisticated, there are three basic types of commercial services: sharing a server, using the services of a virtual storefront or sharing a server without appearing to. The first type, sharing space on a commercial Internet service, is where you are one of many people who use that service and share space on that server. This is the most appropriate choice for a casual Web publisher, or someone with information to share, but who doesn't need a high profile or have a great interest in developing a unique identity. This option is discussed later in "Sharing Space."

A second option is to use the services of a virtual storefront, or mall. Typically, these services cater to the needs of a business with a product or service to sell, and who want a way to sell it on the Internet. These services may also provide you with advertising and are more aggressive in promoting you and other companies on their server. A final type of server service is one in which you appear to have your own server and identity. With this kind of service, the fact that you share your service is not apparent, allowing you the freedom to develop your own home page with its own unique look and feel. Often, though, these services won't be able to provide the credit card and security services provided by a virtual storefront.

Finally, you need to consider any additional Internet service you may want to provide to your customers or readers. For example, do you distribute software and need an anonymous FTP capability? Or perhaps you want to allow text searching of your pages. Also, almost every image map or CGI interface requires adjustments and configuration on the Web server. Is your service provider willing to do this for you? At the end of the chapter is a list of questions you may want to ask your service provider when shopping for a server to publish your Web pages. As you read through the chapter, decide which features are important to you so that when you start researching service providers, you're armed with a ready list of requirements.

Deciding Between Service Providers & Going it Alone

Without a doubt, you can get the most control over your World Wide Web pages and other Internet services if you run your own server. For most individuals and many companies, however, this option is an economic impossibility. Although providing your own Web server is covered in detail in Chapter 12, "Servers at Your Service," this is a good time to stop and examine your options.

Connections to the Internet at this time are the single biggest expense when you consider ongoing maintenance of a directly connected Web site. For decent commercial-grade performance, you'll want at least a 56,000 bit-per-second link (56 kbps) and a full-time link so that people can reach you any time of the night or day. While the cost of a link like this from your business or home to the closest Internet service provider varies widely, you should figure you won't get away for less than $200-$400 dollars per month. It doesn't take much more calculation than that to realize a private Internet connection is out of the question for most people. And, unfortunately, even though you are paying for this line 24 hours a day, the actual amount of time you have data going over the line is far, far less—unless, of course, you have a very popular site or have more activity than just your Web server. By using the services of a commercial Internet provider, the costs of the lines to the Internet are spread out over many, many users. Remember, although you are sharing your Internet connection, the average load on the service provider's Internet line still permits your customers to retrieve information from your pages very rapidly.

Most of the time Internet providers have line speeds of a T-1 (1.544 megabits per second) or greater. Of course, if the service provider has *too* many customers, the average link load goes up—and your individual performance goes down.

Perhaps one of the biggest advantages for having your Web pages on a commercial service is that it doesn't matter where the service provider is located. You can be in California, but you could use a service provider in Chicago, if it has the price and services you want.

Sharing Space

Many companies and individuals get by just fine with this simplest of options. The idea of sharing space on a provider's computer is very simple: you have your own "home" directory, and you put your HTML pages in that directory or in subdirectories of your home directory. The most rudimentary service of this type is found on many UNIX-based systems, where there are many individuals who have accounts on the system, and any of the users can add Web pages directly in their own account's space. Each user can have an HTML link to the master home page of the service provider simply by putting an HTML file with a specific name, such as index.html, in his or her home directory. The service provider then scans the users' home pages on a regular basis and creates a list of everyone who has an HTML page in his or her home directory.

How Much Does it Cost?

Sharing space on a service is about the cheapest option for having a Web presence. A typical charge is $65 per quarter with a 10-megabyte disk space limit. You can fit a *lot* of Web pages into 10 megabytes of disk, too.

What Does My Address Look Like?

In most cases, when sharing space, the URL to your HTML page would look something like this:

http://www.servprovidr.com/~yourlogin/index.html

The important issues to remember about this URL are that (1) the name of the system is *your service provider's name*, and (2) people reach you through a reference to your login: *~yourlogin*. If you just want to get information to the Internet community, this may be the fastest and cheapest way to do it. The drawbacks for a company, however, are that it is unlikely a casual browser would stumble across your latest sales brochure, or that someone who knows your company's name would think to look on the system owned by your service provider.

On the other hand, there are many Web searching programs and indexes available to the Internet community, and these programs will eventually find you and your home page. If you've chosen the words used in page titles and text carefully, you can ensure that people who are interested in the product you're selling or service you're providing can find you. Also, there are ways you can specifically seed search databases with your URL and inform the Internet community about your site. For example, the Lycos search engine at http://lycos.cs.cmu.edu/ has a form you can fill out that lets their search engine know about your site. The Yahoo directory will accept candidates to be included in its list, which is arranged by category. This directory is indexed as well. Go to http://www.yahoo.com/yahoo/bin/add/ and fill out a form requesting placement on their lists. For general advertising to the Internet community, you can send information about new sites to the moderated USENET newsgroup comp.internet.net-happenings.

What Other Services Can I Get?

You may be interested in Internet services besides a basic Web server, such as anonymous FTP and USENET news. If you are distributing software, for example, you could use anonymous FTP as a way to distribute shareware or software updates. In some cases, you might want customers to upload files to you. You should ask your service provider if it can make an anonymous FTP service available to your customers.

Having the ability to access USENET newsgroups is very common and can be a great benefit if you want to scan the newsgroups for topics that concern your business or interest. Often, you can find people who are inquiring about some product or service you offer and can reply to them via e-mail.

Handling Image Maps & CGI Interfaces

When you share a server, you also share the HTTP server and its associated services. If you want to use an image map, for example, you'll need to add information about your specific image map to a configuration file on the shared server. The configuration file contains information about the "hot" areas on your images, so that when a browser clicks on an image, the server will know what to do. Find out if this is something you can do yourself, or if you need to have your service provider add the information.

Forms require the use of back-end CGI programs. Find out if your service provider will allow you to create your own CGI programs, or if they must be installed in a protected area that only the service provider can access. Many service providers offer consulting and programming services to help with the creation of CGI back-ends, so even if you are allowed to write your own programs, you may not want to.

Cybermalls

Being part of a collection of companies on a commercial system, often called a *cybermall,* is another way to bring your pages to the Internet. In this model, you are one of many companies that share space on a Web server that is specifically set up to house many "stores." In this storefront or mall analogy, a person interested in buying something or learning about your product would first enter the "mall" by going to the main home page for the service provider. From that point, the browser is led to your page by lists or a directory of stores on that server. Once at your home page, the user can look at whatever materials you've put on display. Very often, the service provider for the mall will also provide a way for people to pay for merchandise you have for sale.

As a small business, this is a great way to get started. The service provider takes care of setting up the server, creates a front-end for the mall that will attract people to browse, and provides you with a way to actually make sales over the Internet. Since the service provider is responsible for the security and authentication of the consumer, you're off the hook for the use of credit card numbers or setting up customer accounts. Some of the Web servers now on the market offer encrypted transaction protocols and offer a secure way to conduct business on the Internet. Security on the Web is a tricky business—especially when financial transactions are involved—and your customers will always expect you to bear the ultimate responsibility for the privacy of their information. You should always be familiar with the security techniques used by your provider.

Similar to the previous example of sharing space on a commercial Web site, the various Web indexes will eventually pick up trails to your pages; it's also likely that your mall service provider will make an effort to link its storefront to as many other Web pages as possible. Also, security remains the job of the Internet provider, but in this case since the entire mission of the service provider is commercial, it is likely that it will be running with a high degree of emphasis placed on privacy and security.

How Much Does it Cost?

The cost of being part of a cybermall can vary widely depending on the level of service provided by the mall owner, but as an example, the introductory pricing for the service provider Open Market (http://www.openmarket.com/) is $75 per month for up to 5MB of storage (about 100 pages), a $500 set-up fee, plus per-transaction fees (for when your customers actually buy something) of between 3 percent and 7 percent. Another provider, First Virtual, offers an information-selling service with service charges of between 2 and 10 percent based on the way the service is configured, plus a $10 setup fee. This server is focused on information that can be transmitted electronically.

What Does My Address Look Like?

Just as if you were in a real mall, people find you by going to the virtual mall site first. You can still be reached directly, however, by using a full URL that points straight to your page. For example, Lexis/Nexis has a storefront, and their "direct" address is http://www.openmarket.com/lexis-nexis/. While it's the responsibility of the mall operator to properly advertise their site, you can still get listed on Web search sites and directories by listing your direct URL.

National Public Radio, which also uses First Virtual as a service provider, offers their transcripts for sale at http://www.infohaus.com/access/by-seller/National_Public_Radio/. NPR is an example of an organization that actually has their own Web server (at http://www.npr.org/) but is getting help from First Virtual to handle the sales of transcripts, because they don't want to get into the business of handling the sales themselves.

Having Your Own Server—Without Your Own Server

This kind of service is fairly new to the Internet and is perfect for the company or person who wants an identity on the Internet, but still doesn't want to go through the expense and bother of running a site.

How Much Does it Cost?

The cost for this service is comparable to that of the virtual storefront, at under $100 per month, plus a $150 setup charge, with no usage fees. This compares favorably with the cost of a private 56kbps private line, which *starts* at over $100 month and can be many times that depending on how far you live from the telephone company's switching office and what your local telephone company charges for private lines.

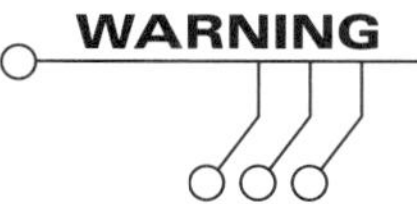

Be careful when shopping for a service provider. Some service providers charge you based on how many bytes are transmitted for you over the Internet, which in turn depends on how complicated your pages are and how many people access your Web pages. Since the number of accesses cannot be predicted, you leave yourself open for a huge end-of-the-month bill!

What Does My Address Look Like?

In this case, the service provider still shares a common system among many users, but through some clever programming of the HTTP server, you can actually support multiple IP addresses on one host. In this way, you get your own unique IP address and name, such as www.mycompany.com, but when people connect to this computer, they are actually connecting to a computer that has many identities on the Internet. In this way, your little company can have the same Internet name stature as AT&T, DEC or IBM, without actually having its own computer on the Web!

For many Web users, a common way to locate a company they're interested in is to create a URL that starts with "www," put your company's name or initials in the middle and end with ".com". When you establish your service, work with your Internet service provider to pick a name that people would think of when trying to find you. You may find that your perfect name is already taken, so be prepared with a few additional options.

An example of a virtual server is Macro Computer Solutions, a commercial provider located in Chicago (http://www.mcs.com/vserv/index.html). In their offering, called VSERVE for Virtual Service, they currently have The Underground Network (http://underground.net/), Internet Training and Consulting Services (http://www.itcs.com/), IT Solutions (http://www.its.com/) and Cybersight (http://cybersight.com/cgi-bin/cs/s?main.gmml/).

There's no way for anyone to tell if these four companies are on four different systems, or all on the same system. With a shared service such as this, you're still left with the problems of setting up your own way of selling products and conducting secure transactions. If, however, you aren't trying to conduct actual business transactions over the Internet just yet, the Virtual Presence solution may be perfect for you.

Server Services & Web Pages

Although this book is mostly about creating your own HTML pages, you may decide that you don't want to go it completely alone. Many server services have close relationships with consultants willing to help with almost any aspect of HTML page creation. For example, if you're not artistically inclined, a server service can direct you to an HTML design service. Most service providers can also hook you up with local programming talent if you don't want to create your own HTML pages, or need help with a back-end CGI program.

Going Shopping

Now that you've read about the different options available when choosing a provider, here's a list of questions to ask when shopping for a service provider or server service.

The Basics

- Do you offer a Web server, and can I control my own Web pages? How do people find me on your server?
- What is the cost of this account? Is there a time limit that I have to watch out for? If so, how do I know what I've already used?
- What services do you offer to the public? Can I have anonymous FTP space that anyone can read from? Is there a place for "incoming" files, and is it visible or hidden? Do you limit the size of files placed in an "incoming" anonymous directory?
- Can I also send and receive electronic mail? What about USENET newsgroups? Can you alias my e-mail account to use a more personal system name?
- How fast is your link to the Internet? How fast is your equipment? Do you measure the load on your links, and when do you add capacity?
- How do you handle disk storage? What's my limit, and is it advisory or enforced?
- How much experience does your system administration staff have, and how do we reach you?
- How secure is my data? What's your policy on backups?

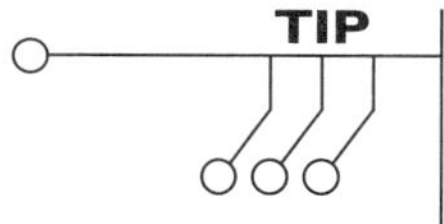

Even though your data may be backed up by your service provider, you should always keep a copy of your Web pages on your own computer, and on your own backup media. This way, you can be sure the pages will never be destroyed.

- How often do system outages or partial outages occur? Do you have records, and can I look at them? What is your policy on repairing the system during off-hours? Can I report system problems 24 hours a day?
- What billing methods do you support? Can I use a credit card? Will you bill me?
- Do you keep credit card numbers on the computers that are connected to the Internet?
- Can I create and manage my own image maps? How quickly can I make changes if I need to ask you to update your server?
- Can I create CGI programs and control them myself?
- What kind of Web server hardware and software are you using? (If you plan on writing your own CGI scripts, this can be very important!)

For Virtual Storefronts

- What methods are available for collecting money from my customers? Credit cards? Individual accounts?
- What is your charge for purchase transactions?
- What is your security scheme? Do clients need a special Web browser to conduct secure transactions?
- Do you provide an alternate way to accept orders if a customer doesn't want to leave a credit card?
- Do you keep my customer's credit card numbers on an Internet-connected system, or do you transmit them to a protected system?

For Private Rented Systems (Virtual Servers)

- Do I get to pick my own URL name? Do I use a standard IP port number for my Web server?
- Do I share hardware with others, or is this my own machine? If I share space, can others measure the volume of information being offered by my Web server?
- Do you charge me a flat rate? Or do you measure the amount of information sent over the Internet?

Moving On

Using a commercial service provider for your Web pages has many advantages over using your own server, particularly if you have no other reason to have a full-time connection to the Internet. Based on your needs and budget, there are several options you can choose from, and a wide variety of commercial service providers available. See Appendix D, "Resources," for a listing of numerous service providers and server services. For a comprehensive listing of Internet service providers in the United States and many other countries, check out http://www.teleport.com/~cci/directories/pocia/pocia.html.

If you have other reasons to be connected to the Internet that would justify the cost of a private line, or if you want to selectively share HTML documents with friends or other people on the Internet with a modem dial-up line, read the next chapter about setting up your own Web server. Using your own server provides you the ultimate amount of control and privacy over your small part of the Web, and can be lots of fun. With Windows NT and Windows 95 you have lots of choices of servers, and a variety of ways to provide information to the Internet community. With the information in the next chapter and the servers provided on the Companion CD-ROM, you can get started today!

12

Servers at Your Service: Publishing on Your Own

Just as there are instances when you would want to use the services of a commercial Internet provider, there are very good reasons for running your own server. Setting up a server on your computer not only lets you publish Web documents for the general public, it gives you more flexibility for controlling access to your system. Maybe you have sensitive information that you don't want to share. By setting up a server on your own, you can selectively share Web documents with friends and business associates without a dedicated (24-hour) connection. This chapter describes setting up and working with the main Windows 3.*x* and Windows NT HTTP servers to give you complete control over the way your information is presented to selected readers or the entire world.

Providing Your Own Server

What do you need to get started? If you expect to publish Web pages for the general public to read, you will need a full-time connection to the Internet plus a computer to host your Web server. A full-time connection can come in a variety of speeds, ranging from a slow 14.4kb/s leased line through the more common 56kb/s lines up to T-3 (45mb/s) lines. As you would expect, the faster the line, the more expensive the monthly charge. It is almost impossible to quote rates for leased lines on a national basis, because every telephone company prices the lines differently, and the price you pay will also depend on how far you are from the central telephone switching office. The best way to determine the cost of a line is to contact several Internet service providers in your area and ask them to help you get rates from the phone company. Your service provider can tell you exactly where you will need to connect, and will either set you up or put you in touch with the right person at the phone company.

Of course you can also publish your Web pages without a dedicated connection. This is especially helpful in the process of creating and testing Web pages or sharing information with selected individuals. In order for the person to view your Web pages, you must have your Web server set up, be connected to your service provider and have turned on your Web server.

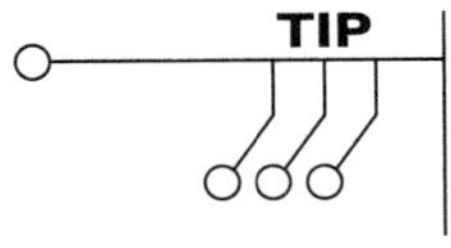

Look for the introduction of a new kind of Internet service in the near future: a dial-out *ISDN connection. With this service, you would have a regular dial-up ISDN line, and use it only when you need it. The key to this service is that your Internet service provider knows* your *ISDN number, and when someone tries to contact your system, the service provider automatically dials you up to complete the connection. This way, you are paying for the connection only when you need to dial out* or *someone is trying to reach you.*

If you are already connected to the Internet through your business or school, then all of this may be taken care of already. All you will need is a connection to your local area network and a computer that supports a Web server. Web servers are often called HTTP servers, since HTTP (HyperText Transfer Protocol) is the name of the protocol used primarily on the World Wide Web. You have a number of choices of operating systems, including most UNIX-like variants, Windows 3.1, Windows NT and Macintosh. The primary focus of this book is Windows-based systems, so this chapter will discuss servers that are available for Windows 3.1 and Windows NT.

In this chapter, you will learn about a number of different servers that run on Windows for Workgroups 3.11 and Windows NT 3.5. There are two servers included on the Companion CD-ROM: a 16-bit Windows server written by Robert Denny, and a 32-bit Windows NT server written by the European Microsoft Windows NT Academic Centre (EMWAC). The complete server setups for both are provided, so you can try everything out for yourself. In addition to these two servers, there are a few other really fine NT-based servers that you can look into, and which are described later in this chapter.

Each of the available servers provides basic Web server services, and all do so very well. Where you have a choice in the NT servers, you'll probably wind up making a decision based on a particular feature you want, or a level of documentation or support you need. As this book was being written, the commercial servers' releases were still in development. Because it is unfair to compare performance of beta products, or pick out specific bugs in developing products, the coverage of these products is limited to the features and benefits of each. For the most up-to-date information, check in the USENET newsgroup comp.infosystems.www.providers, or get demonstration copies from the publishers.

WinHTTPD 16-bit Version

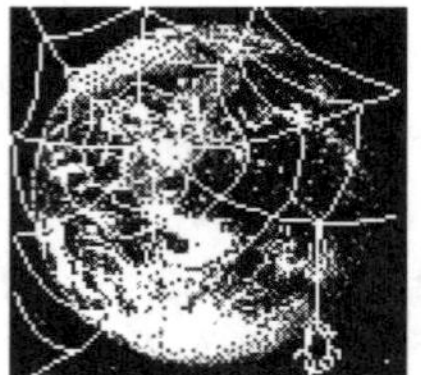

When all you have is lemons, make lemonade. Even though Windows 3.11 isn't exactly a lemon, it isn't the operating system most people think of when selecting a multi-user host system. And when you start up an HTTP server, that is exactly what you'll be providing. The good news is that with WinHTTPD by Robert Denny, your Windows system can do a remarkable job of being that multi-user system. According to Denny's tests, this system, tested on a 486DX/66 with 8 MB of memory, can handle 8 requests per second with an average request size of 4kb. This data rate will exceed by over four times the capacity of a 56kb/s leased line, and will even max out many a local ethernet adapter. So you can see that if you are using anything slower than a fractional T-1, this server can provide data faster than your link can handle it.

This Web server provides an extremely simple setup procedure. Even if you've never set up a Web server before, you can have the "demo" system up and running in a matter of minutes. It comes with documentation that is adapted from the NCSA HTTP server, with modifications that reflect the unique Windows features, including an experimental CGI interface (see Chapter 9 and later in this chapter for information on this).

This server is included on the Companion CD-ROM, and you can install it right now. It is shareware, and in this case this means if you are using the server for a business you will have to pay a $99 shareware fee. It is free for personal use.

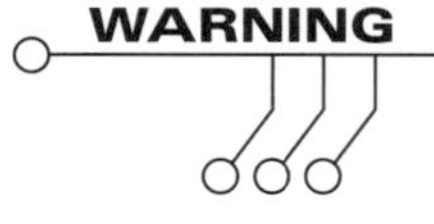

Many TCP/IP protocol stacks were designed for and largely tested with client applications, not server applications. Using your windows PC as a server will stress the TCP/IP stack in new ways, and you may find that there are problems with the stack. Before giving up, see if the supplier of the TCP/IP stack has an updated version. Also, if you are connected to a LAN-based TCP/IP network, try the Microsoft TCP/IP for Windows for Workgroups 3.11. This protocol has been revised (release "a" or later) to fix some of

the bugs uncovered when using WinHTTPD, and is now a very reliable protocol stack for WinHTTPD. Some people have reported occasional crashes of their systems when running WinHTTPD. If what you need is a highly reliable commercial system, you should probably consider using a Windows NT-based server.

The list of features for this server is impressive:

- HTTP/1.0 protocol.
- Very fast, can deliver well over 25,000 requests/hour on a fast system such as a 486DX/66.
- Dual-mode CGI interface: CGI 1.1 (modified) script interface using DOS Virtual Machine and an experimental Windows CGI interface with form field decoding.
- Server-generated directory indexes with type-specific icons, conforms to formatting of current CERN and UNIX NCSA servers.
- Automatic extract of <TITLE>...</TITLE> string from HTML documents for directory index descriptions.
- Automatic mapping of HTTP protocol MIME types to DOS file extensions. This means that a filename with a .gif extension, for example, is sent to the Web browser identified as an "image/gif" type. See the Options>>Preferences >> Helper Applications menu in Netscape for a long list of MIME types (shown under the heading "File Type").
- NCSA "imagemap" support (Windows CGI port), preconfigured global and local document access controls.
- Access authentication.
- Large integrated set of HTML documentation, including authoring and administration references and primers.
- Configurable network port assignment.

Not only is there an impressive list of features, if you must run 16-bit Windows, this is your only choice. Good thing for you it's a great choice. For up-to-date information about WinHTTPD, visit the Web server at http://www.city.net/win-httpd.

Installing the WinHTTPD Server

This server is included on the Companion CD-ROM. You can get started right away running a Web server by installing WinHTTPD on your Windows system.

What You'll Need The basic requirements are: a PC running Windows 3.1 or Windows for Workgroups 3.11 (Windows NT is *not* an option for this server); a solid TCP/IP stack with a specification-compliant Winsock interface; and a connection to the Internet, or the network to which your users are attached.

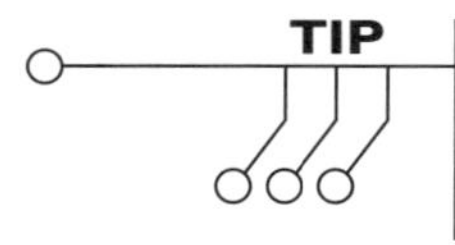

If a group of people in your building or on your campus are already connected to a LAN you don't need to be connected to the Internet. You do still need all the PCs (and other types of systems) to be running a TCP/IP stack.

The specific requirements on the PC system depend largely on the use you'll be putting the server to. If what you're after is a test bed to create your Web masterpiece, then almost any system that can run Windows will do. Even though the instructions that come with the server say a 486/33 with 8 MB of memory, we tested this system on a 386/16, and it was faster across a local network than any modem-based network connection we tested. However, if you expect any serious use, you'll want to stick to the recommendation in the installation instructions.

Getting Started Before you even run the setup program, you'll want to set the TZ variable in your AUTOEXEC.BAT file. A typical setting for the Eastern United States would be: SET TZ=EST5EDT, which means the time zone is called EST (Eastern Standard Time) and is five hours later than Universal Coordinated Time. For the West Coast this is PST8PDT. This variable is used by the server to create log entries, which according to the format of the NCSA log files, must be in Universal Coordinated Time (UCT ... formerly GMT). If you don't use Daylight Saving Time in your state, omit the second three-letter time zone abbreviation.

From the CD-ROM directory /WINHTTPD, double-click on SETUP.EXE. This will run a standard Windows setup process, and will install all the executables and samples on your hard disk. When that is completed, all you need to do is start up the server from the icon that was created in your program manager. At that point, you can connect to the server from any computer on the network, including the same system the server is running on.

In addition to the basic HTTP server, WinHTTPD comes with a performance monitoring utility based on Visual Basic and Microsoft Access that allows you to monitor the usage of your server extremely easily, and even create automatically generated HTML statistics pages. This is as easy to set up as the basic server.

Additional WinHTTPD Utilities

Polyform The Polyform program from Willow Glen Graphics is a fast way to get started with forms processing when you just want to collect information, and aren't interested in programming a back-end CGI program yourself. Polyform is a shareware program, and is provided on the Companion CD-ROM. Polyform takes input from a form you create, stores the information sent from the form in a file on your Web server, returns a confirmation page to the Web browser and optionally mails the results to a user you specify, or mails a form letter to an address specified on the form. To use Polyform, follow the installation instructions provided in the README.TXT file that comes with the program on the Companion CD-ROM.

VBStats VBStats is a wonderful Web server statistics program (actually a suite of programs) available at the same location as WinHTTPD that allows you to extract a number of parameters about your server's use from the log files. You can find it at http://city.net/win-httpd/lib/uti-support/. The file name is vbstat31.zip. It is based on Visual Basic and Access, but you don't need either program to make this run. The heart of the system is the Access database that contains the items in the following table.

Table	Function
Accesses	Each access to the server, from a line in the log.
AuthUsers	Each unique user that authenticated via the server.
Objects	Each unique URL target that was accessed.
PastTotals	Weekly totals generated by previous report runs.
RestrictPats	Contains patterns used for visibility restriction.
Sites	Each unique client host name or IP address.

The VBStats program reads this database to provide data to you and to your Web browser clients in a number of ways, including charts and graphs—we all love charts and graphs.

Wincron The Wincron program will automatically run programs of your choice at preselected times under Windows. It is included in the WINHTTPD package so that you can cycle the log files on a daily basis and run the VBStats program automatically.

EMWAC HTTPS for Windows NT

European Microsoft Windows NT Academic Centre

Although the WinHTTPD for Windows 3.1 is a great HTTPD server, you may prefer to use a more robust operating system than DOS as the underpinning of your Web server service. Windows NT 3.5 provides many advantages beyond those of 16-bit Windows, including increased local security, multi-threading and process space memory protection.

If you are interested in trying out a server for Windows NT, the EMWAC HTTP server is included on the Companion CD-ROM. This product offers a fully functional Web server for free that you can use for any purpose you want. It is missing some of the more sophisticated features of the professional NT servers that are discussed later in this chapter, such as access control and proxy server capabilities, but for many organizations this is not an issue.

EMWAC is the European Microsoft Windows NT Academic Centre, which is an integral part of the Computing Services of the University of Edinburgh. The most recent information about EMWAC and the Windows NT Toolchest can be found at http://emwac.ed.ac.uk/html/internet_toolchest/top.html.

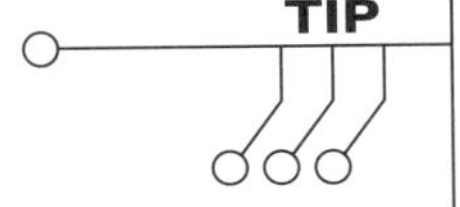

In addition to the HTTP server, you can get freeware versions of a Gopher server, a WAIS server and a WAIS toolkit that supports the HTTP server. An alternate way to obtain these tools is to purchase the Microsoft Windows NT 3.5 Resource Kit, or get programs for the Resource Kit (which includes these servers) from the Microsoft FTP server at ftp://ftp.microsoft.com/bussys/winnt/winnt-public/reskit/nt35/i386.

This Web server is simple to install (as are all the Windows NT servers) as a service on your Windows NT 3.5 system. It does not come with a getting started "web" as do the other servers, so you need to jump right in and start creating your own pages.

The EMWAC HTTPS server comes with some sample CGI host programs (written in C) to get you started. You are restricted to command-line programs with this server, so you can't use Visual Basic or other application level programs as you can with WinHTTPD. You can, however, use the many command-line facilities available with Windows NT. For example, you can use the perl port for NT, which can be obtained via anonymous FTP from a number of sites, including the EMWAC site mentioned earlier.

In addition to the basic EMWAC server, a very handy add-on that is also available from EMWAC and is on the Companion CD-ROM is a WAIS search engine. WAIS stands for Wide-Area Information Service, but in this case, we are using it only for its local search capabilities, and the Web server returns the results to the user.

Installing the EMWAC Server

The EMWAC server is included on the Companion CD-ROM, so if you have an NT system, you can set up a Web site right away.

What You'll Need Clearly, you'll need a Windows NT system, but either a workstation or server system will do. There are no hard-and-fast rules for memory requirements or system speed, so you'll have to judge for yourself if the response time you get from the server is OK. We have tested this server on a 386/33 system and it ran just fine, even though that is below the recommended minimum for NT all by itself. As with any HTTP server, if you want to provide a public service, you'll need an Internet connection.

Getting Started The EMWAC server comes with documentation in PostScript (.ps) and Microsoft Write (.wri) formats. You should read them over once before starting just so you understand the "big picture" of how the server works. To install the server,

1. Log in to your Windows NT system as a user with administrative privileges.
2. The HTTP Server is distributed in three versions, for the Intel, MIPS and DEC Alpha architectures. In each directory are the following files:

HTTPS.EXE	The HTTP Server itself.
HTTPS.CPL	The Control Panel applet.
HTTPS.HLP	The Control Panel applet help file.
HTTPS.DOC	The manual in Word for Windows format.
HTTPS.PS	The manual, in PostScript format ready for printing.
HTTPS.WRI	The manual in Windows Write format.
EGSCRIPT.ZIP	A sample CGI script programs.
COPYRITE.TXT	The copyright statement for the software.
READ.ME	A summary of new features, etc.

Choose the version that matches your computer, and copy the files into a directory. A good choice is the \WINNT\SYSTEM32 directory, which is where many other services reside, but you can choose any directory you wish. Using the Security/Permissions menu option in the File Manager, verify that the SYSTEM user has read permission for the file.

3. Move HTTPS.CPL and HTTPS.HLP to the \WINNT\SYSTEM32 directory if they aren't there already. Start the Control Panel from the Program Manager to verify that the HTTP Server applet is represented as an icon in the Control Panel.
4. Check the IP address of your machine using the command:

   https -ipaddress

   This will display the name of your machine (e.g., emwac.ed.ac.uk) and its IP address(es) as reported by the Windows Sockets API. If this information is incorrect, you need to reconfigure the TCP/IP software on your machine.

   The HTTP Server will not work if this address (or list of addresses if your machine has more than one network interface) is wrong.
5. Install https into the table of Windows NT Services (and simultaneously register it with the Event Logger) by running the program from the Windows NT command line, specifying the -install flag. (Note: It is vital that you execute this command using the copy of HTTPS.EXE that you placed in the \WINNT\SYSTEM32 directory, and not using some other copy that you plan subsequently to delete.) For example, enter **https -install**.

   The program will register itself with the Service Manager and with the section on installation problems in the documentation.

6. To verify that the installation has succeeded, start the Windows NT Control Panel and double-click on the Services icon. The resulting dialog box should list HTTP Server as one of the installed services. If so, see the Configuration section of the documentation for further instructions.

Setting Options The few options available for the EMWAC server are set through the Windows Control Panel. Once you install the server, you'll find a new icon in the Control Panel for the HTTP server. Opening this program reveals the options you have for the server. The server options are well documented in the help file that comes with the server, HTTPS.HLP.

Additional HTTPS Utilities

WAIS Toolkit In addition to the basic HTTP server, EMWAC provides a number of other tools for use with Windows NT. In particular, you'll probably want to use the WAIS Search toolkit, which is included on the Companion CD-ROM. To use the WAIS Search capabilities, create an HTML page that has the "ISINDEX" field that you read about in Chapter 9, "Forms, Databases & CGI." When a user enters a search term in the text field of the ISINDEX form and submits the form, the HTTPS server automatically executes the WAISLOOK program to search the WAIS database with the same name as the HTML page you created. For example, if you create a page called "myindex.htm," then the server will submit a query to the WAISLOOK program with the "myindex" database specified. You can set up indexes of parts of your site, or the entire Web on your site with very little effort.

Like the HTTP server, the WAIS toolkit comes with documentation for its use, and the HTTPS server documentation explains how to integrate the WAIS search engine with the Web server.

WebSite

If you liked WinHTTPD by Robert Denny for Windows 3.1, you'll love this NT-hosted server. Denny wrote this server, which is supplemented with companion programs written by others, for sale and distribution by O'Reilly and Associates. You can ask for more information by writing to website@ora.com. Denny took all the best parts of his WinHTTPD and with his colleagues added additional features that a commercial Web site would need. A small sampling of the features offered by this fine server include:

- Runs as an application *or* a service.
- Supports Windows NT 3.5 or Windows 95.
- Supports Windows CGI for access to Windows application resources (such as Visual Basic's database and mail access).
- Offers complete and transparent support of NT-command prompt CGI programs, NT-perl scripts and UNIX-like Korn shell scripts (as provided through the POSIX capabilities of NT).
- Identifies user by ID and password.
- Offers group affiliation for users.
- Allows access control by user and by group.
- Allows access control by IP address or sub-network.
- Uses built-in URLs for system information functions such as usage statistics.
- File directory browsing access control.
- Extended file directory displays, including:
  Directory page headers,
  Directory page footers,
  Icons to identify different file (MIME) types,
  Hidden file support,
  Descriptions of HTML files pulled from HTML titles, and
  Extended file descriptions available via hyperlinks in the directory listing.

- Extensive tracing options.
- Many CGI program examples, including Visual Basic and perl scripts.
- Configurable network port assignment.
- Integrated add-on programs and easy system maintenance.
- Uses Windows 95–style tabbed index for server settings application.

There are two feature that are really cool. One is the built-in URL function. Certain URLs that start with a tilde (~), such as /~stats, instruct the server to provide internally generated HTML pages for special functions. The /~stats function, for example, provides a page that shows server usage statistics. The other feature is the ability to choose the mode in which the server operates. You can have the server run as an application or as a service. You decide how the server should run based on your CGI needs and how you want to operate your server. The announced price for WebSite is $499 per copy.

Additional HTTPS Utilities

In addition to the features offered in the main server product, three utilities included with the server make creating a Web server almost easy: Mapedit, Webview and Webindex.

Mapedit is a utility that allows you to create image maps out of any GIF file. It provides a point-and-click interface that lets you define almost arbitrarily shaped regions on a bitmap image, and then define jump-to destinations for those regions. See Chapter 7, "Getting Graphic With Images," for all you'll need to know about image maps.

Webview is a terrific program that scans all the Web pages at your site and creates visual cues for every type of link and image. It verifies each link that you have on your site, both internal and external. It clearly shows invalid links so that you can repair them before a user complains about it. This makes Webview an essential tool for maintaining your Web server.

Webindex is a replacement for a WAIS search engine. It provides a simple interface to indexing all the documents on your server, and allows you to add ISINDEX lines to your documents to access the search engine.

You have two options for running this HTTP server under NT: running it as a service or as a user-level application program. The option you choose will be driven largely by your needs and preferences about which is "better" for a World Wide Web server.

A service under Window NT runs in the background and is controlled by the operating system (with your guidance). A service is turned on when you start the NT system, and has nothing to do with a user login. Examples of services that come with Windows NT include the FTP server. The FTP server is available as soon as the NT system initializes, and stays running as long as the system is turned on. A service can only interact with other services and programs written to be used from the command prompt.

An application program, on the other hand, is typically run by a user or when a user logs in. An application program can interact with services, command-line programs and other application programs via all types of program communications, including standard Windows messages.

Purveyor

Purveyor is a professional version of the EMWAC server for NT. Starting from the stable and well-tested base of the EMWAC server gives Purveyor the advantage of not really being a "release 1.0" product. This is the *only* server currently available for Windows NT that can act as a caching proxy server (for firewall proxy applications in companies that maintain strict controls over Internet access from internal network connections).

This server offers a complete set of features, including:

- Proxy service: This allows the server to cross corporate firewall router boundaries.
- Caching on proxy: This speeds repeat page requests.
- Runs as a service.
- Can operate on Intel and Alpha platforms.
- Identification of user by ID and password.
- Group affiliation for users.
- Access control by user and by group.
- Access control by IP address or sub-network.
- Access control is integrated in the Windows File Manager.
- Configurable network port assignment.
- Full transaction logging, including date, time, HTML page and IP address of the requester.

Worthy of mention is the integration of Purveyor with the NT File Manager. Although all of the professional level servers provide access control, none are as easy to use as the Purveyor method. The Purveyor setup program adds a menu item called "Purveyor" to your File Manager. (You'll need to restart the File Manager before seeing the new menu item.) To change the Access Control List, you select the file or directory you want to control access to, and then select the Purveyor menu item. By choosing Edit Access Control you are presented with a dialog box that allows you to select the specific type of access control you want: by user, group or network IP address.

Purveyor also comes with a full-text searchable online help system that makes finding information about the server a breeze. For more information about Purveyor, go to the Process Software Web site at http://www.process.com/prodinfo/purvdata.htm. In addition to its Web server, Process Software makes a fine NFS server for Windows NT that you may find useful if you operate in an environment with UNIX systems. Both the Web server and the NFS server are available free for an evaluation period of 30 days. After that you need to pay for the products if you want to continue using them. The announced price for Purveyor is $1,995 per copy.

ALIBABA

ALIBABA is the HTTP server from Computer Software Manufaktur, a company in Austria. It offers all the features you expect in a professional level HTTP server, including access control, MIME file-type mapping for directory listings and multi-threaded operation. It also offers a Windows CGI interface that is very similar to that included with the O'Reilly server. For more information about this server, you can check out http://www.csm.co.at/csm/. A summary of major features is as follows:

- Multithreaded NT service operation.
- HTTP 1.0 protocol.
- Directory listings can be provided to the Web browser.
- CGI 1.0 with all environment variables supported.
- Configurable network port assignment.
- GET and POST commands.
- Configurable network port.
- Many configurable set-up parameters (server root directory, default document name, etc.).
- Directory ignores.
- Up to 40 alias names.
- Up to 40 script alias names.
- Up to 200 icon/gif extensions for directory listings.
- Up to 400 mime/type extensions.
- Access logging (Common Logformat 1.2).
- Error logging.
- Some HTTP error messages are definable (some with variables).
- NCSA format image maps.

CGI Server Programs for Windows CGI

One of the more interesting features of the two servers written by Robert Denny is his use of an extension to CGI—the Windows CGI. Although Windows 3.1, Windows 95 and Windows NT have many powerful features, their built-in command line is not one of them. To get around this problem, and to allow access to the broad range of services available from Windows programs, Denny created an extension to CGI called Windows CGI. This interface uses many of the same concepts as standard CGI, including the use of environment variables to pass information. But, instead of putting all the information in the "standard in" data stream, this method creates files that can be read by any program. Once the temporary data file has been created, the server starts up your CGI support program, which can be a Windows executable. The Windows program can read the temporary files that contain the information passed in from a form, and then create an HTML page that is saved in a temporary output file, which is passed back to the Web browser. In Chapter 9, we created a simple MAPI interface program to send mail when a comment form was filled out. On the Companion CD-ROM you will find a program that interrogates an Access Database file containing a list of books about the Internet, and returns a list of matching titles to the user. All of the source files you need to duplicate and expand this example can be found on the Companion CD-ROM.

To start with, the example is based on the Visual Basic example that Robert Denny includes with his servers. The example uses the same CGI.BAS file as found with the server. A new module, called CGIACC.BAS, has been created to perform the database look-ups.

To get the example program running, follow these steps:

1. Copy the files from the CD-ROM in the book's example directory to the WinHTTPD cgi-win directory.
2. Move the access.htm file from there to the htdocs directory. Move all the .dll files to your Windows system directory, ensuring that you do NOT copy over files that are newer or the same date in your Windows system directory.

3. Ensure that the WinHTTPD server is running, and open the access.htm page from your Web browser with the URL http://yourhost/access.htm. (Where *yourhost* is the name of your machine.)
4. Enter a search term in the field labeled Title, and press the Search on Title button.

If everything is installed correctly, you will receive a page with the results of your query.

CGI Server Programs for Windows NT

POSIX Shell Scripts

The batch language capability for Windows NT is not by itself very useful for creating CGI scripts, mostly because it does not allow the use of the "<" or ">" characters, even in quoted strings. Fortunately, Microsoft has provided a POSIX shell utility, sh.exe, which uses a scripting language that is very useful for creating small CGI scripts. The shell sh.exe is available for free as part of the Windows NT 3.5 Resource kit on the Microsoft FTP server. The precise way you access the alternate shell depends on the server you are using, and because this CD-ROM contains the EMWAC server, the script example in this chapter will support that server. The Purveyor server is based on the EMWAC server, so the example also works with Purveyor. The scripting for WebSite has a bit more flexibility.

To create a shell script for the EMWAC server, first create a form that will call the script testcgi.sh. This shell script is shown here:

```
echo "Content-type: text/html"
echo
echo "<HTML><HEAD><TITLE>Shell CGI Test</TITLE>
</HEAD>"
echo "<BODY><H1>Posix Shell CGI Test
</H1>\n<HR>Environment Variables:<PRE>"
set
echo "</PRE><HR></BODY></HTML>"
```

This script doesn't do anything but echo the environment variables, so the form can be pretty much anything you want. The important aspect of the form is the FORM tag is that it must use the following structure:

```
<Form METHOD=POST
ACTION="/directory-name/sh.exe?/directory-name/
TESTCGI.SH">
```

The directory-name refers to the subdirectory, relative to the root of the HTML documents directory, that contains the scripts. To make this work, you must have a copy of sh.exe in the same directory as the script file. The first part of the ACTION is the executable file sh.exe, which is the program the server actually runs. The second part (which is passed as a query parameter) is the script that sh.exe will run, in this case TESTCGI.SH. The data from the form is presented in the standard input stream, which you would need to access from the shell script.

The key issues to note are:

1. You must use POST.
2. The POSIX shell sh.exe must be in the same directory as the script file, and be pointed to by the ACTION parameter.
3. POSIX is case sensitive, so the name of the script *must* be in the correct case.

Perl Scripts

For many users of UNIX-like operating systems such as Solaris, perl is a familiar and very powerful script programming language. If you are such a person, you'll be happy to find that there is a version of perl that works with Windows NT. You can get it from the EMWAC FTP site for free, and install it on your system. Using perl scripts is very similar to using shell scripts when you create forms. As with shell scripts, the FORM tag must be set up very carefully:

```
<Form METHOD=POST
ACTION="/directory-name/perl.exe?/directory-name/
test.pl">
```

where directory-name is the sub-directory off the root documentation directory that contains the scripts. To make this work, you must have a copy of perl.exe in the directory. The first part of the ACTION is the executable file perl.exe which is what the server actually runs. The second part (which is passed as a query parameter) is the perl script that perl.exe runs, which in this case is test.pl. The data from the form is presented in the standard input stream, which you need to access from the perl script.

The shell script itself must return the HTML or plain text page. In this case the content of test.pl appears as follows:

```
#!./perl
print "Content-type: text/html\n";
print "\n";
print "<HTML><HEAD><TITLE>Perl CGI Test</TITLE>
</HEAD>\n";
print "<BODY><H1>Perl CGI Test</H1>\n<HR>Environment
Variables:<PRE>\n";
foreach $var (sort keys(%ENV)) {
        print $var, ": ",$ENV{$var},"\n";
}
print "</PRE><HR></BODY></HTML>\n";
```

There are many perl scripts written as CGI scripts, but remember that most of them are UNIX scripts, so you may need to make changes to them to adapt them to Windows NT.

Command-Line Executable Programs

Command-line executable programs are the simplest to execute from forms, because you call them directly, instead of indirectly, through the use of a command-line parameter as with sh.exe and perl.exe. The disadvantage, of course, is that you must write an executable program and compile it. There are two sample programs provided with the EMWAC server, and they are available on the Companion CD-ROM. The programs must be command-line programs—not graphical windows programs, or system services.

Moving On

You currently have at least five choices for servers on Windows-based systems. Each of them is a product worth considering for commercial Web server operation. The explosive growth in the Windows market along with the increasing stability of the Windows NT operating system makes the use of one of the NT-based products extremely attractive, even though various kinds of UNIX operating systems have been the proving ground in the past. If one of the programs described in this chapter doesn't meet your needs, keep checking around. With the tremendous growth in the Windows and Windows NT markets, there will certainly be more HTTP servers to come. Also, the servers described in this chapter are new and are undergoing continuing development. Always check with the manufacturer for the latest price, feature and availability information.

Although we've finished our discussion of publishing on the Internet, it is in no way the last word on Web publishing. As you continue to traverse the Web, you are bound to come upon many exciting, new Web publishing features and vehicles. The more you continue to explore the possibilities of Internet publishing, the greater the rewards. The next move is up to you, but fortunately you have the Web publishing world at your fingertips and the next step it is only a hyperlink away.

SECTION IV

Appendices

About the Online Companion

Publish on the World Wide Web! The *Publishing on the Internet Online Companion* is an informative tool as well as an annotated software library. It aids in your understanding of HTML authoring and publishing on the World Wide Web while at the same time providing you with the resources and utilities you need to accomplish these tasks. The *Publishing on the Internet Online Companion* hyperlinks Chapter 10 of the hard-copy book to the World Wide Web sites it references. So you can just click on the reference name and jump directly to the resource you are interested in.

Perhaps one of the most valuable features of the *Publishing on the Internet Online Companion* is its Software Archive. Here, you'll find and be able to download the latest versions of all the freely available software mentioned in *Publishing on the Internet*. This software ranges from HTML editors, converters and templates such as HotMetaL, Microsoft's Internet Assistant and HTML TagWizard to many of your basic publishing essentials, such as MapEdit, a tool for making image maps, and GoldWave, an editor for audio files. Also with Ventana Online's helpful description of the software you'll know exactly what you're getting and why, so you won't download the software just to find you have no use for it.

The *Publishing on the Internet Online Companion* also links you to the Ventana Library where you will find useful press and jacket information on a variety of Ventana Press offerings. Plus, you have access to a wide selection of exciting new releases and coming attractions. In addition, Ventana's Online Library allows you to order online the books you want.

The *Online Companion* represents Ventana Online's ongoing commitment to offering the most dynamic and exciting products possible. And soon Ventana Online will be adding more services, including more multimedia supplements, searchable indexes and sections of the book reproduced and hyperlinked to the Internet resources they reference.

Before you use the *Online Companion* for the first time, you must register with Ventana Online. To register, run Netscape (one of the programs included on the CD-ROM) and click the Register link on the opening page. Your registration number can be found on the card that is inserted behind the CD-ROM in the back of the book. Follow the instructions onscreen to complete your registration.

Free voice technical support is offered but is limited to installation-related issues and is available for 30 days from the date you register your copy of the book. After the initial 30 days and for non-installation-related questions, please send all technical support questions via Internet e-mail to help@vmedia.com. Our technical support staff will research your question and respond promptly via e-mail.

To access, connect via the World Wide Web to http://www.vmedia.com/piw.html

About the Companion CD-ROM

The CD-ROM included with your copy of *Publishing on the Internet for Windows* contains a wealth of valuable software, including Netscape Navigator, HoTMetaL PRO from SoftQuad, Internet Assistant from Microsoft and Paint Shop Pro. Also included are many photo clip-art images, sample HTML templates, and programs, such as a CGI back-end routine that let users query an Access database from a World Wide Web page. In short, this CD offers virtually everything you'll need to start publishing on the Internet today.

To install the CD-ROM, load the CD and with Windows running, select **File**, **Run** from the Program Manager. Then type **D:\SETUP** (where D: is your CD-ROM drive) in the command-line box and press Enter. The setup routine creates a program group called Internet Publishing. Double-click on the Publishing CD program item. You'll see a menu screen offering several choices. Click on the appropriate menu items to explore the contents of the CD-ROM. For a summary description of the CD's contents, click on the Overview button.

To use a particular product or program, access the contents of the CD using the File Manager in Windows. Each product or program has a separate folder with a README document describing how to install and use that software. For the latest information on the software products and other topics related to this book, please refer to the *Publishing on the Internet for Windows Online Companion*.

Below is a list of folders and their contents for the *Publishing on the Internet* CD-ROM.

Folder	Contents	Description
NETSCAPE	Netscape Navigator	WWW browser
HOTMETAL	HoTMetaL PRO	HTML editor
PANORAMA	Panorama	SGML document reader
MSWORDIA	Microsoft Internet Assistant/Word Viewer	HTML add-on to MS Word
RTF2HTML	RTF2HTM WRTF2HTM	converter, DOS version converter with Windows front-end
CANYON	Drag And Zip, Drag And View, Drag And File	Utilities
ACROBAT	Adobe Acrobat Reader	portable document reader
HTTPDSRV	Freeware Windows HTTPD server	server
NTSERVER	Freeware EMWAC HTTP server for Windows NT and WAIS Toolkit	server and utilities
GIFTOOL	GIFTool	interlaces GIF files and creates transparent backgrounds
	WGIFTool	GIFTool is DOS version; WGIFTool runs under Windows NT 3.5 and Windows 95
GIFTRANS	giftrans.exe	GIF transparency program
MAPEDIT	mapedit.exe	image mapping software
POLYFORM	Polyform	CGI forms program
NOHANDS	Common Ground MiniViewer	portable document viewer
PAINTSHP	Paint Shop Pro	complete image enhancement and paint software
GOLDWAVE	GoldWave	editor for audio files

Folder	Contents	Description
CMCDPHOT	CMCD	photo clip art
IMAGECLB	Image Club Graphics	photo clip art
TEMPLATE	Sample HTML templates for chapter examples	
PROGRAMS	Sample and CGI back-end programs	

Free voice technical support is limited to installation-related issues and is available for 30 days from the date you register your copy of the book. After the initial 30 days and for non-installation-related questions, please send all technical support questions via Internet e-mail to help@vmedia.com. Our technical support staff will research your question and respond promptly via e-mail.

Illustrated HTML Reference

The HyperText Markup Language (HTML) is composed of a set of elements that define a document and guide its display. This chapter presents a concise reference guide to HTML, listing almost all of the elements and giving a brief description and illustration of each one.

You should be aware that HTML is an evolving language, and different World Wide Web browsers may recognize slightly different sets of HTML elements. In particular, the Netscape browser included on the Companion CD-ROM uses an extended set of HTML codes. These codes are indicated in this list by **N Netscape Extensions:** after the section heading where the new extension tag information is located.

HTML markup elements fall into two classes: *markup tags* and *character entities*. Markup tags define elements of the document that require special display or presentation. Character entities define special characters that are used within the document. The list here is divided into three sections. The first section displays all the standard document markup tags and extended tags. The second section lists the special markup tags that are used in HTML forms. The third section lists all the character entities. Within each section, the items are listed alphabetically by tag for easy reference. This means, for example, that the Anchor tag <A> comes before the Address tag <ADDRESS>.

Uniform Resource Locator

The URL (Uniform Resource Locator) is not a tag, but is a standard method for inserting document linking information into an HTML document. The structure of a URL may be expressed as:
resource_type://host.domain:port/pathname
where the possible resource types include: file, http, news, gopher, telnet, ftp and wais, among others. Each resource type interprets the pathname in its own way. Note that each resource type relates to a specific server type. The domain name may be optionally followed by a colon, followed by an integer TCP port number, used when a server is listening on a non-standard port. If the port number is absent, the standard port number is used. Most URLs don't require a port number.

For example, a link to the home page for the National Center for Supercomputing Applications at the University of Illinois (home of the Mosaic network navigator) is given by:

```
http://www.ncsa.uiuc.edu/SDG/Software/Mosaic/
NCSAMosaic.html
```

To point to a local home page on the C drive in the http directory, a system would use the following URL:

```
file:///c:/http/home.html
```

Notice that the URL section containing the host and domain name is missing in this reference, since this file is located on the local host. In this case, the two forward slashes separating the host and domain name section from the pathname are directly before the single forward slash marking the beginning of the pathname.

Markup Tags

An HTML markup tag may include a name, some attributes and some text or hypertext. Each markup tag has a specific name and is bracketed by the < (less than) and > (greater than) symbols. Tag names are not case-sensitive, so that the tag <DL COMPACT>, for example, is exactly the same as <dl compact>. For ease of reading, all tags presented here will be in capital letters.

The tag will appear in an HTML document in one of three formats, depending on the type of the tag:

<tag_name>
<tag_name>. . .</tag_name>
<tag_name attribute_name="argument">. . .</tag_name>

The first type of tag indicates a tag that stands alone and affects the information that follows in some way. For example, the <DD> tag marks the following item in the document as a definition description.

The second type of tag encloses some portion of the document, which may consist of text, graphics, or other HTML commands—or all of these. For example,

```
<TITLE> My Home Page </TITLE>
```

creates a title element in a document.

The last type of tag also encloses some portion of the document but also includes attribute information within the tag itself. Attributes may be used in either of two formats. The first format is simply the attribute name itself, like this:

```
<tag_name attribute_name>
```

For example, the tag <DL COMPACT> defines a definition list that is presented in a compacted form, as indicated by the attribute COMPACT.

In the second format, the attribute has an argument associated with it, like this:

```
< tag_name attribute_name="argument">
```

For example, the anchor tag <A NAME="Tag1"> defines an anchor tag that marks a location that is named "Tag1". Arguments that are text information usually must be enclosed in double quotation marks; attributes that are numbers usually may be inserted without quotations. However, most browsers will accept quotations around any argument, so inserting them, even if they are not required, is usually acceptable.

Because HTML is an evolving standard, not all documents will use all these tags or follow all these rules. In a similar way, not all browsers or servers will understand and present information with all of these tags. The listings here will give you a way to determine the use and visual presentation of most standard HTML tags for your documents. In particular, to allow older HTML documents to remain readable, the <HTML>, <HEAD> and <BODY> tags are optional within HTML documents.

ANCHOR TAG

<A>. . .</A>

A [HREF:] /A

Purpose
Defines an anchor tag. An anchor is either the origin or destination of a link within the document.

Syntax

```
<A NAME="Anchor_Name" | HREF="[URL|#Anchor_Name |
URL?search_word+search_word]" [ REF="relationship"
|REV="relationship" |
TITLE="HREF_document_name" ] >Hypertext</A>
```

Attributes & Their Arguments
The Anchor tag has two attributes: HREF and NAME. An anchor must include either a NAME or an HREF attribute, and may include both.

NAME="anchor_name"

The "anchor_name" defines a target location in a document. This target location can be referenced by other anchors in the document by using the "anchor_name" as part of an HREF attribute within another anchor tag.

HREF="#anchor_name"

Links to a location in the same document.

HREF="URL"

Links to another file or resource.

HREF="URL#anchor_name"

Links to a target location in another document.

HREF="URL?search_word+search_word"

Sends a search string to a server. Different servers may interpret the search string differently. In the case of word-oriented search engines, multiple search words might be specified by separating individual words with a plus sign (+).

In addition to these, there are three optional attributes: REV, REF and TITLE. However, these attributes are not widely used in the Anchor tag.

REF="relationship"

Defines the relationship between this document and the link URL given in the HREF attribute. Possible relationship entries are: ["next" | "previous" | "parent" | "made"].

REV="relationship"

Defines the relationship between the link URL given in the HREF attribute and this document. This is the reverse of the specification provided by the REF attribute. Possible relationship entries are: ["next" | "previous" | "parent" | "made"].

TITLE="HREF_document_name"

Indicates the document title of the document pointed to by the HREF attribute. This is not used much by current browsers. It is most useful when the link is to a document, such as a Gopher menu, that does not have an internal name. By using this, the menu can be displayed on the browser window with a name.

Examples

A link to a page at another location
The following includes an HREF that links to Ventana Media's home page.

```
<A HREF="http://www.vmedia.com/">Ventana Media
Online</A>
```

A local link to a file
The HREF points to the local file product.zip in the files directory.

```
<A HREF="/files/product.zip">Our Product listing</A>
```

A link within a page
The following example includes the HREF attribute to specify the destination anchor named end.

```
<A HREF="#end">Jump to Conclusions</A>
```

In order to move to the destination labeled end, the document must also include the anchor with the NAME attribute set to end.

```
<A NAME="end"></A>
```

A link to a target location in another document
Similar to a link within a page, this link must also include the HREF attribute to specify the document (order.html) as well as the destination anchor (feedback).

```
<A HREF="order.html#feedback">Place an order</A>
```

In order to move to the destination, the document order.html must exist and include an anchor with the NAME attribute set to feedback.

```
<A NAME="feedback"></A>
```

See Also
LINK, URL, IMG and FORM

ADDRESS TAG

<ADDRESS> . . . </ADDRESS>

ADDRESS /ADDRESS

Purpose
Defines a signature or address. This tag is normally used at the bottom or top of a page to provide address, signature or other author information.

Syntax
<ADDRESS>Signature</ADDRESS>

Attributes & Their Arguments
None.

Example
The following would insert the author's name and e-mail address on two separate lines.

```
<ADDRESS> Brent Heslop <BR>
bheslop@isdn.bookware.com </ADDRESS>
```

See Also
BLOCKQUOTE, BODY, BR and FORM

BOLD TAG

<B> . . . </B>

Purpose
Presents the text within the tags in boldface type. The Strong tag is preferred.

Syntax

```
<B>Text</B>
```

Attributes & Their Arguments

None.

Examples

The following markup defines the enclosed text to be displayed in a bold font.

```
<B>Ventana Media Online</B>
```

See Also

EM, I, STRONG and TT

BASE TAG

```
<BASE>
```

BASE [HREF:] /BASE

Purpose

Specifies the pathname to be used to resolve relative addresses within the document. This is useful when link references within the document do not include full pathnames (i.e., are relative pathnames).

Syntax

```
<BASE HREF="URL">
```

Attributes & Their Arguments

The Base tag has one required HREF attribute.

```
HREF="URL"
```

Links to another server or system.

Examples

A pointer to a remote server or system
Generally, all pointers used in a document for local links use relative addressing. This means that the links within the document will work even when the document and its associated files are moved to a different location. However, if the server cannot find a link, the Base tag provides a pointer to the original location of the links. For example, this HREF points to the files directory at Ventana Media's server.

```
<BASE HREF="http://www.vmedia.com/files">
```

With this as a base, all relative anchor references in the document would use this as a base when accessing relative file information if a reference could not be found on the local server. For example, an HREF that points to the local file product.zip would be inserted into the document as:

```
<A HREF="product.zip">Our Product listing</A>
```

The server would first look for this file in the current directory that holds the document; if it was not found there, the server would concatenate the anchor tag and the base information to access the following reference:

```
http://www.vmedia.com/files/product.zip
```

See Also
A and HEAD

BASEFONT TAG (NETSCAPE EXTENSION)

```
<BASEFONT>. . .</BASEFONT>
```

BASEFONT /BASEFONT

Purpose
Defines the size of the base font used in the document. All subsequent font changes are based on this size. Note that Netware does not require the ending </BASEFONT> tag, but does allow it. If

the ending tag is present, the basefont setting applies only to text within the tags. If the ending tag is absent, the setting applies to all the remaining fonts used in the document.

Syntax

```
<BASEFONT SIZE=number >Text</BASEFONT>
```

Attributes & Their Arguments

```
SIZE=number
```

Establishes the desired size for the font used to display the document. The number argument must be between 1 and 7; the default value is 3.

Example

The following defines the basefont for the enclosed text to be slightly larger than the standard size.

```
<BASEFONT SIZE=4><P>This is larger type for easier reading.</P></BASEFONT>
```

See Also

FONT

BLINK TAG (NETSCAPE EXTENSION)

```
<BLINK>. . .</BLINK>
```

BLINK /BLINK

Purpose

Causes the text within the tags to blink when displayed.

Syntax

<BLINK>Text</BLINK>

Attributes & Their Arguments

None.

Example

The following displays the text within the tags as a blinking element in the same font as the body text.

```
<P>One portion of this sentence is <BLINK>blinking text
</BLINK> to create emphasis.</P>
```

See Also

EM, STRONG, I and B

Block Quote Tag

```
<BLOCKQUOTE> . . . </BLOCKQUOTE>
```

BLOCKQUOTE /BLOCKQUOTE

Purpose

Includes a section of text quoted from some other source.

Syntax

```
<BLOCKQUOTE>Block of text</BLOCKQUOTE>
```

Attributes & Their Arguments

None.

Examples

The following block quote displays as an indented, single-spaced block of text, which is separated from the body text by a paragraph break.

```
<BODY>A recent press release from Canyon software tells
you about their new software.
<BLOCKQUOTE><I>Drag And Zip</I>, Drag And File's built-
in Zip Manager, links directly to Internet World Wide Web
browsers including Mosaic and Netscape. Drag And Zip
also supports files compressed with PKZIP, LHA and GZIP
programs and has a built-in virus scanner.
</BLOCKQUOTE></BODY>
```

See Also
BODY, P and PRE

Body Tag

<BODY>. . . </BODY>

BODY > < /BODY

Purpose
Defines the part of the document that represents the actual document contents. Distinguished from the Head section of the document.

Syntax

```
<BODY>Text of document, including additional HTML tags
if desired</BODY>
```

Attributes & Their Arguments
None.

Examples
The Body tag defines the display elements of the document. For example,

```
<BODY>This is a minimum of text to be inserted into the
body of a document. It will display as a single paragraph
</BODY>
```

N Netscape Extensions:

Syntax

```
<BODY [BACKGROUND="image_URL"
BGCOLOR="#rrggbb" TEXT="#rrggbb" LINK="#rrggbb"
VLINK="#rrggbb" ALINK="#rrggbb"] >
```

Attributes & Their Arguments

BACKGROUND="image_URL"

Allows you to specify a URL that points to an image to be used as background for the body of the document. The image is tiled to fill the background viewing area.

BGCOLOR="#rrggbb"

Allows you to specify a background color for the body of the document. The argument "#rrggbb" is a set of three hexadecimal numbers that specify the color that you wish displayed.

TEXT="#rrggbb"

Allows you to specify the color of all text in the document that is not specially colored to indicate a link or other special attribute. The argument "#rrggbb" is a set of three hexadecimal numbers that specify the color that you wish displayed.

LINK="#rrggbb"

Allows you to specify a color for body text that gives link information. The argument "#rrggbb" is a set of three hexadecimal numbers that specify the color that you wish displayed. The default color is blue (#0000FF).

VLINK="#rrggbb"

Allows you to specify a color for body text showing a link that has already been visited. The argument "#rrggbb" is a set of three hexadecimal numbers that specify the color that you wish displayed. The default color is purple (#FF00FF).

ALINK="#rrggbb"

Allows you to specify a color for body text showing a link that is currently activated. The argument "#rrggbb" is a set of three hexadecimal numbers that specify the color that you wish displayed. The default color is red (#FF0000).

See Also

HEAD and HTML

Break Tag

Purpose
Forces a line break immediately and retains the same style.

Syntax

Attributes & Their Arguments
None.

Examples
The following would insert the author's name and e-mail address on two separate lines. The Break tag forces a new line immediately after the name, but retains the Address tag style for the e-mail address.

```
<ADDRESS> Brent Heslop <BR> bheslop@bookware.com
</ADDRESS>
```

N Netscape Extensions:

Syntax
<BR [CLEAR="keyword"] >

Attributes & Their Arguments
CLEAR="keyword"
Allows you to specify how to insert the break after a floating image. The CLEAR attribute specifies whether to take floating images into account when producing a break. Possible keyword entries are: ["left" | "right" | "all"]. CLEAR="left" inserts a line break in the text and moves vertically down until the left margin is clear . CLEAR="right" inserts a line break in the text and moves vertically down until the right margin is clear. CLEAR="all" inserts a line break in the text and moves vertically down until both margins are clear.

See Also
P and PRE

CENTER TAG (NETSCAPE EXTENSION)

<CENTER>. . .</CENTER>

CENTER /CENTER

Purpose
Centers the enclosed text.

Syntax

```
<CENTER>Text</CENTER>
```

Attributes & Their Arguments
None.

Example
The following shows an example of centered text.

```
<CENTER>This text will be centered on the document
line.</CENTER>
```

See Also
IMG and TABLE

CITATION TAG

<CITE>. . .</CITE>

CITE /CITE

Purpose
Style tag for display of a citation. Text is typically displayed in italics or underlined.

Syntax

<CITE>Citation text</CITE>

Attributes & Their Arguments

None.

Example

The following shows a typical citation as it might appear in a document:

<CITE>Caesar: The Gallic War; English Translation by H. J. Edwards, C.B.; Loeb Classical Library, Cambridge, MCMLXXIX </CITE>

See Also

B, EM, IT, STRONG and TT

CODE TAG

<CODE>. . .</CODE>

CODE /CODE

Purpose

Defines a text element to be rendered in a format suitable for computer program text. Text is usually rendered in a monospaced font.

Syntax

<CODE>code_text</CODE>

Attributes & Their Arguments

None.

Example

The following is a sample of computer code rendered in a Code tag.

<CODE>class CErectorView : public CView</CODE>

See Also
PRE and TT

DEFINITION TAG

<DFN>. . .</DFN>

Not supported by HoTMetal PRO

Purpose
Provides a definition of a term or phrase within a text block. Similar to the Strong tag. This is a new tag and may not be supported by all browsers.

Syntax

```
<DFN>Text</DFN>
```

Attributes & Their Arguments
None.

Example
The following includes a definition item within a normal text paragraph.

```
<P>In Windows, <DFN>resources</DFN> are user-interface
items, such as menus, icons, dialog boxes, and so on, that
are used to interact with the user. </P>
```

See Also
VAR, STRONG, DL, B, I and U

DIRECTORY LIST TAG

<DIR>. . .</DIR>

Purpose
Defines a list of directory items. A directory list is an unordered list consisting of one or more List Item tags. List items in this type of list should be less than 24 characters long. The intention is to generate a short, concise list. This limit is not generally enforced by browsers. If you exceed this limit, however, the displayed list may not look as you intended. Note that directory lists should not be nested.

ASSOCIATED TAG: LIST ELEMENT TAG

<LI>. . .

Purpose
Defines an element in a list. Note that this tag should never be used outside a list definition tag as it may not be correctly displayed by a browser. Also notice that this tag does not have a matching termination.

Syntax

```
<DIR><LI> List_element</DIR>
```

Attributes & Their Arguments
None.

Example
The following displays a directory list with three entries.

```
<DIR> <LI>First Directory Entry <LI>Second Directory Entry
<LI>And so on... </DIR>
```

See Also
DL, MENU, OL and UL

Definition List Tag

<DL>. . .</DL>

Purpose
Presents a list of items and their definitions; it may also be used to present a glossary. A definition list is an unordered list consisting of one or more Definition Term tags and an associated Definition Description tag. These tags always occur together in the list, and each list element is composed of one set of tags.

Associated Tag: Definition Term Tag

<DT> . . .

Purpose
Marks a term to be defined within a Definition List. Note that this tag should never be used outside a Definition List tag as it may not be correctly displayed by a browser. Also notice that this tag does not have a matching termination. Must be followed by a Definition Description tag.

Associated Tag: Definition Description Tag

<DD>. . .

Purpose
Provides the definition text for the associated Definition Term tag within a Definition List. Note that this tag should never be used outside a Definition List tag as it may not be correctly displayed by a browser. Also notice that this tag does not have a matching termination. Must be preceded by a Definition Term tag.

Syntax

<DL [COMPACT]> <DT>Defintion_term <DD>Definition_text </DL>

Attributes & Their Arguments

The Definition List tag has one optional attribute.

COMPACT

This attribute presents a definition list or glossary that uses a minimum amount of indentation and white space when displayed.

Example

The following displays a definition list with two entries.

<DL> <DT>First Term <DD>Definition of First Term <DT>Second Term <DD>Definition of Second Term </DL>

The same list can be compressed for display by using the following argument.

<DL COMPACT> <DT>First Term <DD>Definition of First Term <DT>Second Term <DD>Definition of Second Term </DL>

See Also

DIR, MENU, OL and UL

EMPHASIS TAG

<EM> . . . </EM>

Purpose

Presents the text within the tags in emphasized format. This is usually underlined, but may appear in italics. The important point is that the emphasized text be noticeably different from the surrounding normal text.

Syntax

<EM>Text</EM>

Attributes & Their Arguments
None.

Examples
The following markup creates a text element that is emphasized (usually in italic font).

```
<EM>Ventana Media Online</EM>
```

See Also
BOLD, I, STRONG and TT

FONT TAG (NETSCAPE EXTENSION)

```
<FONT>. . .</ FONT>
```

FONT /FONT

Purpose
Changes the size of the enclosed text from the size set by the Basefont tag (or from the default size if no Basefont tag has been set).

Syntax

```
<FONT SIZE=number>Text</FONT>
```

Attributes & Their Arguments

SIZE=number

Establishes the desired size for the font used to display the document. The number argument may be an integer between 1 and 7 that sets the font to the new size. The number may be preceded by + or - to indicate a relative change to the basefont size. The default basefont size is 3.

Example
The following defines the font for the enclosed text to be slightly larger than the current basefont size.

```
<FONT SIZE=+2><P>This is larger type for easier reading.
</P></FONT>
```

See Also
BASEFONT

HEADER TAGS

<H1> . . . </H1> Most prominent header
<H2> . . . </H2>
<H3> . . . </H3>
<H4> . . . </H4>
<H5> . . . </H5>
<H6> . . . </H6> Least prominent header

H1 /H1

H2 /H2
H3 /H3
H4 /H4
H5 /H5
H6 /H6

Purpose
Defines the data contained between the tags as a text header. The headers are defined in six descending categories. The first Header tag, <H1>, is the most prominent header, with each successive level being less prominent but still distinct from the normal text and from each other. Headings are generally distinguished by size and bold type, but a browser may use another method of display if required.

Syntax
<H*n*>Header_text</H*n*>

Attributes & Their Arguments
None.

Examples

The following shows a series of headers.

```
<H1>Major Heading</H1>
<H2>First sub-heading</H2>
<H3>Minor heading</H3>
<H3>Another minor heading</H3>
<H2>Final sub-heading</H2>
```

See Also

BODY and HEAD

HEAD TAG

```
<HEAD>. . . </HEAD>
```

HEAD /HEAD

Purpose

Defines the part of the document that contains general data about the page. Distinguished from the Body section of the document.

Syntax

```
<HEAD>Header information</HEAD>
```

Attributes & Their Arguments

None.

Examples

The Head tag defines the page description and information elements of the document. These are placed ahead of the body of the document. For example:

```
<HEAD><TITLE>Minimum Page</TITLE></HEAD>
<BODY>This is a minimum of text to be inserted into the
body of a document. It will display as a single paragraph
</BODY>
```

See Also

BODY and HTML

HORIZONTAL RULE TAG

<HR>

HR ——— /HR

Purpose
Draws a horizontal rule across the width of the document. The individual browser controls the size and presentation of the line, and some browsers may render a line of fixed length.

Syntax

```
<HR>
```

Attributes & Their Arguments
None.

Example
The following would insert a horizontal line the width of the browser window between the two paragraphs of text.

```
<P> This is two paragraphs of text divided by a single,
horizontal line. </P> <HR> </P> This is the second para-
graph of text. </P>
```

N Netscape Extensions:

Syntax

```
<HR [ALIGN="keyword" NOSHADE SIZE=number
WIDTH=value] >
```

Attributes & Their Arguments

ALIGN="keyword"

For rules that are not the full document width, the ALIGN attribute specifies where the rule is to be placed. Possible keyword entries are: ["left" | "right" | "center"].

NOSHADE

Specifies that you want a solid rule instead of the default Netware horizontal rule, which is a shaded, engraved line.

SIZE=number
Defines the vertical size of the rule in pixels.

WIDTH=value
Specifies the width of the rule. The default rule is automatically the width of the page. The value argument is [number | percent], which allows you to specify the width of the rule in pixels or as a percentage of the document width.

See Also
BR and P

HTML TAG

<HTML>. . . </HTML>

Purpose
Defines the data contained between the tags to be in HTML format.

Syntax
```
<HTML>Document_data</HTML>
```

Attributes & Their Arguments
None.

Examples
The HTML tag defines entire document. These tags are placed around the contents of the document. For example,

```
<HTML>
<HEAD><TITLE>Minimum Page</TITLE></HEAD>
<BODY>This is a minimum of text to be inserted into the
body of a document. It will display as a single paragraph
</BODY>
</HTML>
```

See Also
BODY and HEAD

ITALIC TAG

<I> . . . </I>

Purpose
Presents the text within the tags in italic type.

Syntax

```
<I>Text</I>
```

Attributes & Their Arguments
None.

Examples
The following markup defines the enclosed text to be displayed in an italic font.

```
<I>Looking Good in Print, R. Parker, Ventana Press</I>
```

See Also
B, EM, STRONG and TT

IMAGE TAG

<IMG>. . .</IMG>

IMG [SRC:] /IMG

Purpose
Embed a graphic image in the document.

Syntax

<IMG SRC="URL" [ALT="textstring" ALIGN="keyword" ISMAP] >

Attributes & Their Arguments

The Image tag has one required attribute: SRC, and three optional attributes: ALT, ALIGN and ISMAP.

SRC="URL"

Specifies the location of the image that is to be rendered by the browser in the document at the point where the Image tag is located.

ALT="textstring"

Allows a text string to be put in place of the image in browsers that cannot display images.

ALIGN="keyword"

Specifies a position relationship to surrounding text. Possible keyword entries are: ["top" | "middle" | "bottom"].

ALIGN="top" aligns the image with the top of the tallest element in the line of surrounding text.

ALIGN="middle" aligns the center of the image with the baseline of the line of surrounding text.

ALIGN="bottom" aligns the base of the image with the baseline of the surrounding text.

ISMAP

If ISMAP is present and the image tag is within an anchor, the image will become a "clickable image." The pixel coordinates of the cursor will be appended to the URL specified in the anchor if the user clicks within the ISMAP image. The resulting URL will take the form "URL?*m*,*n*" where *m* and *n* are integer coordinates.

Examples

A simple image

The following is a typical Image tag that might be used to display a picture of the author of a page.

```
<H3> <IMG HREF="author.gif" ALIGN="top" ALT="Brent
Heslop"> My Picture </H3>
```

An image within an anchor tag

A better way to use the image might be to link the Image tag to an Anchor tag that references a resumé, for example.

```
<A HREF="bio.html"> <IMG HREF="author.gif" ALIGN="top"
ALT="Brent Heslop"> My Resum$eacute; </A>
```

N Netscape Extensions:

Syntax

```
<IMG SRC="URL" [ALT="textstring" ALIGN="keyword"
ISMAP BORDER=value HSPACE=value VSPACE=value
WIDTH=value HEIGHT=value] >
```

Attributes & Their Arguments

ALIGN="keyword"

Specifies a position relationship to surrounding text. Possible keyword entries are: ["left" | "right" | "top" | "texttop" | "middle" | "absmiddle" | "baseline" | "bottom" | "absbottom"].

ALIGN="left" defines a floating image. The image is rendered at the left margin and subsequent lines of text are wrapped around the right side of the image.

ALIGN="right" defines a floating image. The image is rendered at the right margin and subsequent lines of text are wrapped around the left side of the image.

ALIGN="top" aligns the top of the image with the top of the tallest element in the line of surrounding text. This is the same as the standard behavior.

ALIGN="textop" aligns the top of the image with the top of the tallest text in the line of surrounding text. This is usually, but not always, the same as ALIGN="top".

ALIGN="middle" aligns the center of the image with the baseline of the line of surrounding text. This is the same as the standard behavior.

ALIGN="absmiddle" aligns the center of the image with the center of the surrounding text line.

ALIGN="baseline" aligns the base of the image with the baseline of the surrounding text line. This is the same as ALIGN="bottom".

ALIGN="bottom" aligns the base of the image with the baseline of the surrounding text line. This is the same as the standard behavior.

ALIGN="absbottom" aligns the base of the image with the bottom of the surrounding text.

BORDER=value

The integer value argument defines the thickness of the border around the image. The value argument may be 0, indicating no border. Note that BORDER=0 on images that are also part of an Anchor tag may confuse users who are accustomed to seeing a colored border around active images.

HSPACE= value

For a floating image, the integer value argument defines the amount of space to be allocated between the alignment margin and the image and between the image and the text adjoining it.

VSPACE=value

For a floating image, the integer value argument defines the amount of space to be allocated between the bottom of the text line and the top and bottom of the image.

WIDTH= value HEIGHT=value

Both attributes take an integer value that indicates the width and height of the image. These values are provided to speed up the display. They allow the browser to allocate the image area and calculate its size while the image is still being loaded.

See Also

URL, A and FORM

INDEXED TAG

<ISINDEX>

ISINDEX /ISINDEX

Purpose
Specifies that the current document describes a database that can be searched using the index search method appropriate for whatever client is being used to read the document. This tag occurs in the Head section of the document. This tag is meaningful only if the document resides on a server that provides indexing services. For this reason, you should be careful about adding this tag manually. Most servers that support searching will add this element automatically to the document when they send it.

Syntax

```
<ISINDEX>
```

Attributes & Their Arguments
None.

Examples
The following markup defines an indexable document:

```
<HEAD> <TITLE>An Indexable Document</TITLE>
<ISINDEX></HEAD>
```

N Netscape Extensions:

Syntax

```
<ISINDEX [PROMPT="text"] >
```

Attributes & Their Arguments

PROMPT="keyword"

Specifies the message that should appear in front of the search window. The default message (used by the standard Search tag) is "This is a searchable index. Enter search keywords:"

See Also
HEAD and TITLE

KEYBOARD INPUT TAG

<KBD>. . .</KBD>

KBD /KBD

Purpose
Defines a text element that defines a sequence of characters to be entered by the user from a keyboard. This is intended for use in instructional or other text as a distinctive graphic element to show users what to enter. This is not a fill-out section of a form. Text is usually rendered in a monospaced font.

Syntax

```
<KBD>user_entry_text</KBD>
```

Attributes & Their Arguments
None.

Example
The following is a sample of keyboard code rendered in a Keyboard Input tag.

```
<P>When requested, enter your user name at the login:
prompt, like this <KBD>login: dh</KBD></P>
```

See Also
FORM and PRE

LINK TAG

<LINK>

LINK [HREF:] /LINK

Purpose
Defines a link with another document. The link tag allows you to define relationships between the document containing the link tag and the document specified in the HREF attribute. A link tag must contain an HREF attribute.

Syntax
```
<LINK HREF="URL" [ REF="relationship" |REV="relationship"
|
TITLE="HREF_document_name" ] >
```

Attributes & Their Arguments
The link tag has one required attribute: HREF, and three optional attributes: REF, REV and TITLE.

HREF="URL"

Defines the link between this document and another entity, usually specified by the REF or REV attributes.

REF="relationship"

Defines the relationship between this document and the link URL given in the HREF attribute. Possible relationship entries are: ["next" | "previous" | "parent" | "made"].

REV="relationship"

Defines the relationship between the link URL given in the HREF attribute and this document. This is the reverse of the specification provided by the REF attribute. Possible relationship entries are: ["next" | "previous" | "parent" | "made"].

TITLE="HREF_document_name"

Indicates the title of the document pointed to by the HREF attribute. This is not used much by current browsers. It is most useful when the link is to a document, such as a Gopher menu, that does not have an internal name. This lets you display the menu on the browser window with a name.

Example

A simple link
The following includes an HREF that points to Ventana Media's home page and indicates that Ventana Media was the maker of this document.

```
<LINK HREF="http://www.vmedia.com/" REF="made">
```

A link within a series
The following example shows links for a document that represents Chapter 2 (chapt2.html) in a series of chapters.

```
<HEAD> <TITLE>Chapter 2: How I grew up</TITLE> <LINK
HREF="http://www.myserver.com/Bio/chap3.html"
REF="next" <LINK HREF="http://www.myserver.com/Bio/
chap1.html" REV="previous" </HEAD>
```

See Also
A, URL and FORM

Listing Tag

```
<LISTING> . . . </LISTING>
```

LISTING /LISTING

Purpose
Example computer listing; similar to the Preformatted Text tag except that no embedded tags will be recognized. To preserve formatting, the text is displayed in a monospaced font. This is an obsolete tag; the Preformatted Text tag is preferred.

Syntax

```
<LISTING>Text</LISTING >
```

Attributes & Their Arguments
None.

Examples
The following shows how you may use text in a listing text block.

<LISTING>This is sample listing <LISTING> text</LISTING>

See Also
XMP and PRE

MENU TAG

<MENU>. . .</MENU>

Purpose
Defines a list of menu items. A menu list is an unordered list consisting of one or more List Item tags. Each item in this type of list should be a single line. The list generated on a browser may be rendered more compactly than an Unordered List. Note that menu lists should not be nested.

ASSOCIATED TAG: LIST ITEM TAG

<LI>

Purpose
Defines an element in a list. Note that this tag should never be used outside a list definition tag as it may not be correctly displayed by a browser. Also notice that this tag does not have a matching termination.

Syntax
<MENU><LI> List_element</MENU>

Attributes &Their Arguments
None.

Example
The following displays a menu list with three entries.

```
<MENU> <LI>First Menu Item <LI>Second Menu Item
<LI>Third Menu Item </MENU>
```

See Also
UL, OL, DL and DIR

NOBREAK TAG (NETSCAPE EXTENSION)

<NOBR>. . .</NOBR>

NOBR /NOBR

Purpose
Forces enclosed text to stay together, without any line breaks.

Syntax

```
<NOBR>Text</NOBR>
```

Attributes & Their Arguments
None.

Examples
The following shows a single line of text that will be kept together on one line by use of the Nobreak tag.

```
<NOBR>This text must always stay together on one line.
</NOBR>
```

See Also
BR and WBR

ORDERED LIST TAG

<OL>. . .</OL>

OL LI /LI /OL

Purpose
Defines an ordered (numbered) list consisting of one or more List Item tags.

ASSOCIATED TAG: LIST ITEM TAG

<LI>

Purpose
Defines an element in a list. Note that this tag should never be used outside a list definition tag as it may not be correctly displayed by a browser. Also notice that this tag does not have a matching termination.

Syntax

```
<OL><LI> List_element</OL>
```

Attributes & Their Arguments
None.

Example

A simple ordered list
The following displays an ordered list with three entries.

```
<OL> <LI>First List Item <LI>Second List Item <LI>And so
on... </OL>
```

An ordered list nested with other lists
The following list has three items, with the first item being a sub-list with two items. The numbers start over for each nested list.

```
<OL> <LI>First List Item <OL> <LI>First Sub-Entry Item
<LI>second Sub-Entry Item </OL> <LI>Second List Item.
This is a long entry to show how the browser handles list
elements that are longer than a single line. In fact, a list
element may be a significant block of text. <LI>And so on...
</OL>
```

N Netscape Extensions:

Syntax

<OL [TYPE="keyword" START=number]> <LI [TYPE="keyword" START=number]> List_element</OL>

Attributes & Their Arguments

TYPE="keyword"

Allows you to specify how you want list items marked. Use of the TYPE attribute in the List tag affects the entire list. Use of the attribute in a List Item tag affects that tag and all subsequent tags. Possible keyword entries are: ["a" | "A" | "i" | "I" | "1"].

TYPE="a" uses small letters for list elements.
TYPE="A" uses capital letters for list elements.
TYPE="i" uses small Roman numerals for list elements.
TYPE="I" uses capital Roman numerals for list elements.
TYPE="1" uses numbers for list elements. This is the default.

START=number

Allows you to specify an index number that should be used when starting the list. The index number specifies the starting point of the list elements in the sequencing method selected by the TYPE attribute. For example, using START=3 will start the list at c, C, iii, III or 3 depending on the setting of TYPE.

See Also

UL, DL, DIR and MENU

PARAGRAPH TAG

<P> . . . </P>

Purpose

Presents the text within the tags as a single paragraph. In an obsolete form, this tag might be used alone (as </P>) to mark the end of a paragraph; preferred usage is to include the paragraph text within the tags.

Syntax

<P>Text</P>

Attributes & Their Arguments

None.

Examples

The following displays two separate paragraphs of text, divided by a horizontal rule.

<P> This is two paragraphs of text divided by a single, horizontal line. </P> <HR> <P> This is the second paragraph of text. </P>

See Also

BR and PRE

Preformatted Text Tag

<PRE> . . . </PRE>

PRE /PRE

Purpose

Identifies text that has already been formatted (preformatted) by some other system and must be displayed as is. Preformatted text may include embedded tags that will be interpreted for rendering, but not all tag types are permitted. The Preformatted Text tag can be used to include tables in documents. To preserve formatting, the text is displayed in a monospaced font. The Preformatted Text tag is preferred to the obsolete Listing <LISTING> and Example <XMP> tags.

Syntax

<PRE>Text</PRE>

Attributes & Their Arguments
The Preformatted Text tag has one optional attribute.

WIDTH="value"

This attribute tells a browser the maximum width to be expected in the block of preformatted text. This allows the browser to adjust the window, and perhaps the font and size of the displayed text, to improve rendering.

Examples
The following shows how you may use text in a preformatted text block.

```
<PRE>
        Act Three, Scene Two
<I>Antony:</I> Friends, Romans, countrymen, lend me your
ears;
            I come to bury Caesar, not to praise him.
            The evil that men do lives after them,
            the good is oft interred with their bones.
</PRE>
```

See Also
BR, P, CODE, LISTING and XMP

SAMPLE TAG

<SAMP>. . .</SAMP>

Purpose
Defines a text element that represents a series of literal characters. Text is usually rendered in a monospaced font.

Syntax

```
<SAMP>sample_text</SAMP>
```

Attributes & Their Arguments
None.

Example
The following is a sample of sample text.

```
<SAMP>This is a sequence of sampled characters</SAMP>
```

See Also
CODE, KBD and PRE

STRIKEOUT TAG

```
<STRIKE> . . . </STRIKE>
```

not supported by HoTMetaL PRO

Purpose
Presents the text within the tags in strike-out format (with a line through the text).This is a common style used in legal documents and in revisions and editing of text. This is a new tag and not supported by all browsers. If a browser does not support this tag, the text is generally rendered just like normal text.

Syntax

```
<STRIKE>Text</STRIKE>
```

Attributes & Their Arguments
None.

Examples
The following markup creates a display with the text enclosed by the tags with a line through it.

```
<P>You can use type-specific tags to show edits by
<STRIKE>striking out</STRIKE> text rather than removal.
</P>
```

See Also
EM, STRONG, I and B

STRONG TAG

<STRONG> . . . </STRONG>

STRONG /STRONG

Purpose
Presents the text within the tags with a stronger emphasis than the Emphasis tag. Usually, the text is displayed in bold. This tag is preferred to the Bold tag.

Syntax
<STRONG>Text</STRONG>

Attributes & Their Arguments:
None.

Examples
The following markup displays the enclosed text in a very different manner than the body text (usually in bold font).

<STRONG>Pay Attention. This is important.</STRONG>

See Also
B, EM, I and TT

TABLE TAG (NETSCAPE EXTENSION)

<TABLE>. . .</TABLE>

not supported by HoTMetaL PRO

Purpose
Defines a table. A table is an ordered set of data presented in rows and columns. Tables may be nested.

Associated Tag: Table Row Tag

<TR>. . .</TR>

Purpose
Defines a row of a table. This tag should never be used outside a table definition tag. The number of rows in a table is equal to the number of Table Row tags that it contains.

Associated Tag: Table Data Tag

<TD>. . .</TD>

Purpose
Defines a data cell in a table. Table data must appear within a table row. Each row need not have the same number of data cells; short rows are padded with empty cells to the right.

Associated Tag: Table Header Tag

<TH>. . .</TH>

Purpose
Defines a header cell in a table. Header cells are identical to data cells except that text or data in header cells is presented in a bold font. Table headers must appear within a table row.

Associated Tag: Caption Tag

<CAPTION>. . .</CAPTION>

Purpose
Defines the caption for the table. Caption tags are optional. If used, they must appear between the Table tags but outside of table rows or cells. Captions are horizontally centered with respect to the table.

Syntax

```
<TABLE [BORDER | BORDER=value | CELLSPACING=value |
CELLPADDING=value | WIDTH=value]>
<CAPTION [ALIGN="keyword"]> Caption_text </CAPTION>
<TR [ALIGN="keyword" | VALIGN="keyword"]>
<TH | ALIGN="keyword" | VALIGN="keyword" | NOWRAP |
COLSPAN=value | ROWSPAN=value | WIDTH=value>
Table_heading_text </TH>
</TR>
<TR [ALIGN="keyword" | VALIGN="keyword"]>
<TD | ALIGN="keyword" | VALIGN="keyword" | NOWRAP |
COLSPAN=value | ROWSPAN=value | WIDTH=value>
Table_element </TD>
</TR>
</TABLE>
```

Attributes & Their Arguments

Many attributes are available in several different tags used in tables. Each attribute listed below describes any special effects that depend on the tag it is associated with. The general rule is that attributes at a lower level override any previous attribute settings. For example, the default alignment of a table is ALIGN=:"left". This is overridden for any given row by specifying the ALIGN attribute for that row. Within a row, the ALIGN attribute specified for a cell or header overrides the alignment for that row.

ALIGN="keyword"

Sets the alignment of the data controlled by the tag. For the <CAPTION> tag, the ALIGN attribute specifies where the caption text is to be placed. Possible keyword entries are: ["top" | "bottom"]. The default setting is ALIGN="top". For the <TR>, <TH> or <TD> tags, the ALIGN attribute specifies where the data is to be placed. Possible keyword entries are: ["left" | "right" | "center"]. The default setting is ALIGN="left".

BORDER[=value]

Specifies that you want a border around the table and all table cells. If absent, the table is drawn without borders, but space is allocated for the border by default. This means that a table without the BORDER attribute will occupy the same space as one with the BORDER attribute but without a value argument. The optional value argument allows you to specify the size of the border. If a value of 0 is used, the table will not have a border and no space will be saved for the border, making the table more compact than simply eliminating the BORDER attribute.

CELLPADDING=value

Controls the padding around the data in a cell. The cell padding is the space between the borders of the cell and the contents of the cell. The default CELLPADDING is 1. Note that using CELLPADDING=0 in a table with visible borders is not recommended, as the data in the cells may touch the border.

CELLSPACING=value

Controls the spacing between cells of the table. The default CELLSPACING is 2.

COLSPAN=value

Specifies how many columns of the table this cell should span. The default COLSPAN is 1.

NOWRAP

Prevents the data within the cell from being broken to fit the width of the cell. The resulting cell may be larger than a standard cell to accommodate the data.

ROWSPAN=value

Specifies how many rows of the table this cell should span. The default ROWSPAN is 1. The rows spanned must be defined by Table Row tags. An attempt to extend a cell into a row not specified with a <TR> tag will be truncated.

VALIGN="keyword"

Sets the alignment in the vertical direction within the cell for the data controlled by the tag. Possible keyword entries are: ["top" | "middle" | "bottom" | "baseline"]. The default setting is VALIGN="middle".

WIDTH=value

Specifies the width of the overall table or of a specific cell within a table. The default width for tables and cells is determined by complex algorithms within the browser. The value argument is [number | "percent"] which allows you to specify the width of the element in either pixels or as a percentage of the document width (for a table) or of the table width (for cells).

Example

The following displays a three-column table with two rows and a caption.

```
<TABLE BORDER>
<CAPTION>A Table</CAPTION>
<TR><TH> Heading 1 </TH> <TH COLSPAN=2> Heading 2
</TH></TR>
<TR><TD>Item Name</TD> <TD ALIGN="center"> 100
</TD> <TD ALIGN="center"> 200 </TD> </TR> </TABLE>
```

See Also

OL, UL and PRE

TITLE TAG

```
<TITLE> . . . </TITLE>
```

TITLE Document Title: /TITLE

Purpose

Specifies a title for an HTML document. This tag occurs in the Head section of the document and is required by HTML standards. Note that the title will not appear directly on the document as is customary on printed documents; instead, it will usually appear in a window bar identifying the contents of the window where the document information is displayed. HTML Header tags perform the functions usually reserved for titles in printed documents.

Syntax

```
<TITLE>Text</TITLE>
```

Attributes & Their Arguments

None.

Examples

The following markup defines a title for an HTML document.

```
<TITLE>Sample Document</TITLE>
```

See Also
HEAD and BODY

Typewriter Tag

<TT> . . . </TT>

Purpose
Presents the text within the tags in a monospaced font (usually Courier) that looks like a typewriter.

Syntax
<TT>Text</TT>

Attributes & Their Arguments
None.

Examples
The following markup displays the enclosed text in a monospaced font (usually Courier or a variant of that font).

```
<TT>This is simple, monospaced text that looks like a
typewriter.</TT>
```

See Also
B, EM, I and STRONG

Underline Tag

<U> . . . </U>

not supported by HoTMetaL PRO

Purpose
Presents the text within the tags underlined.

Syntax

<U>Text</U>

Attributes & Their Arguments

None.

Examples

The following markup defines the enclosed text to be displayed underlined.

```
<P>You can use type-specific tags to force
<U>underlining</U> when you require that and nothing
else.</P>
```

See Also

B, I, EM and STRONG

Unordered List Tag

<UL>. . .</UL>

Purpose

Defines an unordered (bulleted) list consisting of one or more List Item tags.

Associated Tag: List Item Tag

<LI>

Purpose

Defines an element in a list. Note that this tag should never be used outside a list definition tag as it may not be correctly displayed by a browser. Also notice that this tag does not have a matching termination.

Syntax

```
<UL><LI> List_element</UL>
```

Attributes & Their Arguments

None.

Example

A simple unordered list

The following displays an unordered list with three entries.

```
<UL> <LI>First List Item <LI>Second List Item <LI>And so
on... </UL>
```

An unordered list nested with other lists

The following list has three items, with the first item being a sub-list with two items. Many browsers will show different bullet types to indicate the level of indentation within an unordered list.

```
<UL> <LI>First List Item <UL> <LI>First Sub-Entry Item
<LI>second Sub-Entry Item </UL> <LI>Second List Item.
This is a long entry to show how the browser handles list
elements that are longer than a single line. In fact, a list
element may be a significant block of text. <LI>And so on...
</UL>
```

N Netscape Extensions:

Syntax

<UL [TYPE="keyword"]> <LI> List_element</UL>

Attributes & Their Arguments

```
TYPE="keyword"
```

Allows you to specify how you want list items marked. Use of the TYPE attribute in the List tag affects the entire list; use of the attribute in a List Item tag affects that tag and all subsequent tags. Possible keyword entries are: ["disc" | "circle" | "square"].

TYPE="disc" uses the default solid round bullet for list elements.
TYPE="circle" uses an open circle bullet for list elements.
TYPE="square" uses a square bullet for list elements.

See Also

UL, DL, DIR and MENU

VARIABLE TAG

<VAR>. . .</VAR>

VAR /VAR

Purpose
Provides a variable term or phrase within a text block. Similar to the Emphasis tag.

Syntax
```
<VAR>Variable_text</VAR>
```

Attributes & Their Arguments
None.

Example
The following includes a variable item within a normal text paragraph. The variable term is displayed with emphasis within the text.

```
<P>In C++, <VAR>variables</VAR> may be private, public,
or protected. </P>
```

See Also
DFN, STRONG, DL, B, I and U

WORD BREAK TAG (NETSCAPE EXTENSION)

<WBR>

WBR /WBR

Purpose
Allows Netscape to break a word or text block at the tag if necessary.

Syntax

```
<NOBR>Text el<WBR>ement</NOBR>
```

Attributes & Their Arguments

None.

Examples

The following shows a single line of text that will be kept together on one line by use of the Nobreak tag but may be broken at the Word Break tag if necessary.

```
<NOBR>This text must stay together <WBR>on one line if
possible.</NOBR>
```

See Also

BR and NOBR

EXAMPLE TEXT TAG

<XMP> . . . </XMP>

XMP /XMP

Purpose

Similar to the Preformatted Text tag, except that no embedded tags will be recognized. To preserve formatting, the text is displayed in a monospaced font. This is an obsolete tag; the Preformatted Text tag is preferred.

Syntax

```
<XMP>Text</XMP>
```

Attributes & Their Arguments

None.

Examples

The following shows how you may use text in an example text block.

```
<XMP>This is sample example <XMP> text</XMP>
```

See Also
LISTING and PRE

COMMENT TAG

<!. . .>

not supported by HoTMetaL PRO

Purpose
Allows you to insert comment data into the HTML document without displaying it on the screen. Often used to provide information about the author, revision data and so on. Some browsers have problems with comments that are longer than a single line. For best compatibility, you should make multiline comments into several comment lines.

Syntax

```
<!Text >
```

Attributes & Their Arguments
None.

Examples
The following shows a typical use of comments. Note that the comment has been broken into several different lines, with each line an individual comment.

```
<! Created by: David Holzgang >
<!  using HoTMetaL Pro 1.0 >
<!  on 23 February 1995 11:22 >
<!  Revised: dh 1 Mar 95 16:35>
```

See Also
HEAD and TITLE

HTML Forms

The HTML forms interface allows document creators to define HTML documents containing information to be filled out by users. When a user fills out the form and presses a button indicating the form should be "submitted," the information on the form is sent to a server for processing. The server will usually prepare an HTML document using the information supplied by the user and return it to the browser client for display.

A form may contain any of the standard HTML tags. In addition, forms have certain special tags that are only used, and recognized, within a form document. The following tags define and implement the forms interface:

<FORM>...</FORM>
<INPUT>
<SELECT>...</SELECT>
<OPTION>
<TEXTAREA>...</TEXTAREA>

The last four tags are only valid within a Form tag.

FORM TAG

<FORM>. . .</FORM>

FORM [ACTION:] /FORM

Purpose
Defines a form within an HTML document. A document may contain multiple Form tags, but Form tags may not be nested. Note that non-form tags can be used within a Form tag.

Syntax
<FORM ACTION="URL" METHOD=[GET|POST]> Text of form, including additional standard HTML tags and form tags if desired </FORM>

Attributes & Their Arguments
Forms have two required arguments.

ACTION="URL"

The URL location of the program that will process the form.

METHOD=method

The method may be either GET or POST. This is the method chosen to exchange data between the client and the program started to process the form.

Example
The is an example of how a Form tag might be used to define a registration form for a university.

```
<FORM ACTION="http://kuhttp.cc.ukans.edu/cgi-bin/regis-
ter" METHOD=POST> . . . </FORM>
```

See Also
URL and BODY

INPUT TAG

```
<INPUT>
```

INPUT [SRC:] /INPUT

Purpose
Defines an input field where the user may enter information on the form. Each input field assigns a value to a variable that has a specified name and a specified data type.

Syntax

```
<INPUT TYPE="keyword" [NAME="textstring"
|VALUE="textstring"|CHECKED|SIZE=number|
MAXLENGTH=number]">
```

Attributes & Their Arguments

TYPE="keyword"

Specifies the data type for the variable. Possible values for keyword are [“text” | “password” | “checkbox” | “radio” | “submit” | “reset”].

TYPE=“text” and TYPE=“password” accept character data.

TYPE=“checkbox” is either selected or not.

TYPE=“radio” allows selection of only one of several radio fields, if they all have the same variable name.

TYPE=“submit” is an action button that sends the completed form to the query server.

TYPE=“reset” is a button that resets the form variables to their default values.

NAME="textstring"

where textstring is a symbolic name (not displayed) identifying the input variable.

VALUE="textstring"

where the function of textstring depends on the argument for type as follows:

TYPE=“text” or TYPE=“password”

textstring is the default value for the input variable.

TYPE=“checkbox” or TYPE=“radio”

textstring is the value of the input variable when it is “checked”.

TYPE=“reset” or TYPE=“submit”

textstring is a label that will appear on the submit or reset button in place of the words “submit” and “reset”.

CHECKED

No arguments. For TYPE=“checkbox” or TYPE=“radio”, if CHECKED is present the input field is “checked” by default.

SIZE=number

where number is an integer value representing the number of characters allowed for the TYPE=“text” or TYPE=“password” input fields.

MAXLENGTH=number

where number is an integer value representing the number of characters accepted for TYPE=“text” or TYPE=“password”. This attribute is valid only for single line “text” or “password” fields.

Examples

A simple text input area
The following provides an input area for entering a user's name.

```
<P>Please enter your name:</P> <INPUT TYPE="text"
NAME="username" SIZE=30 >
```

Using input for submission of data
These two Input tags add the necessary buttons to submit data accumulated in the form or cancel it.

```
<INPUT TYPE="submit" VALUE="Send Form">
<INPUT TYPE="reset" VALUE="Clear Form">
```

Using radio buttons as input
The following example defines four radio buttons. The third button is checked by default when the form is first displayed.

```
<P> Please select one of these destinations:
<INPUT TYPE="radio" NAME="S1" VALUE="CANADA">
Canada
<INPUT TYPE="radio" NAME="S1" VALUE="GB"> Great
Britian
<INPUT TYPE="radio" NAME="S1" VALUE="USA"
CHECKED> United States of America
<INPUT TYPE="radio" NAME="S1" VALUE="AUS">
Australia</P>
```

See Also
FORM

SELECT TAG

```
<SELECT>. . .</SELECT>
```

SELECT OPTION /OPTION /SELECT

Purpose
Defines and displays a set of optional list items from which the user can select one or more items. This element requires an <OPTION> element for each item in the list.

Associated Tag: Option Item Tag

<OPTION>

Purpose

Defines an element in a selection list. Within the Select tag the Option tags are used to define the possible values for the select field. Note that this tag should never be used outside a Select tag as it may not be correctly displayed by a browser. Also notice that this tag does not have a matching termination.

Syntax

```
<SELECT NAME="textstring" [SIZE=value MULTIPLE]
<OPTION [SELECTED]>Option_item </SELECT>...
```

Attributes & Their Arguments

NAME="textstring"

where textstring is a symbolic name (not displayed) identifying the input variable.

SIZE=value

The argument for SIZE is an integer value representing the number of <OPTION> items that will be displayed at one time.

MULTIPLE

If present, the MULTIPLE attribute allows selection of more than one <OPTION> value.

SELECTED

If this attribute is present, then the option value is selected by default.

Example

In the following example all three options may be chosen but bananas are selected by default.

```
<SELECT MULTIPLE>
<OPTION>Apples
<OPTION SELECTED>Bananas
<OPTION>Cherries
</SELECT>
```

See Also
FORM

TEXTAREA TAG

```
<TEXTAREA>. . .</TEXTAREA>
```

TEXTAREA /TEXTAREA

Purpose
Defines a rectangular field where the user may enter text data. If a default text element is present, it will be displayed when the field appears. Otherwise the field will be blank.

Syntax

```
<TEXTAREA NAME="textstring" ROWS=value
COLUMNS=value >default_text</TEXTAREA>
```

Attributes & Their Arguments

```
NAME="textstring"
```

where textstring is a symbolic name (not displayed) identifying the input variable.

```
ROWS=value COLS=value
```

Both attributes take an integer value that represents the lines and number of characters per line in the text area to be displayed.

Example
The following demonstrates the use of a Textarea tag.

```
<P>Please enter your comments below:<BR> <TEXTAREA
NAME="tree_data" ROWS=5 COLUMNS=40>I like trees
because...</TEXTAREA></P>
```

See Also
FORM

Character Entities

One problem that occurs when transmitting text across computer systems is the problem of how to represent punctuation marks, accented characters and other characters that may be commonly used in one language or system and not in another. Each computer system has some method for handling these problems. For example, on the Macintosh, you can generate an e with an acute accent—the last é in the word resumé—by pressing the Option key and the "e" key, followed by the "e" key again. However, the character generated in this way cannot be displayed correctly on any system that isn't a Macintosh, so if you use this character within an HTML document, the recipient will probably not see the correct character. This is one type of character display problem.

Another problem is how to display certain punctuation marks. For example, the HTML language uses the characters "<" (the less-than sign) and ">" (the greater-than sign) to signal HTML commands within a document. For obvious reasons, you cannot insert these same characters in the text of the document without causing problems when the document is displayed. You need another method for displaying these characters in your text.

To solve this problem when using an HTML document, the HTML language defines character entities that are used instead of these special characters. These may take one of two formats.

&keyword;

Displays a particular character identified by a special keyword. For example the entity *&* displays the ampersand character, (&), and the entity *<* displays the less than (<) character. Note that the semicolon following the keyword is required, and the keyword must be one from Table A-1 shown below. The definitive list of acceptable keywords is presented at http://info.cern.ch/hypertext/WWW/MarkUp/Entities.html.

&#ascii_equivalent;

Uses a character from the ISO Added LATIN I character set identified by the decimal integer ascii_equivalent. Again note that the semicolon following the ASCII numeric value is required. Table A-2 shows the character and gives the ascii_equivalent value for all the characters in the ISO Added LATIN I character set that are not available from the keyboard and do not have a character keyword. Note that Table A-1 shows the integer ascii_equivalent for the characters as well as the keyword. You can use either method (keyword or ascii_equivalent) to insert these into your text; however, the keyword is considered the better alternative.

When using HoTMetaL PRO , you can insert any of these characters without worrying about how to encode them. HoTMetaL PRO allows you to simply insert most special character entities that you want by using the Insert Character Entity command in the Markup menu (Ctrl-E). This displays a HoTMetaL Insert Entity dialog box that shows you the most common characters that you might want to use in your text as keys. Simply press the key for the character that you want and HoTMetaL PRO inserts the correct encoding for that character entity in your text. HoTMetaL PR0 also automatically supplies the correct encodings if you type either of the special characters "<" or "&" from the keyboard, as these cannot be allowed in any HTML text, for obvious reasons. For all other character entities, you need to use the Insert Entity dialog box as described here or type the entity directly into the text.

Mnemonic	As Displayed	Description	Decimal ASCII Equivalent
AElig	"Æ"	capital AE diphthong (ligature)	#198
Aacute	"Á"	capital A, acute accent	#193
Acirc	"Â"	capital A, circumflex accent	#194
Agrave	"À"	capital A, grave accent	#192
Aring	"Å"	capital A, ring	#197
Atilde	"Ã"	capital A, tilde	#195
Auml	"Ä"	capital A, dieresis or umlaut mark	#196
Ccedil	"Ç"	capital C, cedilla	#199
Eth	"_"	capital Eth, Icelandic	#208
Eacute	"É"	capital E, acute accent	#201
Ecirc	"Ê"	capital E, circumflex accent	#202

Mnemonic	As Displayed	Description	Decimal ASCII Equivalent
Egrave	"È"	capital E, grave accent	#200
Euml	"Ë"	capital E, dieresis or umlaut mark	#203
Iacute	"Í"	capital I, acute accent	#205
Icirc	"Î"	capital I, circumflex accent	#206
Igrave	"Ì"	capital I, grave accent	#204
Iuml	"Ï"	capital I, dieresis or umlaut mark	#207
Ntilde	"Ñ"	capital N, tilde	#209
Oacute	"Ó"	capital O, acute accent	#211
Ocirc	"Ô"	capital O, circumflex accent	#212
Ograve	"Ò"	capital O, grave accent	#210
Oslash	"Ø"	capital O, slash	#216
Otilde	"Õ"	capital O, tilde	#213
Ouml	"Ö"	capital O, dieresis or umlaut mark	#214
Thorn	"_"	capital Thorn, Icelandic	#222
Uacute	"Ú"	capital U, acute accent	#218
Ucirc	"Û"	capital U, circumflex accent	#219
Ugrave	"Ù"	capital U, grave accent	#217
Uuml	"Ü"	capital U, dieresis or umlaut mark	#220
Yacute	"Y"	capital Y, acute accent	#221
aacute	"á"	small a, acute accent	#225
acirc	"â"	small a, circumflex accent	#226
aelig	"æ"	small ae diphthong (ligature)	#230
agrave	"à"	small a, grave accent	#224
agrave	"à"	small a, grave accent	#224
amp	"&"	ampersand	#38
atilde	"ã"	small a, tilde	#227
auml	"ä"	small a, dieresis or umlaut mark	#228
ccedil	"ç"	small c, cedilla	#231
eacute	"é"	small e, acute accent	#233
ecirc	"ê"	small e, circumflex accent	#234
egrave	"è"	small e, grave accent	#232
eth	"∂"	small eth, Icelandic	#240
euml	"ë"	small e, dieresis or umlaut mark	#235
gt	">"	greater than	#62
iacute	"í"	small i, acute accent	#237
icirc	"î"	small i, circumflex accent	#238
igrave	"ì"	small i, grave accent	#236

Mnemonic	As Displayed	Description	Decimal ASCII Equivalent
iuml	“ï”	small i, dieresis or umlaut mark	#239
lt	“<“	less than	#60
ntilde	“ñ”	small n, tilde	#241
oacute	“ó”	small o, acute accent	#243
ocirc	“ô”	small o, circumflex accent	#244
ograve	“ò”	small o, grave accent	#242
oslash	“ø”	small o, slash	#248
otilde	“õ”	small o, tilde	#245
ouml	“ö”	small o, dieresis or umlaut mark	#246
quote	“‘“	single quote	#62
szlig	“ß”	small sharp s, German (sz ligature)	
thorn	“_”	small thorn, Icelandic	#254
uacute	“ú”	small u, acute accent	#250
ucirc	“û”	small u, circumflex accent	#251
ugrave	“ù”	small u, grave accent	#249
uuml	“ü”	small u, dieresis or umlaut mark	#252
yacute	“y”	small y, acute accent	#253
yuml	“ÿ”	small y, dieresis or umlaut mark	#255

Table A-1: *Character keywords in HTML.*

Number	As Displayed	Description
#161	“¡”	inverted exclamation mark
#162	“¢”	cent sign
#163	“£”	pound sign
#164	“¤”	general currency sign
#165	“¥”	yen sign
#166	“¦”	broken (vertical) bar
#167	“§”	section sign
#168	“¨”	umlaut
#169	“©”	copyright sign
#170	“ª”	ordinal indicator, feminine
#171	“«”	angle quotation mark, left
#174	“®”	circled R/registered sign
#175	“¯”	macron
#176	“°”	degree sign

Number	As Displayed	Description
#177	“±”	/pm B: plus-or-minus sign
#178	“2”	superscript two
#179	“3”	superscript three
#180	“´”	acute accent
#181	“µ”	micro sign
#182	“¶”	pilcrow (paragraph sign)
#183	“·”	/centerdot B: middle dot
#184	“ ¸ ”	cedilla
#185	“1”	superscript one
#186	“º”	ordinal indicator, masculine
#187	“»”	angle quotation mark, right
#188	“ _ ”	fraction one-quarter
#189	“ _ ”	fraction one-half
#190	“ _ ”	fraction three-quarters
#191	“¿”	inverted question mark

Table A-2: *ISO Added LATIN 1 character entities with only a numeric representation.*

APPENDIX D

Resources

The following sections list Internet publishing related programs and periodicals. The topics include TCP/IP software, Web browsers, HTML editors and converters, portable document viewers, graphic editors, 3D rendering applications, clip art, multimedia applications, Web servers, CGI programs and utilities. This resource guide also lists some Web design companies and server services as well as service providers who will let you publish your pages at their site.

If you don't find what you're looking for here, we recommend you use a Web directory or a Web searching facility. You can use the Yahoo directory or search program by entering the URL: http://www.yahoo.com. The top of the page includes a search option and the bottom of the Yahoo home page lists additional general Internet directories, such as WWW Virtual Library and EINet Galaxy.

TCP/IP Software

BW-Connect TCP for DOS and Windows
Beame & Whiteside, Ltd.
606 Hillsborough Street
Raleigh, NC 27603-1655
Voice: (800) 463-6637
Voice: (919) 831-8989
Fax: (919) 831-8990
URL: http://www.bws.com
E-mail: sales@bws.com

Chameleon
NetManage, Inc.
10725 North De Anza Boulevard
Cupertino, CA 95014
Voice: (408) 973-7171
Fax: (408) 257-6405
URL: www.netmanage.com
E-mail: info@netmanage.com

Distinct TCP/IP Tools
Distinct Corporation
12901 Saratoga Avenue
P.O. Box 3410
Saratoga, CA 95070
Voice: (408) 366-8933
Fax: (408) 366-0153
E-mail: mktg@distinct.com

Intercon TCP/Connect II
InterCon Systems Corporation
950 Herndon Parkway, Suite 420
Herndon, VA 22070
Voice: (800) 468-7266
Voice: (703) 709-9890
Fax: (703) 709-5555
URL: http://www.intercon.com
E-mail: comment@intercon.com

Internet In A Box
Spry, Inc.
316 Occidental Avenue South, Suite 200
Seattle, WA 98104
Voice: (800) 777-9638
URL: www.spry.com
E-mail: info@spry.com

O'Reilly and Associates, Inc.
103 Morris Street, Suite A
Sebastopol, CA 95472
Voice: (800) 998-4269
URL: http://www.gnn.com
E-mail: info@ibox.com

Internet Membership Kit
Ventana Communications, Inc.
P.O. Box 2468
Chapel Hill, NC 27515
Voice: (919) 942-0220
Fax: (919) 942-1140
URL: http://www.vmedia.com/wimk.2.html
E-mail: help@vmedia.com

LAN WorkPlace for DOS
Novell Inc.
2180 Fortune Drive
San Jose, CA 95131
Voice: (800) 243-8526
URL: http://www.novell.com
E-mail: info@novell.com

PathWay Access on DOS/Windows
The Wollongong Group Inc.
1129 San Antonio Road
P.O. Box 51860
Palo Alto, CA 94303
Voice: (800) 872-8649 (Outside CA)
Voice: (800) 962-8649 (CA)
URL: http://www.twg.com
E-mail: sales@twg.com

PC-NFS
SunSoft
Two Elizabeth Drive
Chelmsford, MA 01824
Voice: (508) 442-2300
Fax: (508) 250-2300
URL: http://www.sun.com

PC/TCP OnNet for DOS/Windows
FTP Software, Inc.
100 Brickstone Square
North Andover, MA 01810
Voice: (800) 282-4387
Voice: (508) 685-4000
Fax: (508) 794-4477
URL: http://www.ftp.com
E-mail: info@ftp.com

Piper/IP & Acadia/VxD
Ipswitch, Inc.
81 Hartwell Avenue
Lexington, MA 02173
Voice: (617) 861-1411
Fax: (617) 861-8788
URL: http://directory.net/ipswitch
E-mail: info@ipswitch.com

SuperHighway Access for Windows & SuperTCP Pro
Frontier Technologies
10201 North Port Washington Road
Mequon, WI 53092
Voice: (800) 929-3054
Voice: (414) 241-4555
Fax: (414) 241-7084
URL: http://www.frontiertech.com
E-mail: info@frontiertech.com

Trumpet Winsock
Shareware
Author: Peter R. Tattam (University of Tasmania)
E-mail: peter@psychnet.psychol.utas.edu.au
URL: ftp://ftp.utas.edu.au/pc/trumpet/

World Wide Web Browsers

Cello
Freeware
FTP: fatty.law.cornell.edu
Directory: /pub/LII/Cello
Filename: cello.zip
URL: http://ftp.law.cornell.edu/pub/LII/Cello

Enhanced NCSA Mosaic for Windows
OEM licences to commercial firms
Spyglass Inc.
1800 Woodfield Drive
Savoy, IL 61874
Voice: (217) 355-6000
Fax: (217) 355-8925
URL: http://www.spyglass.com/
E-mail: info@spyglass.com

InterAp (Internet Applications)
California Software Incorporated
4000 Civic Center Drive, 4th Floor
San Rafael, California 94903
Voice: (415) 491-4371
Fax: (415) 491-0402
Support@calsoft.com
FTP: ftp://ftp.calsoft.com
URL: http://www.calsoft.com
E-mail: Sales@calsoft.com

Internet In A Box
Spry, Inc.
316 Occidental Avenue South, Suite 200
Seattle, WA 98104
Voice: (800) 777-9638
Voice: (206) 447-0300
Fax: (206) 447-9008
E-mail: info@spry.com

O'Reilly and Associates, Inc.
103 Morris Street, Suite A
Sebastopol, CA 95472
Voice: (800) 998-4269
URL: http://www.gnn.com
E-mail: info@ibox.com

Lynx
URL: ftp://ftp2.cc.ukans.edu/pub/WWW/lynx

NetCruiser
NETCOM
3031 Tisch Way, 2nd Floor
San Jose, CA 95128
Voice: (800) 353-6600
Voice: (408) 345-2600
Fax: (408) 241-9145
URL: http://www.netcom.com
E-mail: info@netcom.com

Netscape Navigator
Shareware/Commercial
Netscape Communications
501 E. Middlefield Road
Mountain View, CA 94043
Voice: (415) 254-1900
URL: http://home.netscape.com
E-mail: info@netscape.com

The Pipeline
150 Broadway, Suite 1710
New York, NY 10028
Phone: (212) 267-3636
Fax: (212) 267-4380
URL: http://www.pipeline.com
E-mail: info@pipeline.com
Modem: (212) 267-6432 (login as guest)

Quadralay WebWorks
Quadralay Corporation
8920 Business Park Drive
Austin, TX 78759
Voice: (512) 346-9199
Fax: (512) 346-8990
URL: http://www.quadralay.com
E-mail: info@quadralay.com

Quarterdeck Mosaic
Quarterdeck Office Systems, Inc.
150 Pico Blvd.
Santa Monica, CA 90405
Voice: (310) 314-4263
Fax: (310) 314-4218
URL: http://www.qdeck.com
E-mail: bob@qdeck.com

SlipKnot
MicroMind, Inc.
150 Broadway
New York, NY 10038
Voice: (212) 267-3636
URL: http://interport.net/slipknot/slipknot.html
E-mail: slipknot@macromind.com

Super Mosaic
Luckman Interactive
7035 Bee Caves Road, Suite 200
Austin, TX 78746
Voice: (512) 329-5242
Fax: (512) 329-5420

WinWeb
Freeware
EINet Windows Software
MCC
3500 West Balcones Center Drive
Austin, TX 78759-6509
URL: ftp://ftp.einet.net/einet/pc/winweb/
File: winweb.zip
E-mail: winweb@mcc.com.

HTML Editors & Convertors

ANT_HTML & ANT_PLUS
Author: Jill Swift
P.O. Box 213
Montgomery, Texas 77356
URL: ftp://ftp.einet.net/einet/pc/ant_html.zip
E-mail: jswift@freenet.fsu.edu

CU_HTML.DOT
Author: Kenneth Wong and Anton Lam
E-mail: anton-lam@cuhk.hk
Computer Services Centre
The Chinese University of Hong Kong
URL: http://www.cuhk.hk/csc/cu_html/cu_html.htm
File: cu_html.zip

GT_HTML.DOT
The Georgia Tech Research Institute (GTRI)
Authors: Jeffrey L. Grover, John H. Davis III and Bob Johnston
URL: http://www.gatech.edu/word_html/release.htm
E-mail: gt_html@gatech.edu

HoTMetaL
Shareware
URL: ftp://ftp.ncsa.uiuc.edu/Web/html/Windows/HotMetal
File: hotmetal.exe

HoTMetaL PRO
Commercial
SoftQuad Inc.
56 Aberfoyle Cresent
Toronto, Ontario, CANADA M8X 2W4
Voice: (416) 239-4801
Fax: (416) 239-7105
URL: http://www.sq.com
E-mail: hotmetal@sq.com

HTML Assistant & HTML Assistant Pro
Shareware/Commercial
Brooklyn North Software Works
25 Doyle Street
Bedford, Nova Scotia
Canada B4A 1K4
Voice: (902) 835-2600
Fax: (902) 835-2600
E-mail: harawitz@fox.nstn.ns.ca

HTMLed
Shareware
I-Net Training and Consulting
URL: ftp://pringle.pnta.ca/pub/HTMLed/
File: htmed09a.zip

HTML HyperEdit for Windows
Shareware
Author: Steve Hancock
URL: ftp://info.curtin.edu.au/pub/internet/mswindows/hyperedit
File: hypedit.zip
E-mail: s.hancock@info.curtin.edu.au

HTML Writer
Author: Kris Nosack
376 North Main Street
Orem, Utah 84057
URL: http://wwf.et.byu.edu/~nosackk/htmlwrit.html
E-mail: html_writer@byu.edu

Microsoft Internet Assistant
One Microsoft Way
Redmond, WA 98052-6399
Voice: (800) 426-9400
Voice: (206) 882-8080
URL: http://www.microsoft.com/pages/deskapps/word/ia/default.htm

PostScript to HTML
Florence Research Area and Electromagnetic Research Institute of National Research Council
Author: Alessandro Agostini and Stefano Cerreti
URL: ftp://ftp.area.fi.cnr.it/pub/dos/misc/ps2html
File: ps2html.exe
E-mail: agostini@server.area.fi.cnr.it
E-mail: ced@server.area.fi.cnr.it

Quarterdeck Web Author
Quarterdeck Office Systems, Inc.
150 Pico Blvd.
Santa Monica, CA 90405
Voice: (310) 314-4263
Fax: (310) 314-4218
URL: http://www.qdeck.com
E-mail: bob@qdeck.com

RTF to HTML
Freeware
Author: Chris Hector
URL: ftp://ftp.cray.com/src/WWWstuff/RTF/latest/binaries/
File: dos.zip

TagWizard for Word 6.0 for Windows
NICE technologies USA
2121 41st Avenue, Suite 303
Capitola, CA 95010
Phone: (408) 476-7850
Fax: (408) 476-0910
URL: http://infolane.com/nice/nice.html
E-mail: nicetech@netcom.com

Portable Document & Other Document Viewers

Adobe Acrobat Reader, Exchange and Network Distiller
Adobe Systems Incorporated
1585 Charleston Road
P.O. Box 7900
Mountain View, CA 94039-7900
Voice: (800) 862-3623
Voice: (800) 833-6687
Fax: (415) 961-3769
URL: http://www.adobe.com
URL: ftp://ftp.adobe.com/pub/adobe/Applications/Acrobat

Common Ground 2.0
No Hands Software
1301 Shoreway Road #220
Belmont, CA 94002
Voice: (800) 598-3821
Voice: (415) 802-5800
Fax: (415) 593-6868

Envoy
Novell Inc.
2180 Fortune Drive
San Jose, CA 95131
Voice: (800) 526-5011
Voice: (801) 429-7000
URL: http://wp.novell.com/
E-mail: info@novell.com

GhostView & GhostScript
Freeware
Author: Russell Lang (GhostView)
Free Software Foundation, Inc.
675 Mass Ave.
Cambridge, MA 02139
E-mail: Russell Lang <rjl@monu1.cc.monash.edu.au>

Microsoft WordView
Freeware
One Microsoft Way
Redmond, WA 98052-6399
Voice: (800) 360-7561
Voice: (206) 882-8080
URL: http://www.microsoft.com/pages/deskapps/word/viewer/wordvu.htm

Replica
Farallon Computing, Inc.
2470 Mariner Square Loop
Alameda, California 94501
Voice: (510) 814-5100
Fax: (510) 814-5020
URL: http://www.farallon.com/
E-mail: info@farallon.com

GRAPHIC APPLICATIONS & UTILITIES

Adobe Photoshop
Adobe Systems Incorporated
1585 Charleston Road
P.O. Box 7900
Mountain View, CA 94039-7900
Voice: (800) 862-3623
Voice: (800) 833-6687
Fax: (415) 961-3769
URL: http://www.adobe.com

CorelDRAW! 5
Corel Corporation
1600 Carling Avenue
Ottawa, Ontario CANADA K1Z 8R7
Voice: (613) 728-8200
Fax: (613) 728-9790
URL: http://www.corelnet.com

Fractal Design Painter
Fractal Design Corporation
335 Spreckels Drive
Aptos, CA 95003
Voice: (408) 688-5300
Fax: (408) 688-8836

giftool.exe
Author: David Kobalas
Home Pages, Inc.
257 Castro Street, Suite 219
Mountain View, CA 94041
URL: http://www.homepages.com/tools/
E-mail: info@homepages.com

giftrans.exe
Author: Andreas Ley
URL: ftp://ftp.rz.uni-karlsruhe.de/pub/net/www/tools/
or
URL: http://melmac.corp.harris.com/files/
File: giftrans.exe
E-mail: ley@rz.uni-karlsruhe.de

Graphic Workshop for Windows
Shareware
Alchemy Mindworks, Inc.
Post Office Box 500
Beeton, Ontario LOG IAO CANADA
Voice: (800) 263-1138
Voice: (905) 729-4969
Fax: (905) 729-4156.
URL: http://uvnorth.north.net:8000/alchemy/html/alchemy.html
File: gwswn11k.zip

HiJaak Graphics Suite
Inset
71 Commerce Drive
Brookfield CT 06804-3405
Voice: (203) 740-2400
Fax: (203) 775-5634

Kai's Power Tools
HSC Software
6303 Carpinteria Avenue
Carpinteria, CA 93013
Voice: (805) 566-6200
Fax: (805) 566-6385

LView Pro
Freeware
Author: Leonardo Haddad Loureiro
URL: http://www.ncsa.uiuc.edu/SDG/Software/WinMosaic/
E-mail: mmedia@world.std.com

Paint Shop Pro
Shareware
JASC, Inc.
10901 Red Circle Drive, Suite 340
Minnetonka, MN 55343
Voice: (612) 930-9171
Fax: (612) 930-9172
URL: http://www.winternet.com/~jasc/index.html
E-mail: jasc@winternet.com

WinGIF
Shareware
Author: Kyle Powell
SuperSet Software Corporation
P.O. Box 50476
Provo, UT 84605-0476
E-mail: 76704,12@compuserve.com.

Clip Art & Digital Photography

CMCD
CMCD Inc.
600 Townsend Street, Penthouse
San Francisco, California 94103
Voice: (800) 664-2623
Fax: (415) 703-0711
URL: http://www.cmdesign.com

Corel Professional Photos
Corel Corporation
1600 Carling Avenue
Ottawa, Ontario CANADA K1Z 8R7
Voice: (800) 772-6735
Voice: (613) 728-3733
Fax: (613) 761-9176
URL: http://www.corelnet.com

Image Club Graphics Inc.
729 24th Avenue Southeast
Calgary, Alberta CANADA T2G 5K8
Voice: (800) 387-9193
Fax: (403) 261-7013
URL: http://www.adobe.com/imageclub/
E-mail: imageclub@aol.com

Instant Buttons & Controls
stat Media
7077 East Shorecrest Drive
Anaheim Hills, CA 92807-4506
Voice: (714) 280-0038
Fax: (714) 280-0039

Multimedia Applications & Utilities

Adobe Premiere
Adobe Systems Incorporated
1585 Charleston Road
P.O. Box 7900
Mountain View, CA 94039-7900
Voice: (800) 833-6687
Fax: (415) 961-3769
URL: http://www.adobe.com

Cambium Sound Choice
Cambium Development
P.O. Box 296-H
Scarsdale, NY 10583-8796
Voice: (800) 231-1779
Voice: (914) 472-6246
Fax: (914) 472-6729

Director for Windows
Macromedia
600 Townsend Street
San Francisco, CA 94103-9632
Voice: (800) 288-4797
Voice: (415) 252-2000
Fax: (415) 626-0554

GoldWave
Author: Chris Craig
P.O. Box 51
St. John's, NF CANADA A1C 5H5
URL: http://web.cs.mun.ca/~chris3/goldwave/
E-mail: chris3@garfield.cs.mun.ca

Intel Smart Video Recorder Pro
2200 Mission College Boulevard
P.O. Box 58119
Santa Clara, CA 95052-8119
Voice: (800) 538-3373
Voice: (408) 765-8080
Fax: (800) 525-3019
URL: http://www.intel.com

InterActive
HSC Software
6303 Carpinteria Avenue
Carpinteria, CA 93013
Voice: (805) 566-6200
Fax: (805) 566-6385

Media*Studio*
Ulead Systems Inc.
970 West 190th Street, Suite 520
Torrance, CA 90502
Voice: (310) 523-9393
Fax: (310) 523-9399

Microsoft Video for Windows
Microsoft Corporation
One Microsoft Way
Redmond, WA 98052-6399
Voice: (206) 882-8080
Fax: (206) 883-8101
URL: http://www.microsoft.com

Movie Line/Movie Machine Pro
Fast Electronic
One Twin Dolphin Drive
Redwood City, CA 94065
Voice: (415) 802-0772
Fax: (415) 802-0746

MPEGPlay
Shareware
Author: Michael Simmons
34 Shillington Way
Thornlie WA 6108
Australia
URL: http://www.ncsa.uiuc.edu/SDG/Software/WinMosaic/
File: mpeg32e.zip

MusicBytes
Prosonus
2820 Honolulu Avenue, Suite 268
Verdugo City, CA 91046
Voice: (800) 999-6191
Voice: (818) 766-5221
Fax: (818) 248-9417

QuickTime for Windows & QuickTime Development Kit (APDA, #R0453LL/B)
APDA Apple Computer, Inc.
P.O. Box 319
Buffalo, NY 14207-0319
Voice: (800) 282-2732
Voice: (800) 637-0029 Canada
Voice: (716) 871-6555 Intl
URL: http://www.apple.com
E-mail: APDA@applelink.apple.com

ReelMagic MPEG Playback Card
Sigma Designs Inc.
46501 Landing Parkway
Fremont, CA 94538
Voice: (510) 770-0100
Fax: (510) 770-2640

ReelMagic Producer
Sigma Designs Inc.
46501 Landing Parkway
Fremont, CA 94538
Voice: (510) 770-0100
Fax: (510) 770-2640

SoundTrack
Access Softek
2550 Ninth Street, Suite 206
Berkeley, CA 94710
Voice: (800) 386-4272
Voice: (510) 848-0606

WAVE for Windows
Turtle Beach Systems
Cyber Center #33
1600 Pennsylvania Avenue
York, PA 17402
Voice: (800) 645-5640
Voice: (717) 767-0200
Fax: (717) 767-6033

WHAM
Author: Andrew Bulhak
21 The Crescent
Ferntree Gully Vic 3156
Australia
E-mail: acb@yoyo.cc.monash.edu.au.

WPLANY
Author: Bill Neisius
URL: http://www.ncsa.uiuc.edu/SDG/Software/WinMosaic/
File: wplany.zip
E-mail: bill@solaria.hac.com.

XingCD
Xing Technology Corporation
1540 West Branch Street
Arroyo Grande, CA 93420-1818
Voice: (800) 294-6448
Voice: (805) 473-0145
Fax: (805) 473-0147

3D Rendering, Morphing & Animation

Animator Pro
Autodesk
2320 Marinship Way
Sausalito, CA 94965-9910
Voice: (800) 879-4233
Voice: (415) 491-8398
Fax: (415) 491-8398

Elastic Reality
Elastic Reality Inc.
925 Stewart Street
Madison, WI 53713
Voice: (608) 273-6585
Fax: (608) 271-1988

Morph Studio
Ulead Systems Inc.
970 West 190th Street, Suite 520
Torrance, CA 90502
Voice: (310) 523-9393
Fax: (310) 523-9399

PhotoMorph 2
North Coast Software Inc.
P.O. Box 459
Barrington, NH 03825
Voice: (603) 664-6000
Fax: (603) 664-7872

3D Studio
Autodesk
2320 Marinship Way
Sausalito, CA 94965-9910
Voice: (800) 879-4233
Voice: (415) 491-8398
Fax: (415) 491-8398

trueSpace
Caligari Corporation
1955 Landings Drive
Mountain View, CA 94043
Voice: (415) 390-9600
Fax: (415) 390-9755

Visual Reality & Simply 3D
21731 Ventura Boulevard, Suite 310
Woodland Hills, CA 91364
Voice: (800) 669-7318
Voice: (818) 883-7900
Fax: (818) 593-3737

Web Servers, CGI Programs & Utilities

ALIBABA
CSM - Computer Software Manufaktur
Bindergasse 5-9/24
A-1090 Wien
Austria, Europe
Voice: ++43-1-319 42 46
Fax: ++43-1-317 30 40
URL: http://www.csm.co.at/csm/
E-mail: sales@csm.co.at

EMWAC HTTPS for Windows NT
Author: Chris Adie
European Microsoft Windows NT Academic Center (EMWAC)
Computing Services
30-38 George Square
Edinburgh EH8 9LJ
URL: http://emwac.ed.ac.uk./html/internet_toolchest/top.html

HTTPD
Shareware
Author: Robert B. Denny
221 South Oak Knoll Avenue, Suite 207
Pasadena, CA 91101
URL: http://www.city.net/win-httpd
E-mail: rdenny@netcom.com

Map Edit
Shareware
Author: Thomas Boutell
URL: http://sunsite.unc.edu/boutell/mapedit/mapedit.html
URL: ftp://sunsite.unc.edu/pub/packages/infosystems/WWW/tools/mapedit/
File: mapedit.zip
E-mail: boutell@netcom.com

Polyform
Shareware
Author: Mark Bracewell
Willow Glen Graphics
URL: http://wgg.com/
E-mail: mcb@wgg.com

Purveyor
Commercial
Author: Chris Adie
European Microsoft Windows NT Academic Center (EMWAC)
Sold by:
Process Software Corporation
959 Concord Street
Framingham, MA 01701
Phone: (800) 722-7770, (508) 879-6994
FAX: (508) 879-0042
URL: http://www.process.com/prodinfo/purvdata.htm
E-mail: info@process.com

VBStats
Author: Robert B. Denny
221 South Oak Knoll Avenue, Suite 207
Pasadena, CA 91101
URL: http://www.city.net/win-httpd/lib/util-support/
File: vbstat31.zip
E-mail: rdenny@netcom.com

WAIS Toolkit
European Microsoft Windows NT Academic Center (EMWAC)
Computing Services
30-38 George Square
Edinburgh EH8 9LJ
URL: http://emwac.ed.ac.uk./html/internet_toolchest/top.html

WebSite
Commercial
Author: Robert Denny
O'Reilly and Associates, Inc.
103 Morris Street, Suite A
Sebastopol, CA 95472
Voice: (800) 998-9938
Voice: (707) 829-0515
URL: http://website.orn.com/
URL: http://www.city.net/win-httpd/
E-mail: website@ora.com

ZBServer
Author: Bob Bradley
URL: http://bbgun.at.utm.edu/zbs/zbs.htm

Compression Utilities

Drag And Zip
Shareware
Canyon Software
1537 Fourth Street, Suite 131
San Rafael, CA 94901
Voice: (415) 382-7999
Fax: (415) 382-7998
Modem: (415) 453-4289
URL: http://www.acs.oakland.edu/oak/SimTel/win3/archiver.html
File: dz50.exe

GnuZip
Freeware
Author: Jean-loup and Gaillu and many others
URL: ftp://prep.ai.mit.edu/pub/gnu
E-mail: jloup@chorus.fr

PKZip
Shareware
Author: PKWARE
URL: http://www.acs.oakland.edu/oak/SimTel/win3/archiver.html
File: pkz204g.exe

Web Document Design Services

American Information Systems Inc.
911 North Plum Grove Road, Suite F
Schaumburg, IL 60173
Voice: (708) 413-8400
Fax: (708) 413-8401
URL: http://www.ais.net
E-mail: info@ais.net

Audio Online Inc.
8672 Heritage Road
Norval, Ontario CANADA L0P 1K0
Voice: (905) 451-2804
URL: http://www.audio-online.com/ao/
E-mail: dave@audio-online.com

Beverly Hills Software
469 S. Bedford Drive
Beverly Hills, CA 90212
Voice: (310) 843-0414
Fax: (310) 843-9917
URL: http://bhs.com/
E-mail: sales@bhs.com

Bonsai Software
2582 Old First Street
Livermore, CA 94550-3155
Voice: (510) 606-5701
Fax: (510) 606-5702
URL: http://www.bonsai.com
E-mail: ksedgwic@bonsai.com

EPublish
2806 Union St.
Madison, WI 53704
Voice: (608) 243-8000
URL: http://www.fullfeed.com/epub/index.html
E-mail: office@epublish.com

Free Range Media, Inc.
117 South Main, Suite 400
Seattle, WA 98104
Voice: (206) 340-9305
Fax: (206) 340-0509
E-mail: info@freerange.com

Internet Design Group
Voice: (415) 424-0747
URL: http://www.mall.net/homepage.htm
E-mail: idg@mall.net

Knossopolis
Voice: (604) 988-4770 (John Maxwell)
URL: http://www.knosso.com/
E-mail: knossopolis@wimsey.com

Michele~Shine Media
1800 Market Street, Suite 204
San Francisco, CA 94103
Voice: (415) 621-0299
Fax: (415) 621-5023
URL: www.internex.com/MSM/home.html
E-mail: crmk@netcom.com

NPiX Interactive Web Marketing
Voice: (404) 892-1971
URL: http://www.com/npix
E-mail: info@npixi.com

Tecnation Digital World
555 Bryant Street #257
Palo Alto, California 94301
Voice: (415) 327-4332
Fax: (415) 327-1910
URL: http://www.tecnation.com/tecnation/
E-mail: hello@tecnation.com

Thunderstone Software — EPI, Inc. (Information Retrieval)
11115 Edgewater Drive
Cleveland, Ohio 44102
Voice: (216) 631-8544
Fax: (216) 281-0828
URL: http://www.thunderstone.com
E-mail: info@thunderstone.com

UniPress W3 Services Division
UniPress Software, Inc.
W3 Services Division
2025 Lincoln Highway
Edison, NJ 08817
Voice: (800) 222-0550 x920 (Clay Webster)
Voice: (908) 287-2100
URL: http://www.unipress.com/w3/
E-mail: w3@unipress.com

Webvertising
2727 Nasha Road 1, Suite 615
Seabrook, TX 77586
Voice: (713) 326-4886
Fax: (713) 326-3952
URL: http://www.sccsi.com/welcome.html
E-mail: whitney@sccsi.com

Xynergy
ElectoMedia Interactive Web Design
136 Piedra Loop
Los Alamos, NM 87504
Voice: (505) 470-2589
Voice: (505) 982-8383, ext. 20
URL: http://www.nets.com/xynergy.html
E-mail: electromedia@nets.com

Young Ideas
207 2nd Street, Suite B
Sausalito, CA 94965
Voice: (415) 331-3128
Fax: (415) 331-9620
E-mail: indy@bonsai.com

Internet & Web Related Publications

Boardwatch Magazine
Newstand/Subscription
8500 W. Bowles Avenue, Suite 210
Littleton, CO 80123
Voice: (303) 973-6038
Fax: (303) 973-3731
URL: http://www.boardwatch.com
E-mail: jack.rickard@boardwatch.com

Digital Video Magazine
Newstand/Subscription
80 Elm Street
St. Peterborough, NH 03458
Voice: (800) 441-4403
Voice: (603) 924-0100
Fax: (516) 562-7406
Subscriptions: (800) 998-0806
E-mail (subscriptions): subs@dv.com

Internet Business Journal
Strangelove Internet Enterprises, Inc.
208 Somerset Street East, Suite A
Ottawa, Ontario CANADA K1N 6V2
Voice: (613) 565-0982
Fax: (613) 569-4432

The Internet Letter
NetWeek LLC
1294 National Press Building
Washington DC 20045
Voice: (202) 638-6020
Fax: (202) 638-6019
URL: http://www.infohaus.com/access/by-seller/Internet_Letter
E-mail: info@netweek.com

Internet World
Newstand/Subscription
Mecklermedia Corporation
20 Ketchum Street
Westport, CT 06880
Voice: (203) 226-6967

Matrix News
Matrix Information and Directory Services
1106 Clayton Lane, Suite 500W
Austin, TX 78723
Voice: (512) 451-7602
Fax: (512) 452-0128

NetGuide
Newstand/Subscription
600 Community Drive
Manhasset, NY 11030
Voice: (516) 562-5000
Fax: (516) 562-7406
URL: http://wais.wais.com:80/techweb/ng/current/
E-mail: netmail@netguide.cmp.com

Net Week Inc.
220 National Press Building
Washington, DC 20045
Voice: (202) 638-6020
Fax: (202) 638-6019
E-mail: netweek@access.digex.net

New Media
Newstand/Subscription
901 Mariner's Island Boulevard, Suite 365
San Mateo, CA 94404
Voice: (415) 573-5170
Fax: (415) 573-5131

ONLINE ACCESS
Newstand/Subscription
900 N. Franklin, Suite 310
Chicago, IL 60610
Voice: (312) 573-1700

PC Graphics & Video
Newstand/Subscription
201 East Sandpointe Avenue, Suite 600
Santa Ana, CA 92707
Voice: (714) 513-8400
Fax: (714) 513-8412

Publish
Newstand/Subscription
501 Second Street
San Francisco, CA 94107
Voice: (415) 978-3280
Fax: (415) 975-2613
E-mail: 76127.205@compuserve.com

WIRED
Newstand/Subscription
544 Second Street
San Francisco, CA 94107
Voice: (415) 904-0660
Fax: (415) 904-0669
URL: http://www.wired.com
E-mail: info@wired.com

Service Providers & Server Services

Automatrix, Inc. (Server Service)
P.O Box 196
Rexford, NY 12148
Voice: (518) 372-5791
Voice: (518) 877-7270
URL: http://www.automatrix.com

BBN Planet
3801 East Bayshore Road
Palo Alto, CA 94303
Voice: (800) 662-4770
Voice: (415) 934-2655
Fax: (415) 934-2665
URL: http://www.bbnplanet.com
E-mail: info@bbnplanet.com

Best Internet Communications Inc.
421 Castro Street
Mountain View, CA 94041
Voice: (415) 964-2378
Fax: (415) 691-4195
URL: http://www.best.com
E-mail: info@best.com

BizNet Technologies (Server Service)
Corporate Research Center
1872 Pratt Drive, Suite 1725
Blacksburg, VA 24062
Voice: (703) 231-7715
URL: http://www.BizNet.com.blacksburg.va.us/index.html
E-mail: biznet@bevnet

Branch Infomation Services (Server Service)
2607 Patricia
Ann Arbor, MI 48103
Voice: (313) 995-8783
Fax: (313) 995-1931
URL: http://branch.com:1080
E-mail: jon@branch.com

CCI Networks
4130 95th Street
Edmonton, Alberta Canada T6E 6H5
Area code(s): 403
Voice: (403) 450-6787
URL: http://www.ccinet.ab.ca
E-mail: info@ccinet.ab.ca

CCnet Communications
Area code(s): 510
Voice: (510) 988-0680
190 N. Wiget Lane, Suite# 291
Walnut Creek, CA 94598
Voice: (510)988-0680
URL: http://www.ccnet.com
E-mail: info@ccnet.com

CERFnet
Area code(s): 619, 510, 415, 818, 714, 310, 800
P.O. Box 85608
San Diego, CA 92186-9784
Voice: (800) 876-2373
Voice: (619) 455-3900
URL: http://www.cerfnet.com
E-mail: sales@cerf.net

CICNet
Area code(s): 312, 708, 800, 313, 309, 217
2901 Hubbard Drive
Ann Arbor, MI 48105
Voice: (800) 947-4754
Voice: (313) 998-6703
Fax: (313) 998-6105
URL: http://www.cic.net
E-mail: info@cic.net

Clark Internet Services, Inc. (Server Service)
10600 Route 108
Ellicottt City, MD 21042
Voice: (800) 735-2258
Fax: (410) 730-9765
URL: http://www.clark.net
E-mail: info@clarknet

Colorado SuperNet
Area code(s): 303, 719
One Denver Place
999 18th Street
Denver, CO 80202
Voice: (303) 296-8202
Fax: (303) 296-8224
URL: http://www.csn.org
E-mail: info@csn.org

Computing Engineers (Server Service)
P.O. Box 285
Vernon Hills, IL 60061
Voice: (708) 367-1870
Fax: (708) 367-1872
URL: http://www.wwa.com/
E-mail: info@wwa.com

CRL
Box 326
Larkspur, CA 94977
Area code(s): 213, 310, 404, 415, 510, 602, 707, 800
Voice: (415) 837-5300
Voice: (415) 381-2800
Fax: (415) 381-9578
URL: http://www.crl.com
E-mail: info@crl.com

CTS Network Services (Server Service)
4444 Convoy Street, Suite 300
San Diego, CA 92111
Voice: (619) 637-3637
Fax: (619) 637-3639
URL: http://www.cts.com
E-mail: support@cts.com

CTS Network Services (CTSNet)
Area code(s): 619
4444 Convoy Street, Suite 300
San Diego, CA 92111
Voice: (619)637-3637
Fax: (619)637-3630
E-mail: info@crash.cts.com

CyberGate
Area code(s): 305
662 South Military Trail
Deerfield Beach, FL 33442
Voice: (305) 428-4283
Fax: (305) 428-7977
URL: http://www.gate.net
E-mail: info@gate.net

Cyberspace Development (Server Service)
3700 Cloverleaf Drive
Boulder, CO 80304
Voice: (303) 938-8684
Fax: (303) 546-9667
URL: http://marketplace.com
E-mail: office@marketplace.com

Cybersight (Server Service)
2162 NW Everett, Office #2
Portland, OR 97210
Voice: (503) 228-4008
Fax: (503) 224-1749
URL: http://cybersight.com
E-mail: imi@cybersight.com

DATABANK, Inc.
1473 Hwy 40
Lawrence, KS 66044
Voice: (913) 842-6699
Fax: (913) 843-8518
URL: http://www.databank.com
E-mail: info@databank.com

Digital Express: Group, Inc.
Area code(s): 301, 410, 609, 703, 714, 908, 909
6006 Greenbelt Road, Suite 228
Greenbelt, MD 20770
Voice: (800) 969-9090
Voice: (301)220-2020
URL: http://www.digex.net
E-mail: info@digex.net

Echo
97 Perry Street, Suite 13
New York, NY 10014
Area code(s): 212, 718
Voice: 212-255-3839
URL: http://www.echonyc.com
E-mail: info@echonyc.com

Engineering International, Inc.
2313 Headingly, N.W.
Albuquerque, NM 87107
Voice: (505) 343-1060
Fax: (505) 243-1061

GEMS (Global Electronic Marketing Service) (Server Service)
200 Elmwood Davis Road, Suite 102
Liverpool, NY 13088
Voice: (315) 453-2912
Fax: (315) 453-3052
URL: http://www.gems.com/index.html
E-mail: info@gems.com

Global Enterprise Services
3 Independence Way
Princeton, NJ 08540
Voice: (800) 358-4437
Voice: (609) 897-7300
Fax: (609) 897-7310
URL: http://www.jvnc.net/
E-mail: info@jvnc.net

HoloNet
Information Access Technologies, Inc.
46 Shattuck Square, Suite 11
Berkeley, CA 94704
Voice: (510) 704-0160
Fax: (510) 704-8019
URL: http://www.holonet.net/
E-mail: info@holonet.net (automated)
E-mail: support@holonet.net

IDS World Network
Area code(s): 401, 305, 407
3 Franklin Road
East Greenwich, RI 02818
Voice: (800) 437-1680
Voice: (401) 884-7856
URL: http://www.ids.net
E-mail: info@ids.net

Infoboard (Server Service)
3 Grant Road
Swampscott, MA 01907
Voice: (617) 592-6675
Fax: (617) 592-3042
URL: http://www.infoboard.com/infoboard
E-mail: infoboard@infoboard.com

Institute for Global Communications/IGC Networks
Area code(s): 415, PDN
18 De Boom Street
San Francisco, CA 94107
Voice: (415) 442-0220
Fax: (415) 546-1794
URL: http://www.igc.apc.org/igc/igcinfo.html
E-mail: igc-info@igc.apc.org

InterAccess Co.
Area code (s): 312, 708, 815
9400 W. Foster Avenue, Suite 111
Chicago, IL 60656
Voice: (800) 967-1580
Voice: (708) 671-0111
Fax: (708) 671-0113
URL: http://www.interaccess.com/
E-mail: info@interaccess.com

Internet Direct, Inc.
1366 East Thomas, #210
Phoenix, CA 85014
Voice: (602) 274-0100
Fax: (602) 274-8518
URL: http://www.indirect.com
E-mail: info@indirect.com

Internet Express
Area code(s): 206, 303, 505, 602, 719, 800
1155 Kelly Johnson Boulevard, Suite 400
Colorado Springs, CO 80920
Voice: (800) 748-1200
Voice: (719) 592-1240
Fax: (719) 592-1201
URL: http://usa.net
E-mail: service@usa.net

Internet Media Services (Server Service)
644 Emerson Street, Suite 21
Palo Alto, CA 94301
Voice: (415) 328-4638
Fax: (415) 328-4350
URL: http://netmedia.com
E-mail: info@netmedia.com

Internet Presence & Publishing Corp. (Server Service)
World Trade Center, Suite 1700
Norfolk, VA 23510
Voice: (800) 638-6155
Voice: (804) 446-9060
Fax: (804) 446-9061
URL: http://www.shopkeeper.com/cgi-bin/shopkeeper
E-mail: info@tcp.ip.net

InterNex Information Services, Inc. (Server Service)
2302 Walsh Avenue
Santa Clara, CA 95051
Voice: (408) 496-5466
Fax: (408) 496-5485
URL: http://www.internex.net
E-mail: info@internex.net

Kalidospace (Server Service)
P.O. Box 341556
Los Angeles, CA 90034
Voice: (310) 399-4349
Fax: (310) 396-5489
URL: http://kspace.com
E-mail: editors@kspace.com

Macro Computer Solutions
1300 West Belmont, Suite 402
Chicago, IL 60657
Voice: (312) 248-8649
Fax: (312) 248-9865
URL: http://www.mcs.com
E-mail: info@mcs.com

Merit Network/MichNet
2901 Hubbard Pod G
Ann Arbor, MI 48105
Voice: (313) 764-9430
Fax: (313) 747-3185
URL: http://www.merit.edu
E-mail: info@merit.edu

Metasystems Design Group, Inc. (Server Service)
2000 North 15th Street, Suite #103
Arlington, VA 22201
Voice: (703) 243-6622
Fax: (703) 841-9798
URL: http://www.tmn.com
E-mail: info@tmn.com

MIDnet
201 North 8th Street, Suite 421
Lincoln, NE 68588
Voice: (402) 472-7600
Fax: (402) 472-0240
URL: http://www.mid.net
E-mail: nic@mid.net

MRNet
511 11th Avenue Box 212 South
Minneapolis, MN 55415
Voice: (612) 342-2570
Fax: (612) 344-1716
URL: http://www.mr.net
E-mail: info@mr.net

MSEN, Inc.
Area code(s): 313, 810, 800
628 Brooks Street
Ann Arbor, MI 48103
Voice: (313) 998-4562
Fax: (313)998-4563
URL: http://www.msen.com
E-mail: info-request@msen.com

Mulitmedia Ink Designs (Server Service)
14544 High Pine Street
Poway, CA 92064
Voice: (619) 679-8317
URL: http://mmink.cts.com/mmink/mmi.html
E-mail: rdegel@ctsnet.cts.com

MV Communications, Inc.
Area code(s): 603
P.O Box 4963
Manchester, NH 03108
Voice: (603) 429-2223
URL: http://www.mv.com
E-mail: info@mv.com

NEARNET
BBN Technology Services, Inc.
10 Moulton Street
Cambridge, MA 02138
Voice: (800) 632-7638
Voice: (617) 873-8730
Fax: (617) 873-5620
URL: http://www.near.net
E-mail: nearnet-join@near.net

Neosoft
Area code (s): 713, 504, 314, 800, SprintNet
3408 Mangum Street
Houston, TX 77092
Voice: (713) 968-5800
URL: http://www.neosoft.com
E-mail: info@neosoft.com

Netcom On-Line: Communications Services
Area code(s): 206, 212, 214, 303, 310, 312, 404, 408, 415, 503, 510, 512, 617, 619, 703, 714, 818, 916
4000 Moorpark Avenue, Suite 209
San Jose, CA 95117
Voice: (800) 501-8649
Voice: (408) 554-8649
Fax: (408) 241-9145
E-mail: info@netcom.com

Net+Effects (Server Service)
Net+Effects
6475 Dwyer Court
San José, CA 95120
Voice: (408) 739-0557
URL: http://www.net.effects.com
E-mail: info@net.effects.com

NetIllinois
1840 Oak Avenue
Evanston, IL 60201
Voice: (708) 866-1825
Fax: (708) 866-1857
URL: http://www.illinois.net
E-mail: info@illinois.net

North Bay Network
20 Minor Court
San Rafael, CA 94903
Voice: (415) 472-1600
Fax: (415) 472-2461
URL: http://www.nb.com
E-mail: info@nb.com

North Shore Access
Area code(s): 617, 508
Voice: (617) 593-3110
URL: http://www.shore.net
E-mail: info@shore.net

NorthWestNet
15400 S.E. 30th Place, Suite 202
Bellvue, WA 98007
Voice: (206) 562-3000
Fax: (206) 562-3791
URL: http://www.nwnet.net
E-mail: info@nwnet.net

Nuance Network Services
Area code(s): 205
904 Bob Wallace Avenue, Suite 119
Huntsville, AL 35801
Voice: (205) 533-4296
URL: http://www.nuance.com
E-mail: info@nuance.com

OARNet
Area code(s): 614
1224 Kinnear Road
Columbus, OH 43212
Voice: (614) 292-8100
Fax: (614) 292-7168
Voice: (800) 627-8101
URL: http://www.oar.net
E-mail: info@oar.net

Panix Public Access UNIX & Internet
Area code(s): 212, 516
Voice: (212) 741-4400
Fax: (212) 741-5311
URL: http://www.panix.com/
E-mail: info@panix.com

Performance Systems International, Inc. (PSI)
Area code(s): Send e-mail to: numbers-info@psi.com for list
510 Huntmar Park Drive
Herndon, VA 12180
Voice: (800) 827-7482
Voice: (703) 620-6551
Fax: (703) 620-4586
Faxback: (800) 329-7741
URL: http://www.psi.net
E-mail: info@psi.com

Phantom Access
1562 First Avenue, Suite 351
New York, NY 10028
Voice: (212) 989-2418
Fax: (212) 989-8648
URL: www.phantom.com
E-mail: info@phantom.com

Pipeline
Area code(s): 212, 718
150 Broadway
New York, NY 10038
Voice: (212) 267-3636
URL: http://www.pipeline.com
E-mail: infobot@pipeline.com

Portal Communications Company
Area code(s): 408, SprintNet
20863 Stevens Creek Boulevard, Suite 200
Cupertino, CA 95014
Voice: (408) 973-9111
Fax: (408) 725-1580
URL: http://www.portal.com
E-mail: info@portal.com

PREPnet
305 S Craig Street, 2nd Floor
Pittsburg, PA 15213
Voice: (412) 268-7870
Fax: (412) 268-7875
URL: http://www.cmu.edu/
E-mail: prepnet@cmu.edu

South Coast Computing Services, Inc.
1811 Bering, Suite 100
Houston, TX 77057
Voice: (800) 770-8971
Voice: (713) 917-5000
Fax: (713) 917-5005
URL: http://www.sccsi.com/
E-mail: info@sccsi.com

Spry Consulting Group (Server Service)
316 Occidental Avenue South
Seattle, WA 98104
Voice: (206) 447-0800
Fax: (206) 447-9008
URL: http://www.spry.com
E-mail: info@spry.com

Studio X (Server Service)
1270 Calle de Comercio #3
Santa Fe, NM 87505
Voice: (505) 438-0505
Fax: (505) 438-1816
URL: http://www.nets.com
E-mail: webmaster@nets.com

SURAnet
8400 Baltimore Blvd.
College Park, MD 20740
Voice: (800) 787-2638
Voice: (301) 982-4600
Fax: (301) 982-4605
URL: http://www.sura.net
E-mail: marketing@suranet.net

Systems Solutions Network
Area code(s): 302
1254 Lorewood Grove Road
Middletown, DL 19709
Voice: (302) 378-1386
Fax: (302) 378-3871
E-mail: sharris@marlin.ssnet.com

Teleport
Area code(s): 503, 206
319 SouthWest Washington #803
Portland OR 97204
Voice: (503) 223-0076
Fax: (503) 223-4372
URL: http://www.teleport.com
E-mail: info@teleport.com

Telerama Public Access Internet
Area code(s): 412
P.O. Box 60024
Pittsburg, PA 15211
Voice: (412) 481-3505
Fax: (412) 481-8568
URL: http://www.telerama.com
E-mail: info@telerama.com

Texas Metronet
Area code(s): 214, 817
860 Kinwest Parkway, Suite 179
Irving, TX 75063-3440
Voice: (214) 705-2900
Voice: (817) 543-8756
Fax: (214) 401-2802
URL: http://www.metronet.com
E-mail: info@metronet.com

UUNET Technologies, Inc.
3060 Williams Drive
Fairfax, VA 22031
Voice: (800) 258-4039
Voice: (703) 206-5600
Fax: (703) 206-5601
URL: http://www.uu.net
E-mail: info@uunet.uu.net

VNet Internet Access, Inc.
Area code(s): 704, 919, Public Data Network (PDN)
1206 Kenilwratch Avenue
P.O. Box 31474
Charlotte, SC 28231
Voice: (800) 377-3282
Voice: (704) 334-3282
URL: http://www.vnet.net/
E-mail: info@vnet.net

XNet Information Systems
3080 East Ogden Avenue, #202
Lisle, IL 60532
Area code(s): 312, 708, 815
Voice: (708) 983-6064
URL: http://www.xnet.com
E-mail: info@xnet.com

Index

A

B

C

D

E

F

G

H

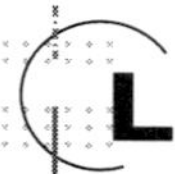

M

N

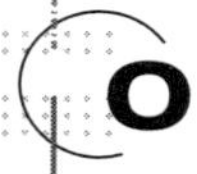

O

P

Q

R

S

T

U

V

W

Colophon

This book was created on a Power Macintosh 8100 using PageMaker 5.0. Graphics were produced and edited in Adobe Illustrator 5.5, Adobe Photoshop 3.0 and Aldus Freehand 3.1. The body text is set in Adobe Palatino. Subheads are set in DTC Bembo. Chapter titles, running heads and sidebars are set in Adobe Univers. Tables are set in Adobe Franklin Gothic. Page proofs were printed on a LaserJet 4 printer and final film output was produced on a Linotronic 330.

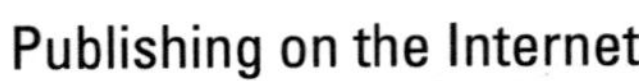

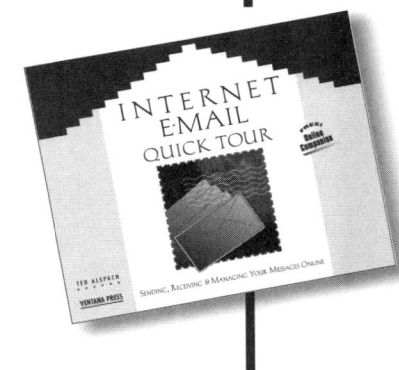

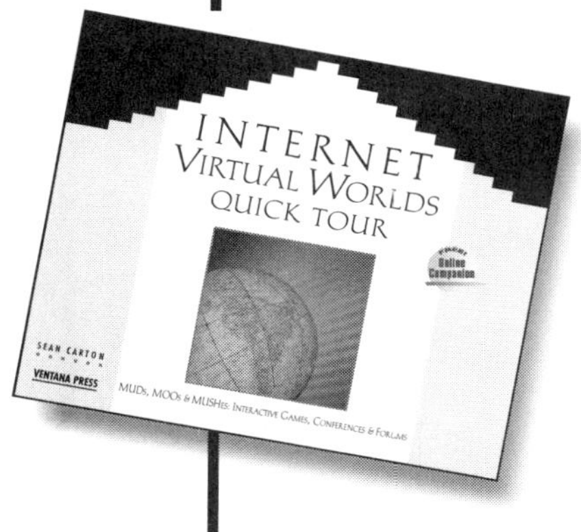

Internet Virtual Worlds Quick Tour

$14.00, 224 pages, illustrated

Learn to locate and master real-time interactive communication forums and games by participating in the virtual worlds of MUD (Multi-User Dimension) and MOO (MUD Object-Oriented). *Internet Virtual Worlds Quick Tour* introduces users to the basic functions by defining different categories (individual, interactive and both) and detailing standard protocols. Also revealed is the insider's lexicon of these mysterious cyberworlds.

Internet Roadside Attractions

$29.95, 384 pages, illustrated

Why take the word of one when you can get a quorum? Seven experienced Internauts—teachers and bestselling authors—share their favorite Web sites, Gophers, FTP sites, chats, games, newsgroups and mailing lists. Organized alphabetically by category for easy browsing with in-depth descriptions. The companion CD-ROM contains the entire text of the book, hyperlinked for off-line browsing and online Web-hopping.

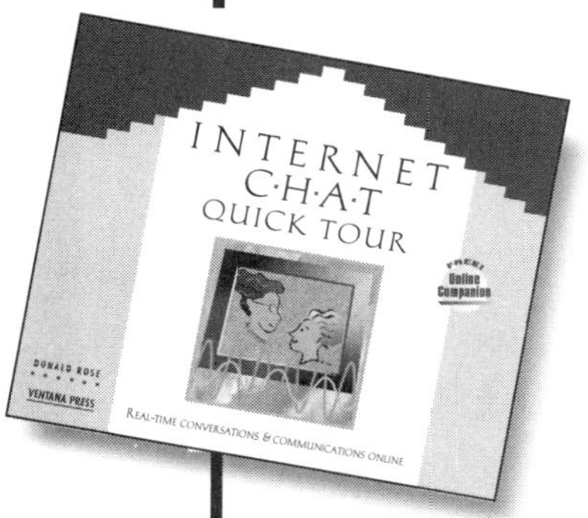

Internet Chat Quick Tour

$14.00, 200 pages, illustrated

Global conversations in real-time are an integral part of the Internet. The worldwide chat network is where users find online help and forums on the latest scientific research. The *Internet Chat Quick Tour* describes the best software sites for users to chat on a variety of subjects.

Books marked with this logo include a free Internet *Online Companion™*, featuring archives of free utilities plus a software archive and links to other Internet resources.

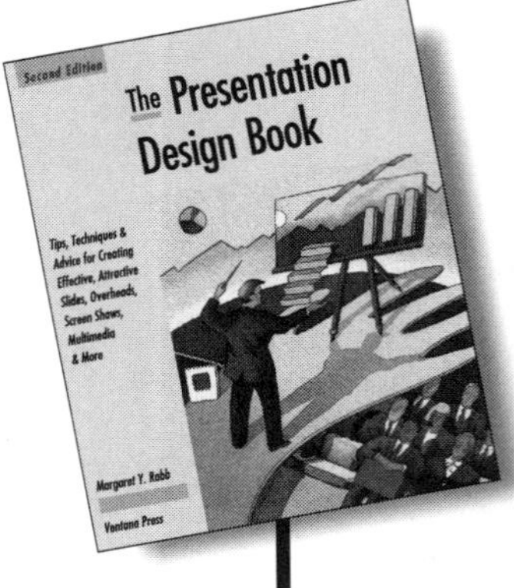

Second Edition
The Presentation Design Book
Margaret Y. Rabb
Ventana Press

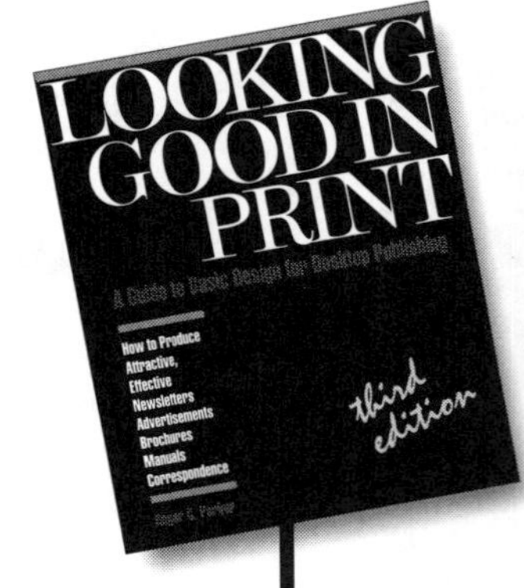

LOOKING GOOD IN PRINT
third edition

Looking Good in Color
The Desktop Publisher's Design Guide
Ventana Press
Gary W. Priester

Looking Good With QuarkXPress

$34.95, 544 pages, illustrated

Looking Good With QuarkXPress showcases the graphic devices, layouts and design tools built into the latest version of QuarkXPress. The basic principles of graphic design are brought to life on every page with examples of newsletters, brochures and more in a straightforward guide that is accessible to users at all levels. The companion CD-ROM features valuable templates, fonts, clip art, backgrounds and XTensions for both Macintosh and Windows users.

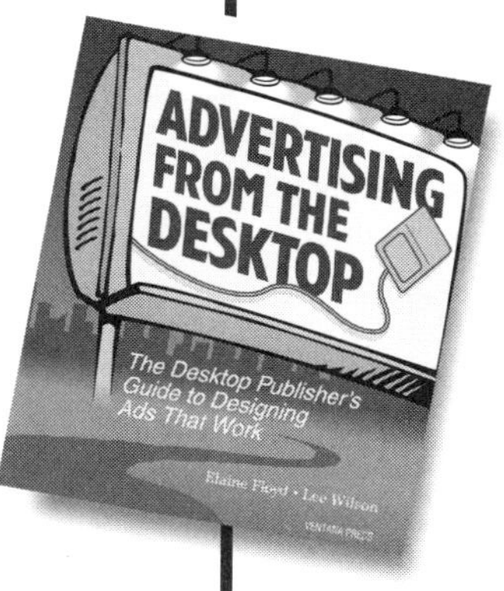

Advertising From the Desktop

$24.95, 464 pages, illustrated

Advertising From the Desktop offers unmatched design advice and helpful how-to instructions for creating persuasive ads. With tips on how to choose fonts, select illustrations, apply special effects and more, this book is an idea-packed resource for improving the looks and effects of your ads.

Newsletters From the Desktop, Second Edition

$24.95, 392 pages, illustrated

Now the millions of desktop publishers who produce newsletters can learn how to improve the designs of their publications. Filled with helpful design tips and illustrations, as well as hands-on tips for building a great-looking publication. Includes an all-new color gallery of professionally designed newsletters, offering desktop publishers at all levels a wealth of ideas and inspiration.

Check your local bookstore or software retailer for these and other bestselling titles, or call toll free: 800/743-5369

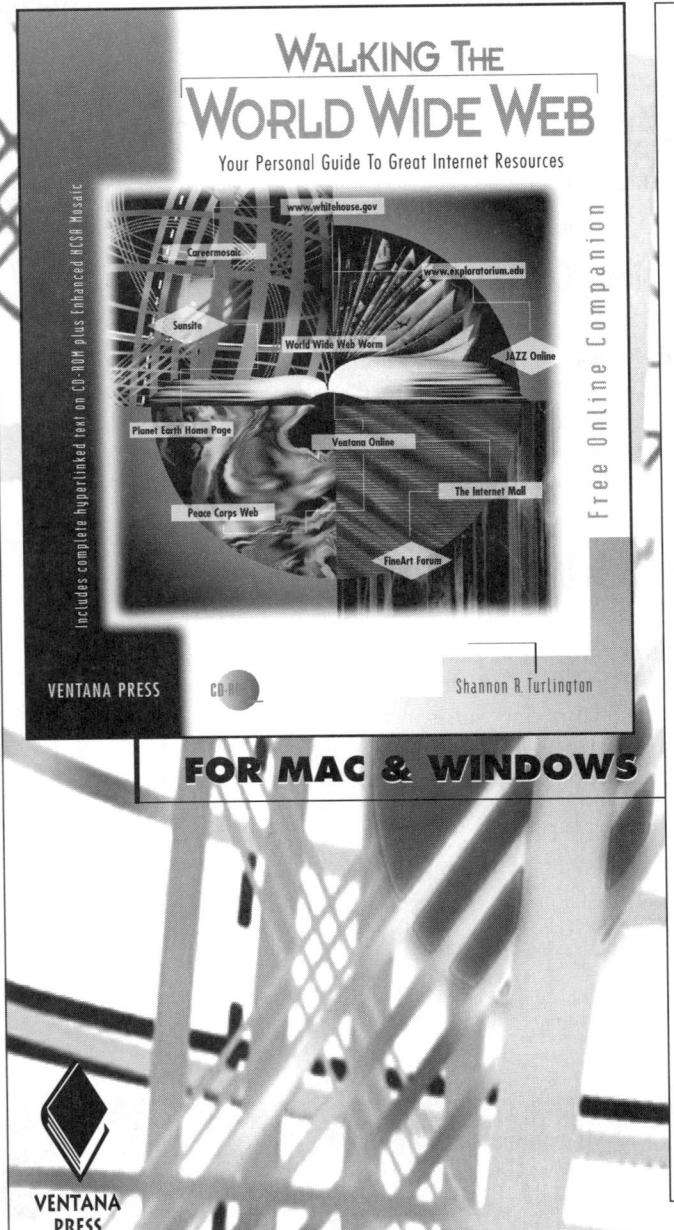